Archbishop Laud (1940)
The Last Days of Hitler (1947)
Men and Events (1957)
The Rise of Christian Europe (1965)
The Crisis of the 17th Century (1968)
The Philby Affair (1968)
The Plunder of the Arts (1970)
Princes and Artists:
The Patronage of the Habsburg Courts (1976)

Hermit
of Peking

Hermit
of Peking

THE HIDDEN LIFE OF
SIR EDMUND BACKHOUSE

Hugh Trevor-Roper

ALFRED A. KNOPF

NEW YORK

1977

THIS IS A BORZOI BOOK
PUBLISHED BY ALFRED A. KNOPF, INC.

Copyright © 1977 by Hugh Trevor-Roper

All rights reserved under International and Pan-American Copyright
Conventions. Published in the United States by Alfred A. Knopf, Inc.,
New York. Distributed by Random House, Inc., New York. Originally
published in Great Britain as A Hidden Life: The Enigma of Sir
Edmund Backhouse by Macmillan London Ltd., London. Copyright
© 1976 by Hugh Trevor-Roper.

LIBRARY OF CONGRESS CATALOGING IN PUBLICATION DATA

Trevor-Roper, Hugh Redwald.   Hermit of Peking.
First published in 1976 under title: A hidden life.
Includes index.
1. Backhouse, Edmund Trelawny, Sir, bart., 1873–1944. 2. Sinologists
—Great Britain—Biography. I. Title.

DS734.9.B3T73 1977   951′.007′2024 [B] 76-47921
ISBN 0-394-41104-8

MANUFACTURED IN THE UNITED STATES OF AMERICA
PUBLISHED APRIL 20, 1977
REPRINTED ONCE
THIRD PRINTING, JULY 1977

'I have had an interesting life, though in a
hidden way – behind the scenes, I mean.'
  Edmund Backhouse to J. O. P. Bland, 1933

'The greatest genius it has ever been my
privilege to know.'
                    G. E. Morrison, 1909

'The most remarkable scoundrel ever known
in the Far East.'
                    G. S. Hall, 1917

Contents

Four pages of photographs
will be found following page 114.

Acknowledgments

I am grateful to all those who have assisted me in my pursuit of Sir Edmund Backhouse, even though many trails proved false and delusive. I have expressed certain particular obligations in the text. Here, I offer my general thanks to those who have answered my letters, supplied personal information, allowed me to quote copyright matter, or pointed the way to other sources, and who may well be somewhat surprised at the total picture to which they have contributed: viz.:

Sir Harold Acton; Sir John Addis; Mr S. A. M. Adshead of the University of Canterbury, Christchurch, New Zealand; Sir Jonathan Backhouse, Bart.; Mr Alan Bell, Assistant Keeper of Manuscripts at the National University of Scotland; Mr M. W. Bryan of Oriel College, Oxford; Sir Colin Crowe; Mrs Hope Danby; Mr Mark Elvin of St Antony's College, Oxford; the Lord ffrench; Mr Philip Fox of G. C. Fox & Co., Falmouth; Mr Kenneth Gardner, Deputy Keeper of Oriental MSS and books, the British Library; Mr Peter Gwyn, archivist of Winchester College; Mr J. R. Highfield of Merton College, Oxford; Mr Robert Rhodes James; Sir Lionel Lamb; the late Mr W. E. Lewisohn; Laetitia, Lady Lucas-Tooth; M. Roland de Margerie, Ambassadeur de France; Sir James Marjoribanks; Mr Frederick Müller, officer in charge of the Search Room of the Department of Official Receivers, Royal Courts of Justice; Mr Michael Moss, archivist of Glasgow University; Mr Francis Noel-Baker; Sir Alwyne Ogden; Sir Humphrey Prideaux-Brune; Eva, Countess of Rosebery; Dr A. L. Rowse; Mr Peter Shaw, Secretary of King's College, London; Mr Gardner D. Stout; M. Henri Vetch of Hong Kong; Commander Clare Vyner; Mr Edward H. Weitzen, Chairman of the Bank Note Company of New York; Sir Dick White.

I am also grateful to Miss Caroline Hobhouse of Macmillan London Ltd for her imperturbable patience and assistance and to my wife for her care and devotion in preparing the index.

Hermit
of Peking

Prologue

ON the roll of honour of the Bodleian Library at Oxford – that neo-Jacobean marble tablet upon which are inscribed the names of its most munificent benefactors – there appears, together with those of Humfrey, Duke of Gloucester, Sir Thomas Bodley, Archbishop Laud, Oliver Cromwell, Paul Mellon and the Rockefeller Foundation, the name 'Edmundus Backhouse, baronettus'. Sir Edmund Backhouse, second baronet (1873–1944), is certainly worthy of his place on that record, for in 1913 he presented to the Library a collection of 17,000 volumes* of Chinese printed books and manuscripts, some of them (we are assured) exceedingly rare and valuable, some quite unique, and in the course of the next eight years he added another 10,000 volumes, making the Backhouse collection – according to the experts – by those gifts alone, one of the finest Chinese libraries in Europe. So handsome a gift deserves appropriate recognition. It also raises questions. Who was the donor? How did he acquire these treasures? What motive impelled his generosity? The scope and provenance of any great collection is part of its history, and as we honour our benefactors, so we should also seek to know about them, as a just recognition of their generosity.

Sir Edmund Backhouse, at the close of his life, was particularly anxious that we should know his true history. He then wrote, for publication – he insists frequently on his desire for publication –

* Chinese books are counted in *chüan*, being the stitched 'gatherings' which make up a book. The word is generally rendered 'volumes', and I have therefore kept to this usage.

[Explanatory notes have been set at the foot of the page. Source notes will be found on pp. 303–6.]

two volumes of memoirs. These memoirs, which are unlikely to be published, differ profoundly from the only public record of his life at present in print: the brief entry in *The Dictionary of National Biography* written by his friend Mrs Hope Danby. In offering a third account, which differs totally from both his and hers, I hope that I shall approach nearer to the truth. It may be that he will appear, in this book, a little less respectable than in Mrs Danby's article; but at least he will seem a great deal more respectable than he would himself have us believe.

Sir Edmund Backhouse was a sinologist. He earned his fame and acquired his collection in China. If he is known in the world, it is by two books which he wrote in collaboration with J. O. P. Bland: *China under the Empress Dowager*, published in 1910, and *Annals and Memoirs of the Court of Peking*, published in 1914. The first of these, the first scholarly life of the last significant ruler of imperial China, has long been regarded as a classic, and is regularly cited as an authority by Western writers. Nothing can replace it in the immediacy of its documentation, the vividness of its detail, the ease and readability of its style. The latter is a similarly documented anthology of scenes from court history under the Ming Emperors and their successors, the last dynasty of China, the Manchu dynasty of the Ch'ing.

For a summary of Backhouse's life it is convenient – indeed necessary – to begin with the only published source, Mrs Danby's brief biography. Mrs Danby is a painter and writer who lived in Peking from 1926 to 1942 and who counted Sir Edmund Backhouse as one of her oldest friends there. In her article on him, which is based on 'personal knowledge', she related Backhouse's immediate parentage; his education; his extraordinary flair for languages; his long residence in China; his service as translator to the embassy; his teaching appointments; his publications; his generosity to the Bodleian Library; and the honours bestowed upon him. Distinguished posts, she tells us, were offered to him in Europe, 'but China called', and in China he stayed. 'As time went on', we learn, he became a recluse, devoting his whole days to study and writing. 'In his house in the West City of Peking, he lived the life of a Chinese scholar, even wearing the long native robes. Little by little, he gave up all social contacts with his European and American friends, and would receive only two or three of them; thus he gained the reputation of being something of a mystery man. But he continued to see his Chinese friends, among whom were scholars, officials and members of the old imperial family.' He was working, it seems, upon an Anglo-Chinese dictionary and upon personal histories of the Ch'ing Emperors. But a disastrous accident prevented the completion of these works. 'When the Japanese invaded Peking in 1937 Back-house was forced to leave his Chinese home, and he took refuge in the compound of the former Austrian Legation, later going to live in a house in the British Embassy grounds. The Japanese, deeply suspicious of all written documents, made a bonfire of his papers and manuscripts, among them the dictionary and the histories, and so the priceless records and labour of nearly half a century were lost.' In his last years, she concludes, Backhouse 'turned to religion', and became a Roman Catholic. When war broke out between Japan and Britain in December 1941, he refused the offer of repatriation, and died in the French hospital in Peking on 8 January 1944.

To this formal account Mrs Danby has added a few picturesque details in a volume of memoirs of her own life in China which she published in 1955. Here Backhouse features as a benevolent, absent-minded professor with an 'intimate knowledge of Chinese history', whose dignified white beard, and the 'long, heavy, white silk Chinese gown' which he wore even in the heat of summer, made him resemble one of the Jesuits at the early Manchu court. These external details create an agreeable picture of the *émigré* English baronet who had gone native, but they do not bring his personality any nearer to us. We still do not know what caused him to live in Peking, what was the real subject of his secret study, the motive of his secluded life. The mystery man is a mystery man still.

One of the mysteries concerning Backhouse surrounds the Chinese diary, the diary of Ching-shan, which, as he tells us, he himself discovered in 1900, during the Boxer Rising, and after-wards translated for inclusion in *China under the Empress Dowager*. The debate about the authenticity of this work, the original manu-script of which is now in the British Museum, began during his lifetime and has never been entirely settled. The late Victor Purcell, in his authoritative book on *The Boxer Uprising*, published in 1963, devoted a special appendix to the document, which, if genuine, must be regarded as an irreplaceable primary source for the historian. He concluded that the diary was forged, but by whom and for what purpose he could not determine. Mrs Danby, in her brief biography of Backhouse, does not mention this controversy, on which, however, any final judgment of his character must depend. I venture to think that the evidence which I shall submit will settle that controversy.

I confess, I would have been happy to leave Backhouse in his self-engendered cloud of mystery had it not been for a strange chance. In the summer of 1973, a distinguished Swiss scientist, the director of an international medical institute, wrote to me, in somewhat guarded terms, asking me whether I would receive and, if I thought fit, transmit to the Bodleian Library for preservation there, a substantial work by Backhouse, which had recently come into his hands. In explanation of his request, my correspondent enclosed a history of the document and the written opinions of two distinguished scholars to whom it had been shown. These scholars agreed that it was of great literary and historical value, although it was clear, from their reports, that it was also somewhat obscene. The document was destined for the Bodleian Library as a natural companion to the collection of books and manuscripts already given by the author; but it was thought that it should first be examined by a British historian, and I was thought most appropriate since it was believed that, like Backhouse, I had spent some time in the British Secret Service. I accepted the proposal and since, for some reason, it was thought inconvenient to entrust such a parcel to the post, it was placed ceremoniously in my hands at Basel airport, through which, in August 1973, I happened to pass.

When I arrived back in Oxford, I unpacked the parcel, and found that it consisted of two works, neatly typed on quarto paper, each contained in an elegant case of Chinese manufacture, and prepared, in every detail – dedication, table of contents, illustrations – for the printer. Both works were in English. The first was entitled 'The Dead Past'; the second, which was liberally sprinkled with Chinese ideograms, had a French title, 'Décadence Mandchoue'. To each was prefixed a solemn – some might say an over-solemn – protestation of scrupulous veracity. Suitably impressed, I decided to start at once, and to begin with the more solid-looking volume 'Décadence Mandchoue'.

I had not read far before I realised why the Swiss custodians of these volumes had preferred not to entrust them to the post. How, I asked myself, would a right-minded and conscientious customs officer react if he were to open and read these works? The text would surely be confiscated, and perhaps the law would inconveniently take note of the sender and the addressee. For the volumes were of no ordinary obscenity. Reading them, I was reminded of the phrase of A. J. A. Symons when he discovered, with equal surprise and dismay, the pornographic Venetian letters of Frederick Rolfe, Baron Corvo: 'letters', he called them, 'that Aretino might have written at Casanova's dictation'. This parallel, which immediately struck me at my first reading of Backhouse's memoirs, was often to recur to me as I afterwards studied his strange personality. In the end, I was to find it far closer than I had any reason to foresee.

But it was not merely the obscenity of these two volumes which startled me as I read. Far more, it was the story which they told. Backhouse's scrupulously veracious memoirs recorded, in detail, a life so extraordinary, and touched, at so many points, the literary and social history of late Victorian England and late Manchu China, that having once embarked upon them, I felt obliged to go on. It was not that they were compulsive reading. Rather, I was perplexed by the personality behind them. Just as Symons was driven, by those obscene Venice letters, to pursue the elusive and preposterous personality of their author, so I felt driven, by these obscene memoirs, to study the no less elusive and preposterous character which had created them. I embarked on a 'quest for Backhouse' comparable with his *Quest for Corvo*.

Besides, there was a practical motive. How, I asked myself, could I allow such explosive documents to be preserved in the Bodleian Library, and in other public repositories, without attempting to check, as far as I could, the surprising historical statements which they contained: statements which, whether they were true or false, equally demolished the accepted portrait of the devoted scholar and raised, by implication, serious questions about his work as a scholar and benefactor?

But if one is to check the autobiography of a recluse, against what external sources is one to check it? At first I attempted to follow the clues provided by the memoirs themselves. In them, Backhouse wrote of his close friendship, even intimacy, with the English and French literary men, and the English statesmen, of the 1890s. This being so, it seemed reasonable to suppose that some trace of him would appear in their papers. But when I examined their available papers, I found that these distinguished men were remarkably – perhaps in some cases understandably – reticent on the subject. In fact, as far as I could discover, they did not mention him at all. Moreover, some of the statements, or confessions, in Backhouse's memoirs were so remarkable that I judged it prudent not to rely too implicitly on any statement that came solely from them.

I therefore decided to build up Backhouse's history, as far as possible, solely from external sources, without any reference to his memoirs, even as a starting point. I consulted those of my friends who had been in China in Backhouse's lifetime, and soon found myself in correspondence with a number of persons who might well have seen, and sometimes even had seen, the elusive baronet. Sir Harold Acton directed me to M. Henri Vetch, the French publisher in Peking, now in Hong Kong, who had published the 1939 Peking edition of *China under the Empress Dowager* and had thus been in touch with its author. M. Vetch directed me to Mr William Lewisohn, former *Times* correspondent in Peking, who was now living in retirement, being ninety years old, but *encore très lucide*, in Marlow on the Thames. Mr Lewisohn, besides giving me useful information, directed me to several retired British diplomatists who had served in Peking in the 1920s and 1930s. Mrs Danby supplemented her published accounts by some vivid touches. My friend M. Roland de Margerie confirmed some of the details already supplied to me and added some fascinating personal reminiscences. I am grateful to all these persons for their help. But in the end, what could they say? They could bring the elusive form briefly to life. They could confirm that he existed.

Prologue

Perhaps they had caught a glimpse of him – seen him pass in a
rickshaw, in his Chinese clothes, hastily covering his face lest he be
observed by profane Western eyes. Perhaps they had met him over
some necessary business – a translation, his allowance, his safety.
Then they had noted his intense nervous fear of company, his
suspicion that he was being dominated but also his unfailing courtesy and charm, his exquisite manners and feminine movement.
Or they had merely heard of him, as the fabulous hermit in the
Tartar city. Not one of them had any idea of his true personality,
or why he had come to China, or what he did there. He was an
institution – or rather, since that word implies a certain stability,
a continuous furtive presence, like some shy night-animal which
lives in a far corner of the park, and has lived there since time out
of mind, but is seldom seen, although once or twice, in times of
drought or dearth, to the astonishment of all, it has come to the
house to be fed.

Seeking to penetrate behind such superficial impressions, I
naturally looked for papers. But Backhouse left no personal
papers, and there are (I am informed) no Backhouse family papers.
Everything which he himself had written and kept with him up
to 1939 disappeared in the mysterious holocaust of that year,
which Mrs Danby has ascribed, perhaps too readily, to the
Japanese.* After that date there were only the memoirs. However,
there was one institution with which he must surely have corresponded, at the time of his great benefactions: the Bodleian Library.
I therefore turned to the archives of that Library. There I was
rewarded by finding my first solid evidence of his existence and
activity before he disappeared into his almost total oriental
seclusion.

This evidence consisted of two volumes of correspondence
concerning the Backhouse collection, kept by two successive
librarians: Falconer Madan, who was librarian till 1919, and his
successor Arthur Cowley. These two volumes shed a new and

* Mrs Danby ascribes the episode to the year 1937, and thus to Japanese pressure.
She has evidently conflated two distinct episodes: Backhouse's temporary withdrawal from Japanese pressure in 1937 and his abandonment of his house in 1939.
It was on the latter occasion that his papers were destroyed, and there is no evidence
that the Japanese had any hand in their destruction. The episodes will be described
below.

7

disconcerting light on Backhouse's activities between 1912 and 1923 and strengthened the conclusions to which I was already being driven by a critical study of his memoirs. But of course these two volumes did not go back beyond 1912 when Backhouse first approached the Bodleian with his handsome offer of Chinese books and manuscripts. He was then already in his fortieth year, and had already lived – as I deduced – at least fifteen undocumented years in China: undocumented, that is, except by his own memoirs, which, being themselves on trial, could not be used as a source.

Since the public documents of those early years did not mention him, it was clear that I must seek out private documents. There were two persons whose correspondence should have shed light on Backhouse's life in China before 1913. One of these was his collaborator, J. O. P. Bland, the co-author with him of those two books, *China under the Empress Dowager* and *Annals and Memoirs of the Court of Peking*. At the time of their first collaboration, Bland was correspondent of *The Times* in Peking. The other was Bland's superior (and rival) in the hierarchy of *The Times*, the well-known political correspondent and expert on China, Dr G. E. Morrison.

Since Morrison knew everybody in Peking, it seemed to me inconceivable that he did not know Backhouse, and as he was never inhibited by discretion, it seemed to me unlikely that he did not, at some time, express his opinions about him. I was therefore surprised and disappointed to find, in Mr Cyril Pearl's life of Morrison, no mention whatever of Backhouse as a person, or indeed of Morrison's relations with his own colleague, Backhouse's collaborator, Bland. However, on discovering from Mr Lewisohn that Morrison's own diary, though prepared for publication, had been found unpublishable precisely because of his outspokenness, I was not discouraged. I asked my friend Mr S. A. M. Adshead, who was in Australia at the time, to help me by looking at certain boxes of Morrison's original papers; for these papers are all now at the Mitchell Library in Sydney. He kindly did so, and his transcripts have been invaluable to me. They provided the earliest evidence of Backhouse's activities in Peking, evidence since supplemented by Dr Lo Hui-min's scholarly edition of Morrison's selected correspondence, of which the first volume appeared when my book was already in the publisher's hands.

More important even than Morrison's papers would be the personal papers, if any still existed, of J. O. P. Bland. Morrison died in 1920; Bland outlived Backhouse, dying in 1945. But were there any Bland papers? At first I presumed that there were not, for in 1963, in his book *The Boxer Uprising*, which I have already mentioned, Victor Purcell wrote that he had 'not, so far, been able to trace any private papers of J. O. P. Bland'. However, I soon learned that in 1970 – five years after Purcell's death – Bland's literary executor had presented his papers to the University of Toronto, where they are now to be found in the Thomas Fisher Rare Book Library. I therefore wrote to the librarian, who kindly sent me microfilms of all the papers which I needed. They included Bland's copious correspondence, his detailed diaries, and his unfinished memoirs. This rich archive proved the most valuable single source which I had yet discovered. Together with the Morrison papers, it enabled me to reconstruct an almost continuous biography of Backhouse from 1899 to 1914, and occasionally beyond.

These three manuscript sources, then – the Bodleian papers, the Morrison papers and the Bland papers – provided me with the essential material for my independent study of the life of Sir Edmund Backhouse from the time of his arrival in China until the outbreak of the Second World War. After that, there was a fourth source in his last patron and protector, the Swiss consul-general in Peking, Dr Reinhard Hoeppli, the 'editor' and only begetter of the memoirs which had been placed in my hands in Basel. The contribution of Dr Hoeppli will become apparent in due course. He was to play an important part in this story.

When I found myself in possession of these four major sources, I believed that I was in a position to reconstruct and perhaps explain the life of Backhouse. But soon it became apparent that that life, whatever relation it bore to the life described in the memoirs, was far more extraordinary and mysterious than was openly admitted in any of these documents, or perhaps even known to any of their writers. Bland, Madan, Cowley, Hoeppli, though surprised by individual manifestations of Backhouse's character, were all quite unaware of his true nature, or his full career. Even Morrison, with his rough perceptions, only saw certain obvious aspects of that character. If I were really to discover the springs of his action, I must penetrate more deeply. Fortunately, one of these four major sources supplied me with certain essential hints.

The crucial document, without which I would never have been able to break through this second barrier, was a summary account drawn up by Morrison, two years before his death, of the remarkable entrepreneurial activities of Backhouse in the years 1914–18. Nothing that I had hitherto read had given any suggestion of such activities, which, on first reading, seemed to me, as they seemed to others at the time, quite incredible. The only way to test them was to examine the records, if they were available, of the two companies which were shown to have employed Backhouse as their agent in China. These two companies were John Brown Shipbuilding and Engineering Company, of Clydeside, and the American Bank Note Company of New York. To these companies I therefore addressed my enquiries.

John Brown Shipbuilding and Engineering Company, of Clydeside, was a subsidiary of John Brown & Co., of London, and, as such, enjoyed little autonomy. The records were therefore likely to be held by the parent company in London. Most of the evidence which I found showed that Backhouse's activities were in any case controlled by the parent company, whose chairman was Charles McLaren, first Lord Aberconway. This parent company still continues, but my attempts to penetrate its records were firmly blocked. I was informed that the company almost certainly had no archives going back to the years in question, and anyway had no time to 'rummage' among past papers to look for them. However, I found that some of the documents relating to the shipbuilding activities of the company had either remained with the subsidiary company on Clydeside or had been sent to it when that company was absorbed, in 1968, into the consortium of Upper Clyde Shipbuilders, and that afterwards, when that consortium had gone into liquidation, these documents had passed into the library of Glasgow University. There the Archivist, Mr Michael Moss, kindly examined them for me and, thanks to him, I was able to reconstruct at least the outline of Backhouse's activities during his seven years on the company's pay-roll. A fuller account, based on the central records of the company, would no doubt be more colourful; but at present it is not to be had.

My application to the second of these two companies, the American Bank Note Company, was very differently received. The Chairman of its Board, Mr Edward H. Weitzen, showed an immediate interest and personally ordered the archives of the company to be examined for me. The company's researcher, Mr A. Zecher, rummaged very thoroughly, and supplied me with a series of fascinating transcripts which both confirmed and supplemented the revelations in Morrison's documents, and enabled me to establish, in some detail, the story of Backhouse and the Chinese bank notes. Afterwards, Mr Mark Elvin drew my attention to a third source which turned out to bear on the same episode. It is a file among the archives of the Foreign Office, entitled 'Affairs of Sir Edmund Backhouse.' On inspection, I found it to be a file opened in October 1917 on the orders of the British Minister in Peking, Sir John Jordan. The circumstances in which it was opened will become clear later in this book. At present it is enough to say that it provided me with the final and conclusive evidence on that curious episode: an episode which is of obvious importance in view of the disputes surrounding some of Backhouse's literary exploits.

Historical enquiry never ends. I had already, as I thought, completed my text and had sent it to the publisher, when Mr Elvin drew my attention to the Peking file. On first reading that file, I fondly believed that I need only add some details and qualify others in my chapter on Backhouse's entrepreneurial activities. But on looking more closely I soon saw that there had been another even more extraordinary episode in Backhouse's life during the First World War. The reference to it came in a confidential note by the Minister himself. This note clearly implied that Backhouse had indeed been a secret agent of the British government, and had been involved, as such, in a mysterious and protracted operation of which the Minister did not afterwards wish to be reminded. This operation evidently concerned the secret purchase of arms, probably in the summer of 1915.

At first, I must admit, I was tempted to leave it at that: to point to the mystery, declare it mysterious, and say no more. My text was complete; my publisher was ready to print it; other avocations beckoned me away. Had I not spent enough time on Backhouse? Was not his character now sufficiently illustrated, my conclusion sufficiently proved? How glad I am that I did not yield to that temptation of indolence! A few more visits to the public records soon pierced the veil of mystery and revealed the incredible story – surely the most fantastic even of Backhouse's exploits – which I shall describe in the seventh chapter of this book.

When I consider how deeply I had studied the life of Backhouse, and how nearly I had sent it to press, without having discovered any trace of this extraordinary and crucial episode, which obliged me to write a complete new chapter and re-orient my whole book, my confidence almost failed me. How could I be sure that other episodes, no less strange, were not hidden away, equally inaccessible, in the dark corners of that apparently hermit life? For assuredly there are many such dark periods, many unstirred depths in which similar slumbering monsters may yet uncoil and heave. There are the restless journeys between England and China undertaken almost every year before 1921. There are the long periods of unbroken seclusion in Peking after 1921. There are the sinister adventures in America to which George Hall alluded, as events long past, in 1917. Above all, there are the missing years between 1895, when Backhouse left Oxford, and 1898, when he arrived in China. Though I have tried hard to penetrate them, those three years, which may have been so important in the formation of his character and tastes, and in the direction of his later life, remain, surprisingly, a total blank.

I have decided to leave them a blank. No doubt, somewhere, there are documents which would shed some light, even if it were only indirect light, obtained by deduction or from retrospective allusion, on those missing years. But some archives have proved impenetrable to me, and others have been destroyed.* After many fruitless applications and illusory trails, a historian must often be content to suspend judgement and to leave obstinate problems unanswered. There is anyway, in historical research, after a certain point, a law of diminishing returns: if a problem will not yield to direct assault, it may be wisdom to pass it by and tackle another, which may indirectly serve our purpose, rather than lay a long and futile siege to an impregnable fortress. I hope that, in spite of many questions still unanswered, this brief study will nevertheless fulfil its purpose: that it will answer certain questions which have long been discussed about Backhouse's work, and provide a truer history than has hitherto been available about the mystery man whom a Chinese scholar has described to me as 'though a recluse, certainly the most interesting and colourful of the Europeans of his time in China'.

* The private papers which might have shed light on Backhouse's early years in China are those of Lord ffrench, with whom Backhouse was closely connected in 1908–9; of Percival Yetts, who was both a Chinese scholar and, while legation doctor, Backhouse's medical adviser; and of Sir Reginald Johnston, the Confucian scholar and Chinese administrator who, as we know, had unstated reasons for disliking Backhouse and was in China at the same time. But no ffrench papers have survived and we know that both Yetts and Johnston caused their own papers to be destroyed. Sir Sidney Barton, who knew Backhouse well in Peking seems to have left no personal papers. Two men whose personal judgements on Backhouse as a man and as a scholar would be of interest are Sir John Jordan, British minister in Peking 1906–1920, and Arthur Waley; but I have been unable to trace any private papers of Jordan, and Waley's papers disappeared in mysterious, not to say scandalous, circumstances after his death.

CHAPTER ONE

The Wild Oats

EDMUND TRELAWNY BACKHOUSE was born in 1873. The
Backhouse family had risen gradually from humble origins in
Lancashire. From their earliest recorded ancestor, John Backhouse of Yealand Redman, yeoman, in the time of Cromwell, they
had been Quakers: indeed, they must have ranked as one of the
oldest continuously Quaker families, coming, as they did, from
the original home of Quakerism at the time of its first founder,
George Fox. By the nineteenth century, the Backhouse family
had risen in the world of commerce. Their headquarters were
now in Darlington, where they owned a family bank; they also
had interests in collieries and railways; and business and matrimony had carried them into other counties. But always, hitherto,
they had kept within the Quaker fold. Their marriages had been
with other prominent Quaker families – Foxes in Cornwall, Fells of
Lancashire, Norfolk Gurneys – and they were involved, in one way
or another, with many of the famous Quaker mercantile dynasties:
Frys, Hoares, Barclays, Hodgkins, Peases. Several of the family
had written works of Quaker piety, and one of them was a Quaker
missionary.

Among these related Quaker dynasties there was one whose
connexion with the Backhouse family was particularly close. This
was the Fox family of Falmouth: a prolific and close-knit family
which had prospered in commerce and shipping since the eighteenth century. They controlled a shipping agency in the town,
which still survives, and the different branches of the family
established themselves in substantial country houses in the
neighbourhood. Several members of the family obtained literary
or intellectual distinction. In particular, there was Robert Were

14

Fox, F.R.S., of Penjerrick (1789–1877) and his younger brother
Charles Fox of Trebah (1797–1878), scientists and scientific
writers. Children of both these brothers married into the Backhouse family. Robert Barclay Fox, the only son of Robert Were
Fox, married Jane Gurney Backhouse, and Juliet Fox, only child
and heir of Charles Fox, married Jane Gurney Backhouse's
brother Edmund, the grandfather of our hero, thus bringing
Trebah into the possession of the Backhouse family. This Edmund
Backhouse was preoccupied, for most of his life, in the North,
and was Liberal Member of Parliament for Darlington from 1868
to 1880; but then, having inherited Trebah from his grandfather,
he moved to Cornwall. He was then known as Edmund Backhouse of Trebah, and was a J.P. for Cornwall. He died at Trebah
in June 1907.

Edmund Backhouse's son, Jonathan Edmund, was the first
member of the Backhouse family to be brought up, and to marry,
outside the Quaker world. He was born in Darlington in 1849,
but he must have spent much of his early life with his grandparents
and parents in Cornwall, and he married into a Cornish family
well known in Anglican history. His wife was Florence, daughter
of Sir John Salusbury-Trelawny, ninth baronet. But although he
had these Cornish connexions, and ultimately inherited Trebah
(which he then sold), his main interests remained in the North.
He sold the family banking business to the Barclay family and
himself became a director of Barclay's Bank. He then set up as a
country gentleman in the North. Apart from his town house,
Uplands in Darlington, he had a country house, the Rookery, at
Middleton Tyas, just over the Yorkshire border. He held offices
of dignity in the county and in 1901 would be made a baronet for
his services to the Liberal Unionist party.

Jonathan and Florence Backhouse had five sons, one of whom
died young, and a daughter. The four surviving sons, between
them, repudiated all the peculiar Quaker articles of faith: pacifism,
veracity and thrift. Of Edmund's extravagances we shall soon
hear. He was the eldest son. His three brothers all served in
the armed forces. Oliver, born in 1876, would become an
admiral. The third and fourth brothers, Roger and Miles, were
twins born in 1878. Roger would have a distinguished career in

the Navy, ending as Admiral of the Fleet; Miles (who shared Edmund's spendthrift tastes) became a soldier. The daughter, Harriet Jane, would marry Sir John Findlay of Aberlour House, Banffshire, Lord-Lieutenant of his shire and proprietor of *The Scotsman*. Findlay's sister Dora would marry Sir Roger Backhouse, the Admiral of the Fleet.

We know nothing about Edmund Backhouse's childhood, but it is probable that some of it was spent at his grandparents' home in Cornwall among his Fox relations. Certainly the interests which he acquired were less akin to those of his Backhouse predecessors, with their somewhat oppressive Quaker piety, than to those of the Foxes, who could number, apart from scientists and shipping agents, the diarist Caroline Fox, the friend of Carlyle and John Stuart Mill, and, in an earlier generation, the eccentric orientalist Charles Fox. Shipping agency, diaries, literary friendships and eccentric orientalism were to provide the substance of Edmund Backhouse's life. There was also, among his Fox relations, a more curious character. This was Charles Masson Fox, of Rosehill, Falmouth, whose grandfather, Alfred Fox, was a brother of Robert Were Fox of Penjerrick and Charles Fox of Trebah. Charles Masson Fox was a director of the family shipping agency and a timber-merchant. Thanks to his business interests, he was appointed Russian and Swedish consul in Falmouth. He was a pious Quaker bachelor living a somewhat secluded life, and entertaining himself with local affairs, chess-problems and gardening. His few friends were united by literary and homosexual interests. He also had a strong but furtive taste for homosexual pornography. In fact, it was for him that Baron Corvo wrote those outrageous 'Venice letters' to which I have referred.

In 1882 Edmund (or Trelawny, as he sometimes preferred to call himself) was sent to school at St George's, Ascot. This was a very fashionable school run by a clergyman, the Revd Herbert Sneyd-Kynnersley. Sneyd-Kynnersley has won an unfortunate fame because the success of his school drew to it several boys who afterwards became either famous or articulate or both, and who described his least attractive features: his *snobisme*, his fanatical toryism (Mr Gladstone was burnt in effigy every year on Guy Fawkes night), and his sadistic passion for beating bare buttocks. Winston Churchill, Roger Fry, Maurice Baring – their accounts supplement and overlap each other. However, the fullest account, which is also the most objective, comes from a German pupil, Harry, Count Kessler, who was afterwards well known as a liberal diplomatist and author. Kessler does not deny the savage beating (which he himself was spared), but he does show (as does Roger Fry) some of the more attractive characteristics of the school: the headmaster's genuine interest in the boys, his expeditions with them to discover the country, his enthusiasm for natural history, and the high standard of teaching. The school was a seminary for the great public schools, and it inculcated, by traditional methods, their traditional virtues: the virtues of the English gentleman, good manners and absolute truthfulness. All his life, Backhouse would strike all observers as a perfect gentleman; he was infallibly courteous; and he always professed a scrupulous regard for the truth: as he would write in 1943, 'I have ever been veracious'.

In 1886 Backhouse went from St George's to Winchester College, where he was elected a scholar, and thence, in 1892, to Merton College, Oxford, as a 'postmaster' – that is *portionis magister*, a scholar of the foundation. He read classics; but already he had discovered a linguistic genius and he began, as an under-graduate, the private study of Asiatic as well as European languages.

His career at Oxford evidently began well. He took a prize for excellent work in his third term; he narrowly missed a first class in Classical Moderations in March 1894; then he transferred to the newly established School of English Literature. However, he never completed the course. He himself ascribed this failure, which he greatly regretted, to 'a protracted and severe nervous breakdown'. The records of Merton College show that he was absent from Oxford for two terms – the Trinity and Michaelmas terms of 1894. On 10 December 1894 the college decided that he be allowed 'to return into residence on condition that a confidential servant be constantly in residence with him and he be under the supervision of an Oxford doctor'. He kept two terms after his return, but went down in the summer of 1895 without taking a degree.

In his first year at Oxford, Backhouse became a friend of Max Beerbohm who was also at Merton College and two years older than he. The few references which Max made to him in his letters to Reggie Turner do not suggest a close friendship; indeed they suggest that Backhouse was regarded as a rich, or at least spendthrift, follower who could conveniently be exploited. On one occasion he describes an unidentified 'Mr Pigeon' (presumably a nickname), who was to be held 'till I can come back and pluck his plumage at leisure', as 'the best thing we have been on since Trelawny Backhouse'. William Rothenstein, who came to Oxford to draw the inhabitants in 1893, and became a member of Max's circle, has also left a notice of Backhouse. 'I also drew Trelawny Backhouse,' he wrote, 'an eccentric undergraduate of Merton. He would entertain Max and myself and, in the middle of dinner, would make some excuse and leave us for the rest of the evening. He worshipped Ellen Terry; once he engaged a whole row of stalls which he filled with undergraduate friends. He collected jewels and later, in London, he would bring priceless emeralds to show me. Then he disappeared. Years after, I heard he was living in China, when with J. O. P. Bland, he produced a masterpiece, a book on the Empress Dowager.' We shall hear more of his jewels – as also of his tendency to withdraw from society, and his sudden vanishing tricks. In May 1895 we catch another brief glimpse of Backhouse. By now he is at the end of his undergraduate career, and we find him raising money for the defence of Oscar Wilde, at that time facing his famous prosecution. Raising money would also be one of his regular preoccupations in later life.

For, generally speaking, Backhouse was better at spending than at getting. In him, long generations of Quaker frugality at last took their revenge. Throughout his career at Oxford he spent lavishly. At the end of it the creditors began to press, and soon it became clear that they could not be satisfied. Backhouse's debts, incurred in three years as an undergraduate, are said to have amounted to the huge sum of £23,000.

The ugly facts were revealed in December 1895 when Backhouse was formally declared bankrupt. In the documents of the court he is described as 'Edmund Trelawny Backhouse of

Merton College, Oxford, late of the National Liberal Club, Whitehall Court, S.W.1'. The court proceedings dragged on through 1896 and 1897. The receivers were discharged on 3 November 1897, but the discharge was suspended for two years while settlements were made with the creditors, and it was not till 3 November 1899 that the creditors, having received payment of one-tenth of their claims, were declared to be satisfied. By that time, Backhouse was in Peking.

Where had he been in the meantime? We do not know. We can only conjecture. We can only say that there is some evidence that he had been abroad, for when he arrived in Peking he already knew a number of foreign languages, including Russian, Japanese and modern Greek, which can hardly have been acquired without serious study and foreign travel. His sister stated, in a newspaper interview after his death, that after taking his Oxford degree – by which presumably she meant (since he did not in fact take a degree) after leaving Oxford – he went to America and there spent three months in a nursing-home. Among his fellow patients, she said, were a Russian and a Japanese, and it was from them that he learned those two languages. This is no doubt what she heard from him. At any rate, it is evidence that he had been to America; for his sister would have known that. At times of crisis Backhouse tended to disappear and declare himself gravely ill, and it may well be that when the bankruptcy proceedings were brought, he was conveniently abroad.

This conjecture can be supported by another conjecture. For how, we may ask, did his father face this unfortunate affair? Jonathan Backhouse was, by all accounts, exceptionally careful of money, and he would naturally be indignant at his son's outrageous extravagance. On the other hand he was also a very respectable banker, who could not, with equanimity, have seen his son and heir declared publicly and legally bankrupt. In the event, the affair was managed discreetly and no fact was published which stated the connexion between the bankrupt son and the banker father. But we may suppose that, however reluctantly, Mr Backhouse would have sought to prevent the bankruptcy proceedings, had he been able. The fact that they went forward, and that no current address in England was given for Edmund, suggests that he had already gone abroad. The address given in the documents, 'of Merton College, Oxford', merely indicates that these were undergraduate debts. The second address, 'late of the National Liberal Club', implies that he was no longer there.

Further, the Bankruptcy Act of 1869, which was in force at the time, declared that bankruptcy was incurred if a debtor had, 'with intent to defeat or delay his creditors . . . departed out of England, or, being out of England, remained out of England'. It seems probable, in all the circumstances, that this is precisely what Backhouse had done, and that this is how the bankruptcy proceedings were initiated. In other words, having left Oxford and established himself briefly in London, and finding himself pursued by creditors in both places, Backhouse sought refuge abroad; his creditors thereupon appealed to the law; he was declared bankrupt; and his family were left to repair the damage as best they could. Between parsimony, prudence and care for the reputation of his family, his father handled the matter skilfully enough. The creditors were bought off cheaply; the unfortunate facts were successfully suppressed; and Jonathan Backhouse seems to have committed himself to a future policy: he would provide his son with a modest allowance, while warning him that he could no longer expect a customary inheritance. Edmund's prospective capital had been anticipated in the cost of his bankruptcy, and he could not be trusted to manage an estate.

So we have brought our hero to China: somewhat mysteriously, we must admit, and through dangerous domestic rifts and economic shoals; but he is there. Why he came, on what conditions, or with what hopes, we do not know. Of his first appearance there we have one brief and tantalising notice. It comes in the correspondence of Sir Robert Hart, the Ulsterman who effectively created the Chinese Imperial Maritime Customs.

Hart was by now a man of great power in China, which had been his home almost continuously for forty-four years. He lived in great splendour in Peking, dispensing lavish hospitality and maintaining a brass band; and many men who became prominent in Chinese affairs had begun by serving under him. Backhouse evidently hoped to begin that way too, for on 26 February 1899 Hart wrote to a friend that 'a very good candidate' for his department had arrived in the city, namely, Mr Edmund Back-house, the son of a director of Barclay's Bank. Hart added that Backhouse was aged twenty-five, knew Russian and Chinese, and had come with letters of recommendation from Lord Salisbury, the Duke of Devonshire, and Joseph Chamberlain. Lord Salisbury was Prime Minister at the time, the Duke of Devonshire was Lord President of the Council and Joseph Chamberlain was Colonial Secretary. Such powerful sponsorship seems too good to be true. It makes us ask what Backhouse, whom we last saw as a disgraced wastrel, can have been doing in the last three years to deserve it. Unfortunately we cannot answer this question, so we must leave it in suspense. Anyway, powerful though it might be, it was not powerful enough. Hart admitted that Backhouse would be a very desirable addition to his service, but he added that 'at present I can't afford it'. However, it seems that he en-couraged Backhouse to hope that a vacancy would be found.

In fact Backhouse never found a place in the Imperial Customs. How he lived in Peking at first is not clear. It is possible that he acted, for a time at least, as a 'student-interpreter' at the British legation and that he translated occasional documents for British officials. Certainly any Englishman who had a good knowledge of Chinese had plenty of opportunities at that time. For Back-house arrived in China at a time of great excitement. 1898, the year of his arrival, was the year of 'the Hundred Days' Reform', the beginning of a chain of events which would culminate in the revolution of 1911 and the overthrow of the Ch'ing Dynasty. It was the greatest crisis in the long reign of Tzŭ-hsi, the Empress Dowager.

In 1898 the Empress Dowager had reigned, *de facto*, under the form of successive 'regencies' for thirty-seven years. A member of the Manchu clan of Yehonala, chosen as concubine of the third class for the young Hsien-fêng Emperor, she had found herself, at his early death in 1861, in exile and defeat at Jehol, suddenly within reach of political power: for she was the mother of the heir to the throne, now five years old. At the time of the Hsien-fêng Emperor's death, the court was in convulsion. There was foreign invasion, palace conspiracy, and internal rebellion. But by prompt and ruthless action, and with the support of her

Manchu kinsman Jung-lu, who was to become her constant adviser, Tzŭ-hsi prevailed over all opposition and established her first regency. Theoretically it was a joint regency with the late emperor's legitimate widow, 'the Eastern Empress' Hsiao-chên, and of course it was limited to twelve years, till her son, the new T'ung-chih Emperor should be of age. But the Eastern Empress was a cypher, and when the twelve years were up, Tzŭ-hsi, having tasted power, was not disposed to abandon it. The opportune death of her son, the equally opportune suicide of his pregnant widow, and some careful dispositions of force, enabled her to procure the succession of another infant emperor, and for herself a second regency. The new emperor was her nephew, Tsai-t'ien, who now reigned as the Kuang-hsü Emperor. In due course he too came of age, but Tzŭ-hsi contrived to ensure that this did not make much difference – at least until the summer of 1898.

For by 1898 China had suffered a series of humiliating defeats at the hands of the imperialist powers both of the West and of the East. The Russians had imposed their control over Manchuria, the French had seized Indo-China, the Japanese had detached Korea and Formosa, and all the Western powers had set foot in the seaports. Shaken by these disasters, and by the clear evidence that the Celestial Empire was no longer an independent power, Chinese patriots and intellectuals, especially in the south, where Manchu rule had seldom been appreciated, had looked for the cause of decay and discovered it in the corruption of the court. The defeat by Japan in 1894 had been the last humiliation, because Japan, in Chinese eyes, was a barbarian country, a cultural dependency of China. But the Japanese victory also offered a lesson. If an Eastern society could become powerful by borrowing Western methods, China could be regenerated too, by the same means. So there arose, in southern China, and particularly in Canton, the Young China movement of Reform – reform on a Western model, or at least by the adoption of Western methods. By 1898 the reformers had a party in the imperial palace, and they saw their opportunity in palace politics. They resolved to capture the puppet Kuang-hsü Emperor and to encourage him to emancipate himself, as their ally, from the archaic and indeed illegitimate despotism of his old aunt and her irreparably corrupt court.

For a brief period they succeeded. The docile Kuang-hsü Emperor accepted his role. Decree after decree was issued, reform after reform set out. The ancient system of education and examination was abolished. Modern subjects, a modern university, were authorised. Sinecures in the armed forces and in the state were to be abolished. So were the special privileges of the Manchus as a ruling caste. The fleet was to be reorganised, industries promoted, Western technology and means of communication introduced. It was even rumoured that the palace was to be drastically purged, the eunuch system abolished, the empire itself nationalised, and the Empress Dowager quietly removed from power. Such projects naturally caused alarm among those whose vested interests were at stake, and they rallied, in self-defence, round the threatened Empress Dowager. They were lucky in that treason came to their aid. Yüan Shih-k'ai, Judicial Commissioner of Chih-li, the general on whom the reformers relied, and who had pledged his loyalty and obedience to the Emperor, promptly revealed all their plans to the Empress's confidant, the Grand Secretary Jung-lu. It was an act of treachery that would be of great significance. Its immediate effect was no less important. Thus alerted, the old lady showed once again that she could strike first. By a bold *coup de main* the Emperor was arrested, imprisoned, and forced 'spontaneously' to beg his aunt to resume the functions of Empress-regent. Only the warnings of the Western diplomatic corps, and particularly of the British minister, Sir Claude Macdonald, saved him from execution. His life was spared, but it was clear that unless he should survive his formidable aunt (which for that very reason seemed unlikely), he would never be a force in politics again. 'The Hundred Days' of reform were over. The third regency of the Empress Dowager had begun.

Almost immediately, she had to cope with a new threat. 1898 had been the year of the pro-Western enthusiasts, of the progressive Young China reformers. 1899 was the year of the anti-Western fanatics, of the reactionary 'Boxers'. Throughout that year, in province after province, the Boxer movement gathered strength. Its leaders declared themselves invincible, even invulnerable; they claimed magical powers; and they appealed to

Chinese patriots to rise and destroy the foreigners, their missions, their religion, their innovations, their ideas. By the end of the year the movement had become so powerful that the imperial court had to face the problem which it posed. Should it oppose the Boxer movement and thus appear to be the creature of the foreign powers which were destroying the Chinese empire? Or should it declare itself the patron of the movement and use this new and seemingly powerful force to emancipate both China and itself from the domination of those foreign powers?

The party of reaction at court naturally supported the latter course, and three of the imperial princes openly allied themselves with the Boxers. One of them, Tsai-i (Prince Tuan), became the new confidant of the Empress, the director of her policy. On 24 January 1900, the Empress showed her support for the Boxers by appointing Tsai-i's eldest son, P'u-chun, as heir apparent: heir not to the reigning Kuang-hsü Emperor but to his predecessor, her son, the T'ung-chih Emperor. Clearly the deposition of the unsatisfactory Kuang-hsü Emperor was intended – if the Boxers should win. By the summer of 1900 it seemed that the Boxers might well win, provided that the imperial government acted quickly to forestall Allied intervention.

For already a foreign expeditionary force was preparing to intervene. In mid-June the crisis came to a head. Almost simultaneously, the Allies occupied the coastal forts at Taku, which commanded the entry to Tientsin and the route to Peking, and the Empress and Tsai-i connived at the entry of the Boxer army into Peking. The opposition at court was overruled, and foreign envoys were ordered to leave the city. Next day the German Minister, Baron von Ketteler, was murdered. While the Allied powers protested and assembled their forces to strike, the Boxers took over the city and a massacre of foreigners and Chinese Christians began.

The result was the famous 'siege of the legations'. The foreigners in Peking took refuge in their legations, and for fifty-five days, under the direction of the British minister, Sir Claude Macdonald, who had come to diplomacy after a military career, they barricaded themselves against the successive assaults of the Boxers and the mob. When the Allied forces finally entered

Peking and broke up the siege, the Empress Dowager fled hurriedly with her court on 'an autumn tour of inspection' to the ancient city of Sian in the province of Shensi. On her way she issued edicts, in the name of the helpless Emperor, assuming to himself the entire blame for events. He was, after all, expendable. The court remained in Sian for a year. Meanwhile the Allied troops occupied the abandoned capital and exacted heavy retribution for their past sufferings. The Boxer leaders were executed, the Boxer princes forced into suicide or exile. Indemnities were exacted. Cut off alike from the reformers whom it had crushed and from the reactionaries whom it was now forced to disown, the imperial court was isolated, at the mercy of its foreign conquerors. The independent Chinese *ancien régime* had been destroyed, and could never be restored.

Politically, however, the Western powers were obliged to compromise. Much though they hated the Empress and her court, whose responsibility for the events in Peking was clear, their freedom of action was limited by their own mutual rivalries; and seeing no tolerable alternative they invited the chastened Empress back, though on severe terms. She returned in September 1901 to find much of the city in ruins; for the destructive savagery of the Boxers had been followed by indiscriminate looting by native mobs and foreign soldiers, in which officers, and officials, even ambassadors, were not ashamed to participate. However, under the protection of the powers, and by their mutual jealousies, the form of the old court was preserved. This last defeat had made it more fragile than before, more subservient to the West, more open to Western influence. Any thought of practical independence was forgotten. The new heir apparent was deposed. The Kuang-hsü Emperor retained his shaken and shadowy throne. But internally the court remained the same. It was still the court of the Empress Dowager. With its archaic etiquette, its incorrigible, universal corruption and its government by eunuchs, it entered its last, twilight phase unreformed.

Such were the dramatic public events of Backhouse's first three years in Peking. From his arrival he was inevitably exposed to them and, to some extent, involved in them. They also brought him his first patron in China, Dr George Ernest Morrison.

CHAPTER TWO

The Scholar

GEORGE ERNEST MORRISON was an Australian of Hebridean ancestry. He was a forceful, not to say aggressive, personality who was already, in 1898, a significant figure in the Western colony in Peking. Born in Geelong, and educated in Melbourne, he had discovered an early taste for adventurous travel and from the age of seventeen he had carried out a series of remarkable journeys of exploration, on foot or by canoe, in his native continent. Aged twenty, he had crossed Australia from north to south on foot, alone, without a compass, covering 2000 miles in 123 days. He had then gone on an expedition to New Guinea, got himself involved in a skirmish with a party of natives, and been speared by them. Carrying the barbed spear-head in his body, he had travelled to Edinburgh University, where it was removed and where he completed his interrupted medical studies and took a doctor's degree. He had then resumed his travels. He had knocked about the South Seas, walked across Jamaica, worked in copper-mines in Spain, taken a further medical course in Paris, been court physician to the Shereef of Wazan in Morocco and house-surgeon in a hospital in Ballarat; and in 1894, wearing a Chinese cap and gown, and with only eighteen pounds in his pocket, he had walked, 'leisurely, inarticulate and unarmed'* through the whole breadth of China, from Shanghai to Rangoon. This last exploit, which he commemorated in a book, stood him in good stead when he decided, at the age of thirty-five, to become a journalist. In 1895, in London, he was recommended to Moberly Bell, the managing director of *The Times*, and was taken on by the foreign

---

* The phrase is from Bland's (unpublished) memoirs. There is a touch of malice in the adjective 'inarticulate', which refers to Morrison's inability to speak Chinese.

department, then headed by the most famous and influential of *Times* correspondents, Valentine Chirol. Chirol sent him back to the Far East, first to Indo-China and Siam to report on French penetration, then, in 1897, to Peking. For the rest of his life Peking would be his base. By his energy and political flair he would very quickly become famous in the European colony there, feared by all his rivals, hated by the German and Russian diplomatic representatives, one of the most valued of Chirol's correspondents. He would be known summarily as 'Chinese Morrison', 'Morrison of Peking'.

After his return to China in 1897, Morrison threw himself into his new task with his usual energy. He very quickly got to know everyone – or at least all the foreign diplomatists and officials. He built up a network of informants. He also continued his travels and adventures. He could soon claim to know personally every province of China except the forbidden sanctuary of Tibet. As part of the process of self-education, he built up a large library of books on China in Western languages. This library became famous, and Morrison, who welcomed any means of self-advertisement, let it be known that he intended to leave it in China as a token of his disinterested love of the country. That was when he was still a bachelor. Later, when he was over fifty, he would marry his secretary and would change his mind about the library: he would then sell it for £35,000 to a Japanese aristocrat and it would be dispersed in Japan.

To the other members of the European community in China, who seldom left the coastal cities, Morrison was legendary for his understanding of China and Chinese affairs, on which he spoke with unanswerable authority. He claimed that his views were entirely objective and rational, being 'impervious to all sentimental or personal considerations'. That being so, he did not easily suffer contradiction. The asperity of his language about all whose interpretation differed from his own sometimes shocked his employers on *The Times* and Chirol was often driven to remonstrate with him about it. He would describe them as 'cackle-headed asses', hirelings of foreign powers, liars and dunces, and he would not scruple to wreck their careers rather than allow their independent opinions. In consequence, he was more respected for his ability and feared for his influence than loved for his character; and at the end of his life, though he had enjoyed a great reputation, he would have few friends.

Morrison's great virtues, as a correspondent, were his energy in collecting information, his realism in interpreting it, and his clarity of expression. However, he had one great handicap, the Achilles heel in an otherwise invulnerable body. He could neither read nor speak Chinese. This defect, which he never made any attempt to repair, naturally put him at an initial disadvantage in relation to the other experts in Peking. Fortunately, he himself did not regard it as a defect. In his own eyes it was more than compensated by another quality, which raised him above all possible rivals: his unerring political judgment. Lord Curzon once ascribed to him – ironically it is true, but it was accepted as a tribute – a remarkable capacity for 'the intelligent anticipation of events'. This unerring judgment was based not on a profound knowledge of China, nor even on a deep interest in China, but on a strongly held personal point of view. He knew where he stood.

In political terms Morrison was a radical imperialist. His imperialism was unhesitant, uncomplicated, ruthless. He believed in beneficent British power which, being beneficent, was entitled to govern and modernise the world. In China *per se* he showed little interest: what interested him was China as a theatre of competing imperialisms. From the moment of his arrival in Peking, he threw himself into this 'great game' of imperial power politics. He did not intend merely to report events: he proposed to make them. That meant to establish British influence as against that of the French and the Russians, the Germans and the Japanese. 'Our true heritage', he wrote, a few months after his arrival, 'is all South-East Asia up to and including the Yang-tse valley.' To ensure that result, he was an unashamed war-monger. From the beginning, he worked openly to promote a Russo-Japanese war, and when that war came, it would be known as 'Morrison's war'. His philosophy was not that of a journalist: it was that of an empire-builder: a Cecil Rhodes or a Milner in the Far East. His ultimate ambition was to be, like them, an imperial statesman: he would be Prime Minister of Australia, or wield proconsular power as British minister in China.

Meanwhile, what of the Chinese? Morrison's concern with the internal politics of China was entirely subordinate to his imperialism. He made no attempt to understand the Chinese point of view. He was quite unaware of the ideological ferment that was working among the Chinese intelligentsia. He would be taken by surprise by both the great Chinese insurrections which occurred in his time – the Boxer Rising of 1900 and the revolution of 1911. In general, he did not see any danger, or need, of revolution. Of course he believed in reform: the archaic government of China must be modernised, westernised, anglicised; but he believed that this could be done without difficulty: the ruling native government merely needed to take his advice and introduce 'a constitutional form of government'. So he would invest successively in a series of *de facto* rulers – in 'that grand old woman', the Empress Dowager, in the politicians of her imperial successor, in the Southern Reform Movement, ultimately in that treacherous and unscrupulous adventurer to whom he would become political adviser, President Yüan Shih-k'ai. Always, as he said, 'essentially optimistic', always ready to see reform round the corner, he would adapt his views to every change of circumstance. This involved him in naïve idealisation of unlikely persons hardly distinguishable from political sycophancy.* It would also involve him in 'volte-faces' which would precipitate a revolution in *The Times*.

All this was in the future. When Backhouse arrived in Peking, Morrison had but recently established himself there. But already he had made himself famous and formidable. If his political intelligence was naïve, that had not yet been shown. What was clear, and what would compensate for any such naïvety in purely Chinese affairs, was the dynamism of his personality, the efficiency of his political intelligence system, the clarity and trenchancy of his views and, it must be added, his skill and ruthlessness as an operator. He sought power; he knew where power lay, and did not shrink from using the necessary means to reach it.

---

* Thus Morrison, when adviser to Yüan Shih-k'ai, swallowed whole Yüan's account of his treachery to the reformers in 1898. This treachery had ruined the Reform movement in which Morrison believed. Morrison's naïvety in this matter – or his sycophancy to present power – is too much even for his biographer, Mr Pearl.

With Morrison, serving under him as correspondent of *The Times*, was another man who was to become even more closely associated with Backhouse than he: John Otway Percy Bland. Bland was an Ulsterman who, in 1883, as an undergraduate at Trinity College, Dublin, had been offered a post in the Chinese Imperial Maritime Customs by his fellow-Ulsterman, Sir Robert Hart. He had served as secretary to Hart; then in 1896 he had left to become secretary to the Municipal Council of Shanghai: a corporation which was dominated by the British colony and run on British lines. Here he became useful to Morrison and was employed as a part-time correspondent of *The Times* in Shanghai. In 1904 he would give up his position as secretary of the Municipal Council of Shanghai and become agent there for an important financial company, the British and Chinese Corporation, which combined the main British business interests in China; but he continued to act as correspondent of *The Times*.

A genial extrovert, of sporting tastes and some literary interests, a fluent, prolific and elegant writer, expansive and sociable, Bland was very different from the nervous, egocentric, aggressive Morrison, and this difference would gradually grow into mutual dislike. Bland disliked Morrison's arrogance, his self-conceit, his ruthless methods, his monopolising spirit which would brook no rival, no independence; and Morrison disliked Bland precisely because he could be a rival and was of an independent spirit. They also disliked each other's political views. So long as Morrison reigned in Peking and Bland was confined to Shanghai, this mutual dislike did not lead to open friction. But when they collided, there would be trouble. Ultimately their relations would become so strained that China could not hold two such forceful men with such radically opposed philosophies.

Bland was a lifelong tory, with a deep sympathy for tradition. While admitting Morrison's 'genius' and political flair, he disliked him for his political dogmatism, which paid so little heed (as he thought) to social realities, and for his aggressive imperialism. He also despised him for his superficiality, his assumption that he could understand all Chinese problems without knowledge of the language or real sympathy with the people and their traditions. Bland himself was a competent scholar in Chinese and could seldom resist the temptation to emphasise Morrison's ignorance in this field. In fact, Morrison's great value to *The Times* did not depend on his understanding of China: it depended rather on his understanding of the aims of foreign imperialism in China. China, in England, was not news. The penetration of China by foreign powers was.

Bland, on the other hand, was chiefly interested in China, and there his views were completely different from those of Morrison. Both as a tory and as a friend of China, he was radically opposed to 'the great game' of imperialist power politics. Fundamentally, he was opposed to the policy of 'spheres of influence': he believed in the older policy of 'the Open Door' and peaceful trade with China. He wanted Anglo-Russian agreement, not a Japanese war against Russia in Britain's interest. 'After all', he would protest to Morrison, 'we are in China for trade first, and not only to gain victories over the Russian or German diplomatists in Peking'. And he was morally disgusted by the brutality of the imperialist powers, 'the atrocious behaviour of so-called civilised countries in China'. What he hoped to see was not a victorious contest with other imperialist powers over the spoils of China, which would simply play into the hands of the corrupt Chinese mandarins, but the internal reform of Chinese administration; for 'we are in China, not Germany, and it is the policy and behaviour of the Chinese that chiefly affects us and our trade'.

Morrison seemed to argue that 'if we get the best of the German and the Jap, we shall have things our own way' and be able to dictate such internal reform. But Bland did not share Morrison's easy optimism. Morrison's idea that China was 'well suited for constitutional government' seemed to him quite unrealistic. He believed that the ancient structure of the Chinese empire could not be reformed overnight by a mere political decision, and that any real reform would entail profound change, probably a revolution, 'which must either mend or end the body politic'; and on the whole, being of a somewhat pessimistic cast of mind, he believed that it would end it, at least in its present form. The ultimate heirs, he believed, would not be the 'westernised' Chinese of the southern cities, cut off from the reality of Chinese life and foreign to Chinese traditions. He did not believe in the

long-term westernisation of China: he believed that China would
always survive foreign domination, foreign influence. He had no
respect for those missionaries and other Western idealists who
sought to impose their imported alien ideals on an independent
civilisation. He disliked the Kuomintang and its Christianised
leaders, Sun Yat-sen and Chiang Kai-shek. He regarded Sun Yat-
sen as a self-seeking charlatan and his 'three principles' as 'amazing
piffle' which no Chinese took seriously except 'for purposes of
fooling the foreigner'. When the Kuomintang came to power, he
would see it as a corrupt government doomed ultimately to be
swept aside by a revived monarchy based on the peasantry. But
his greatest contempt was for the high-minded, 'invertebrate',
'Chatham House' liberals, the sentimental internationalists of the
'Foreign Office School of Thought' who, in the 1930s, insisted
on seeing Kuomintang China as a Western liberal democracy,
striving, with their help, to attain their ideal of liberal virtue. His
particular *bêtes noires*, in this respect, were Lord Robert Cecil,
Lionel Curtis and Arnold Toynbee.

Bland's views remained consistent all his life. In Europe, in the
1930s, he would be equally contemptuous of those 'liberal'
British conservatives who, being inspired by the same general
philosophy – that all men are ultimately pursuing, and will be
saved by, the same ideals – thought that they should, and could
'appease' Hitler. In his later years he would be a vigorous propagandist against the policy of appeasement. He would regard
British political writers who pretended to understand Nazism
without having read its basic documents with the same contempt
with which he had once regarded Morrison, who pretended to
understand China without being able to read Chinese; and he
would press for an unexpurgated edition of *Mein Kampf*.

Morrison and Bland were to play a great part in the life of
Backhouse. They would be rivals as his patrons and would fight
fiercely for the sole control of his services. Their opposition to
each other would be intense and at times unscrupulous. They came
to hate each other personally. But behind all personal antipathy,
their mutual hatred was essentially ideological. Morrison believed, with the missionaries, the capitalists and the democrats,
that China could only be saved by westernisation under British

influence. Bland believed that westernisation would fail, that China must and would reassert its independence, must rediscover its historic identity and reform itself on that base.

It is unprofitable now to decide between them. In a sense, both were proved wrong, because their programmes were too exclusive. Bland was right in supposing that the westernised, Christianised, mission-trained Chinese of the southern cities would never impose their programme on the vast peasant society of China. He was right to see that their government, when it was established, was too narrowly based, too corrupt, to solve the problems which faced it. But even the peasant monarchy which has replaced it is a monarchy which has adopted the technology, though not the political institutions or ideals, of the West. To that extent the Westerners, like Morrison, were right. Westernisation was a stage on the way to the new Celestial Empire of Mao Tse-tung.

To Morrison in Peking, faced with exciting new developments in Chinese politics, and unable to read the Chinese evidence, the newly arrived Backhouse was a great discovery. Already, at the beginning of 1899, we find Backhouse working for Morrison, reading Chinese newspapers for him, translating official Chinese documents, and acquiring thereby an intimate knowledge of Chinese politics and political habits. He seems to have lived near Morrison, in the Chinese city, and to have become devoted to him. Then, in April 1899, he suffered one of those accidents to which, all his life, he was prone. He was bitten by a dog which, according to him and to Morrison, was 'undoubtedly rabid'. Morrison sent him to Shanghai, with a letter of introduction to Bland, asking him to send Backhouse to an English doctor there, Dr Stanley. It was thus that Backhouse first met his future collaborator.

In his letter of introduction, Morrison described Backhouse as 'a gentleman of Quaker family, father a banker for many years, M.P., cousin of Peases and other Quakers of Darlington. . . . He is an exceptionally gifted fellow. Speaks, reads and writes, among other languages, modern Greek and Russian, and knows 3000 Chinese characters. Very well informed, and I am much attached to him. He is to get the first vacancy in the Customs. He is very unassuming.' Indeed, Backhouse was more than unassuming: his letters, throughout his life, could be excessive in their humility. This humility, combined as it was with extraordinary abilities, often aroused protective impulses in more robust spirits. But it had its reverse side: it could be sycophantic in itself, and it could be the mask for other, more real and less attractive qualities.

Bland looked after Backhouse in Shanghai, but did not send him to Dr Stanley, whose last case of rabies had died horribly under his treatment. Backhouse returned to Peking very grateful for Bland's care of him, and was received back with affection by Morrison, who regarded him as 'a very fine fellow' and cherished him anxiously: for this brilliant and devoted linguist was a treasure which he intended to keep for himself.

Next year, when the Boxer Rising broke out, Backhouse was still in Peking, working for Morrison. He was among those Westerners besieged in the legations; but he made very little impact on the minds of his colleagues. 'I doubt whether he was much help to anyone,' says one of his relations, 'as I heard that he had managed to shoot his own sergeant-major' – another of the accidents to which he was prone. Apart from that, we hear nothing of him till the relieving Western armies had entered and occupied Peking. Then he took part in the looting. In a contemporary note, Morrison records that Backhouse and one Peachey were arrested by Russian soldiers 'on a charge of blackmailing, looting and robbery'. The blackmail was presumably in the interest of the loot: threats to denounce Chinese as Boxers unless they delivered their possessions.

When the Russians arrested Backhouse it cannot have been out of any objection to looting in principle. The Russians themselves joined enthusiastically in the general scramble, and stripped the Summer Palace bare. Presumably Backhouse's crime consisted in looting in their area: for at that time he was living in temporary quarters in the street, Wang Fu Ching, which Europeans afterwards named after its most famous inhabitant, Morrison Street; and this street was now under Russian control. On his release, he decided to move into the British section, inside the Imperial City, and obtained permission to occupy part of the house belonging to a Chinese court official, Ching-shan. Here too he would find opportunities for loot: opportunities which would be the beginning of a long and tortuous story.

Nor should we detect any note of disapproval in Morrison's record of the fact. As Bland would afterwards write, 'everyone was in the hunt: Ministers plenipotentiary, Customs staff, journalists, even missionaries.' The connoisseurs made straight for the houses of rich Manchus and well-known Chinese collectors of porcelain and jade. If Morrison himself was relatively unsuccessful, that was only because he had been immobilised by a gunshot wound in the thigh, which he had received while defending an exposed position during the siege. He afterwards complained bitterly of this untimely immobilisation: with his exceptional local knowledge he might otherwise, as he said, have emerged richer in plunder than all the other connoisseurs. But he managed nevertheless to secure some notable relics from the Palace, amongst them the jade prayer-book from the Empress Dowager's bedroom.

However, if Morrison's wound deprived him of the lion's share of the loot, the siege did bring him some indirect gain. At one moment it was announced in England that the legations had been captured and the defenders massacred. *The Times* thereupon published an obituary notice of him so laudatory that, as he himself afterwards remarked, they simply had to raise his salary when he emerged alive and would never be able to dismiss him afterwards. In particular, the writer of the article remarked that 'with extraordinary judgment, amounting almost to genius, in an atmosphere which he used himself to describe as "saturated with lies", he discriminated with unfailing accuracy between what was true and what was false.' We shall have particular occasion, in due course, to notice an instance of this extraordinary judgment.

When all was over and order had been restored in Peking, Backhouse was well established as Morrison's translator. They would sit up together, late at night, Backhouse translating Chinese documents and Morrison turning them into despatches. The relationship was cordial, even affectionate. Backhouse's letters to Morrison breathe a spirit of devoted loyalty. 'It is not likely, while you are so good as to be willing to see me', he wrote on 21 November 1903, 'that I should ever wish to keep away,' and again, next year, 'I was very sorry not to see you again before leaving, that I might have thanked you for all your kindness to me, and the great help you have so freely given to me in difficulty;' and later, in 1905, 'nobody was ever so generous to his friends as you'. Under Morrison's protection, Backhouse, the unobtrusive scholar, already noted for his hermit tendencies, studied constantly to improve his languages.* In September 1904 Morrison wrote to Bland that 'Backhouse now speaks Mongol with the greatest fluency and will quickly have mastered Manchu, speaking it, reading it, writing it. No one in Peking approaches him in the ease with which he can translate Chinese.'

Morrison was not the only man to make use of Backhouse's remarkable linguistic attainments. Immediately after the suppression of the Boxer Rising, Sir Claude Macdonald, the British minister, was recalled from Peking. This was no doubt a necessary diplomatic move. Macdonald had taken so prominent a part in defending the legations – and indeed, afterwards, in arranging for the auction of the loot – that it would hardly have been tactful to retain him as accredited envoy to the restored Empress. If the past was to be buried, a new envoy, unidentified with the violent events of 1900, was needed. The British government therefore made a neat switch of its envoys in the Far East. It transferred Macdonald from Peking to Tokyo and brought Sir Ernest Satow from Tokyo to Peking to replace him. Satow was a scholar as well as a diplomatist, well-versed both in Chinese and in Japanese. He remained in Peking for six years, and during those years Backhouse was evidently employed by him to translate documents for the British legation. He was also occasionally attached as interpreter to British military units. But his principal patron was Morrison.

It seems that Backhouse worked for Morrison without payment. Morrison was his patron, not his employer, and the admiration seems to have been mutual. Besides, by this time, Backhouse had a useful post in Peking, which he may have owed to Morri-

* Mrs Danby suggests that Backhouse only became a recluse late in life; but although the tendency grew, it was always there. In 1922 Francis Norris, the Anglican bishop in Peking, who had known Backhouse since his arrival in Peking in 1898, wrote that he had been 'a recluse for 20 years'; and Bland refers frequently, in the period 1908-10, to Backhouse's hermit character.

son's patronage. In 1901 he was appointed Professor of Law and Literature at the newly founded university of Peking, the sole lasting result of 'the Hundred Days' Reform'. This was a part-time post and probably of no great weight, but it shows that the Chinese government, which made the appointment, regarded him as an adequate scholar in both subjects. He was certainly well-read in literature; and he had, or could mug up, enough knowledge of the law for the purpose. For the purpose of the new university was to introduce into the curriculum Western subjects such as law and legal institutions, of which the Chinese themselves knew little, and of which competent teachers were hard to find. As a foreign scholar with a considerable knowledge of Chinese, Backhouse would have been an obvious choice. He had the qualifications; he was on the spot; and Morrison, who had an interest in keeping him in Peking, would have been a useful sponsor. Of Backhouse's duties and success in this post, which he held for ten years, we know nothing: the documents of the university of Peking have disappeared from human, or at least from Western, sight.

In 1905 Morrison visited Britain, and Backhouse gave him letters of introduction to his father and to his sister, Lady Findlay. To Sir Jonathan Backhouse he no doubt went, in part, as an emissary of peace, to show that the wastrel Edmund had made good and settled down. To Lady Findlay, who retained a lifelong affection for her wayward brother, he would take a more personal message. Morrison performed his mission with success. He wrote to Backhouse from London that Sir Jonathan had received him 'with the utmost cordiality, and it was delightful to me to see how cordial was the admiration which he had for you. He wrote to me and thanked me for my unfailing kindness to you. I replied saying that so far from being indebted to me, you had rendered me services which I never could forget and had laid both myself and *The Times* under great obligation. I think I spoke to your father in the way you would have wished. I told him I thought you ought to have a new house in Peking, and I said that £12,000 would enable you to purchase a modest establishment.' Morrison added, 'I should have liked to have seen your father's name among the new peers. It is however quite sure that he will receive a peerage sooner or later.' From all that we know of Edmund Backhouse, he would have liked that too.

Back in Peking, Morrison received a letter from Sir Jonathan which showed that he regarded him as a good influence on his son. 'I hear fair accounts of Edmund,' he wrote. 'He seems still unable to undertake any fixity of work. . . . I attach great importance to your kindly guidance of him.' However, it does not seem that the hint about the £12,000 bore fruit. Sir Jonathan's cordiality did not extend as far as that.

Morrison continued to guide Backhouse, and to use his services as a translator and informant. He also used his expertise in Chinese *objets d'art*. In December 1905, while Morrison was in England, Backhouse wrote to him announcing an important purchase. He had recently acquired, he said, 'an interesting scroll'. He had bought it, through an intermediary, from an impoverished mandarin family of Shansi. The scroll was a specimen of the calligraphy of Huai Su, a Buddhist monk whose elegant 'grass characters' – the informal Chinese cursive script – 'were famous in the T'ang dynasty, and men like the great poet Li Po were anxious to get specimens of his work. The scroll', Backhouse added, 'is dated 746 and is of great value.' He had been offered a large sum for it in the Peking book market. . . . Morrison's appetite was whetted by this description and he agreed to buy a share in the scroll. Afterwards, Morrison advanced a further sum to Backhouse and became the sole owner of this very valuable scroll. We know no more about it, for the scroll has since disappeared; but we may keep the episode in mind, for valuable scrolls, 'grass hands' and partnerships in the purchase of curios will soon recur in our story.

For this guidance and collaboration, Backhouse continued to express to Morrison his somewhat unctuous gratitude. In 1906 he returned to England, travelling with a British medical attendant, Dr Cochrane, who 'has kindly consented to accompany me, as I have been having heart-attacks, and need constant treatment'. Dangerous illnesses, often imaginary, were part of the Backhouse syndrome. 'Some day', he told Morrison, 'I hope to return; but in any case I shall always gratefully remember your exceeding kindness towards me.' Sure enough, he was soon back in Peking, eager 'to translate interesting documents against time for you, as when we translated the Tibetan convention together'. When Morrison returned from abroad and sought out Backhouse, Backhouse was delighted. 'I am indeed grateful to you for your great and unfailing kindness,' he wrote. 'No sooner are you back in Peking, with many important matters to attend to, than you are once more helping me over my difficulties. No words of mine can express what I feel.' That was in 1908. It is well to remember this lyrical language, as a corrective to Backhouse's later statements that he had been ruthlessly exploited by Morrison. At the time he does not seem to have felt that he was exploited; or at least, if he did, his language effectively disguised his feelings.

However, all that was soon to change. Already in 1908 a new relationship had begun to cloud the simplicity of Backhouse's devotion to Morrison. In 1907, while Morrison was abroad, Bland had moved from Shanghai to Peking. From now on, while Morrison roved in the political stratosphere as correspondent-in-chief of *The Times* in China, Bland deputised for him as resident correspondent in the capital; and Backhouse, always dependent upon somebody, fell gradually into dependence on him.

The occasion which brought Bland and Backhouse together for the first time since the bite of the supposedly rabid dog in 1899 was provided by the events of November 1908. In that month the long reign of the Empress Dowager came to an end; and the end was worthy of the beginning, and indeed of the whole reign: for it was theatrical, wrapped in dark suspicion of murder, and, in its outcome, yet another short-term triumph for herself, at the expense of her unfortunate country.

The Empress was now an old woman and the end of her reign was not unexpected; but who could foretell the circumstances, or the political consequences, of her death? For forty-six years she had dominated the political scene in China, and her long reign, punctuated though it had been by disasters, had at least proved her own remarkable capacity for survival. In those forty-six years she had made and unmade puppet-emperors, had emerged victorious from a series of palace intrigues, and had seen all her domestic enemies perish. Now, in 1908, the nominal Emperor was still the Kuang-hsü Emperor whose 'Hundred Days' Reform' had been so brutally reversed ten years earlier. In those ten years the Empress Dowager had ruled, with her eunuch court, by the sufference of the great powers which she had challenged during the Boxer Rising but which, after their victory, could find no substitute for her corrupt and feeble monarchy. In this last period of her reign, she had indeed made some concessions to modernity. She had opened up her court, and become the advocate – in theory – of those very reforms which she had so recently resisted. Western diplomatists and their wives, who had so recently trembled for their lives in the barricaded legations, were now made welcome in the imperial palace; an American lady was allowed to paint her portrait for an exhibition in St Louis; popular books set out to correct the old hostile impression; and the memory of her multiplied crimes and vices was buried beneath the new patina of a graceful old age, heightened by the uncertainty of the future. For by the law of the dynasty, her death would enable the feeble Kuang-hsü Emperor, whom she had so long kept under her control, to come at last into his own.

In fact he never did come into his own. On 13 November the Empress, in consideration of an alleged illness of the Emperor, and of her own advanced age, made further provision for the future. She declared a new heir to the throne in the event of the Emperor's death. This new heir was the Emperor's infant nephew, P'u-i, and his father, Prince Ch'un, the present Emperor's brother, was designated as his regent. Next day, the Emperor's death was announced; and on the day after, the Empress herself suddenly died. By a remarkable coincidence – too remarkable to be natural, it was widely said – she had once again, in the nick of time, prevented the succession of a mature emperor, and imposed instead an infant under the tutelage either of herself, or, if she should die, of her own clan: for the new Regent was her nephew and the new Empress Dowager, Lung-yü, to whom she had decreed special powers, was her niece. Thus, as far as political arrangements could ensure it, the continued domination of the Yehonala clan, her clan, over the empire of China was assured. The only question was, could the empire of China survive these arrangements?

This dramatic sequence of deaths, and their exciting political

implications, naturally caused the greatest interest and speculation among all Western observers in Peking, and of course, in
London, in Printing House Square, the editor of *The Times* was
eager for an authoritative interpretation from its own special
oracle, Dr Morrison. Dr Morrison too must have been eager to
supply such an interpretation, if only to bury the memory of his
unhappy failure at the time of the Boxer Siege, which had taken
him completely by surprise. But alas, on this occasion Dr Morrison
was caught napping once again. By a most unfortunate chance,
when the Emperor and the Empress died, he was away from
Peking.

It was all the result of his sporting tastes. Ironically, he seems
almost to have apprehended it. Six months before, Morrison had
gone away on a wildfowling expedition and, before leaving Peking,
had asked Bland to stand in for him in case anything dramatic
should happen during his absence. Bland had promised to do so.
'Go in peace!' he wrote, 'I shall be on hand here for some time
to come, and in the event of the Old Buddha dying, or any other
interesting event, will keep *The Times* informed. May you shoot
100 snipe, and not get a sunstroke doing it.' In fact, on that
occasion, nothing had happened; but now, by a strange turn of
fate, exactly the same situation had recurred. Morrison had
again chosen to go off for a week's wildfowling, in Kwantai on
the Yellow River; and on this occasion the Old Buddha did die,
and the Emperor too. When Morrison returned, all was over.
Moreover, on this occasion, Bland could not stand in for him
after all. He was in Peking, but by another unfortunate chance,
he was incapacitated, being in bed with a fever. However, in this
crisis, he knew what to do. He appealed to one of his closest
friends in Peking, Lord ffrench.

Lord ffrench was an Irish peer who had recently come to
Peking as the chief representative of Pauling & Company, a
British railway construction firm. His arrival was the result of a
recent development in the 'battle of concessions'. In an attempt
to limit the Japanese penetration of Manchuria, the Chinese
government had conceded to a British-American syndicate the
right to build a railway line, known as the Fakumen railway, in
Manchuria. The financiers involved were the Morgan Harriman

group, whose representative was a young American, Willard Straight. Straight had been in the Far East for some years, first working under Sir Robert Hart in the Imperial Maritime Customs, then as Reuter's correspondent during the Russo-Japanese war, and from 1906 to 1908 as American consul-general in Mukden. He had become a close friend of Bland, and at this moment was illustrating Bland's book *Houseboat Days in China*, which would be dedicated to him. Like Bland, Straight wished to save China from further dismemberment by Russia and Japan, and the project of an Anglo-American railway in Manchuria was designed for this purpose. Pauling & Co. were charged with the construction of the railway, which was naturally looked upon with disfavour by the Japanese. ffrench soon became intimate with Bland, and Bland, ffrench and Straight formed a close group of friends. Backhouse also soon became known to ffrench – only last week the two had gone together to buy Tibetan sacred books as a speculation. So, in the crisis caused by the imperial deaths, the absence of Morrison, and his own illness, Bland asked ffrench to find Backhouse. In such a concurrence of accidents, only Backhouse, Morrison's expert, the real writer of so much of Morrison's despatches, could save the reputation of *The Times*.

Backhouse was found and responded. His services, Bland wrote, were invaluable. With his intimate knowledge of Chinese etiquette, of all the traditional rites of the court, he was able to write, or at least to draft, the whole report. He was constantly with Bland during those critical days. 'Backhouse gave me much useful help,' Bland recorded in his diary: 'really a wonderful man, but fearfully timid . . . more of a classical Chinaman than an Englishman.' All that Bland had to do was to revise, to polish up, Backhouse's report. In signing it as his own he felt that he was guilty of plagiarism. He poured out his thanks to Backhouse and wrote to *The Times* praising him by name. But Backhouse, with his almost excessive humility, always deprecated such gratitude. He would merely thank Bland for 'improving' his raw matter. It was a pleasure, he wrote, to look after Bland in his illness. He declined any remuneration: it was quite enough if Bland would occasionally help him with magazine articles – in providing the external polish and carrying the finished product to market.

Meanwhile he would continue to send Bland documents and translations, and for these services he accepted payment. It was a novel experience, he wrote, to be paid for translations made to oblige a friend. Morrison had never paid him a penny. But he would accept no credit. He protested that he merely supplied the 'dry bones, and you furnished them with what they lacked, by imparting to my dull record the living interest of your exquisite style.'

Thus began the famous co-operation between Backhouse and Bland. In many ways it was an alliance of opposites. A Chinese physician, who observed them both after the publication of their work, and who knew nothing of their earlier co-operation, was astonished that such an ill-matched pair should ever have come together. 'Bland', he wrote, 'typified the self-assertive and arrogant Britisher of the treaty ports, while Backhouse looked the scholarly Oxford don whose mission in life appeared to be to "learn, teach, and be of service to the coming generation".' Appearances can be deceptive, and neither description is quite fair. Bland, though robust and extrovert, was neither assertive nor arrogant: his writings show him to have been a humane and kindly man who always, even when most exasperated, treated his wayward partner with patience, tact and consideration. We shall be able to consider Backhouse's scholarly services to posterity later. Of all Backhouse's personal relations, his friendship with Bland, begun over the death of the Empress Dowager, lasted longest. As he wrote to Bland soon after that event, 'I cannot help feeling that the Empress Dowager's decease, however lamentable in other respects, was a lucky event for me, in that it gave me the chance of being privileged to make your acquaintance.'

It also led to closer relations with their intermediary, Lord ffrench, and his firm, Pauling & Co. As head of a busy firm in China, building railways for the Chinese government, ffrench too needed experts, interpreters and translators. He also needed informants with access to, or understanding of, Chinese political circles. Backhouse was an expert translator and he also had, or claimed to have such access. Almost immediately after the old Empress's death, we find Backhouse working privately for ffrench, translating documents and supplying confidential information from friends and informants in high or secret places. One of these highly placed friends was Liang Shih-i, a prominent financier, entrepreneur and political operator in the last years of the Empire, who was of particular interest to Pauling & Co. as Director-General of Railways. On 27 December 1908, Backhouse informed ffrench that Liang had written him a most appreciative letter and accompanied it with the gift of a rare book. As evidence of their close relations, he sent ffrench a translation of the letter. Another such friend was an even more important politician, Hsü Shih-ch'ang, the Grand Secretary. We shall hear more of both Liang Shih-i and Hsü Shih-ch'ang: they were destined to play an important part in Chinese politics, and in the affairs of Backhouse, in the following years.

Apart from these prominent public figures, Backhouse relied for regular information on an unnamed informer described simply as 'Backhouse's friend', 'Backhouse's pal', or 'Backhouse's spy', who was evidently exceptionally well-placed at court: for he was able to report the most intimate details of politics, intrigue and corruption. As ffrench had to outmanoeuvre foreign contractors who were equally eager to build railways in Manchuria and Mongolia, and, in particular, to resist the intrigues of the Japanese, these day-to-day reports could obviously be most useful to him, and at the end of 1908 he proposed to Pauling & Co. that he should engage Backhouse as a regular salaried agent.

The company agreed, and almost at once, ffrench was able to report a new breakthrough to the seat of power. Backhouse, he wrote, had been invited to dinner 'with a number of Manchus, some of them rather prominent here: it will be interesting to hear what they have to say.' From now on, the reports from 'Backhouse's friend' came in thick and fast. ffrench was informed of debates in the Grand Council, the in-fighting of Chinese politicians, the machinations of the Japanese, the obstructions and delays which were holding up those important contracts. 'Backhouse's friend', ffrench reported on one occasion, 'ascribes the delay to the intrigues of Mr Yu Chuan-pu, conducted by Liang Shih-i, who hates Chang.' 'Backhouse's friend', he would write on another, 'has written that there is great confusion in the

Palace, and that he is much upset, and asking Backhouse to go and see him. I fear the young Emperor is about to peg out.' And again, 'Backhouse has just come from seeing his friend, who assures him that Chang told the Regent that he was now sure of arranging the money in a few days through the Yokohama Specie Bank.' The Regent, according to Backhouse's friend, had applied to Backhouse for a map of Manchuria, presumably so that he could study the location of the proposed railway. . . . Thus Backhouse, through his anonymous friend, was gradually inserting himself into the secret councils of the Empire, in the interest of Pauling & Co. Lord ffrench was much impressed: 'Backhouse's friend', he wrote, 'has been right all along, except when it came to dates and some small matters.'

These dealings between Backhouse and ffrench were, of course, known to Bland, as ffrench's closest friend and ally, and indeed it is from Bland's correspondence that we know about them; but Backhouse was very anxious that no news of it should reach Morrison, who seems to have exerted an almost irresistible influence over him, and to have claimed an absolute monopoly of his work. 'I am especially anxious', Backhouse wrote to Bland in February 1909, 'that a distinguished friend of ours whose name I need not mention (he is now away), should never know of my doing this work for Lord ffrench.' On one occasion, Backhouse even forbade ffrench to say anything to Bland, so terrified was he of a possible leak to the dreaded Morrison.

At the same time, Backhouse was evidently working occasionally for Willard Straight and his group of American bankers. Straight employed Backhouse in his negotiations with the Chinese. Whether Morrison was allowed to know of Backhouse's activity for Straight is not clear. Probably he was not. By this time, Straight, ffrench and Bland were working in close personal harmony, while Morrison was a law to himself.

In Morrison's absence from Peking, Backhouse was evidently feeling his way towards freedom – or at least towards alternative dependence. A few days after imposing secrecy on Bland, he took a further step in that direction. It seems that Bland had suggested that they should collaborate, not now on an article, but on a book about the Empress Dowager. As a practised journalist and author, Bland would organise the book, while Backhouse, as a scholar, would supply the documentary material. Backhouse now responded eagerly to the suggestion. He already possessed ample material, he said, beginning with the accession of Tzŭ-hsi's infant son, the T'ung-chih Emperor, and the Palace conspiracy of Su-shan. These were the events which had first brought Tzŭ-hsi effectively to the throne of China. 'If you had time to compose the narrative,' he wrote to Bland, 'I could supply the translations and a certain amount of personal anecdote as well, which you would embellish with your style.' In particular, Backhouse could supply a very interesting Chinese diary which gave a personal account of events during the Boxer Rising, and which, by itself could make a distinct chapter or two of such a book. But Bland, a practised author, must find the publisher: Backhouse himself could never do that.

Bland was delighted with the project. He replied at once, declaring that he would be proud to collaborate with Backhouse in such a venture. It would enable him to repay him for that article on the Empress's death – for in this new work he envisaged himself merely as the editor and presenter of Backhouse's work: 'I shall be very pleased to slip in, on the distinct understanding that I take no credit for your work this time. I shall simply be the recording clerk.' He also welcomed the suggestion of making a few chapters out of the diary which Backhouse had mentioned. Indeed, he considered that the diary could form, in some respects, the centrepiece of the whole book, which now began to assume shape, around it, in his mind. But before Backhouse would commit himself to the project, he imposed one absolute condition. Just as with the work for Lord ffrench, so also with the work for Bland, nothing was to be revealed to Morrison. Backhouse explained that Morrison had treated him abominably in the past, but he feared his rage if he should discover that Backhouse had dared to work on his own account with anyone but himself.

On this basis the partnership was agreed, and Bland wrote at once to the London publisher Edward Arnold, who had recently published Bland's book, *Houseboat Days in China*. 'I am now preparing', wrote Bland, 'in collaboration with a very noted Chinese scholar, who possesses exceptional sources of information and many unique documents, a life of the late Empress Dowager, intended to throw light on many unexplained incidents in Chinese history. It will be about 400 pages with illustrations and we hope to get it done in the autumn or winter at latest. My collaborator is a student and a man of laborious days, and as my part is only to revise and put the thing into an attractive form, you are not likely to have any such delays as have occurred in the case of *Houseboat Days*. . . .' For throughout the preparation of the book, Bland always insisted that he was little more than the editor of Backhouse's material in Backhouse's translation. 'We shall make a fine book of it', he wrote to Backhouse in January 1910, 'but the work will be all yours,' and he wished Backhouse's name to appear before his on the title-page: this, he believed, would be 'more polite and seemly'.

Was Bland right to represent himself merely as the editor of Backhouse's material? Afterwards, in the controversies which followed publication, Bland stated, and Backhouse admitted, that the 'inspiration of the work' was his, that it was he who thought of building the book round the Chinese diary which Backhouse had discovered, that it was he who had all the trouble of the business arrangements. Bland in fact was the intellectual force which created the book out of the material supplied and translated by Backhouse. But the material was undoubtedly all supplied by Backhouse. He obtained the imperial edicts and other documents. He translated them, and he vouched for their authenticity. 'Every work in the manuscript', he wrote, 'has authority: in a few cases oral, but usually written.' In other words, it was a true partnership: both partners were essential to it. Without Backhouse, the material would not have been available; without Bland, it would not have been moulded into a book.

So the collaboration began: a collaboration which was to make Bland and Backhouse a famous partnership in the sinological and literary world. It was a partnership which was to generate two well-known works and many controversies, and from whose consequences neither partner, to the end of his life, was to be entirely free.

CHAPTER THREE

The Historian

ONCE the partnership had been agreed, Backhouse set to work and worked fast. By the end of April 1909 he had made good progress and he then decided to make a visit to London. 'I expect to start today fortnight,' he told Bland, 'with ffrench's permission'; and he proposed to visit Arnold, the intended publisher, himself. Bland wrote to Arnold to prepare him for the visit. Backhouse, he explained 'is very shy and nervous, and horribly afraid of publishers and businessmen generally, being imbued with the philosophic attitudes of the early Sung dynasty; but perhaps you may be able to lure him to a meeting, and thus see a sample of the work, which is certain to create a sensation of the biggest kind.'

Unfortunately, the sample which Arnold saw did not convince him of its sensational quality. Even the famous diary, 'an authentic record of the highest historical value', as Bland called it, did not excite him. He declined the book. Thereupon Backhouse, advised by Bland, took it to another publisher, John Murray, who at first showed great interest. He was especially impressed by the diary: he and his father, he told Bland, had read it 'with great interest', and believed that it alone would sell the book. But afterwards Murray too cooled off, and in April next year Bland passed the text, now complete, to a literary agent. This agent submitted the work to William Heinemann, and quickly obtained from him the terms which Bland had demanded. Heinemann was willing to grant these terms, he said, on the strength of the diary alone.

This diary played so large a part in the making and selling of the book, and was to be the centre of such long and heated controversies afterwards, that we must here say something about it.

It was entitled by Backhouse 'The Diary of His Excellency Ching-shan'.

Ching-shan, the author of the diary, was a Manchu scholar of a courtly family related to the Empress Dowager and 'in close touch with all the leading nobles'. He therefore, as Bland and Backhouse wrote, 'had exceptional opportunities of knowing all the gossip of the court, of learning opinions and watching the movements of the high officials, Chinese and Manchu, who stood nearest the throne'. He held office as Assistant Secretary of the Imperial Household.* He was also tutor to some of the imperial princes who were most closely involved in the Boxer movement. On 15 August 1900, after the entry of the Allied troops into Peking and the flight of the Empress Dowager to Sian, Ching-shan's wife, his senior concubine, and one of his daughters-in-law committed suicide, and he himself, soon afterwards, was murdered by his unfilial son, who pushed him down a well in his own courtyard. He was then seventy-eight years old. The son, En Ch'un, was afterwards shot by British troops for harbouring Boxers.

Three days after Ching-shan's death, Backhouse, according to his own account, moved into his house. We have seen the background to this move: how Backhouse, having been arrested by the Russians for looting in their sector of the city, had decided to move into the British sector and had applied for permission to occupy this house. There, he now stated, he had entered the study and had discovered the late owner's diary and saved it, 'in the nick of time', from being burnt by a party of Sikh soldiers who were already guarding the house. Having taken possession of it, he had kept it in his own hands for nine years and he had now translated selected parts of it to be one of the documents – indeed, the central document – in his book.

At different times, Backhouse gave several accounts of his discovery of Ching-shan's diary, some more, some less detailed, but all consistent with each other. The earliest of these accounts

---

* Bland and Backhouse describe him as Comptroller of the Household but in fact, as Sir Reginald Johnston afterwards pointed out (*Chinese Social and Political Science Review* October 1926, pp. 950 foll.), this is incorrect: Ching-shan never rose to be higher than Assistant Secretary.

is in a letter to Bland of 14 April 1910. The diary, he then wrote, had been rifled by the Sikhs 'out of a camphor-wood Chinese escritoire which stood on the k'ang in the old man's inner room. The leaves were all strewed on the k'ang in great confusion, and some had already been used by the Sikh guard for packing papers and other base purposes. His books and possessions were all scattered about, as they had been looking for valuables.' Bland then asked Backhouse to write a formal account of the discovery of the document for insertion in the book, and this he readily undertook to do.

The great importance of the diary arose from the fact that there was at that time no account, from inside the imperial court, of the impact on it of the Boxer movement in the period of its success. Inevitably, at that time, the court was deeply divided. Those who believed anyway in the necessity of reform, on the Western model, were bound to oppose the anti-Western Boxer movement. Others would oppose it for tactical reasons, believing that the Boxers could not win and that the rebellion, therefore, could only do harm. On the other side, there were politicians and courtiers who believed that the Boxers were, as they claimed to be, invincible, or at least that they would or could win; and if this were so, then there were other reasons why the imperial court, whose power was threatened by reform, should support the rising. Nationalism and reaction united might succeed in driving out the Westerners and gaining a further lease of life for the archaic absolutism of the Manchu dynasty. To foreign observers a document which revealed these internal debates and dissensions of the Manchu court would be invaluable, not only historically but politically; for the court having survived the crisis, the Western powers were still dealing with some at least of the politicians who must have been involved in those debates. The Grand Secretary Jung-lu, for instance, was very anxious for it to be believed, after 1900, that he had been a pro-Westerner during the Boxer crisis. Whether he had been or not was not known, for no such document was available. As Sir Robert Hart wrote to the American missionary Arthur Smith a year after the defeat of the Boxers, 'It would be interesting to get a really reliable Chinese account of Palace doings – and Peking doings –

during 1900. As it is, we are all guessing and inferring and putting this and that together, but we have not got at the facts yet. It's all a question, with no finality in it.'

How Hart would have welcomed Ching-shan's diary, had he known of it! For Ching-shan's diary was precisely the kind of document whose lack he was deploring. It showed, incidentally, that Jung-lu had been a consistent supporter of moderation, had sought to prevent the attack on the legations, and had tried to mitigate the bloodthirsty edicts of the pro-Boxer party. This being so, it was somewhat extraordinary that Backhouse, having found the document in 1900, had not handed it over (as his duty required him to do) at the time, but had sat on it for nine years. He maintained that he had not realised its importance: it was only when he showed it to Bland and ffrench, he said, and when they got excited about it, that he realised its value. That was in 1909. By that time the document had lost its political importance. Jung-lu had died in 1903. But it remained a unique historical document, and as such gave new historical value to Bland's and Backhouse's book.

While the book was in preparation, Backhouse sent the original manuscript of those parts of the diary which he had translated to Bland who was now in England. He had been recalled to England by *The Times*, under pressure from Morrison, and would not in fact return to China, although that was not yet clear. Bland took the manuscript to the British Museum, where he wished it to be available to scholars. At first he proposed to sell it to the Museum, but was told that the Museum had no funds with which to buy it. He then deposited it there, so that its genuineness could be confirmed by scholars. It was in the Museum by August 1910, and has been there ever since.

The collaboration of authors is seldom painless, and Backhouse and Bland experienced some of the usual difficulties and mis-understandings implicit in such a partnership. But considering the differences in their characters, and the difficult nature of Back-house (whom Bland had to excuse to their publishers as 'a some-what erratic gentleman'), we should be struck, during the period of gestation, rather by their general harmony than by their occasional divergences. This harmony was largely due to Bland's tact and patience in dealing with his partner. On Backhouse's side, some of the difficulties which arose could be ascribed, and were ascribed by him, to the uncertainties of his financial position. For in spite of his university salary, his allowance from England, and his periodic payments from Bland, ffrench and Straight, he was always, apparently, in need; and need sometimes drove him to desperate expedients which, since he was so liable to misfortune, generally proved counter-productive.

The first misfortune involved his relations with the firm of Pauling & Co. In 1909, when Backhouse returned to England, it was with the permission of ffrench, and he evidently had some commission to perform for ffrench. He had been very close to ffrench for the last year. ffrench had lent him money privately, and Backhouse had stayed in ffrench's house in Peking. In London he stayed with an office friend of ffrench. But the firm of Pauling & Co. had its internal intrigues, and ffrench had a rival, one Ginnell, who evidently sought to undermine him. Ginnell was an Irishman and an engineer, who was eager, and no doubt competent, to build the railways for Pauling & Co., but who (according to ffrench) had no social or diplomatic gifts and no capacity to deal with Chinese officials. However, he was ambitious, and evidently thought that he could effectively displace ffrench and himself take charge of the company's affairs in China. In order to do so, he would of course need a diplomatic intermediary to handle his relations with the Chinese, and he evidently reckoned on seducing Backhouse. Backhouse, always eager to improve his own income, and always labile in his loyalty, evidently lent himself to the intrigue.

It is not clear whether Backhouse committed himself to Ginnell's conspiracy before leaving China, but once he had arrived in London, and discovered that Ginnell had secured support at the head office of the firm, he seized his opportunity. Ginnell's friends courted him, and he responded. Writing to Bland, he reported that the company now considered him indispensable: 'ffrench can't get on without me, which is flattering'; and he evidently insinuated to Pauling's that they were in danger of losing his services since Bland wanted to secure them for his own schemes – presumably on behalf of the British and Chinese

Corporation. This was in fact untrue and absurd, for (as ffrench wrote to Bland) 'your schemes were intended to work in with Pauling & Co.' Having thus taken note of his value, and raised his price, Backhouse submitted a memorandum to Pauling & Co., in consequence of which the company signed a separate agreement with him, undertaking to send him back to Peking in an enhanced position, with a contract for a year and an option on his services for the following year. Backhouse was thus to become independent of ffrench, responsible direct to London, and would probably be entitled to claim part of ffrench's commission on contracts secured.

When this was reported to him in Peking, ffrench, not unnaturally, was very angry. He wrote firmly back to his head office saying that he was in command in Peking and that he would not co-operate with Backhouse, or on the new project, unless it was first made quite clear that Backhouse was under his orders, and that there was to be no reduction in his own commission. The firm surrendered at once. In an involved letter, indicating some embarrassment, ffrench was assured that all employees of the firm sent out from Europe to China were of course under his orders, and especially 'a gentleman like Mr Backhouse, who is not in the ordinary run of persons engaged for business matters, although of unique value from the Chinese standpoint'. If this had not been made unmistakably clear, he was assured, that was simply because it had not seemed necessary or proper to rub it into a man of such 'modesty and gentlemanly feelings' as Backhouse, who would naturally take it for granted, etc. etc. Backhouse's 'unique value' lay, of course, in his remarkable contacts with the Chinese court and government.

Thus the plot failed, and Bland and ffrench, who had kept in close touch throughout, released their emotion in private correspondence. The real villain, they agreed, was Ginnell. 'If Ginnell is at all representative of the class which would come into power if Home Rule were granted to Ireland,' wrote ffrench, 'then I am a Unionist.' The affair 'certainly seems pretty bad', replied Bland: 'a typical piece of low Irish blackguardism'. Since Bland, ffrench and Ginnell were all Irish, we are reminded of Dr Johnson's remark, 'The Irish, sir, are a *fair* people: they never speak well of one another.' But inevitably Backhouse came in for a share of the blame. ffrench conceded that he might have an explanation, but the plain fact was that 'he has not altogether played the game with me'. Pauling & Co. had thought that they could side-track ffrench and 'run the show with Backhouse'; 'Backhouse was not loyal to me and practically turned on me when he thought that the firm meant to support Ginnell; but he is a weakling and one does not expect anything.'

The result was that Backhouse returned to China in the autumn somewhat crestfallen, with a contract for three months only, and no confidence that it would be renewed. ffrench now regarded him as 'a dangerous cuss and a mischief-maker'. Backhouse did indeed have his explanations: he had been the innocent victim of Ginnell's conspiracy. But the language in which his explanation was quoted does not suggest that it was wholly believed, and it seems that ffrench never fully trusted him again.

It was against this economic background, at the time when his employment with Pauling's seemed likely to lapse, that Backhouse made a new proposal to Bland about their book. In October 1909 he wrote to Bland offering to renounce his own financial interest in the book in exchange for £200. Bland replied that he could not assume that the book would make £400 for them, but he advanced £100 and six months later, in answer to a further request, he added another £50. John Murray afterwards confirmed that the book would never make more than £300, and indeed, on that account, declined to publish it. On this basis, Backhouse surrendered to Bland his whole property in the book, including his translations and the manuscript of Ching-shan's diary in so far as it had been used for the book: that is, that part of the manuscript which Bland would afterwards deposit in the British Museum.

He also wished to remove his own name from the title-page. This too bore some relation to his economic position. In 1910, having completed the text, Backhouse again came to England 'with ffrench's sanction, for a month or two'. Although he had just negotiated a valuable contract for Pauling's, he was aware that his own contract with the firm, which was now running out, might not be renewed. While in Scotland, staying with the

Findlays, he received what he described as 'a very disagreeable letter from Pauling's'. In it, the firm offered to renew his contract, but the terms seemed to him inadequate and the language used was insufficiently 'flattering'. Perhaps ffrench had seen to it that Backhouse's position was now more narrowly defined and more clearly subject to his control. Perhaps Backhouse sensed the distrust which ffrench by now felt for him. At all events, he did not accept the contract and never had any further business relations with Pauling's. When he returned to Peking, ffrench noticed that he avoided meeting him.

At the same time, he had a disagreeable breach with his other employer in Peking, Willard Straight. Just before leaving China, he wrote to Bland from the Imperial Hotel, Tientsin, saying that he was 'worn out' negotiating two contracts, one for Pauling's the other for Straight. But Straight's group seemed no more grateful than Pauling's for Backhouse's hard work. They paid him £200, which he thought inadequate. Since he had (as he said) been in charge of all the negotiations, he expected £500; and he asked Bland for advice. Bland sensibly observed that everything depended on the conditions originally made. If Backhouse had afterwards been required to do more than had originally been envisaged, he should have made a separate contract; but surely they would not contest his claim for further remuneration 'if you have done more than was originally intended'. Bland undertook to write personally to Straight and settle the matter diplomatically. Straight, however, was adamant: Backhouse was told that he would not receive another penny. He was deeply hurt. 'I hate quarrelling with people', he wrote, 'and yet I always seem to manage to offend.' He really believed that he had earned a bonus. However, he conceded, Straight was at least 'more liberal than Morrison, who never paid me a *sou*'. Bland again interposed his diplomacy, but apparently without effect. Backhouse's business relations with Straight, as with Pauling's, were now over.

Thus it began to seem that Backhouse, if he returned to China, might be without economic resources and more than ever dependent on Chinese goodwill. In these circumstances, was it wise, he asked himself, to appear as the author, even as the co-author, of a book on the Empress Dowager which must necessarily refer, and might give offence, to persons still alive and powerful in Chinese life? The Empress Dowager had only been dead for two years. The present Empress Dowager, Lung-yü, was her niece, and – according to Backhouse – not only modelled herself entirely on her revered aunt, but had a particularly nasty temper. Other members of the Yehonala clan had positions of influence. Na-t'ung, who had played a critical part during the Boxer rebellion, and had been revealed in Ching-shan's diary as 'a damnable cold-blooded rogue and villain', was now high in the Chinese Grand Council and Associate President of the Wai-wu Pu, or reformed Foreign Office. The more Backhouse thought about the situation in China, the more apprehensive he felt about his book. All through the spring of 1910, from the time when he had completed the manuscript, his letters to Bland express his doubts. However, by the summer, his confidence returned. He now seemed to think that there was no danger. After all, there was nothing objectionable in the book; only Na-t'ung could complain, 'and he doesn't matter, so long as he doesn't bring a libel action'.

Backhouse could afford to swallow his doubts because at this moment he was thinking that he would not, after all, return to China. On 22 June he lunched with Bland in Bland's London club, and set out his position. Bland recorded the conversation in his diary. After arguing the pros and cons of having his name on the title-page, Backhouse said that he was now of independent means, having made 'arrangements with his father'. He 'was *not* going to accept employment from a certain shipbuilding firm who want him to go and negotiate.' ('Nous verrons', added the sceptical Bland.) He said that 'he was sorry that neither ffrench nor Straight were quite pleased with him – this with reference to the Chinese and Ginnell's treachery, etc. He asked me to go and see his father and also to shoot with Findlay, his brother-in-law. I said I would with pleasure.' After lunch, Backhouse and Bland went together to see Heinemann. Nothing was said about removing Backhouse's name. Bland then set off to fish in Ireland and Backhouse went to Darlington to stay with his father.

Ten days later, Bland, in Ireland, was surprised by a letter from Backhouse which revealed a complete volte-face. Backhouse now insisted that his own name must not appear in the book. At the most he would allow his initials, but he much preferred absolute anonymity. He was afraid of reprisals by Na-t'ung against his Chinese servants. Perhaps he himself would be forbidden to return to Peking. . . . Bland deplored this change of attitude. Chinese officials, he protested, would never read the book. Even if they did, they would attach no more importance to it than to any other barbarian production. They could not forbid Backhouse to live in Peking, or molest his servants. Na-t'ung's name could always be omitted: Bland would see to that at once. Anyway, why go back to China at all? Would it not be far better to stay in England? However, Backhouse stood his ground, and after further vain attempts to dissuade him, Bland surrendered, merely remarking that anonymity was futile since 'some of your good friends, e.g. Morrison, will inevitably let the Chinese know of its authorship'.

Bland obediently wrote to Heinemann asking that Backhouse's name be omitted. Heinemann replied that it was now too late: the prospectus of the book had already gone out 'to all parts of the world', with Backhouse's name in it: it must stand. 'Backhouse will be in a horrid state of distress', Bland noted dryly in his diary. ' . . . I fear he will make difficulties, being a flabby mortal and timid.' Backhouse would indeed make difficulties in the future, as we shall see, though not of the kind expected; but for the present there was nothing to do. However, to please him, Bland secured the omission of the damaging references to Na-t'ung from Ching-shan's diary.

Backhouse's sudden change of front had its reasons. He was now staying with his father, and Sir Jonathan had put his foot down. The promised – or, more probably, imagined – 'independent means' had evaporated. If Sir Jonathan had used such words, he had not used them in the sense in which Edmund understood them. He had meant that he had fixed him up with a settled job; and it was that job with that shipbuilding firm which Edmund had decided *not* to accept. Moreover, that job would take him back to China. He was to be the agent, in Peking of the great shipbuilding firm of John Brown.

Sir John Brown, who had died in 1896, was the pioneer of

iron-plate manufacture. He was a Sheffield man, and had begun as a cutler; but his great achievement had been the development of armour-plating for warships. This development had transformed the Royal Navy and the firm of John Brown Ltd of Sheffield became the great supplier of armour-plating for modern vessels for those powers with which Britain was friendly. Before the end of the century, the firm had taken over the shipbuilding business of J. and G. Thomson on the Clyde, and had set up a subsidiary firm of John Brown & Company, shipbuilders, at Glasgow. It was this subsidiary firm which had now acquired the services of Edmund Backhouse as its representative in Peking.

This was not what Backhouse had wanted. He had hoped that his father would make some financial provision for him which would make him 'independent of labour *in partibus*'. But Sir Jonathan's money-bags had remained tightly closed and Edmund dutifully went from Darlington to Glasgow to be interviewed and recruited. The prospects of the post, as presented to him, were exciting and the offer, as he told Bland, was 'far more flattering' than anything he had received from Pauling & Co. John Brown & Co. had been told by the Chinese consul-general in London that the Chinese government had raised six million pounds by internal taxation, and was going to raise another four million pounds in the next two years, in order to build a modern navy. Backhouse was to direct the orders to the Clyde and receive a commission on sales. A mirage of vast riches floated before his eyes. How dreadful if all should be ruined by some misconstrued passage in his book! In such circumstances, anonymity might well be the more prudent course.

Naturally Sir Jonathan Backhouse, who at last thought that his wastrel son was settled in honest commerce, would hold the same views. A few months later, as pre-arranged with Backhouse, after fishing and shooting his way through Ireland and Scotland, Bland called on Sir Jonathan in London. He had luncheon with him and his naval son, Oliver, at the Carlton. Presumably he felt his way, seeking to encourage the old man's generosity towards his scholarly but unbusinesslike son. But Sir Jonathan did not respond. He 'was snuffy', Bland reported to ffrench, 'and did not appeal to me in any way. Openly parsimonious.' In his diary,

Bland was more outspoken. 'He made a dreadful fuss over the bill', he recorded, '(23/6d. for the lot!), insisting on paying it in silver because, he explained, "he never broke a fiver or gave gold if he could help it", and tipped the waiter *sixpence*! Whew!' No wonder Edmund's huge debts at Oxford had pierced that parsimonious heart.

Incidentally, Sir Jonathan told Bland 'that he had been instrumental in arranging for our Edmund's agreement, which works out at about £4,500 a year for four years. And Edmund (this between you and me) writes me that his expenses are so high that he will be out of pocket on his work. That settles my opinion of the pleas of poverty with which he used to regale you and me.' Edmund, however, continued to insist that this father was 'quite wrong about my salary': he would be lucky, he said, if he saved £500 a year. However, he had to admit that he was receiving £2,000 in advance, and 'the terms seem liberal'.

It seems that Backhouse obtained the post with John Brown, partly at least by emphasising those grand contacts in Chinese court politics which had enabled him to be so useful to Pauling & Co., and particularly his friendship with the Grand Secretary Hsü Shih-ch'ang. It was therefore with a shock that he learned, in August 1910, while he was still at his father's home in Darlington, that the Grand Secretary had fallen from power. He wrote in dismay to Bland, 'The Grand Secretary's downfall is a heavy blow to me, for he has written most graciously to me to assure me of his willingness to help me. . . . My plans are completely upset by this latest move of the chess-men. I thought, with others, that the Grand Secretary was as secure as the Tai Mountain. . . . Honestly, I don't see much use in going out to China'. However, Bland reassured him: 'I sympathise with you at the loss of Shih Hsu's friendly support, but I am not at all of your opinion that the changes in official circles should prevent your going out. You have lots of friends and much influence outside of the Grand Secretary, and I am sure Brown & Co. could not get a better man to do their work, though I admit to scepticism *in re* their chances of selling any ships to China under present *financial* conditions.' Thus reassured, Backhouse recovered confidence and, on his return to China, would discover that Hsü Shih-ch'ang could be just as useful to him – and therefore to John Brown & Co. – out of office as in it. We shall hear again of Hsü Shih-ch'ang.

The appointment with John Brown began a new syndrome in the life of Edmund Backhouse. From now on, he would feed himself with recurrent illusions of selling battleships to the Chinese and netting, for himself, huge commissions. From the start, Bland tried to disabuse him. The Chinese, he warned him, were always bamboozling foreigners about buying warships, which they had no funds either to buy or to maintain. 'Tell Brown & Co. not to advance one penny, except against definite and binding agreements to conclude business.' He was equally sceptical about the financial capacity of 'the remnants of government' in China and the commercial capacity of Backhouse. Why did Backhouse not stay in England, 'doing such work as the Museum would gladly give you, and leave China for the Chinese?' Let him stay with 'the scholar's work for which you were created' and have 'no nonsense about going out to get shipbuilding contracts from our friends in the City of Dreadful Dust'. 'I wish, my dear Backhouse,' he wrote later, 'that your father would provide for you properly and let you go in for the kind of work that would bring you credit and dignity, rather than these sordid commercial things which don't do any decent man any good, as I know full well.' To ffrench, Bland was more summary. Has 'the worthy Backhouse', he once rhetorically asked, 'any chance of selling anything to anybody?' Backhouse's phantom battleships became a standing joke among the old Peking hands. But Backhouse was not to be deflected. The battleship fantasy became part of his dream-world. He clung to his illusions, and with each change in the Chinese government would see a fleet of imaginary battleships steaming proudly from the Clyde to Tientsin, and leaving a vast commission in his hands.

Meanwhile the book was being corrected for the press; and in October 1910 it was published. It was entitled *China under the Empress Dowager* by J. O. P. Bland and E. T. Backhouse – for the publisher had refused Bland's suggestion that the name of Backhouse should come first. In spite of the gloomy forecasts of Edward Arnold and John Murray, the book proved a great success. It appeared at the right moment; it caught the mood of that moment; and it had a solid content which satisfied, at last, a real and serious need.

For by the end of 1910 the collapse of the Manchu dynasty – perhaps of the whole immemorial Chinese Empire – was predictable. It had been a great dynasty, the dynasty under which China had captured the imagination of 'enlightened' Europe, and although its last half-century had witnessed only decay and dismemberment, that dismal spectacle had, to some extent, been masked by the personality of the extraordinary woman who had ruled it. In retrospect, the disreputable old Empress now seemed the last great figure in Chinese history. She was the old sorceress who, against all reason and probability, had preserved and dominated an archaic, sophisticated and corrupt society and, by her machiavellian arts, postponed for fifty years the inevitable revolution. But how, men asked, had she done it? No satisfactory answer to that question had yet been given. Though a few Western Barbarians had been allowed to penetrate the Chinese court during the last decade, the true history of the pre-Boxer period was deeply hidden by the protective barriers of a strange language and an inveterate habit of contemptuous secrecy. Only the irreverent but no doubt irresponsible Cantonese press offered to illuminate the secret life of the Empress. From such sources, scandalous tales were spread and enlarged. The Empress's court was represented as a private theatre of extravagant debauchery and recondite pleasure. To satisfy the public interest, several popular works were now appearing, and indeed Bland and Backhouse found their work alternately rejected by publishers for failing to achieve the same level of vulgar popularity as one of them and hustled forward in order to forestall another. But their purpose was not to compete with such works: it was to render them unnecessary; and it did.

For what Bland and Backhouse supplied was the first documented and readable public account of the whole reign. It was compiled from authentic Chinese sources, supplied and translated by the profound scholar Backhouse, but addressed to a literate English public by the fluent and efficient journalist Bland. Its virtues were obvious. It published many original Chinese state papers, especially the memorials of the Censors. It quoted private diaries of Chinese court officials and personal interviews with them. It showed an intimate knowledge of Chinese palace politics and personalities; and yet the style throughout is easy and attractive. No other work presents so clear a picture of the decadent Manchu court, with its archaic etiquette, its universal corruption, its impossible dilemmas, or the masterful, narrow, single-minded egotism of its illegitimate but irremovable ruler. A historian might regret that it did not take the reader far outside the court; but that was not its purpose. An exact scholar might complain that the documents in it could not be checked, since there was no system of reference; but the book was not addressed to such exact scholars, nor written in the pedantic style of a university thesis. It was addressed to the intelligent layman, who found it, as he will still find it, both instructive and delightful. When it first appeared, the reviewers were unanimous in its praise. It was, said *The Times*, 'a document more illuminating than perhaps any that has ever come out of China'. The reading public agreed. In the first eighteen months, eight impressions were bought up, and the book was translated into several foreign languages.

One of the features of the book which most excited well-informed readers was the diary of Ching-shan, which, as published, filled the whole of Chapter XVII – some fifty pages – and was often cited as an authority in other chapters. The published parts of the diary, which run mainly from May 1900 until a few hours before Ching-shan's death on 15 August 1900, give a vivid account of the reactions of the imperial court to the Boxer rebellion and the different attitudes adopted by the Empress Dowager and her various advisers. Historically, its most important contribution concerns the attitude of Jung-lu, the Empress's most constant military and political supporter. It was thanks to Jung-lu's troops that Tzŭ-hsi had first established her regency in 1861. He was now commander-in-chief, Grand Counsellor, and close personal adviser of the Empress. According to Ching-shan, Jung-lu constantly opposed the Boxers and sought, in spite of the rival pressures to which the Empress herself yielded, to frustrate their influence and to protect the foreigners against them. He appears in the diary, as he had not previously appeared, as a persistent advocate of moderation, realism and co-operation with the West. For these and other reasons the diary, as published, was welcomed as a very important contribution to history. It conveyed, wrote one reviewer, 'a panorama of Chinese court life in its most poignant moments, such as without doubt has never before been offered to European judgment'. Four years later, Backhouse himself would publicly refer to it as having afforded, 'for the first time, authoritative evidence of the opinion in which Tzŭ-hsi was held by those most competent to judge'. A friend who had served, like him, in the Chinese Imperial Customs wrote to Bland that the diary was 'a real *trouvaille* and should create a sensation. I am very pleased to read your rehabilitation of Jung-lu.' The diary also made the name of the diarist. From now on, the obscure courtier Ching-shan became a well-known figure in recent Chinese history, an essential source for the most critical period of the Manchu court in its agony between aggressive Western imperialism and mounting Chinese revolution.

The unexpected success of their work was naturally gratifying to Bland and Backhouse, and Backhouse might well have regretted his action in selling all his rights to Bland for £150. However, Bland, recognising the value of Backhouse's contribution, decided to disregard this sale, and regularly paid half the proceeds to Backhouse until 1917. This was very satisfactory to Backhouse who always acknowledged Bland's 'great generosity' in the matter. Nor did Backhouse, now back in Peking and busy marketing imaginary battleships, suffer any of the inconveniences which he had apprehended. There was some trouble indeed – or so, at least, he reported to Bland. Some of his friends said that the book was too flippant and should have been suppressed for a generation; others that 'it will ruin us for ever with the Chinese'. Certain Chinese had already shown signs of indignation. Several old friends were 'cold'. Others were 'furious': Li Ching-fang, for instance, the Chinese minister in London, was very angry at a casual but deprecatory reference to him in one of Backhouse's documents. The new Empress Dowager, Tzŭ-hsi's niece Lung-yü, had had the whole book translated 'on yellow paper' (Backhouse was always circumstantial about details) and read aloud to her. She was very annoyed at a reference to herself as 'unattractive', and had forbidden all mention of the book in the Press. The police had visited Backhouse's amanuensis and sought to bribe him to reveal the source of the published documents. 'Naturally', Backhouse reported, 'he said nothing, and, as a matter of fact, I have never told him where they came from.' On another occasion Backhouse reported that armed men had invaded his courtyard on two successive nights: doubtless retainers of his neighbour the young Duke Shan, who was 'returning from the haunts of pleasure' and who, being a clansman of Tzŭ-hsi, was thus expressing his resentment.

So at least Backhouse reported. Bland was sceptical about his reports. 'Backhouse says the Manchus are furious about the book', he recorded in his diary, 'but he exaggerates. They probably don't care a cuss.' And indeed, if Backhouse's reports were true, we must be surprised at the equanimity with which that 'timid', 'flabby' creature responded to all the excitement, even danger. He reported it all without any sign of alarm, almost in a spirit of euphoria. It was the price of fame; and anyway, he now felt, the Manchu dynasty was impotent against him. Quite clearly it was 'finished': it will not last our time; the mandate of Heaven has been withdrawn from it. As if to emphasise his resolution to stand his ground, Backhouse now began to build himself a country house outside Peking. So far was he from any regrets about a book which, flippant or not, impolitic or not, had proved such a success, that he was already envisaging a new project. Could not Bland and he follow up their success by writing a book, *Memoirs of the Manchu Dynasty*, compiled from records, state papers, etc.? Backhouse already had a mass of papers. The work could be done very quickly. It could begin with a long narrative about the last days of the Ming.

But alas, Backhouse's post-publication euphoria was not to last long. In the spring of 1911, while he was enjoying, for the first time in his life, the delicious sense of success and fame, ominous news came from England. The dreaded Morrison was on his way to Peking. For the past few months Morrison had been in Europe, mainly in England, trumpeting the cause of Young China. Now, his mission over, he was returning to the East. 'Morrison goes back next month', Bland had written to ffrench at the close of

1910. 'The Young China party ought to rear him triumphal arches and a dais, and sing psalms in his praise.' Young China might welcome him as a returning hero, but how would the feeble Backhouse be able to stand up to that masterful personality, more powerful than the whole Manchu court? In particular, how would he justify himself for having slipped the noose and collaborated, in guilty secrecy, with Morrison's arch-enemy, Bland?

CHAPTER FOUR

Between Two Patrons

In February 1909, when Backhouse furtively transferred his services as a translator from his original patron, Morrison, to his new friends Bland and ffrench, he persuaded himself that he was escaping from the tyranny of a master who exploited him without reward to a free and profitable partnership. To Bland, he would explain that Morrison had a hold over him: he had discovered about Backhouse's youthful indiscretions – 'that I had gone amuck as a foolish youth a generation ago' – and he had threatened to expose him, and ruin his credit in Peking, unless he laboured for him and for him alone. Whether there was any truth in this or not – and we shall see that it had at least some basis of fact – it was certainly not the whole truth; for Morrison's empire over Backhouse was clearly personal, not merely mechanical. Backhouse, a pliable, feminine character, needed to yield to a master; and Morrison, whose autocratic spirit would bear no brother near the throne, and who would not tolerate the independence of Bland, found in Backhouse an ideal, but also a willing, slave.

For most of the time in which Backhouse and Bland were working on their book, Morrison was out of their way. Bland was in England from 1909; Backhouse was in England or Scotland for much of 1909 and 1910; and although Morrison also came to England in 1910, there was little occasion for them to meet. Besides, Morrison, at this time, had other fish to fry. He had come to England for a purpose. There had been a revolution in *The Times*.

The story begins in 1908, when the proprietors of *The Times*, the Walter family, found themselves forced to sell their property. After a series of complicated manoeuvres, in which the leading

66

spirit was Morrison's original patron, Moberly Bell, the paper was bought by Lord Northcliffe, the megalomaniac tycoon who had created popular journalism and the *Daily Mail*. Bell had kept Morrison informed of the manoeuvres, and Morrison, with his keen eye for power, had seen, in this internal revolution, a means to his own advancement. He quickly ingratiated himself with the new proprietor, who had been very ready to woo him, and then, confident of his support, set out to eliminate his two greatest enemies. These were, first, the Foreign Editor, Valentine Chirol, and secondly, his local rival, Bland.

For several years, Morrison had enjoyed harmonious relations with Chirol. Chirol had appreciated Morrison's reports, and Morrison had praised Chirol, as he had praised Backhouse, to his face, in extravagant terms. 'You are beyond all comparison the greatest correspondent the world has ever seen', Morrison had written to Chirol in 1904, 'and I am proud to know you.' But since that date relations had deteriorated. Chirol could not follow Morrison's abrupt political volte-faces; he was unconvinced by his naïve views on the possibility of instant reform in China; and he was shocked by his violent attacks on his colleagues. Sometimes he even felt obliged to modify or tone down Morrison's reports. Although he always, on these occasions, sent patient explanations to Morrison. Morrison was furious at being 'gagged' and now, after the change of ownership, he resolved to use his influence with the new proprietor to drive Chirol out of *The Times*.

In January 1910 Morrison returned to England and set to work. In private sessions with Northcliffe, he easily persuaded his new patron that Chirol 'was quite unfit to be our foreign editor', and must be removed as the chief obstacle in the way of Northcliffe's ambition to control the paper. Meanwhile, he also set out to remove Bland, who had become intolerable to him on several grounds. First, there was their general disagreement on policy. Secondly, there was that unfortunate chance which had enabled Bland, not himself, to report the dramatic deaths of the Emperor and the Empress. Morrison always looked back with mortification to that ill-timed sporting trip to Kwantai. Thirdly, on Chinese politics, Bland clearly agreed with Chirol – perhaps even was the influence behind Chirol. We are not here concerned with Morrison's war against Chirol: we shall concentrate on the war against Bland.

Morrison had already gained his first point in 1909, when Bland was summoned back to England. This was something, but it was not enough, for even in England Bland was still employed by *The Times* and could threaten Morrison's exclusive position in the Far East which Northcliffe had promised to strengthen. Morrison was determined to stop this; and his determination – little though it needed such stimulus – was sharpened by a particular incident.

In December 1909 the *Fortnightly Review* had praised a 'remarkable and masterly article' about China in *The Times*, which, being signed by 'our correspondent', it ascribed to the famous Dr Morrison. The article was in fact by Bland. Morrison was very angry: angry at being credited with Bland's views, angry at seeing Bland's work and opinions praised, angry that Bland was allowed to write in *The Times* at all. He therefore wrote to Bland, telling him that his views were 'damnably wrong' and must not be fathered on him. Bland duly wrote to the editor of the *Fortnightly Review*, explaining the difference between 'our own correspondent', who was Morrison, and 'our correspondent', who was his deputy, Bland. But Morrison was not appeased, and when he left Peking for England he was determined to force the issue to a conclusion.

Morrison had planned his journey some time ago, and it was to be a leisurely expedition. He left Peking in January 1910 and travelled slowly through China and Russian central Asia. His departure from Peking left Backhouse free to enjoy his new-found freedom, and he expressed his enjoyment in lyrical terms. On 16 January 1910, he wrote to Bland from Peking, 'Morrison has left. I have often regretted doing so much work for him, for he has spoken very unjustly about me, and if ffrench had been a different kind of man, might have done me great harm. He has never forgiven me for helping you with that emergency article about the Old Buddha when he was off on a sporting trip. One doesn't like attacking a man behind his back, although he is always doing it; but he does not seem to understand loyalty in friendship.' Bland understood the position perfectly. Six months later, he learned that Morrison was about to arrive in England. 'I shall not trouble him very much or often,' he wrote to ffrench. 'I wonder how he will like the publishing of the book and how Backhouse will explain his having dared to do it without permission.'

He was soon to be enlightened. No sooner had Morrison arrived in London than Heinemann suggested to Bland that – since Sir Robert Hart had declined – Morrison be invited to write a preface to the book. Bland naturally objected. Either Morrison would write the preface, thereby imposing his patronage and his views, or more probably, he would refuse, 'which would make us lose face'. Happily that dilemma was avoided. But a few days later Bland met Morrison in London, and in conversation – since the matter was no longer secret – told him for the first time about the book on which he and Backhouse were engaged. He also showed him the prospectus, in which reference was made to the central document, the diary of Ching-shan. Morrison (as Bland afterwards recalled) 'read it with a sickly smile' and then began to abuse Backhouse, saying that he must have invented the diary, since Ching-shan had not died in 1900 and the diary could not be his.* A month later Bland met Morrison in a train. Morrison, he recorded, 'simulated great friendship' and invited him to lunch; but he did not accept the invitation.

After the London meeting, Bland wrote to Backhouse and told him about Morrison's criticism of Ching-shan's diary. Backhouse had by this time also come to Britain and was now nestling comfortably in Midlothian. On reading the criticism, he could afford to chuckle. 'The infallible Morrison', he wrote, had confused Ching-shan with the better-known Grand Secretary, Ching-hsin; 'but Morrison says this in order to justify his scepticism, and one might expect something of the sort.' All the same, Backhouse suggested that a note should be inserted in the book

---

* Bland's fullest description of this meeting in London is in a letter to Backhouse of 22 January 1912. He there dates it October 1910 which is clearly a confusion with the luncheon at Shepperton. The date of the London meeting was 7 August 1910 as is shown by Bland's diary and contemporary correspondence. The diary entry is brief: Morrison, says Bland, 'seemed sick at the *Empress Dowager* and damned Backhouse freely'.

emphasising the difference between the two men; 'otherwise Morrison would damn the whole thing *ab initio* on the fictitious grounds that they were the same'. Such a note was duly added to forestall such objections.

Three months later – on 10 October 1910, just after the publication of the book – there was another meeting when Morrison, together with two other guests, came to luncheon with the Blands at their home at Upper Helliford near Shepperton. Bland described the visit in a letter to ffrench. Morrison, he said 'did not say anything, good or bad about the book, but the things he said about Backhouse were simply sulphurous. I have no doubt he says the same sort of thing about me whenever it will do any good. He is really the most amazingly indiscreet person for a *Times* correspondent, and the word "loyalty" is not in his dictionary.'

In his diary, Bland was a little more explicit about Morrison's conversation on that day. 'Morrison', he wrote, 'is evidently intriguing with Northcliffe, and gave me a long account of their friendly relations. . . . He spoke in sulphurous terms of Backhouse, said he had repudiated his Oxford debts and been associated with the Oscar Wilde scandals – had sent lots of jewellery to Ellen Terry and other actresses – had no real friends or acquaintances among the high Chinese officials. But not a word did he say about the *Empress Dowager*! He will never forgive Backhouse for having kept the diary from him all these years.'

We have seen that some of these allegations at least were true. Backhouse had repudiated his Oxford debts. We know from William Rothenstein about his cult of Ellen Terry and his traffic in jewels. We know from Max Beerbohm that he collected money for Oscar Wilde's defence. Evidently it was true also that Morrison did not scruple to use his knowledge, when he wanted, to damage Backhouse, and bring him back to heel.

When Morrison told Bland about his close relations with Northcliffe, he presumably did not enter into all the details of his successful machinations. It is to Morrison's private letters that we must look for those details: how he had spurred Northcliffe on to join him in denunciation of Chirol, 'the most hopelessly unjust and jesuitical foreign editor that can be found in Great Britain', whose removal was essential if Northcliffe were ever to gain full control of the paper, and how he had offered himself as an instrument to be used against 'the old gang' whom Northcliffe had promised, on buying the paper, not to disturb, but whom he was now preparing to eliminate: not only Chirol, but Buckle, the editor, and Moberly Bell, the managing director, to whose efforts Northcliffe owed his success in purchasing the paper. Within a year, all these men would be removed: Bell by premature death, Chirol and Buckle by resignation.

Nor, of course, would Morrison mention to Bland the schemes he was laying for the ruin of Bland himself. Only afterwards, from a friend in the office, would Bland learn what had happened. Attacked by Morrison, Bland had been supported by Chirol; but that, of course, said Morrison, only proved that Chirol was 'prejudiced'. Another umpire had then been called in, and had also pronounced for Bland; which had merely incensed Morrison more. Bland survived this first attack, but he could see well enough what the end would be. 'Can't expect him to love me as long as he is Peking correspondent,' he wrote in his diary. 'Shouldn't be surprised if he insisted on their choosing between us; in which case he would surely get the field to himself.'

When ffrench, in Peking, received Bland's letter describing the luncheon-party and Morrison's 'sulphurous' attack on Backhouse, he may well have been somewhat confused, for he had recently received a letter from Morrison describing his earlier meeting with Bland, speaking warmly of the forthcoming book, for which he prophesied a great success, and soliciting direct contact with Backhouse, who was now back in Peking, and on whom he poured out not sulphur but the softest glycerine. 'I should like exceedingly to hear from Backhouse,' Morrison had written, 'who now for the first time will receive popular applause and public recognition of his extraordinary abilities. He is one of the greatest scholars England possesses. It will be a new role for him, this agency of Sir John Brown.'

This friendly message was evidently passed on to Backhouse, for almost at once Backhouse wrote to Morrison. He described his ambition in life, which was not to be an agent of Sir John Brown but 'to live a student's life in Peking, for which I am fitted'. As for Morrison's kind words about the book, though very grateful, he must disclaim them. He was a mere translator: the whole merit of the work was 'due to Bland's skill and the book is his and his only. . . . My name ought not really to appear at all; indeed I had decided to withdraw it, but found that it was too late to do so.' Then, after describing the finding of Ching-shan's diary, in which Morrison had evidently expressed interest, he returned to his theme-song: 'whatever credit there may be in the book belongs to Bland, and my part is merely mechanical.'

Morrison at once replied, sweeping aside these humble protests. Backhouse, he wrote, was far too modest. The book was splendid and did him the greatest honour. Backhouse was 'the most remarkable genius I know. . . . It is not necessary to say how much I admire your colossal ability, and I shall always be grateful for the help you have so often and so willingly given me.' Thus Morrison, after his 'sulphurous' denunciations of Backhouse to Bland, turned directly to Backhouse and sought to woo him back to himself with honeyed, excessive flattery.

Before leaving London for a short visit to Spain, Morrison did his best to undermine the credit of the new book by repeating, in the London literary world, his doubts about the authenticity of Ching-shan's diary. An article by W. T. Stead, for instance, suggested that the diary was mis-translated. As Stead could give no reason to justify this suggestion, Bland was understandably indignant. The insinuation must have come, ultimately, from Morrison. Then, on 25 November 1910, Bland received an urgent letter from his publisher, Heinemann. Heinemann wrote that it had come to his ears from more than one source that Morrison had declared Ching-shan's diary to be a fake. One of his inform-ants – the editor of a monthly periodical *The World's Work*, published by Heinemann – had been told so categorically by Morrison himself. Morrison had even suggested that the diary was the work of Backhouse's 'boy'. Heinemann insisted that the matter be cleared up, since 'it would damage us and the book very much to leave such a statement by one of Dr Morrison's authority uncontradicted'. Bland at once wrote to Morrison, demanding that he deny the allegations. Then he wrote off to Backhouse in Peking asking for his comments. He hoped that Morrison on his return from Spain would reply satisfactorily. If not, could Ching-shan's hand be identified? The manuscript, after all, was now in the British Museum for all to see.

Backhouse replied somewhat majestically to these allegations. There would be no difficulty in identifying Ching-shan's hand, he wrote: 'I have other specimens, but I suppose people would say they had been faked too.' The idea that his 'boy' had faked it was laughable: it would be more rational to accuse himself. If Bland had doubts, Backhouse suggested that he should get an English sinologist – Hillier or Giles – to look at the manuscript: 'I don't think a Chinese could very well give an unprejudiced opinion, as they are so angry at its publication.' But in general he dismissed the whole affair as an absurdity, a mere nuisance, not to be taken seriously. 'How odd', he added, 'that Morrison should have such an antipathy to me,' especially in view of the flattering letters he had so recently received; but that was the way of the world. 'The surest way to make an enemy of a man is to do favours for him. When I think of all the work I have done for Morrison, I feel rather sore.'

When Morrison returned from Spain, he replied rather evasively to Bland's challenge. He suggested that Bland himself did not believe in the authenticity of the diary and that the reports might well have been started by him. He ascribed Heinemann's action to the motives of a sharp businessman who wanted, by this device, to secure a certificate from the great oracle on Chinese affairs, Dr Morrison. But his letter contained the vital words, 'I have never said Ching-shan's diary was a fake,' and so Bland was able to satisfy Heinemann. Morrison then wrote to Backhouse telling him that Bland ('you know what a mischievous man is Bland') had been making trouble, saying 'that Mr Heinemann had told him (so Bland said, but I do not know if it is true) that I had said Ching-shan's diary was a fake. I have never said any such thing. . . . Bland himself has spoken so wildly about the diary that I believe it is he himself who has created an impression.' Then, having used the episode to sow trouble between Backhouse and Bland, Morrison turned again to flattery of Backhouse: 'you are a genius with powers and gifts that have been given to no other man of my acquaintance.'

What are we to make of this tortuous correspondence? It is

important to be clear about it because of the great controversies which are still to come. There are two problems: first, the relations between Morrison, Bland and Backhouse; secondly, the allegations that Ching-shan's diary was a fake. The active force in both matters was Morrison.

It is clear that Morrison resented the 'damnably wrong' views and the personal independence of Bland. He had done everything possible to neutralise Bland. He had secured his removal from China and (as he thought) the suppression of his views on Chinese politics. It was therefore mortifying to him when Bland published a highly successful and – as Morrison himself grudgingly admitted to third parties – 'valuable' book on Chinese history. But Bland, he rightly believed, could not have done this without the aid of Backhouse. Backhouse, as he wrote to others, was 'our greatest scholar in Peking': he had written 440 out of the 500 pages in the book; the combination with Bland was very effective, 'for Bland linked together the translations in a way Backhouse could never have done'. To Morrison, therefore, with his monopolising spirit, it was essential to separate Backhouse from Bland, partly in order to weaken Bland, partly in order to recover for himself a much needed Chinese scholar who could collaborate but never compete with him. He set about this task with machiavellian cunning. Publicly he said nothing about the book, either praise or blame; to Bland himself he wrote a letter of somewhat hypo-critical congratulation on its success; but privately he undermined the book, denigrated Backhouse to Bland and Bland to Backhouse, seeking to dissolve the partnership; and meanwhile he wooed Backhouse, seeking to draw that feeble creature, whose character he despised, but whose 'genius' he needed, back into dependence on him.

One method of discrediting the book was by declaring its central document a 'fake'. There can be no question that Morrison assiduously spread this report and that his attempt to father it on Bland was disingenuous, for it is clear that Bland never doubted that the document was genuine: 'the man is not born', he wrote, 'who could fake a document like that, and the original is open to anyone's inspection.' When directly challenged, Morrison expli-citly denied, in writing, both to Backhouse and to Bland, that he had ever said that the document was not genuine; but this denial was forced out of him and, however he may have justified it to himself, was essentially a lie. Moreover, as we shall see, he continued, after his denial, to repeat the allegation. Bland believed that he did this out of mere malice: that he was enraged against Backhouse for having kept the diary secret all these years and then given it to Bland instead of to him, and that he was now taking his revenge by declaring it to be a forgery although he knew that it was not. This is of course a hypothetical possibility. But there is also another possibility, less damaging to Morrison's character. It is possible that Morrison genuinely believed, or suspected, the diary to be a forgery, but knew that he could not substantiate his belief.

Certainly Morrison did not attempt to substantiate his charge. The evidence which he offered to Bland, before publication, was clearly worthless: it only showed his own ignorance. Nor could he have based such a belief on internal evidence, for he was no scholar, and anyway he expressed it without ever seeing the document. If he really believed that the document was a fake, it could only be either because he knew that Backhouse's circumstantial account of its discovery was false, or because someone whom he trusted had told him that the document itself was false; and if he declined to assert his belief in public, that must have been because, for some reason, he could not, or would not, produce his witness in court. Here, for a time, we can leave the question in suspense.

Thus the year 1911 opened with Bland in England and Backhouse in China enjoying the universal acclaim of their book and Morrison, intent on destroying their partnership and recovering control over Backhouse, preparing to set out from London, where he had done all the damage he could, to Peking, where his helpless victim had already been softened up for the final attack.

How did Backhouse look forward to the arrival of Morrison, the terrible patron whom he had dared to deceive and desert and who was now luring him back into dependence with such extravagant praise? According to his letters to Bland, Backhouse intended to keep his distance. 'I hope Morrison and I will have no more dealings with one another,' he wrote on 8 January:

' . . . when Morrison arrives, I mean to avoid him entirely.'
Bland was obviously apprehensive. Morrison ought by now to
have reached Peking, he wrote at the end of February: 'I shall be
very interested to hear how he behaves to you.' He had never
written to Bland again since his 'very characteristic denial of the
statements attributed to him. . . . To have anyone but himself
coming forward as an authority on China was naturally unpleasant, and he could not help acting as he did, I suppose.' Next
month Morrison arrived in Peking and Backhouse reported that
he spoke 'very bitterly' about Bland, but that they seldom met:
by now 'he and I are hardly even acquaintances.'

A few days later Backhouse met Morrison and reported a
conversation with him. Morrison, with great show of friendship
and sympathy, had deplored Backhouse's 'neglected chances of
achieving a measure of notoriety' by his work. 'If I had come to
him, he would have written a preface for it and made me famous
for ever, etc., etc. I pointed out that you had generously admitted
the idea and framework of the thing was mine, and that your
contributing to the work gave it its special character and savour
and enabled it to sell well and receive good reviews. Otherwise it
would have been buried in oblivion even if it had found a publisher.' Morrison, said Backhouse, 'attacks you everywhere, but
over-vindictive abuse defeats its own ends. . . . I don't want to
quarrel with him openly because he could do me even greater
injury than he has already inflicted; but I can never regard him as
anything but a bitter and unscrupulous enemy who will rejoice
over my undoing.'

Backhouse's reports on Morrison, and on his own conversations with him, thoroughly alarmed Bland. It was all very well
for Backhouse to protest that he saw through Morrison's pro-
fessions of 'loyal and disinterested friendship'; but if once the
weak Backhouse, through unwillingness to quarrel openly, slipped
into Morrison's grasp, how would he ever avoid becoming his
creature again? Bland was particularly alarmed to learn that
Morrison was playing on Backhouse's vanity, trying to persuade
him that Bland had robbed him of the credit, and even of the
profit, of his work. Of course such a charge was grotesque. Had
not Bland always recognised the importance of Backhouse's con-

tribution, given him public credit for it, begged him not to conceal his name, tried to have his name put before his own, insisted on his receiving full payment even after he had sold out to him? In a long letter of expostulation, he begged Backhouse to stand firm against Morrison's insinuations and blandishments. 'I greatly fear that your ineradicable good nature will lead you again to work for him, as you have done all these years, for his credit, and only to get abused later on. That is Morrison's way. He uses men and then abuses them. I did much work for him, even as you have done, but the moment I presumed to take any credit for it to myself, and thus to deprive him of "the unique position of the Peking correspondent", he proceeded to injure me in every possible and treacherous way; and he has treated Chirol and you in the same way. The things he said of you here last autumn, in the presence of a witness' – that is, the 'sulphurous' comments at Shepperton – 'will not bear repeating; but I warn you against being deceived into rendering him further services. As for me, I have simply wiped him off the slate and care neither for his good nor bad report. Most decent people do in the long run.'

If Bland was alarmed by what Morrison was saying in China, Backhouse was hardly less alarmed about what might be reported back to Bland in England. So he decided to get in first. Morrison, he wrote to Bland on 20 April, 'following his usual practice', had been saying that Backhouse had spoken slightingly to him about Bland. This, protested Backhouse, was quite untrue. 'I have always spoken of you with the greatest sincerity as a good friend, and have invariably spoken of your share in our book as the factor in its success with the public. Any other statement is Morrison's fabrication.' Shocked by these allegations, Backhouse declared that he would never cross Morrison's portals again; and he added that Morrison treated their joint book as non-existent. It was four days after sending this letter that Backhouse proposed to Bland another joint book, *Memoirs of the Manchu Dynasty*. Bland agreed to co-operate, and Backhouse set to work collecting and translating documents.

So far, it seemed – at least by his own account – Backhouse was holding out against Morrison. But then, in June 1911, Bland dined in London with a friend recently arrived from Peking, and received news which alarmed him. According to this visitor, it was being widely said in Peking that Bland had treated Backhouse badly, depriving him of his due share of the profit and the credit of their joint enterprise. Bland was very angry. Of course this was untrue, and of course it all came, ultimately from Morrison. Bland wrote at once to Backhouse urging him to write to Morrison and put the record straight: 'I really think that a poisonous lie of this kind should be jumped on.' If, as was reported, Backhouse was already on the way home, Bland would himself write to Morrison telling him the facts; 'and I shall tell him that his concern for the interests of a man whom he has systematically exploited for years does him infinite credit.' Backhouse replied expressing great distress at this report and protesting that he had always disclaimed any credit for their book, as would be confirmed by their friends in Peking: 'you have no more loyal friend than I am, as I hope you know.'

Backhouse did not come to London that summer or autumn. He stayed in Peking busily collecting matter for the *Memoirs of the Manchu Dynasty*, sending it to Bland, and selling an imaginary battleship. About Morrison he expressed the most orthodox sentiments. He assured Bland that he would never have anything to do with that rogue again: 'his behaviour to me will rankle always, and friendly relations between us are impossible.' Bland replied in kind, approving and encouraging his work, and expressing benevolent scepticism about the battleship. But he was not entirely happy: he knew Backhouse's weakness only too well. Besides, he had detected Backhouse's unmistakable hand in some of Morrison's recent messages to *The Times*. In a letter to Backhouse, he touched lightly on this fact, adding, 'I only hope your assistance will be better rewarded in the future than it has been in the past.'

He also received in October a remarkable letter from Backhouse. It was a complete volte-face. Without any warning, Backhouse had changed his tune. In unusually strong terms, he now demanded that in their new book there must be no room for misunderstanding about his own share of the work, and he complained that he had been denied credit and profit from their previous venture. To Bland, it was only too clear who had called this new tune: 'I smell Morrison at his usual friendly trade,' he wrote in his diary. However, he was careful not to over-react. Once again he wrote back courteously. Of course, he said, Backhouse must receive full credit for his work on the new book, and most of the profit from it, 'for my part of the job would be simply that of editing and arranging your work and placing it to the best advantage'. Then he took steps to check the facts at their source. He turned to his invaluable friend in Peking, Lord ffrench.

'There is one thing', Bland wrote to ffrench, 'that I want to know most particularly, and that is, what are the present relations between Backhouse and Morrison? I suspect that the wily Morrison makes B. work as of old, and that he is doing his utmost to put him against working with me.' Then, after describing Backhouse's 'extraordinary letter', he went on: 'Now, if this is M's work, and if that poor weak creature has been listening to him against me, I will reply that he can write his next book with M. and see what they make of it between them. M's name would sell it all right, but it would be a queer production! And they would fight like blazes over the production and the accounts. That would please me.' As for Backhouse's protestations 'that he has nothing to do with M., that he will never cross his doorstep again', etc., Bland stated firmly that 'I know he is lying, for I see in M's telegrams full proof of daily interviews with B. And so I can hear, quite plainly, B. telling M. how I have done this, that and the other, all serving to show that he has always loved M. and has been led astray by me. And in that case he can go to the Devil and I will write my own books in my own way.' ffrench's reply bore out some at least of these deductions. Backhouse, he wrote, was visiting Morrison daily, and supplying him with translations of edicts 'quite in the old way'. In Backhouse's defence, ffrench explained that Morrison had 'got him cold' – that is, had caught him out trying to bribe Chinese for some nefarious purpose; after which he had a hold on him. 'I don't blame Backhouse,' ffrench added: 'he is such a weakling, and I admire his genius much'; also, 'I must say that he has always spoken of you in the nicest way.'

This seems to have appeased Bland, who wrote back in a tone

of tolerant resignation. It was indeed remarkable, he replied to
ffrench, that Backhouse 'should allow himself to be thus used,
without thanks or reward, but, he is a queer fish and I really
believe that this is a case of Svengali and little Trilby.' So he
resumed his correspondence with Backhouse on an amicable
note. Then, at the end of the year, a new crisis broke out. It was
caused by a review of *China under the Empress Dowager* in the
Journal of the Royal Asiatic Society. The review was signed 'W. E.
L.', who was, in fact, W. E. Leveson, a close friend of Bland, at
that time serving in Shanghai, and it was likely to cause the greatest offence to Backhouse and play into the hands of Morrison; for
it not only ascribed the book exclusively to Bland, whom it
praised extravagantly, making no reference to his collaborator,
but also dismissed the documents, which were in fact Backhouse's
contribution, as 'wearisome interludes'.

Backhouse read the review and was outraged. He drafted a
pompous letter to the editor of the journal and sent a copy to
Bland. Bland was put in a difficult position. He had already
thanked Leveson for the generous review; now he saw the full
implications of that generosity. For did it not exactly confirm
Morrison's allegation, that all the credit for the joint work was
being given to Bland? He now wrote again to Leveson to expostu-
late. Backhouse, he said, was, predictably, 'furious'. 'Nothing I
can say will persuade him, and Morrison, that I had no hand in
inspiring that review. So now see what you have done!' It was
ironical that Backhouse should make such a scene about the
failure to mention his name since he had himself tried so hard to
keep it out of the book; but since it was in, why did Leveson so
completely ignore it? Was it on purpose? If so, what was the
purpose? Bland had told Backhouse 'not to be silly', but, 'seriously, I cannot wonder at the poor fellow taking offence, especially
when you alluded to his translations as "wearisome interludes".
This he calls "mean and cruel innuendo". I call it deliberately
offensive to a sensitive soul.' Bland wrote no less than four letters
to Leveson, begging him to write to Backhouse and calm him
down, but Leveson did not answer. His inspiration, and his
purpose (if he had one) remained obscure.

Meanwhile, Bland sought to soothe the sensitive soul of Backhouse. He wrote in the most emollient tones. He fully appreciated Backhouse's annoyance, he said . . . he had written at once to Leveson pointing out the stupid injustice of the thing . . . he always emphasised Backhouse's share in the work . . . 'you must not make me responsible for the indiscretions of my friends'. . . . Finally, Bland offered to drop the collaboration over the *Memoirs of the Manchu Dynasty*. 'A partnership that is not based on perfect confidence is no good to me, and I cannot help feeling that you are being influenced by a very loyal friend of yours to terminate an agreement which, if continued, is likely to diminish the glory of the only bright light in China.'

Scarcely had Bland posted his letter to Backhouse, than another letter arrived from Peking. It was of icy coldness, and it repeated all the old allegations which had originated with Morrison: that his own part in their joint work had been insufficiently recognised, that he had been defrauded of his due credit, that the order of the names on the title-page was evidence of this, etc., etc. This was too much for Bland, and he decided at last to call Backhouse firmly to order and force him to choose between himself and Morrison.

On 13 January 1912 Bland wrote to Backhouse a long letter – the first of a series of long letters – demanding, in effect, that he face the realities of his own situation. Backhouse's last letter, following as it did his unfortunate letter to the editor of the *Journal of the Royal Asiatic Society*, had confirmed him in a decision to which he had gradually been coming, viz., that so long as Backhouse remained under Morrison's influence, no collaboration between them was possible. For Backhouse, it was clear, had now succumbed completely to that influence – exactly as Bland had predicted. He was repeating statements about his collaboration with Bland which he himself knew to be 'damned lies', 'figments of your easily influenced mind'. Now Bland demanded that he come into the open and prove his allegations – if he could. Then, after setting out the true facts of their collaboration, he ended with an ultimatum: 'and so, my dear Backhouse, with sincere regrets, and hoping that you may achieve "a measure of notoriety" (is that the word you meant?) with the help of your generous and loyal friend, I leave you to give me the proofs for which I ask, and meanwhile, and until you return to this country, let us say no more about joint work.'

If Bland's letters, at this period, seem a little vehement, even neurotic in their insistence, the reason is clear enough. Not only were Backhouse's allegations grossly unjust – Bland particularly resented the insinuation that he had defrauded Backhouse of his financial reward when in fact he had treated him with great generosity – they were also clearly part of a vendetta against him by Morrison. For precisely at this time Morrison had carried his intrigue against Bland in the offices of *The Times* to a victorious conclusion. The desertion of Backhouse, his return to the patronage – the ruthless, exploiting, contemptuous patronage – of Morrison, coincided with the complete victory of Morrison in the offices of *The Times*, the final humiliation of Bland.

The long crisis had come to a head on 19 May 1911, when *The Times* had published an article by Bland – the first of three – on 'Currency Reform in China'. The article was a careful, well-documented survey of a complicated subject, and it is hard to find anything in it to which any exception could be taken; but its mere publication roused Morrison to hysterical rage. Morrison now regarded China as his private fief: he had been invested with it personally by Lord Northcliffe, and nobody else had any rights there. Therefore he was furious that Bland should have written, and *The Times* should have published, such an article; and he decided to force the issue. At first he thought of appealing directly to Northcliffe. He drafted a telegram to Northcliffe. Then, on second thoughts, he changed his plan. He decided that it might be more effective to wave the big stick in the face of smaller men. Chirol had already been driven out of his office, and his duties were being performed, temporarily, by his assistant, Dudley Braham. Braham was clearly in a weak position, and Morrison, strong in the support of the tyrannical new proprietor, believed that he could bully him into subjection – especially since the anti-semitic Northcliffe had told Morrison 'that he would not have a Jew in charge of the Foreign Department of *The Times*'; and Braham was a Jew.

Morrison's letter to Braham, on this occasion, is a horrible document. He denounced Bland and his 'dirty action' in unmeasured terms. He expressed his indignation with *The Times* for allowing it. Bland, he wrote, had done great injury both to Morrison himself and 'to British interests here'. He was 'the most disloyal and treacherous man I know . . . you do not seem to realise what a man he is. His main mission is to revenge himself upon all who have disagreed with him. I am certain now that it was he who set Chirol against me . . . and he has turned Backhouse entirely away from me. In the past Backhouse used often to help me, and I still more helped him. Now he is civil to me, no more. It is impossible, he tells me, to be otherwise, seeing what Bland has written him of what I have said against him, and warning him against having any dealings with me.' Then Morrison proceeded from complaints to thinly veiled threats. He referred to the strength of his own position, his indispensability to *The Times* and his influence with its new proprietor. 'I am the best-known Englishman at present east of India, and I am often told the best-known correspondent in the world. . . . Lord Northcliffe begged of me to communicate with him whenever I felt that things were not going well with me, and he wanted me to draw up a private code so that I could communicate with him confidentially. . . . I have not yet availed myself of this opportunity. I will however not hesitate to do so should I find a repetition of such a malicious act . . .'. Bland, he declared, had made 'a calculated attempt to impair my authority and prestige'; and he ended his letter by demanding protection against 'a correspondent who left behind in the Far East the most unenviable reputation for unscrupulousness, disloyalty and treachery. Excuse this note. I write very frankly. My one wish is to help promote the best interests of the paper.'

Faced by this ultimatum, the establishment of *The Times* surrendered. It seems that Braham tried to save Bland – Bland certainly believed that he did, and was always grateful to him – but the matter was referred to the editor, Buckle, and Buckle yielded to the threat. No doubt he remembered the fate of Chirol – which, in spite of his surrender, he would soon himself incur. At all events, Morrison was informed that Bland would no longer write about China in *The Times*, 'so that you will have field to yourself'. The very phrase recalls Bland's prophecy in his diary six months before, 'shouldn't be surprised if he insisted on their choosing between us; in which case he would surely get the field to himself'. Bland, naturally, felt very bitter about his exclusion. 'Morrison has done me the last bad turn in his power', he wrote to one friend, 'by using his influence with "me Lord" so that I cannot get anything on China into *that* paper'; and to another, 'in view of Dr Morrison's objections to the publication of opinions which conflicted, or might conflict, with his own, the Editor has been unable to avail himself of my services'.

Morrison's letter to Braham shows, incidentally, that up to that time at least – that is, up to 9 June – Backhouse was resisting Morrison's blandishments. It was only after breaking Bland, and boasting to Backhouse that he had broken him, that Morrison was able to turn and subjugate 'that poor weak creature', who nevertheless, as ffrench's account shows, seems to have struggled for a time, continuing to speak well of Bland. But by the autumn the irresistible Morrison had completed his triumph; it was now clear that Bland could no longer exercise any patronage in China or any influence with *The Times*; and Backhouse was once again reduced to total dependence on the victor. In these circumstances Bland might be pardoned for seeing himself as the victim of conspiracy and responding somewhat hysterically to a double persecution.

Bland's firm letter of 12 January drove the wretched Backhouse into an agony of expostulation. In letter after letter, he expressed his regrets. He begged for peace. He wriggled miserably on the hook, protested that he never saw Morrison, tied himself into knots of disingenuous self-justification. But Bland was inexorable. He was prepared to leave some matters over till Backhouse came to England, he said, but on the essential point he would make no concession. He was convinced that Backhouse's behaviour was entirely controlled by Morrison: 'your own letters prove it conclusively'. 'When you escape from that almost hypnotic state to which his influence reduces you, and when you are comfortably at home in England, I shall be glad to resume relations and work with you;' till then all collaboration was suspended, and Backhouse could publish the *Memoirs of the Manchu Dynasty* on his own, where he liked, with a foreword by Morrison. Backhouse's material for that book was at present in Bland's possession. He would now return it. 'Please tell me to whom you wish me to send the stuff.'

Backhouse pleaded and protested, but in vain. All pleas, all protestations were firmly brushed aside, or only elicited from Bland yet another excoriating résumé of the familiar story. In one letter Bland spelt out Backhouse's dilemma with deadly clarity. 'I fear you are between the Devil and the deep sea, for you are being made to suffer for the sins and quarrels of your friends. Let me make myself perfectly clear: I decline absolutely to go in for any further joint work unless you undertake to do no more with or for Morrison. That is what I mean when I say that I will continue the collaboration when you come home, for I do not think you capable of refusing to do anything he asks on the spot.' This insistence, Bland added, may seem strange, but the fact is, 'Morrison has not hesitated, on top of many other treacherous acts, to lay down the condition that I am not to be allowed to write about China in *The Times*. You yourself have told me how he has boasted of this, and I have heard it repeatedly confirmed at the office. Well, he knows best, and *The Times* presumably knows best, whether that sort of thing pays in the long run; but meanwhile I see no reason why I should not object to your working for him.'

It is difficult not to sympathise with Backhouse, that 'sensitive soul' torn apart in the struggle of more powerful personalities. But Morrison's case should not go by default. If Bland had been deserted and traduced, so had he. Bland complained that Backhouse, whom he had befriended and patronised, had then gone over to his rival and joined with him in slandering his former patron. But had not Morrison already been treated in exactly the same way? Before Bland came to Peking, Morrison had been Backhouse's patron, and Backhouse had acknowledged his patronage in the most grateful, not to say sycophantic, terms. Then Bland had appeared and seduced Backhouse away, and Backhouse, encouraged by Bland, had turned about and denounced Morrison, in retrospect, for having exploited his labour and deprived him of credit or reward. Now Morrison was paying Bland back in his own coin. Morrison was perhaps more unscrupulous in his defamation, more cynical in his use of Back-house, whom he now despised; but he felt himself to be the victim of treachery and he was bent on revenge. The worst accusation that could be made against him was that he was still actively disseminating a charge which he could not prove and which, when challenged, he had been forced to deny – that Ching-shan's diary was a 'fake'. That charge, for the moment, we have agreed to leave in suspense.

Under Bland's relentless barrage, Backhouse finally collapsed and surrendered at discretion. He promised to sever himself from Morrison. He announced that he would come to England. Thus encouraged, Bland responded. His answers became softer. He praised Backhouse's writings. He poured balm into his numerous and gaping wounds. He undertook to write, on Backhouse's behalf, to the editor of the *Journal of the Royal Asiatic Society* – although by the time that he wrote he feared that the editor would think 'that we are both a little dotty on the crust'. He agreed that a 'definite rupture' with Morrison, at this moment, might be too difficult, and that it could be postponed; and he decided that 'the best and most graceful way of showing the absolute equality of our partnership will be, in future, to follow the usual practice and put your name first on the title-page' of the new book. That book now sailed happily forward towards completion, provision-ally entitled *The Memoirs*, or the *Rise and Fall*, or the *Secret History of the Manchu Dynasty*.

Backhouse's emancipation from the bondage, or hypnotic spell, of Morrison was perhaps made easier by political events in China. In 1911 the Chinese Revolution broke out, and early in 1912 the Manchu dynasty came to an inglorious end with the voluntary abdication of the new Empress Dowager. Thereupon the Young China party claimed the inheritance. A republic was set up, with Sun Yat-sen, the leader of the Young China movement, as its first President. As a champion of the Young China party, Morri-son enjoyed his apotheosis in those months. His prophecies, it seemed, had come true. His programme would now be carried out. And in *The Times* his voice alone would be heard: for by now he had imposed his complete monopoly on *The Times*, ex-cluding any expression of Bland's views on Chinese affairs.

86

Bland's views, of course, were very different. He looked on the new Republic as a makeshift expedient without staying-power, and he ridiculed Morrison's patronage of it. 'The Only Correspondent, he whose messages go forth from Peking', he had written in December 1911, 'has decided that everything will be for the best in the best of all possible worlds so soon as the Manchus have been expelled.' His own view was that it was not the Manchus who needed to be expelled from the throne but inveterate corruption which needed to be expelled from the official world; and he saw no signs that the Young China party, or its successors, would achieve this. Now, when the Republic had been set up, he ridiculed Morrison, who had 'nailed his colours' to 'this government of a day'. 'It cannot be long before China passes to disruption,' he wrote in May 1912, 'and in the meanwhile the only business of those who assume the functions of government will be to feather their own nests;' and he added, 'I see that Morrison continues to believe in the Republic and Young China. Well, he will live to realise his error.' To Bland, the problems of China were not so much political as social and economic, and Morrison, he observed, knew as much of finance as 'a cow of astronomy'.

Immediately, however, there was no stopping the advance of Progress or of Morrison. After the ephemeral rule of Sun Yat-sen, a more powerful figure strode to the centre of the stage. This was the man whose treachery had been so important in 1898, Yüan Shih-k'ai.

As the reward of his treachery to the unfortunate Kuang-hsü Emperor, Yüan had won the favour of the Empress Dowager, and throughout her last regency had been Viceroy of Chih-li and one of the most powerful of her councillors. But the party of reform had never forgiven him. Nor did the Kuang-hsü Emperor. The Emperor could forgive all others, who had acted against him out of loyalty, or in pursuit of declared interests, but the traitor Yüan was beyond the pale, and it is said that his last message, before his death, was a request to his brothers never to trust Yüan. Certainly his brother, Prince Ch'un, who assumed the regency after the death of the Empress, acted in that spirit. He dismissed Yüan from office and exiled him from Peking. For the last three years of the Manchu Empire, Yüan was in opposition, waiting on events. When the revolution came, he stepped forward to command them. He now placed himself at the head of the Republic in which, for the rest of his life, he would be the dominating personality.

The rise to power of Yüan Shih-k'ai did not impress the sceptical Bland. He could not believe that Yüan had 'the moral qualities' to last, or indeed the desire to preserve the republican form of government. But Morrison, in his enthusiasm, welcomed him as the strong man of China, hailed his accession to power, and in the summer of 1912 accepted the post of political adviser to him. Bland greeted the news of this appointment sardonically. 'I trust the good Yüan may find his newest adviser useful', he wrote, 'and that he may in due time buy his library and thus end a glorious career for Morrison. All the same, for a man who does not speak Chinese to be adviser to a Chinese who does not understand English is a position unique in its way. Yüan will soon either be a corpse or a dictator, and if the latter, Morrison will find it hard to explain his position to his Radical Republican friends of Young China.'

Bland's prophecy was remarkably accurate. In July 1913, after the attempted 'Second Revolution' of Sun Yat-sen, Yüan crushed the Young China movement, increased his own powers, and prepared to make himself Emperor, the founder of a new imperial dynasty. Bland could afford to savour the irony of the situation. 'How are your contracts getting on with Yüan Shih-k'ai?' he would ask Backhouse. 'Now that he is formally established in his seat and has no further need of getting them ratified by the Houses of Parliament, it seems to me that your moment has arrived, and I expect to see him buying battleships by the gross.' A little later he would write to ffrench that Morrison was expected in London, 'and I am looking forward to meeting him in the Office, to hear the latest accurate information about Yüan Shih-k'ai as a Republican'.

Morrison's new post no doubt diverted some of the pressure from Backhouse. It also led to a somewhat tentative *rapprochement* between Bland and *The Times*, for Morrison would now have to give up his position as sole *Times* correspondent in Peking. Bland was willing, if asked, to replace him, and the matter was discussed, though it did not come to anything. Meanwhile Backhouse paid a brief visit to London, where his father was in hospital after a serious operation, and afterwards went to stay at the family home at Darlington. In these circumstances collaboration on the new book was resumed. By the summer of 1913 Bland had completed his editorial work, and the publishers promised that the book would be on sale by mid-January 1914. The title had now been changed – since the subject matter was not confined to the Manchu court but went back to the Ming dynasty – to *Annals and Memoirs of the Court of Peking*; and the names of the authors were given as E. T. Backhouse and J. O. P. Bland, in that order.

Thus, in spite of all the storms which had threatened to disrupt it, the literary marriage of Bland and Backhouse had produced its second birth. No sooner was the book completed than Backhouse, as usual, began to suffer qualms. Just as he had feared that *China under the Empress Dowager* would exasperate the Chinese, and had wished to disown the book on the eve of publication, so now he feared that *Annals and Memoirs of the Court of Peking* would exasperate British readers. Was the book altogether moral? Was there not too much on the uninhibited sexual life of the Chinese court? Were these subjects not too freely, and too tolerantly described? As he looked at certain passages of his work, Backhouse was filled with doubt, although he tried to reassure himself by saying that there was nothing quite so indecent as the account, in the Old Testament, of the activity of Onan. All the same, he felt, there would be trouble. Perhaps a presentation copy ought not, after all, to be sent to Dr Rendall, the headmaster of Winchester, Backhouse's old school: 'I think the book too disreputable to send to a schoolmaster with stern views on morality and feel sure he would return it in disgust.'

The book was not sent to Dr Rendall, but Bland was naturally irritated by Backhouse's sudden fit of retrospective puritanism. He was sorry, he wrote, that Backhouse did not like certain parts of the book – especially the last chapter, which was entirely by Bland – and still more sorry that he should think the work as a whole 'disreputable'; 'but it occurs to me to ask why, if you now think it disreputable, you should have collected the materials for publication. The fact is, my dear Backhouse, you are apt to anticipate, and to dread adverse criticism. One must have the courage of one's convictions and try to keep them single-minded.'

Readers who persevere with this essay, and arrive at Back-house's own memoirs, may well be surprised that he should ever have suffered from puritan inhibitions. But perhaps, in this instance, there was a special reason. In the spring of 1913, when his work on *Annals and Memoirs of the Court of Peking* was complete, Backhouse was preparing a new chapter in his life. He then wrote from Peking to Bland that he was coming home for good. He had had enough of selling hypothetical battleships to insolvent temporary governments. Rumour had it that he was returning to be married, but Backhouse himself said nothing about that. He proposed collaboration on several new books. He was also maturing other plans which required that he should present a respectable, not a 'disreputable', image to headmasters and other established figures. He was preparing to penetrate the groves of Academe. Backhouse the agent of railway-constructors, bankers and shipbuilders was about to be transformed into Backhouse the scholarly professor of Chinese, the munificent benefactor of learning.

CHAPTER FIVE

The Benefactor – One

THE story of Backhouse's spectacular benefactions to Oxford University begins in the summer of 1912. This was the time when he had at last surrendered, or at least undertaken to surrender, to the ultimatum of Bland and had agreed to sever his connexion with Morrison in Peking. It was a time of revolution in China; and it was the time when Sir Jonathan Backhouse had a serious illness which left him, for the rest of his life partly paralysed. The disagreeable pressures of life in Peking, the lack of success in the business of selling ships, and the obvious advantage of reconciliation with a rich and ailing parent, may possibly have contributed to Edmund Backhouse's motives in seeking to settle down in a respectable position in England. Already in February 1912 he had written to Bland that he proposed to resign from his position in Peking – that is, presumably, his agency for John Brown – and return to England. Business prospects, he said, were bad; he would come to London; 'and it may be that a Chinese lectureship may fall vacant one of these days, which would just suit me.'

Backhouse first approached his old university through A. H. Sayce, the Professor of Assyriology. He informed Sayce that he had a number of old books and manuscripts which he had purchased cheaply 'from the imperial library' in Peking and which he now offered to place in the Bodleian Library at Oxford. Sayce at once took up the offer. He wrote to Backhouse asking him to send the books and urged him to continue buying 'any other old books' that might be offered from such a source. If he could not afford to buy them himself, the Bodleian would surely find the means; for, as Sayce wrote to Falconer Madan, Bodley's Librarian, in reporting the correspondence, 'from £5 to £10 is not much for an immaculate copy of a Sung book full of autographs of the Ming Emperors.' Backhouse thereupon sent to Madan the catalogue of the collection which he was offering. The books, he said, had 'belonged to the library of the Ming dynasty and had been kept in the Palace from 1400 until 1644' – that is, until the fall of the dynasty. It included examples of Sung printing, as early as A.D. 1150. Some of these Sung and Ming Palace editions were unique, as were some of the 150 scrolls and autographs of Chinese scholars which were additional to the 17,000 volumes. 'So many famous collections have been destroyed in the recent upheavals and rebellions' that the opportunity of making such a collection would hardly recur. The present value of the books offered, said Backhouse, was probably £4500, 'but these figures are largely guesswork'.

Backhouse's original intention was to deposit the books and manuscripts in the Bodleian, where he hoped to work on them himself, with an undertaking that he would bequeath them, and whatever other works he might collect, absolutely to the Library. He was thus clearly envisaging residence in England. However, finding himself unable to pay the charges for freight, insurance and customs, he soon revised his project, and offered his collection as an outright gift if the Bodleian would pay these charges. This offer was gladly accepted, and in the spring of 1913 the collection was duly sent. It filled twenty-nine crates and weighed 4¼ tons. Included in it were six volumes of the famous Yung-lo Encyclopaedia, a work of great rarity. Backhouse declared that for this work alone he had refused £5000; but he took no credit for his refusal as he hoped, by placing his collection in the Bodleian, and himself studying it there at leisure, to benefit from it quite as much as the university could. Also included in the gift were ninety volumes of Chinese newspaper cuttings illustrating the last years of Manchu rule and the revolution against it. He had been using these cuttings, he said, for a history which he was writing of those times.

Scarcely had Backhouse given orders to send his collection to Oxford when, as so often, he began – as always, too late – to regret his decision. About this time, British friends of China were

trying to set up an Anglo-Chinese League, with a religious basis
and a headquarters at some mountain shrine. The chief supporter
of this League was Reginald Johnston, the Confucian scholar who
was now district officer of Weihaiwei. Backhouse heard about
the League from Percival Yetts, the medical officer at the British
legation, who was to become a distinguished scholar of Chinese
literature and art. At once he expressed interest in it. Yetts
reported to Johnston that Backhouse was 'very sick with himself
for having presented his library to the Bodleian, as he is strongly
in favour of "the League" and would have given his library to
the League instead of to the Bodleian if he had known about it
in time'. However, the gift, once accepted by the university,
could not be revoked. As the League soon fizzled out through
lack of support, this was just as well.

Soon after despatching his collection, Backhouse was visited
in Peking by Sayce. Backhouse told Sayce that the collection he
had sent to Oxford was 'the best collection of old Chinese books
in Europe or America'. The Chinese were very nervous and were
selling off their old treasures for nominal sums: he had just been
offered a Palace copy of the great K'ang-hsi Encyclopaedia for
£250. The British Museum had paid £2000 for its copy. Sayce
himself entered with relish into the game, buying 'a wonderful
harvest' of porcelain and Sung pictures. 'It is an opportunity', he
remarked, 'which will never recur.'

It was indeed. Treasures of all kinds were being picked up,
dirt-cheap, and carried off to Europe and America. Today it is
customary to deplore the plunder of Chinese art which has
distributed it throughout the world, and the custodians of Chinese
museums play a regular gramophone record about the losses
caused by 'U.S. Imperialists and Kuomintang reactionaries'.
Some deplored it at the time; but they were powerless to stop it,
and even they recognised that it was the only means whereby the
artistic heritage of China could be preserved. As Bland wrote to
a friend in April 1914, it was pointless to try to shame the Chinese
or otherwise to prevent the loss of their monuments and treasures.
'In fact, as things are in China, and as they are likely to be for
many years to come, every work of art recovered and brought
away in safety is preserved for the future edification of the whole

world, whereas left in China it must always be in danger. For instance, Aurel Stein's bare-faced looting of the Cave of the Thousand Buddhas has been no loss to China and a great gain to scholars and antiquarians in this country. . . . Nine-tenths of ancient China's treasures are at this moment in Europe and America. If they had not been thus preserved, it is quite certain that most of them would have been destroyed in the upheavals of recent years.'

Backhouse's collection arrived in England in July 1913. When the twenty-nine crates were opened in Oxford, the privileged orientalists who examined their contents uttered appropriate cries of astonishment and delight. It was, they exclaimed, 'a truly magnificent collection'. In extent and value it surpassed anything that they had ever dreamed of. The collection of autograph scrolls was unparalleled outside China. In short, Oxford had, 'at one bound', overtaken all other collections in Europe, and Backhouse similarly, at one bound, had established himself as the greatest benefactor among orientalists.

Meanwhile, the donor himself had arrived in London. This time, he made it clear, he was coming to stay. He had, in effect, taken Bland's advice, to give up those sordid commercial activities in China and realise his undoubted gifts as a scholar at home. He had several projects in hand. One was the revision of Sir Walter Caine Hillier's *Pocket Dictionary of Colloquial Chinese*. Hillier was a distinguished scholar-diplomatist who, after serving as Chinese Secretary in Peking and consul-general in Korea, had returned to England in 1904 as Professor of Chinese at King's College, London. After four years in London, he had returned to China as adviser to the Chinese government after the death of the Empress Dowager, and had published his dictionary at Shanghai in 1910. The work was very successful and reprints were called for. Hillier passed the work of revision on to his own successor as Chinese Secretary in Peking, Sir Sidney Barton, and to Backhouse. By 1914 Barton and Backhouse were so far advanced that Backhouse listed the dictionary among his publications in *Who's Who*; but it did not actually appear till 1918. Backhouse was also, at this time, planning a larger Chinese dictionary which he hoped to see published by the Clarendon Press; he was making further

suggestions of collaboration on 'several new books' to Bland –
who however was not enthusiastic – and he announced his intention of settling in Oxford in order to catalogue and use his
own collection, and to write, presumably, his history of the
Chinese Revolution and the fall of the Manchu dynasty.

This new life of quiet scholarship in England presupposed an
income, and Backhouse decided, since his father would not make
him independent, to seek an academic post. While in London, he
applied, with Hillier's support, for Hillier's old chair of Chinese
at King's College, which happened to be vacant. But what he
really wanted, as he confided to Madan, was to succeed T. L.
Bullock as Professor of Chinese at Oxford. The emoluments of
the Oxford chair were, admittedly, very small – £150 a year, as
against £300 a year at London – but that, he explained, was not
the most material point. He was also aware of a difficulty: having
never completed his undergraduate course at Oxford, he had no
university degree. But that defect could, he hoped, be circum-
vented or overlooked. With these projects in mind he announced
that he would visit Oxford, and discuss matters with Madan. The
day, the time, the trains were duly fixed; but then, at the last
minute, the visit was postponed by telegram and afterwards can-
celled. Then Backhouse suddenly disappeared. He was off again
to Peking. He had heard 'bad news from China', he said: 'my
property there is in danger, and I wish to be in touch with the
political situation, which is particularly interesting.' This was the
time when Yüan Shih-k'ai was making himself virtual dictator of
China and Bland would write to Backhouse that no doubt Yüan
would be buying 'battleships by the gross'.

Backhouse sold no battleships, but at the end of the year his
plans in England bore fruit. First, the University of Oxford
hailed its benefactor. On 2 December 1913, *The Times* published
a lyrical article about his gift to Oxford. The article was by
Lionel Giles, the keeper of oriental books and manuscripts at the
British Museum and son of the famous sinologue H. A. Giles.
Giles rehearsed the treasures which had suddenly almost quad-
rupled the Chinese collection at Oxford and made the university
the owner of the best Chinese collection in Europe. There were
three priceless early printed works which Backhouse, perhaps

over-enthusiastically, ascribed to the Sung dynasty. These were the *Spring and Autumn Annals* of Confucius with Tso's commentary, beautifully printed and preserved; the *Family Sayings of Confucius*; and the *Ku Chin Chi Yao*, 'a very rare and interesting set of biographical records by Huang Chên, with marginal notes from the hand of the Manchu noble Jung-lu, who will be remembered as the favourite Minister of the Empress Dowager at the time of the Boxer Rising'. Giles himself ascribed these last two works to the Ming and Yüan dynasties respectively, but that did not reduce their great interest. Scarcely less precious than these very early books were a number of superb Ming editions of the greatest rarity; there was also, apart from the volumes of the great Yung-lo encylopaedia, a modern shortened version – that is, in only 1620 volumes – of the colossal *Ku Chin T'u Shu Chi Ch'eng* of the Yung Cheng Emperor ('quite one of the wonders of the world and a small library in itself'); and Giles drew attention to the splendid calligraphic inscriptions by great Chinese scholars, 'the strongly executed autographs of "the Old Buddha", Tzŭ-hsi and of the world-renowned statesman Li Hung-chang', and 'a truly magnificent piece of calligraphy by the great Manchu emperor K'ang-hsi who was contemporary with Louis XIV'. This incredibly rich collection, wrote Giles, was 'so extensive that years will be required for its thorough exploration', and he ended by rejoicing that 'Mr Backhouse himself proposes shortly to return to England and devote himself to this congenial task.'

Next day Oxford University published a formal decree of thanks to Backhouse for his munificence. The text of the decree, and the various newspaper cuttings, were sent to him in Peking. He replied announcing the purchase of still further treasures for the Bodleian, and added, 'is there any chance of an honorary degree? It has always been a great grief to me that I do not possess a degree, and possibly the fact of my being offered this chair, *plus* the gift of the books, might be deemed a sound reason.' He planned to return to England in February, he said, and would then begin work on his catalogue. The Clarendon Press was ready – if a subsidy of £5000 could be found – to publish his Chinese dictionary. . . .

Meanwhile, on the very same day, came the announcement of his election to the chair of Chinese at King's College. Everything had worked according to plan. Bland saw his programme realised: Backhouse could now escape from the intrigues of the British colony in Peking, the tyrannical patronage of Morrison, the absurd and undignified attempts to engage in commerce with corrupt Chinese officials, and devote himself to 'the scholar's work for which you were created'. Bland duly wrote to express his pleasure. 'I don't suppose you will have more than three or four pupils', he wrote, 'so that the work will be light and you will be able to devote some time to digging for materials amongst the ancient archives at Oxford and elsewhere.' On accepting the chair at London, Backhouse resigned his part-time post at Peking University.

Next month, Heinemann published *Annals and Memoirs of the Court of Peking*. The reviewers, on the whole, were delighted by it. Some of them did indeed comment, as Backhouse had feared, on the licentiousness of certain texts; but in general the book was regarded as a worthy successor to *China under the Empress Dowager*, and confirmed Backhouse's reputation as a great British sinologist. Everything seemed now to conspire in his favour. He was praised as a patron, a scholar, an author; his name was known to men of letters and men of learning; he had arrived.

Moreover, his next move seemed to be assured. At the very time when Backhouse was appointed to the chair in London, the reversion of the chair in Oxford, the real object of his ambition, was being assigned to him. Lionel Giles, after his visit to Oxford, reported to Reginald Johnston, who was now in England, that Bullock was expected to resign soon and that Backhouse 'is practically certain' to succeed him; and three weeks later, after a visit to Oxford, Johnston reported to his chief in Weihaiwei, Sir James Lockhart, that although Backhouse had accepted the London chair, 'it seems to be an understood thing that he will succeed Bullock as soon as that worthy can be persuaded to resign'. Johnston's advice to his Oxford friends, was that 'they should turn out Bullock as soon as possible and install Backhouse in his place'. For nobody seems to have held a very high opinion of Bullock as a scholar. He was an old consular man who published nothing and described his hobby in *Who's Who* as 'translating the *Peking Gazette*'.

Unfortunately, Bullock had no intention of resigning, and as there was then no compulsory retirement, he could please himself. However, the reversion at least could be assured. As E. H. Parker, the Professor of Chinese at Manchester, wrote, Backhouse was now established as the heir apparent at Oxford, 'but pending Bullock's retirement he is contenting himself with King's'. Meanwhile he had 'got on the soft side of Oxford by presenting them with four tons of Chinese books'. Parker had himself been invited to catalogue the books, but had declined. He had not then known that Backhouse was the donor. He had, like everyone else, the highest respect for Backhouse as a Chinese scholar. No one else, he thought, could compete with him for the Oxford chair.

In this harmonious chorus of recognition, there was only one jarring note. It came from George S. Payne, a well-known Oxford jeweller. On 23 February 1914, Mr Payne wrote to Madan, who was his neighbour and friend in North Oxford, reminding him of certain facts. A few years ago, said Payne, he had promised to give £100 to the funds of the parish church which they both attended 'upon my receiving payment for goods had by Mr Edmund T. Backhouse from me to the amount of £1600'. This debt had been incurred 'nearly twenty years ago' – i.e. at the end of Backhouse's period as an undergraduate at Merton College. But Backhouse, having 'obtained his discharge from the bankruptcy court', had paid no more than two shillings in the pound. Now Mr Payne, hearing of his generous gift to the Bodleian, and considering that he might rather have paid his just debts, 'must reluctantly cancel my promise'.

We have already seen Backhouse, as an undergraduate, collecting jewels and displaying 'priceless emeralds' to William Rothenstein. We have heard of him distributing jewels to Ellen Terry 'and other actresses'. We shall hear a good deal more about this taste for jewellery. Already, with Morrison's aid, stories about it were beginning to circulate in Peking. These stories had not yet reached Oxford, but they would. Meanwhile they found an echo in the solitary voice of Mr Payne.

Apart from that one faint whisper, nothing but praise attended the name of Backhouse in the early months of 1914. His future now seemed assured, and he himself viewed it with some complacency. In April, shortly before leaving Peking for England, he received a visit from Reginald Johnston, who was brought by Harold Harding, the Chinese Second Secretary at the British Legation. Although they were contemporaries and fellow scholars, and had both lived in China for twenty years, Johnston had not previously met Backhouse, and he was apprehensive whether the famous recluse 'will deign to see me or not'. But in fact Backhouse was very gracious and 'unbent to such an extent as to ask me to dinner a few days later'. He spoke of the great dictionary on which he was working and for which he was already soliciting subscriptions. He said that even if he were to hold a professorial chair in England, he intended to spend every summer in Peking. For that purpose he was building himself 'a small bungalow, near Morrison's bungalow'. Clearly, he was still under the spell of that formidable personality.

In fact Backhouse never took up his London chair. As so often, at the moment of decision, he quailed. Just as the imminent publication of each of his two books had filled him with alarm and he had sought to disclaim responsibility for them; just as he had regretted – too late – his gift to Oxford; just as he could never keep to a fixed timetable, but had no sooner announced a journey than he would change it – 'you know what an erratic creature he is', Bland had once written to ffrench: 'I rely not on his going or staying' – so he had no sooner accepted the post at King's College than he began to discover impediments. Already in February – three months before he was due to enter upon his duties – he discovered that something was seriously wrong with his eyes. It was glaucoma, he thought; he must come to London for special treatment; his oculist told him that he must stay in Europe for at least twelve months; he must give up reading. . . . So he wrote to King's College and asked leave to postpone his arrival for a term 'in consequence of trouble with his eyes'. He was 'bowled over' by this eye-trouble, he told Bland; and to Madan he wrote that an academic post was now impossible: 'a year or more of complete rest will be necessary if the sight of even one eye is to be properly preserved.'

Backhouse arrived in London on 16 June, and reported his arrival to Bland on a postcard, 'in which' as Bland wrote to ffrench 'he informed me, in microscopic writing, that his eyes were so bad that he could not see to read or write. He also says that he is going back to China in August' – so much for the twelve-month cure in Europe – 'no doubt to complete the sale of that battleship. I have come to the end of my patience with this gelatinous individual and have no desire for anything but business communications from that quarter Did I tell you that a letter of mine addressed to him in Peking with short postage was returned to me by the Post Office marked "refused by addressee"?' The returned letter, incidentally, had contained a cheque, being half of the royalties from *China under the Empress Dowager* After refusing the letter, as under-stamped, Backhouse had caused his lawyer to write to Bland complaining that he had not received his royalties – to which, of course, he had no legal right We are not surprised that Bland, by this time, had had enough of 'this gelatinous individual'; but if he thought their relations would quietly come to an end, he was sadly mistaken.

If Bland was not eager to see Backhouse, Backhouse, on this visit, evidently was not eager to see Bland. On 8 July he wrote to Bland from London explaining that he had no desire for society. 'As you know', he wrote, 'I am a recluse, and seldom or never visit anyone unless asked to do so. . . . This has been my principle through life. I value the friendship of a few people like yourself, but as a general rule am indifferent to everything and everybody outside my own work and hobbies.' Then he proceeded, as so often, to lament his poverty: poverty which gave an added appearance of eccentricity to his recent munificence to Oxford University.

In August 1914 war broke out in Europe, and Bland made a last, feeble effort to keep Backhouse to his scholarly purpose. 'Will this war increase or reduce your opportunities and prospects of selling a battleship to the Chinese government?' he asked; and himself answered, 'I should think they could now buy German ones second-hand cheaper than anything you can do for them.' Therefore, he should come back to his dignified chair at King's College. But it was unavailing. Backhouse had made up his mind to run out. He wrote to King's College definitely resigning the chair which he had never occupied. He must return to China, he said, 'to rest his eyes'. He did indeed return to China; but on his way, as we shall see, his eyes were sharp enough to spot a new opportunity.

However, if Backhouse had abandoned the prospect of academic life in London, he still longed for academic recognition at Oxford; and having, through his gift to the Bodleian Library, discovered a new friend in the Librarian, he explained his position to him. 'Having no degree', he wrote, 'I am placed at a disadvantage of status as regards sinologues and Oriental scholars in foreign countries;' and again he asked if the University could not make him an honorary M.A. As if to support this modest request, he sent to Oxford a second instalment of Chinese books and manuscripts: seventy-six cases containing 463 *chüan*, or printed volumes, fifteen manuscript rolls, a very fine Chinese pall with printed inscriptions, and one manuscript bound in jade. The total value of this second gift, he claimed, exceeded that of the first: it was worth £9600.

It was a reasonable claim. When the second gift arrived in Oxford, it was seen by Lionel Giles, who, once again, reported ecstatically on 'this wonderful Chinese collection, the like of which will assuredly never come to this country again'. Giles enumerated with astonishment the various items. It is true, there were no Sung editions: Backhouse had been mistaken there; but there were treasures enough, and Giles dwelt particularly on 'that amazing autograph scroll by the great calligraphist Wang Hsi-chih', which 'fairly took my breath away'.

Once again, the gift arrived very opportunely, for in March 1915 Professor Bullock died and Backhouse applied formally to succeed him in the chair of Chinese. In announcing his decision to apply, he informed Madan that he had just sold some Chinese classical paintings in America for £5040; and he asked whether the Bodleian would like some such paintings as a further gift. In another letter he wrote that he would dearly like the chair, 'but I fear an ex-consular man is sure to get it'. His eyes, he added, were now better, and he was anyway planning to leave China, for 'I want to complete my dictionaries before starting the cataloguing of my ex-collection in the Bodleian'.

On all sides it was assumed that Backhouse would be appointed to the Oxford chair. He was unquestionably a scholar – a far more sensitive scholar than the retired consular officials and missionaries who would be his competitors. He had already held a chair in Peking and had been elected to one in London. He was an Oxford man who, by his generosity, had deserved well of Oxford. If the chair had been filled in 1915, he would surely have been elected. But in fact it was not filled. The European war was then raging and the university decided to defer the election till it was over. However, Backhouse had staked out his claim, and his claim had been noted and respected. Eighteen months after Bullock's death, Percival Yetts reported that 'Backhouse is to have the Oxford Chinese chair as soon as the authorities decide to revive it.'

Meanwhile, his second gift to the Bodleian had reinforced his claim. This second gift was duly recorded in the *Bodleian Quarterly*, and Backhouse asked that a copy of that record be sent to his father, at the Rookery, and to his brother-in-law, Sir John Findlay, in Scotland. 'My old father,' he wrote, 'a helpless invalid, would be gratified at the reference to the little gift.' Both Sir Jonathan and Sir John formally acknowledged the document, but whether they were gratified or not we do not know. It may be that they shared the views of Mr Payne the jeweller, and Sir Jonathan may even have detected an ulterior motive behind the gesture. For clearly the old man had not long to live, and his eldest son, no less clearly, hoped that the old threat of disinheritance might not, after all, be enforced. The death of his father would make him a baronet, and surely he would be left enough money to sustain that hereditary dignity.

A gift valued at £4500, a second gift valued at £9600, in the values of 1914 – these show remarkable generosity. How could Backhouse afford such generosity? When we look at his letters to Oxford, he appears as a munificent benefactor showering largess. But when we look at his letters to Bland, how different is the picture! Not only does Backhouse lament his declining health, his incurably weak eyes; he is also, it seems, in direst poverty. Bland was irritated by this querulity, 'I trust that your eyes are better', he wrote in December 1914, 'and that your affairs are prospering. I don't think you really have any cause to let your mind dwell continually on the thought of financial ruin, unemployment, etc. That way lies a morbid state of body and mind. You can always be sure of a competence.' But Backhouse was not to be redeemed from his lamentations. All through the year 1915 his letters are a continuing wail. He has sold his house. He is auctioning his worldly goods. He excuses himself for writing on scrap paper – he is too poor to buy proper writing-paper. A brief visit to London that winter brings no relief. He has had a dreadful time with the doctors. His bladder is giving trouble. He has resigned from his club. His money has all gone. His investments have evaporated. His eyesight is failing, 'and it is doubtful where a nearly blind man can earn his bread', etc., etc. Bland sought again to rally him. 'Seriously, my dear Backhouse,' he wrote, 'you must guard against the growing tendency to parsimony, and your ever-insistent fear of an impecunious old age. That sort of thing, if encouraged, leads to a state of mind which is unprofitable as well for the body as for the soul. It is quite unnecessary in your case, and quite unworthy of you. . . . Go home and do a good burst and defy the foul fiend.' But it was no good: the litany continued. Then, suddenly, silence fell. Once again, Backhouse had mysteriously disappeared.

The mystery began on 7 September 1917, when Reuter informed the press that Backhouse had been appointed Director of Chinese Coolies in France. To those who knew him, the appointment was incredible. Of course it was also untrue. In Peking, Morrison recorded that it was not known how Reuter had been misled into sending such a message, but he assumed that it was by Backhouse himself or an accomplice – that is, presumably, that Backhouse had contrived the publication of the report in order to account for his own disappearance from Peking which happened very soon afterwards. In England, Bland, next year, heard that 'Backhouse has disappeared for the last six months . . . gazetted to be Protector of Chinese Coolies, or something equally lunatic, in France.' No one had heard of him since. 'I think,' added Bland, 'he *must* be dead, because in a letter I wrote him before Christmas, I said that I owed him £52; and if he were alive he would answer that!'

In fact, Backhouse was not dead: he had slipped away from

Peking and, after a brief stay in Japan, had crossed the Pacific and was lying low at the Empress Hotel, Victoria, British Columbia. He was allegedly very ill; but his illnesses were not always to be taken seriously. Meanwhile lawyers in several countries were having a field day.

In the summer of 1918, a faint whiff of the unfortunate affair drifted into Oxford in the form of an agitated, not to say anguished, letter to Falconer Madan from one James Cotton Minchin of Messrs Minchin Garrett & Worley, the London lawyers of the Backhouse family. According to Minchin, his client and old friend Sir Jonathan Backhouse was now dying in Yorkshire and his son Edmund was lying gravely ill in Victoria, British Columbia, and he, Mr Minchin, was left to defend their interests and good name against a most alarming and disagreeable threat. In short, his message to Madan was that Backhouse needed, urgently, a certificate of his competence as an expert in Chinese antiquities. 'To put it *confidentially* and plainly, our friend admitted a "wrong-un" into partnership with him, and we are having terrible trouble with this fellow.' Later Minchin came to see Madan, who wrote a discreet memorandum of the visit. 'What may be written down', he wrote, was that Backhouse was seriously ill in Canada, and that there was 'trouble about a partner of Sir Edmund named Hall'. However, in the end, a settlement was reached; the terrible fellow Hall was somehow persuaded or obliged to withdraw his charges, and 'the lawsuit will not now take place'. What else Madan may have been told, we do not know. At all events, he only heard the version supplied to him by Backhouse's lawyers, and that version, to judge from the sequel, did not cause him to doubt the bona fides of Backhouse, who appeared in it as the injured party. Madan remained the chosen and trusting confidant of Backhouse; and when Madan retired in 1919, and was succeeded as Librarian by Arthur Cowley, himself an orientalist, the relations of trust continued. Madan and then Cowley were the successors, for Backhouse, of Morrison, and then Bland.

We shall come back to the strange affair of 1917–18, the pretended protectorate of Chinese coolies, the sudden flight of Backhouse from China to British Columbia, and the terrible fellow Hall; for that affair needs a chapter to itself. Meanwhile, even at the expense of chronology, we will keep to the thread of our narrative and follow the continuous, if wavering, relations between Backhouse and the University of Oxford, his benefactions and his pursuit of the professorial chair.

Sir Jonathan Backhouse died in Yorkshire on 27 July 1918. He had not been made a peer, as Morrison had confidently prophesied he would be, and his eldest son had to be content to inherit the baronetcy – and a baronetcy, moreover, without endowment. For when his father's will was opened, Backhouse was dismayed to discover no tangible sign of forgiveness. Sir Jonathan had left to his heir a life interest in his house, the Rookery, but nothing else. The trustees of his estate were given wide powers which would effectively protect it against any claim on the new baronet.

Backhouse returned to China in great distress. Economic disappointment engendered psychological disorder, imaginary illness, self-pity – the customary syndrome. 'I am a very sick man', he wrote, ' . . . I fear that my days are not likely to be long.' But he still hoped for the chair of Chinese at Oxford, for which Madan promised his support, and he was still smoothing his way into it by scholarly publication and lavish gifts. In this same year, 1918, the new edition of Sir Walter Hillier's dictionary of colloquial Chinese, revised and enlarged by Backhouse and Barton, was at last published, and in the autumn Backhouse resumed his activities as a benefactor. He announced that he had acquired a full set of the Yung Cheng Encyclopaedia, in 10,000 volumes – a magnificent Palace copy, probably the only complete copy still in existence, printed in Peking in 1726, on fine paper. Only six copies, he wrote, had been printed in this style. A few months later, he reported that he had bought another 5000 volumes, 'mostly splendid editions, many Ming, one or more Yüan, including several rare historical works', all of which he would present to the Bodleian, provided that the Library would pay for packing and freight. All these treasures were duly despatched from Tientsin to Oxford. When Backhouse looked, in imagination, at his collection, he could not but be satisfied with it. It was now, he believed, 'the finest collection existing outside of China and Japan. Indeed, few of the great collections in this unhappy country remain, and here in the capital there is nothing to equal what Oxford now possesses;' and he added that 'as long as I live, I shall lose no opportunities of adding to the collection. Such opportunities come to me frequently, living as I do in touch with scholars.'

Backhouse's respected position among the scholars was recognised, at precisely this time, by one of his rare excursions into publicity. In 1919 Samuel Couling, who for twenty-five years had been a missionary in Shantung and who, in 1917, had published an ambitious *Encyclopaedia Sinica*, began a scholarly sinological periodical, *The New China Review*. The early numbers were illustrated by portraits of men who had distinguished themselves in China, beginning with the two great sinologues H. A. Giles and Edouard Chavannes. In October 1919 the frontispiece was a portrait of Backhouse, who also published some small contributions in the periodical. Appearing, as it did, when the vacant chair at Oxford was about to be filled, the portrait was no doubt timely propaganda. In it, Backhouse appears as a conventional Englishman, clean-shaven, in European clothes, wearing a stiff collar: an eminently respectable candidate for a professorial chair in England.*

Unfortunately this impression of sedate respectability was soon shaken; and the shock was felt in Oxford just as the University was deliberating on the appointment to the chair of Chinese. We therefore return to the events as seen in that university.

* Couling's *New China Review* was short-lived, dying with him in 1922. Backhouse contributed two short items to it: a translation of a brief Chinese poem and a note on the Yung-lo Ta-tien encyclopædia which he had presented to the Bodleian. The portrait of Backhouse is reproduced opposite page 152.

CHAPTER SIX

The Benefactor – Two

AT the close of 1919, while the Librarian of the Bodleian was awaiting the arrival of the 10,000 volumes of the great palace encyclopaedia, Backhouse was straining his eyes – now miraculously improved – towards the distant prospect of the Oxford chair. He confided to his old ally Sayce – the original intermediary of his benefactions – that he was '*very* desirous of becoming Professor of Chinese at Oxford, were it only for a short time, and would be grievously disappointed were he passed over'. Sayce passed on the message. Even if Backhouse were right about his malady, he wrote '(which I doubt), it would not prevent him from lecturing any more than it prevented him from travelling and sightseeing. It did not prevent Max Müller even from enjoying himself at dinner-parties. But I do not think the London specialists will confirm the view of the Peking doctors.' Backhouse's eagerness was duly noted, and the prospects seemed good. Cowley promised his support, as Madan had already promised his. Then a new chain of events began to unwind the carefully lubricated machinery of election.

It began when the famous palace encyclopaedia failed to arrive. The Librarian made enquiries and was told that it had never left Tientsin. Backhouse was informed and at once let out a cry of alarm. He scented a conspiracy. 'I cannot understand the action of the authorities concerned', he wrote, 'they have absolutely no right to hold the same as a lien on me, for they have no sort of claim on me.' Who could be behind this treacherous move? Of course it could only be Sidney Barton, who was now in England. 'I have had to prepare litigation against this gentleman in connexion with a Chinese dictionary brought out under our joint names' – i.e. the revision of Hillier's dictionary – 'but in which he has not done his share under contract. I fancy that *he* has held up the books as a means of punishing me for daring to threaten proceedings;' and he recommended Cowley to take forceful action.

Of course Barton was not responsible at all; it soon became clear that if the encyclopaedia had not been sent, that was merely the result of lack of space. Backhouse quickly sent a candid apology and withdrawal. His accusation had been hasty, he said – the result of worry. The controversy with Barton was now settled: 'we were both at fault, he and I'. However, the original accusation illustrates something of a persecution complex, and must have strengthened the hand of those who doubted the stability of the would-be professor. And might it not be said that this candidate, with his ostentatiously well-timed gifts, was a little too pressing, a little too tactless in his benefactions, as also in his protestations: that he protested a little too much? Backhouse ended his second letter to Cowley with a repetition of his continuing ambition: 'I can assure you that my heart's desire would be to be elected to the Chinese professorship, and it was in this hope that I refused the London chair.' By now he had evidently quite forgotten all that terrible trouble with his eyes.

Three months later, while the electors to the Chinese chair were deliberating, Backhouse once again came forward, offering gifts. He sent a telegram to Cowley, saying that he now had a splendid opportunity of still further enriching the Bodleian. If the Library would advance him £1000 he would obtain six manuscripts and twelve manuscript rolls, of the greatest value and all unique. The Curators agreed to the proposal and Cowley replied accordingly. But then the Regius Professor of Civil Law intervened. Such an advance of money, he said, was contrary to the statutes of the Bodleian. A telegram was sent to Backhouse advising him to hold his hand, but it arrived too late: the Curators were told that the manuscripts had already been bought on the strength of the preceding telegram. Soon they would be on their way to Oxford, with the palace encyclopaedia.

The Curators of the Bodleian were now in some difficulty. To regularise their action, the Librarian and some of the Curators of the Bodleian personally guaranteed the thousand pounds, and a cheque was duly paid, as instructed, into Backhouse's account in Barclay's Bank. Barclay's Bank thereupon declared that they held no such account. The episode was odd, but the matter was set right, and Backhouse assured Cowley that these 'priceless 18 manuscripts', would be 'a κτῆμα ἐς ἀεί [a treasure for ever] to the Bodleian and a sad loss to China, which has ceased to value its ancient relics'. The twelve rolls, he added, had been dutifully offered to the President of the Chinese Republic for $20,000; but they had been refused. Then he added a new request: he wished his name, as the donor of these eighteen new manuscripts, and also of the recent books – presumably the encyclopaedia – to be kept secret. This was a surprising change of tactics: previously he had positively asked that his name be associated with his gifts; but we remember his volte-face about the authorship of *China under the Empress Dowager*: there too he had had cold feet and sought anonymity – for a time.

A few days later, Backhouse wrote again about 'five very precious Chinese manuscripts' for which he had paid altogether £5970 and for which John Pierpont Morgan had offered $5000 apiece. These precious manuscripts he was now obliged to sell at Sotheby's, being collateral security to his bankers. They would go very cheap – probably for only fifteen pounds apiece, 'there being no demand in Europe for Chinese manuscripts'. Could not the Bodleian buy them or get some benevolent patron – say, Lord Curzon – to buy them for it? Backhouse said that his lawyers, Messrs Minchin, Garrett and Worley, would show the manuscripts on demand, but he begged Cowley not to tell even them about his recent gifts, 'because I wish the donor's name not to be published, nor known to any save yourself and the Curators'.

A fortnight later, on 28 June 1920, Backhouse sent another telegram, announcing still further gifts. He informed Cowley that he had just acquired 'the famous Palace Library' of 30,000 volumes and would now send it also to the Bodleian if the freight were paid in advance, before 20 July, when he was due to sail for England. There were 150 cases, he said, and the freight would come to £600. The Librarian was somewhat taken aback by the sudden request during the Long Vacation, but the prize seemed great and the matter was arranged. The Palace Library soon increased in size from 30,000 to 40,000 volumes, and the cost of freight from £600 to £794; but a cheque for the extra £194 was obediently sent. Backhouse's debt to the Bodleian for moneys advanced now stood at £2495.

Meanwhile, the election of a new Professor of Chinese at Oxford had at last taken place. The electors did not, after all, elect Backhouse. For six years, his succession had been regarded as certain, and he had made it more certain by his lavish gifts. But now he was suddenly denied the long-expected prize. What influenced the electors, we do not know. Instead of him, they chose W. E. Soothill, a competent scholar who had formerly been a missionary.

Backhouse took his disappointment well. In spite of this failure, he wrote, he still hoped to come and reside in Oxford; and indeed next spring he came to Britain. He had arranged to stay in Scotland with his sister Harriet and her husband, Sir John Findlay, and on the day of his arrival in London, the Findlays' daughter Laetitia went to Victoria Station to meet him. She could not find him on the platform, and was about to go away when she heard herself greeted from behind and, turning, saw a stranger with a long black beard, dressed in the robes of a Chinese mandarin. It was her uncle, who had now gone native. In this unconventional costume he continued his journey northwards to the Findlays' country home, Aberlour House, in Banffshire. There he settled down for a long stay. Meanwhile the university, still awaiting the arrival of the great Palace collection, passed a second decree of thanks for his continued generosity and resolved to set up the marble tablet commemorating him among the most munificent benefactors of the Library.

To a critical eye, Backhouse's actions in 1920–1 certainly seem somewhat odd. He was obtaining money from the university by telegram for the transport of books and manuscripts of which he had given only the vaguest description and whose number seemed to vary from day to day. He was insisting that his own part in the transaction be concealed even from his own lawyer. And why was he selling at Sotheby's for an estimated fifteen pounds apiece – which was indeed roughly what they fetched – manuscripts which had cost him over £1000 apiece and for which he had been allegedly been offered $5000 apiece? It was all very curious. But his previous gifts had been of unquestioned value and it was difficult for Bodley's Librarian, in the Long Vacation, to turn down, on his own authority, what seemed a magnificent gift from a known and tried benefactor. Unfortunately, after Backhouse's arrival in Britain, the mystery was not cleared: rather it became more mysterious still.

On 21 April 1921, Backhouse wrote to Cowley from Aberlour sending a cheque for £2495 to clear off his debt to the Bodleian. In his letter, he referred again to his recent acquisition of the famous Palace Library, which had now expanded still further in size, to 58,000 volumes. This library, he now explained, had been brought to Peking from the remotest part of West Kansu, over 1600 miles, through a wild region, which lacked proper transport facilities and was now in the throes of rebellion and civil war. Consequently the cost had been enormous. He had himself already spent £4000. The whole collection was now being un-packed in Peking. In view of their generous advance, Backhouse did not ask the Curators to pay these transport charges, but he had to admit that his own funds were now exhausted. He was proposing to come to Oxford in a fortnight and would then discuss the matter. . . . A fortnight later he had not in fact got further than to his brother-in-law's house in Edinburgh, and thence he wrote again asking Cowley not to pay in the cheque for £2495, as it could not yet be honoured. 'I am negotiating the sale of a pearl string', he explained, somewhat ominously, 'which is my property.' He had been offered £3925 for these pearls, but then there had been a sudden agitation about Japanese 'cultured' pearls, which had caused the market for genuine pearls to fall. He would have sent the pearls themselves, but the bank would not accept them as collateral. . . .

The Librarian had already reported to the Curators both Back-house's new gift and the receipt of his cheque. He was therefore somewhat embarrassed by this new development. However, he handled the matter as best he could, and the Curators, in recog-nition of Backhouse's difficulties, found means to reduce his debt to £1841. Backhouse expressed his appreciation and wrote letters of great civility, but he had to admit that his circumstances were now very embarrassed, that he was finding it impossible to sell the pearls, and that, in these conditions, he could only ask for delay. 'Perhaps I was over-ambitious in my purchase of books,' he wrote, 'but it was in a good cause. . . . A business-man would say that I had been rash in over-estimating my resources, but as I have explained, it is not the cost of the books but the cost of transportation that has caused the embarrassment.'

The Curators too were embarrassed. Their action in advancing money for the eighteen manuscripts had been declared to be contrary to statute, and they could be held individually liable for it. How could they face the university's accountants? Moreover, the famous Palace Library of 58,000 volumes, for whose transport they had paid £794, did not arrive. By December 1921 they were worried on both accounts. Backhouse had never appeared in Oxford and by now he had been silent for six months. Cowley wrote to him in Aberlour and again to Edinburgh – his last two addresses; but there was no reply. Once again, as in 1917, he seemed to have completely vanished.

Indeed, he had vanished. His sojourn with the Findlay family, after three months, had come to a sudden, not to say disastrous end. At first, all had gone well. Lady Findlay was devoted to her brother, and Sir John Findlay, though he suffered much from his brother-in-law's eccentricities, was genuinely interested in him. The Findlay children were delighted by their uncle's stories of life in China, Chinese history, and his own familiarity with the imperial court and the old Empress Dowager. However, little by little, Backhouse's eccentricities became too much even for that tolerant family. His indifference to .exact truth became embarrassing. So did his public behaviour. He surprised the natives of Banffshire and the conventional citizens of Edinburgh by walking abroad in his Chinese garb. Then came the affair of the pearl necklace. Backhouse involved his relations in elaborate attempts to sell this valuable necklace, which, he said, had belonged to the Empress Dowager. Ultimately the truth came out: the necklace did not exist. Sir John Findlay was very angry; there was a scene and one day in July Backhouse was found to have disappeared. His family would never see him again.

It was not till October 1922 that Cowley received an answer to the letters which he had addressed to Backhouse. The answer came from Peking. Like the letters to Bland in 1914 and 1915, it was very pathetic in tone. Backhouse began by explaining his apparent silence. He had already written to Cowley via Siberia, he said, but no doubt the Russian censors had held up his letters. Then he explained his own position. 'I am absolutely penniless and stranded here, living with an old friend who is himself in difficulties.' The Anglican Bishop in Peking, Dr Norris, had kindly relieved his wants by giving him the Encyclical Letter of the Lambeth Conference to put into Chinese for publication, and in these and such ways 'I am able to earn a few pounds, but the prospect ahead of me is most gloomy. Our winters here are bitterly cold and even the common necessities have to be forgone. My family (that has benefited at my expense from my father's most unjust will) will do nothing for me.' Too old to work, he was living precariously by 'penny-a-line translations'. As for the Palace Library, the cream of the collection had been sent – and indeed, about this time, the Library did receive six cases of books. The collection which he had already given to the Bodleian, Backhouse went on, had cost him £24,000 in cash. The letter ended with a postscript: 'Please note address. Please also be so kind as to send letters direct here, as I am not on good terms with my brother-in-law, Sir John Findlay, who might not forward letters.' Findlay, like Morrison and Barton, had now joined the ranks of his enemies.

The address which Backhouse asked Cowley to note was 'i/c Chang Ho-chai esquire, 19 Shih-fuma Street, Peking'. This indicated a slight change in his economy. The house was Backhouse's own house in the Tartar City, which he had occupied since 1912, and his hospitable 'friend', Chang Ho-chai, was his Chinese factotum. By this time, Backhouse had passed the ownership of his house to Chang and continued to live there as the tenant, or guest, of his own former servant who now, it seems, had complete control over him. We shall hear more of this servant, and little of it good. Chang, according to one observer, was 'a bad fellow with whom Backhouse was involved in a number of shady dealings in curios and jewellery'.

When the Curators saw this lamentable letter, they realised that the problem of Backhouse would not be quickly or easily solved. They were also in a somewhat delicate position. A year ago they had approved Sir Reginald Blomfield's design for the memorial tablet. They had then considered the names to be inscribed on it. They had decided to omit two names from the list, but that of Backhouse had not been disturbed. By now the tablet had been inscribed and would shortly be set up. It would be inconvenient if, at this precise moment, their relations with Backhouse were to involve them in scandal. When they next met, on 18 December 1922, they decided to proceed cautiously: to carry forward the debt, for the time being, as if it were 'good'; to write to the shipping agents to see if they could trace the missing 150 cases which were alleged to contain the famous Palace Library; to write to Backhouse himself in an attempt to clarify the position; and meanwhile to write privately to Sir John Findlay and enquire 'whether Sir Edmund Backhouse has suffered of late, or is suffering, from any mental trouble', since they found his recent statements 'not in every respect quite intelligble, or reconcilable with one another'. Then they dispersed for the Christmas vacation. Early next term they gathered to witness the ceremonial unveiling, by the Vice-Chancellor, of the memorial tablet. They then turned to the replies gradually elicited by their various letters.

Predictably, the reply of Backhouse, when it arrived, did not clarify the problem. He repeated, with new embellishments, the story of the expensive transport of the Palace Library: it had been carried, he said, by cart through 700 miles of brigand-infested country before it had even reached the rail-head at Kansu. No wonder the cost was enormous. He had already spent some £2500 on that account. Much of the Library had already been despatched by Croft's, the shipping company; the rest would be sent at Backhouse's own expense. As for Backhouse's debt to the Bodleian, that would be paid in full, and with interest, when he had received £30,000 which he was owed by a firm of shipbuilders whom he had formerly represented in China and with whom he was at present in litigation. We recognise this firm of shipbuilders: it was John Brown & Co. who, in 1910, had rashly

Edmund Backhouse aged about forty-five
(New China Review, *October 1919*)

G. E. Morrison
(The Times)

J. O. P. Bland (right), Lord ffrench, and Willard Straight in Peking, about 1909 (original photograph has sustained water damage at right)

Part of the Diary of Ching-shan (British Museum)

Edmund Backhouse near the end of his life
(The Bodleian Library, Oxford)

employed Backhouse as an agent to sell battleships to the insolvent government of China.

Meanwhile Sir John Findlay, discreetly approached by a Curator who had known him as an undergraduate at Balliol, had replied more prosaically. He was not at all surprised, he wrote, by the Curator's question. His brother-in-law had spent some months in Britain in 1921 but had left suddenly in July. Since then, Findlay had had one letter from him and 'in view of the terms of that letter, and his conduct when here', had written to Sidney Barton, of the British Legation in Peking, to enquire after his mental health. Owing to Barton's transfer to Shanghai, he had not yet received an answer. 'On two previous occasions', Findlay added, 'Sir Edmund's mental condition has given cause for concern, and to my mind he is never entirely accountable for his actions. At present he seems to be suffering from one strong obsession, which, in mental cases, is a bad symptom.' Sir John ended by saying that he hoped soon to come to Oxford to visit his son, then an undergraduate at Balliol. He could then, if necessary, discuss the matter further.

At the same time another confidential account of Backhouse was obtained from Peking. It came from Dr Norris, the Anglican Bishop of North China, who had known Backhouse ever since his arrival in China in 1898.* Backhouse was certainly very impecunious, said the Bishop – really poor: 'why, is a question I can't answer'. Things had not gone well for him, and he had been disappointed by his father's will. 'As a matter of fact, Findlay of *The Scotsman*, his brother-in-law, had to advance him *a large sum of money*, not yet repaid.' He was on good terms with his brothers but not with Findlay, though he had lived with him on his last visit to Britain. Was he sane? Yes, quite sane. Odd, of course, having been a recluse so long, but unquestionably sane 'and, if he likes, a very agreeable companion'. Had he any vices? Opium? Drugs? 'I think I am justified in denying it absolutely, without any reservation or hesitation.'

With these somewhat conflicting statements the Curators had

* The Revd. Francis Lushington Norris had been a missionary in Peking since 1889. He became Bishop of North China, succeeding Charles Penry Scott, in 1914 and remained there till 1940.

to be content for the time being. Then, in July 1923, a new character appeared on the stage, and the drama moved forward to a new act. This new arrival was a Mr M. E. Weatherall, an expert on Chinese art, who described himself as a former collaborator of Backhouse. We do not know the nature of their collaboration. Weatherall had come to England on a brief visit from China and he now asked if he might consult, in the Bodleian Library, certain manuscripts alleged to be in Sir Edmund's handwriting. Knowing Backhouse, and his 'peculiar notions' about arrangement, Weatherall was confident that, if given access to the collection, he could find the manuscripts without difficulty. He duly arrived at the Library on 14 September 1923, and, in the absence of the Librarian, was shown the collection by H. E. Craster, the Keeper of Western Manuscripts.

After Weatherall's departure, Craster wrote a memorandum on this visit. Weatherall, he noted, had been interested in two projected undertakings of Backhouse. One was the great Chinese dictionary about which Backhouse had so often spoken and written, and of which (as he had told Weatherall) the complete copy, ready for the press, had been deposited by him in the Bodleian Library. According to Backhouse, all that was now necessary was a subvention which he was trying to raise from the British colony in Peking. The sum mentioned had now grown from £3000 to £10,000. Weatherall clearly entertained some doubts about the reality of this project and suspected that the £10,000, if raised, would be devoted to other purposes; and he had now come to Oxford in order to discover the real state of this famous dictionary on which Backhouse had claimed, ten years ago, to have been working 'for many years' and to have made 'good headway'. He found that it consisted in fact of 'a few notebooks filled with sentences from Chinese classics but unusable except by Sir Edmund'. There was no 'copy' for the press. The other project was the translation of a Chinese diary. Backhouse had told Weatherall that both the complete Chinese original and his own translation of it were deposited in the Bodleian. In fact Weatherall found no Chinese text at all and only two typed pages of 'translation'. This non-existent diary was said by Backhouse to be the diary of the all-powerful Grand Eunuch of the Empress

Dowager, who had ruled her court for forty years, Li Lien-ying. It is a diary of which we shall soon hear more.

Weatherall was obviously not at all surprised at his negative discoveries: it was exactly what he had suspected. Having revealed his suspicions to Craster, he then told him some interesting background details about Backhouse: for instance, how Backhouse sought from time to time to sell a string of pearls which did not really exist. The Library, of course, had heard all about those valuable but imaginary pearls. Then Weatherall asked to see the six cases of books which had recently arrived – the only six which had arrived out of the 150 containing the famous Palace Library so expensively conveyed through bandit-ridden Kansu. Had the Bodleian any 'corroborative evidence' that these books came from a palace library? Of course it had not, and Weatherall himself was very sceptical. In conclusion, Craster noted, 'Mr Weatherall strongly advised us to have no financial dealings with Sir Edmund except upon the strictest business principles, to pay no money except for goods actually received, and to give no receipt for any cheque' until it had been honoured. Backhouse was not really poor, he said (thus unconsciously contradicting Bishop Norris): he had an allowance from his family; but it was vain to imagine that his creditors would ever be paid. 'Sir Edmund, he said, is much in the hands of his Chinese secretary (formerly his boot-black) Chang Ho-chai, who, he asserts, has to date appropriated £25,000 of Sir Edmund's money.' Before leaving, Weatherall gave Craster his address in London and promised to be at the disposal of the Library if he could be of any help while in England.

Five weeks later the Librarian called on Weatherall in London and learned more about Backhouse. Backhouse, he was told, had no 'vices' to account for his lack of funds. 'He is highly nervous and sensitive, with a vivid imagination, which leads him to make statements which are untrue and to commit acts which are fraudulent. The "pearls" have been a figment of his imagination since 1912 at least, when he tried to borrow money on them from Weatherall. The existence of the copy for a Chinese dictionary is equally visionary.' Weatherall was sceptical, among other things, about the alleged imperial edition of the encyclopaedia: was the

Librarian sure that it was genuine and not merely a later reprint of that edition? Nothing that Backhouse said about his finances could be believed. As for recent acquisitions, 'the sums paid for freight (and probably for purchase) are exorbitant, and it looks as though the money was used for other purposes.' On this ominous note Weatherall took his leave and prepared to return to Peking.

All this was very alarming to the Curators, and from now on there were frequent meetings of the special 'Backhouse committee' which they set up to find a way out of their problems. Letters were exchanged, balance sheets drawn up, lawyers and accountants consulted. Weatherall offered to help in China. A copy of the late Sir Jonathan Backhouse's will was obtained. Sir John Findlay was again approached. 'Definite steps' to recover at least some of the money were contemplated. And the committee decided to obtain expert advice on the value of the eighteen unique and priceless manuscripts and scrolls for which the Bodleian had advanced £1000.

Sir John Findlay's reply was discouraging. Backhouse, he wrote, had a small allowance sent by his family and administered for him by Bishop Norris, who looked after him. Apart from this, and a small sum from his father's trustees, he had nothing. No satisfaction was likely. But Sir John asked to be informed before any 'definite steps' were taken. Sir Jonathan's will, when procured, confirmed that there were no assets within the reach of creditors. Then came the report of the expert on the eighteen manuscripts and scrolls.

The report, once again, was by Lionel Giles, the Keeper of oriental books and manuscripts at the British Museum, whose breath had been taken away by Backhouse's first gifts. These documents too, he now reported, would be priceless – if they were genuine. But alas, they were not genuine. In a long and detailed report he showed that all the evidence – the paper, the ink, the calligraphy, the content – proved them to be 'impudent forgeries', clearly manufactured solely 'to be palmed off on some credulous foreigner; for the fraud is too gross and palpable to deceive any educated Chinese'. As for their value, 'finding as I do', wrote Giles, 'that they are forgeries, and not particularly clever ones at that, I have not thought it necessary to estimate their market value; but I think you would be safe in assuming that £4 is nearer the mark than £4000'. This conclusion was endorsed by Soothill, the new Professor of Chinese. Further enquiries also confirmed Weatherall's suspicions about the encyclopaedia: it was not an authentic palace edition of 1726, but a lithographic reprint of 1895–8.

The special Backhouse committee of the Bodleian faced these melancholy facts. It reported that the manuscripts and scrolls were forgeries, by unknown forgers, but that, in view of the large benefactions already received from him, the Curators were not at fault in trusting Sir Edmund Backhouse, and they recommended that the Library bear the loss, but that Backhouse's family be informed of the facts – evidently in the hope that they might contribute towards it. Some of the Curators wished to contribute themselves 'to help the Library and avoid the appearance of blackmail'.

In all this there was no suggestion that Backhouse had been a party to the forgery. Any such suggestion was forestalled by Sir John Findlay, who wrote that although Backhouse had a remarkable knowledge of colloquial and even literary Chinese, he had no expert knowledge of manuscripts, and, 'as I know to my cost, has been repeatedly let down by purchasing them at prices which had no relation to their value'. However, an impartial critic must observe that this argument is not very strong. It is merely a statement that Findlay too had suffered loss through his brother-in-law's speculations in Chinese manuscripts. It proves nothing about the motives of that brother-in-law. Nor would any such explanation have been accepted by Backhouse himself. On 24 March 1924, in reply to the careful and courteous letter which he received from Cowley, explaining the predicament of the Library, Backhouse protested that he could not possibly change his view 'that the eighteen manuscripts are of high value and absolutely genuine', and he added that he spoke with confidence, for 'I have been diligently studying Chinese calligraphy for a quarter of a century, being regarded in China, even by Chinese themselves, as an an authority on the subject'.* If the Curators of the Bodleian

---

* In his entry in the *Peking Who's Who*, Backhouse described his recreations, at this time, as 'Chinese history and Chinese calligraphy'.

did not like his gift, he suggested that they send the manuscripts back and he would sell them and pay his debt out of the proceeds; or they could sell some of his earlier gifts about which the same 'expert' had been so rapturous: for of course he easily identified the authority who had detected the forgery as Lionel Giles.

The Librarian did not hurry to answer this letter. He was concerned with the immediate problem, to which the eccentricities of Backhouse seemed, with each letter, more irrelevant. Besides, Backhouse's letter was soon followed by a letter from Weatherall, now back in Peking; and this letter did not suggest that it would be useful, or even practical, to deal further with Backhouse.

According to Weatherall, Backhouse had now left Peking. He had declared that he was very ill and had persuaded a doctor to say that he must leave China. So he was off, via Canada, to Europe. How he had raised the money for his passage Weatherall could not imagine. It could not be from his own resources, for 'I am confident that he has ruined himself. Whatever money he once may have had has long since been stolen from him by his Chinese servant, who possessed complete authority over him and used his power to enrich himself.' Nor could it be from his family, for although they now paid him an allowance – not much, it was true, $200 a month, 'wholly insufficient for a man of Sir Edmund's character and absolute lack of business sense' – the condition of this allowance was that he did not leave China. The whole affair was very mysterious. As Weatherall complained, 'Dealings with Sir Edmund are not made more easy by his incurable love of mystification, and I am come gravely to doubt whether he is able to separate the true from the untrue in his own mind. He may do so in reflexion; he cannot in speech.' The thought of Backhouse loose in England again thoroughly alarmed Weatherall. 'I fear for him out of China', he wrote; for in the lax, semi-colonial atmosphere of Peking, eccentricities were tolerated which, in England, would soon land him in Wormwood Scrubs. Backhouse's transactions always ended in someone losing money and being left with a grievance. There was absolutely no prospect that the university would recover the money advanced to him: his family would not help – they 'were tired of getting him out of scrapes'. Altogether, Weatherall could see only storms ahead. And yet, like everyone who met him, Weatherall found himself yielding to that unfailing courtesy and charm. 'Sir Edmund was very pleasant to me when we met, and in spite of everything in his disfavour, I like him very much.' Doubtless he had been 'the tool of able and unscrupulous Chinese' who had made him commit acts 'which it is perhaps too kind to describe as foolish' . . . 'Unbelievably, he somehow remains a scholar and a gentleman.'

In fact, when Weatherall wrote this letter, Backhouse had not left China. Perhaps he had merely pretended to leave, in order to throw Weatherall off his tracks. For on 30 May he wrote to the Curators of the Bodleian complaining that he was kept in Peking awaiting a reply to his letter of 24 March to Cowley. Four times (he said) he had postponed his departure in the hope of such a reply, and he was now indignant about it. He was indignant also at the suggestions that his manuscripts were forged, and because he had been given no opportunity to prove their authenticity. He now demanded that the Curators sell his whole collection, pay off his debt, and then split the proceeds with himself. It would be easy to sell it in Japan, he said, to replace the many fine collections destroyed in the recent Tokyo earthquake. He had no doubt that the Curators would gladly sell it, since clearly they took no interest in it. . . . A month later, still having received no reply, he wrote again, more angrily still. His manuscripts he said were 'undoubtedly genuine', and had been pronounced genuine by Chinese scholars. They had cost $20,300. Once again he demanded that the whole collection be sold. A month later he repeated his demand. If the Curators would not sell the whole collection, he would come to England to raise a loan on the security of his life interest and of a life insurance policy which he would take out. Or the Curators could return the disputed manuscripts, which he would then easily sell, 'as their genuineness is beyond doubt'.

The Curators, meanwhile, had almost decided, by themselves, to sell part at least of the collection. As Cowley explained to Weatherall, there was no point in sending the eighteen manuscripts back: 'we should no doubt lose our (forged) manuscripts without getting any return and involve ourselves in a lawsuit which, at that distance, would be costly and difficult.' The only alternative was to sell so much of the collection as would clear the bad debt. But how and where was that to be done? Some of the Curators tried to raise the money privately, and so release the Librarian 'from the bother of selling, the Library from the risk of a forced liquidation, and the university from the scandal of a disclaim which might make donors shy'. Two letters were sent to Sir John Findlay, who, however, did not respond: as one of the Curators put it, he 'sulks like a trout when the water is low'. Sir John had already paid out quite enough and, like the rest of the family, was tired of getting Backhouse out of his interminable scrapes.

In the end, Backhouse was calmed down by the patient and tactful Cowley. His last letter in the Bodleian file is dated 'Lammas 1924'. In it he thanked Cowley for his cordial explanation and apologised for his own querulity, which had been caused (he said) by the damaging stories put about by Weatherall and by 'my fraternal enemy John Findlay K.B.E.'. The former had reported, after his visit to the Bodleian, that 'Backhouse's collection is a white elephant. Only a fraction of the works he promised is here. He has swindled the Library.' The latter had written to Sir Sidney Barton, 'who has been at pains to publish the report *urbi et orbi*', that the Curators of the Bodleian were 'furious' with Backhouse, who had 'robbed and cheated' them. These reports, said Backhouse, 'spread as they are by my manifold enemies all over Cathay, do to me infinite harm'. He then dwelt pathetically on his poverty and the sacrifices he had made to enrich the Library. He could have lived in easy affluence had he not preferred to spend £26,000 on his gifts to the Bodleian. The eighteen manuscripts which he had presented were unquestionably genuine: he had examined them for ten days before deciding to purchase them. As for the infamous Lionel Giles, who had declared them to be forgeries, he would be revenged on him. He would issue writs for libel or slander. Giles, he said, was animated by *odium sinologicum*; he was an ignoramus, no better than his father, H. A. Giles, whose Chinese dictionary 'teems with mistranslations thick as leaves in Vallombrosa'.

Cowley wrote back in emollient terms, and the correspondence died. There was now no point in continuing it. The Bodleian, with the aid of its auditors, found means to clear the debt without selling the collection. But nearly two years later the University caught another, and perhaps a last, glimpse of its wayward benefactor. In March 1926 the Librarian reported 'that he had received a cablegram from Sir Edmund Backhouse, the meaning of which was not clear'. However, there was a possibility of clarification. At that very time, W. E. Soothill, who had captured the Chinese chair from Backhouse, happened to be travelling in the Far East and he proposed, when in Peking, to call on Backhouse. 'Privately I may say', he wrote to Cowley, 'that Backhouse is believed to be entirely under the thumb of a Chinese servant who evidently has some power over him. He sees no one, and when out in a rickshaw, if a European comes in sight, he covers his head and face with a handkerchief. He has disposed of his house in the country and of his carriage and lives in a corner of his old house, his servant controlling the rest of it.' Later, after seeing Backhouse, Soothill reported that he had had 'a most pleasant chat with him. He is a depressing picture, health poor, dishevelled, almost in rags, and with a brain that is abnormal. I suspect the rags are intentional, to indicate poverty!' To Soothill, Backhouse still protested that his manuscripts were authentic and 'that our great encyclopaedia is an original, which it very clearly is not': but even the late-nineteenth-century reprint, Soothill remarked, 'will be extraordinarily valuable in time.' Soothill visited Backhouse at least four times; after his second visit he added a postscript: 'poor fellow, I look on him with the greatest sympathy.'

So ended Sir Edmund Backhouse's relations with the University of Oxford. After 1926 his name, though recorded in such honourable company, was no longer mentioned in its formal documents. There seemed to be almost a conspiracy to forget him. In 1934, when Dr Yüan Tung-li, the Director of the National Library in Peking, visited Oxford, he declared himself particularly impressed by the Backhouse collection, and undertook to send his best pupil, Hsiang Ta, to catalogue the Chinese collection in the Bodleian. Hsiang Ta duly came and worked on the collection for nine months, after which he submitted a report on it. In his report he dwelt on the high value of many of its contents. The twelve volumes of 'the really rare Yung-lo Ta-tien', he observed, were the largest fragment in Europe. He confirmed Soothill's high valuation of the lithographic edition of the encyclopaedia *T'u Shu Chi Ch'eng*: it was, he wrote, 'as is well known, seldom found in China'. These and many other items similarly singled out for praise had come from Backhouse. But the translator and editor of the report, the Revd. E. R. Hughes, University Reader in Chinese, saw no reason to emphasise the origin of these genuine treasures: his only substantial comment was a reminder that the collection of calligraphic scrolls was, 'for the most part, of very dubious authenticity'. Two years later Hughes published an article in the *Oxford Magazine* on the new Chinese Honour School. In this, he referred to all the acquisitions of Chinese books and manuscripts since 1605. He dwelt on the fine collection of Alexander Wylie, which had come to the Library in 1881. But when he came to the year of Backhouse's great gift, he merely remarked that 'in 1913, £1000 was spent in making further purchases'. This, to say the least, seems somewhat ungenerous. In 1944, when Backhouse died, the Bodleian did not notice his death, then or thereafter: no obituary notice, no tributary tear, reminded the university of its erratic but undoubted benefactor.

This melancholy story leaves us asking an obvious question. Did Backhouse himself forge, or cause to be forged, the calligraphic scrolls and other manuscripts, or was he (as Weatherall put it) 'the tool of able and unscrupulous Chinese'? Did he innocently believe in 'the famous Palace collection' brought so expensively from Kansu, or did he invent it, either as a means of raising money for himself, or as a mere fantasy? The more charitable interpretation was expressed by Findlay and by Weatherall and accepted by the Curators – though Findlay may have been preserving the family front and Weatherall added the significant qualification that it was 'perhaps too kind' to describe Backhouse's actions as foolish. And why, we may ask, did Backhouse, in these particular transactions, insist on the concealment of his name, even from his own lawyers? Was he perhaps thinking of the affair of 1918 which had so worried the same lawyers? But perhaps it is best to leave this question unanswered until we have seen more evidence. For ultimately it is the recurrence of a general pattern rather than the details of a particular episode that may illuminate the character of the mystery man; and anyway, we have not yet got to the bottom of the affair of 1918. To do so, we must leave the quiet deliberations of the Bodleian Library and go back, with our hero, to China. There we shall find that he had been leading a far more animated life than could be guessed in the cloisters of Oxford.

CHAPTER SEVEN

The Secret Agent

WE are back in 1915, in the spring of 1915, and the campaigning season is about to reopen in Europe after the first winter of war. The German Blitzkrieg of 1914 has failed, stopped by 'the miracle of the Marne', and the European great powers are preparing to dig in for a long contest. But to the powers of the Entente, who were militarily and industrially unprepared for such a war, there is one great, over-riding problem. It is the shortage of munitions. Neither in the West nor in Russia, after the fierce campaigns of 1914, are there sufficient supplies of guns and ammunition for the battles ahead. In Britain, this problem will lead ultimately to Lloyd George's Ministry of Munitions, and, indirectly, to the fall of the Asquith government. Immediately, that government is scouring the world for ready-made arms. Purchase abroad must supply the gaps of manufacture.

One possible source of supply, rather surprisingly, is China. China has recently been a theatre of war. In Manchuria, Japan has defeated Russia, and during the Chinese revolution large stocks of captured Russian rifles have been sold locally. But now China is at peace under the régime of President Yüan Shih-k'ai, and its external relations have been stabilised. It is neutral in the great conflict in Europe, but its neutrality is benevolent to the Entente powers: the contiguous land-power of Russia and the ubiquitous sea-power of Britain see to that. Why then should not the arms which are lying unused in China be transferred, for immediate use, to Britain or Russia? At the beginning of March 1915, the British War Office asked the Foreign Office to enquire from the British minister in Peking whether these arms could not be bought, for use in Europe.

The British minister in Peking was Sir John Jordan, another of the many Ulstermen who, like Sir Robert Hart and Bland, had made a career in the Far East. He had come out in 1876, as a student-interpreter – the usual beginning of such a career – and had served there ever since. He knew Chinese well and had been Chinese Secretary at the legation before moving to Korea in 1896. He had spent ten years in Korea, the storm centre of Far Eastern politics, as consul-general, chargé d'affaires and then minister. In 1906, on the recommendation of Morrison, then at the height of his influence, he had been brought back to Peking to succeed Sir Ernest Satow as Head of Legation. He had been in Peking ever since. Blunt, even undiplomatic in manner, contemptuous of Oriental dissimulation, he had established himself, by his long experience, his mastery of detail, and his honesty, as the most highly respected member of the diplomatic corps in Peking. Since 1911 he had been doyen of the corps. His weakness, it was said, was his reluctance to impose his informed views on his government at home. There were occasions when he deferred too much to London, even against his own better knowledge.

This was one such occasion. Jordan clearly did not welcome the idea of purchasing arms in China. He told the Foreign Office that the alleged arms could not be traced and that anyway the export of munitions of war was strictly forbidden by the Chinese government.

Nevertheless, the Service Departments at home, having once entertained the idea, would not give it up. They urged the Foreign Office to enquire into the type of machine-gun used in China, and the possibilities of purchase, and refused to be silenced by Jordan's negative reply. The War Office, the Army Council, Lord Kitchener himself pressed for action, and on 17 March, at Kitchener's request a special telegram, 'Private and Secret', was sent to Jordan, pointing out that, the war between China and Japan being over, arms must be available in China. The Foreign Office admitted that the Chinese government could not be asked to commit a breach of its own laws and its professed neutrality, but it suggested that Jordan might 'be able to find a means of effecting a deal through an intermediary from whom the sale to us would not be open to the same objection'. Jordan was asked to consider the matter and report. Copies of this telegram were sent to the King, the Prime Minister, Lord Kitchener, Mr Churchill, Mr Balfour, Sir Edward Grey, and the Ambassador to France. The question of arms from China thus became a high matter of state.

On receipt of this telegram, Jordan saw that he must yield. He replied to the Foreign Office that he saw a slight prospect of success, provided that absolute secrecy was maintained. Then he took counsel with the Chinese Secretary at his legation, Sidney Barton. In due course they evolved a plan of action.

Jordan's plan, as set out two months later in a private and secret telegram to the Foreign Office, was to operate through an unavowed secret agent. This agent would be instructed to purchase the arms in a purely private capacity, without any apparent reference either to the legation in Peking or to the British government, which would however pay the cost, provide the means of communication, and determine the ultimate disposal of the weapons. Provided that the part played by the legation was kept absolutely dark, Jordan believed that his agent could privately purchase 30,000 Mauser and Mannlicher rifles of 1911 and 1912 at £3.10s.od. each, without ammunition. But all arrangements must be left entirely to the agent. This agent had already been chosen: he was to be Backhouse.

On the face of it, the choice was odd. It would have surprised Morrison or Bland. The suggestion probably came from Barton. Barton, as we have already seen, was a friend of Backhouse. They were near contemporaries and had come out to China within a few years of each other. Both were good Chinese scholars, and they were at this moment collaborating on the revision of Hillier's Chinese dictionary. Barton had the reputation of being a blunt, bold man; but he was evidently not an acute diplomatist. He had been brought up in the simple faith of the Plymouth Brethren, to which his father, a military man, was a fanatical convert. After thirty-five years in China, he would end his career as minister in Addis Ababa, and would have the misfortune to be there when Evelyn Waugh visited Abyssinia in 1930: he is thus inevitably identified with that great comic figure, 'the Envoy Extraordinary' in *Black Mischief*. His recommendation of Backhouse as a suitable agent in a delicate operation was to prove another misfortune. But why should he not recommend Backhouse? He could appreciate Backhouse's profound knowledge of China, the Chinese language, and Chinese personalities; and business experience and acumen could be presumed: for was not Backhouse the agent of that world-famous firm of shipbuilders, John Brown & Co.?

In order to secure Backhouse's services, Jordan asked the Foreign Office to 'send for Charles Ellis of John Brown & Company, 8, The Sanctuary, Westminster, and inform him that I am using Backhouse for negotiations, who is treating in the name of his firm by my instructions. Ellis should be requested to observe strict secrecy, and to take no action beyond directing Backhouse by telegram sent through this Legation to act under my orders. If questioned by the Chinese Minister in London, Ellis should reply that Backhouse is acting with authority from the firm.' The purpose of using Backhouse, Jordan insisted, was 'to avoid our name appearing in the matter, which would have been inciting to a breach of neutrality'. In fact, Yüan Shih-k'ai wished to be assured that the British government was the ultimate purchaser, and Jordan therefore asked for permission to state that the British government would cover the President if the transaction should be found out. He asked for this authority at once, 'as I am lunching with the President on Friday'.

This proposal was duly submitted to the Foreign Minister, Sir Edward Grey. Grey did not, at first, like it, and he expressed his doubts. The risks, he thought, were too great. The fact of the sale was bound to leak out, and for the sake of 30,000 rifles it was not worth while to encourage the Chinese government to commit a grave breach of neutrality. So the Foreign Office informed the Army Council that it could not support the project. But Lord Kitchener was not to be put off so easily. If 30,000 rifles were too few to justify the risk, could not the number be increased? If the Foreign Office was so squeamish about breaches of neutrality, might not the arms be supplied to Britain's Eastern ally, Russia? They could then be sent direct to Vladivostok and thence across Siberia to the Eastern Front.

The Foreign Office put this new proposal to Jordan. Did

Jordan think the Chinese government would allow Russia to have the arms on the same terms? If so, the Foreign Office would make appropriate suggestions to the Russians, who 'are not likely to be so scrupulous'. Alternatively, could the number of rifles be increased? In that case British scruples too might be suspended: 'rifles are urgently needed and we might be willing to do for a larger number what would hardly be worth while for so few'.

Jordan had scarcely received this telegram when a new proposal was put to him, this time from the Chinese side. He was approached by Liang Shih-i, the Controller of the Chinese Customs and Head of the Chinese Bank of Communications. We have already met Liang as one of Backhouse's alleged informants in 1909. Having drafted the edict of abdication for the last emperor, he was now the right-hand man and intimate counsellor of President Yüan Shih-k'ai, whom he had served as chief secretary, Minister of Posts and Communications, Head of the Bank of China, and Minister of Finance. He would himself afterwards become Prime Minister of China. In conversation with Jordan, Liang showed no knowledge of the negotiations for Chinese arms, but he made it clear that he knew of Lord Kitchener's need of men, and that he wished to be of service. He suggested that China would supply 300,000 men 'to serve under British officers wherever required, e.g. at the Dardanelles. The men would be shipped as coolies under the 1904 emigration convention, and China would provide 100,000 stand of arms'. Jordan thought the proposal fantastic, but since Liang insisted, he passed it on to the Foreign Office. At the same time, he replied to the specific questions which had been put to him. The Chinese government, he said, was unwilling to supply arms to Russia: it would only supply them to Britain. Therefore he was seeking to increase the Chinese offer in order to make it worth the risk. If the Chinese would forget about the 300,000 coolies but send the 100,000 rifles, then perhaps it would be worth while to give them the assurance that they asked for – i.e. that the arms were destined for use by Britain only and that the British government would indemnify the Chinese government for any unpleasant consequences if the secret should leak out and it should be accused, by the Central Powers, of breach of neutrality.

At the Foreign Office, the Under-Secretary of State was Sir Walter Langley. Under him, the affair of the Chinese arms was handled by Beilby Alston. Alston was a hereditary diplomatist whom the Foreign Office regularly attached to oriental royalty on ceremonial visits. He had personal experience of the Far East, having been Counsellor at the Legation in Peking before the war, and chargé d'affaires during Jordan's absence in 1913. When Alston read of Liang Shih-i's 'extraordinarily fantastic suggestion', he blew it aside with contempt. It was, he minuted, 'a typical example of the working of Liang Shih-i's mind (he is the Machiavelli of China)'. No doubt, he added, it was intended as a hint to Japan and a device to extricate China from her present diplomatic isolation and obtain a seat at the settlement of peace conditions at the end of the war. It was a pathetic suggestion and should be politely refused. However, if the coolies were unwanted, the rifles were not. That part of the offer, he agreed with Jordan, should not be overlooked, especially since the Chinese had themselves raised the number to 100,000. This improved number 'makes it more worth while giving the assurance required'.

The Army Council agreed. The arms, it insisted, were so necessary that Yüan Shih-k'ai should be given the assurances for which he asked. Lord Kitchener himself pressed the Foreign Office to give them. He now wanted 200,000 rifles at least. Yüan could be assured that they were for Britain only; and he begged the Foreign Office to promise full support to China in case of discovery and protest by enemy governments. A telegram was duly sent to Peking in these terms.

In the course of these anxious deliberations with the War Office, the Foreign Office had lost sight of Backhouse. On 25 June it was suddenly, and forcefully, reminded of him. Backhouse had apparently mentioned to John Brown & Co. his proposed work for the legation, and the company, having heard nothing about it from the Foreign Office, was taken by surprise. Backhouse thereupon received an indignant telegram from the company demanding an explanation. The matter was smoothed over. Sir Walter Langley saw Lord Aberconway, the chairman of the company, and explained that the government wished to entrust to Backhouse secret duties of great national importance. Lord

Aberconway responded at once. Having secured from the Foreign Office a formal letter of indemnity 'in respect of anything that Mr Backhouse may do in our names' in the matter of the Chinese arms, he sent a telegram to Backhouse giving him 'full authority to act in negotiations for the British Legation'. The Foreign Office solemnly expressed its thanks to Lord Aberconway for placing Mr Backhouse's services at the disposal of His Majesty's Government, and took full and formal responsibility for his future actions.

Thus by 25 June 1915, Backhouse was established as a secret agent of the British Legation in Peking and entrusted with a mission of the utmost delicacy. Acting purely in his capacity as the representative of a private company, he was to acquire from Chinese sources, and to ship to Britain, in the most profound secrecy, without involving either the Chinese or the British government, at least 200,000 rifles. So great was the need of these arms, and so essential was it to avoid any suspicion of government complicity, that Backhouse had almost complete independence. He alone was to negotiate. He alone was to handle the arms. The less he saw of the Legation the better. Neither the British Legation nor the Chinese government wished, officially, to know about the matter; and although the Legation was to assist him when necessary, and cover him against disaster, and supply him with means of communication to London, only two members of it – the minister himself and the Chinese Secretary – were privy to the operation. In London, the essential stages of this important enter-prise, which had been promoted by Lord Kitchener himself, were reported to the Prime Minister, the Cabinet, and, at times, the King.

The machinery having been thus set up, Backhouse at once set to work. On 30 June he reported to Jordan that he had located, at various places in China, over 150,000 rifles of Austrian and German manufacture. There were 30,000 at Hankow, 45,000 at Hangchow, 30,500 at Mukden, 26,000 at Tientsin, 20,000 at Nanking. At Nanking he had also discovered a particularly useful cache of 100 Skoda maxim guns. The make, year of manufacture, and calibre of all these weapons were exactly reported. 'The final negotiations', Jordan informed the Foreign Office, 'will have to be conducted by Backhouse at the places named, but the Generals Commanding at those places are due in Peking for a conference at the end of this week and advantage can be taken of this opportunity to arrange preliminaries here.'

The War Office was delighted with this news – especially the news about the maxim guns. Unfortunately Backhouse, in declaring his timetable had reckoned without the delays and obstructions inherent in Eastern negotiations; and soon he began to explain complicated difficulties. For instance, he found that the Japanese firm of Mitsubishi was involved in the same game, buying secretly for the Russian government. This competition among allies was most inconvenient, and the Foreign Office instructed the British ambassador in Tokyo to approach his Russian colleague and discover the facts. The Russian ambassador, when approached, professed ignorance of any such activity; which added to the mystery. According to Backhouse, this alleged Russian competition was forcing up the price of the arms, so that the Chinese were able to demand £300 each for the machine-guns. The War Office declared that the price should not exceed £120; but it added that the need was so urgent that cost was a secondary consideration.

Further delays followed, and by the end of July the War Office was showing signs of impatience. Backhouse explained that the main difficulty was 'delay in the arrival in Peking of the generals mentioned'; but he added that there were also unfortunate 'suspicions in certain quarters'. At this, Jordan too became impatient. Unless things could be brought to a head within a few days, he said, he would approach the President's private secretary. Happily this dangerous step proved unnecessary, for suddenly Backhouse announced that the difficulties had disappeared, and Jordan was able to report that 'there is now a good prospect that the contract can be signed between Backhouse and the Military Governor at Hankow, now in Peking', for the sale of not less than 100,000 Mauser rifles with not less than 300 rounds per rifle. All that was necessary was the insertion of a clause stating that the sale was purely private and that the firms concerned – that is, Backhouse's principals, John Brown & Co. and Palmer & Co. – should indemnify the Chinese government if it should find itself obliged to pay compensation to a protesting foreign power. This proposed clause did not worry the War Office at all – indeed it was very welcome – since it omitted any reference to re-sale, and Kitchener was now thinking, once again, of re-selling the arms to Russia. The Legation had previously promised that this would not happen, but now Backhouse's new clause was interpreted as cancelling that promise. Accordingly, on 6 August, on Kitchener's personal orders, a telegram was sent to Backhouse accepting these new terms. The rifles, Backhouse was told, were to be put on a British ship as soon as possible. 'We assume that, in view of the new clause, we need not tell the Chinese their true destination.'

Thus by the beginning of August all seemed set fair. Backhouse (as he told Jordan) had now secured at Hankow over 100,000 rifles and also about 350 Krupp machine-guns (.313 calibre, 1909) and 30,000,000 rounds of ammunition at £200 per gun and £4 per 1000 rounds. The War Office expressed delight and made further suggestions. Could not more Krupp field-guns be found in Chinese arsenals? If so, John Brown & Co. were willing that Backhouse should buy these too in their name. Meanwhile Backhouse was to procure the machine-guns from Hankow, and get them to Hong Kong for shipment to England. Then suddenly the orders were changed. The guns were not after all to be shipped. They were simply to be secured and the Foreign Office was to be told when they were safely in British hands. The reason for this change of plan was that the arms were not now to go to Hong Kong but, most probably, to Vladivostok. Kitchener had decided to send them to Russia.

From now on the pace quickens. Backhouse was in his element, negotiating in profoundest secrecy, with mysterious Chinese officials, giving orders to distant Chinese generals, providing the Legation with lists of guns, calibres, manufactures, organising transport, discovering, explaining and surmounting a continuing series of elaborate oriental obstructions. Those were busy days for the cypher clerks at the Legation and in London. Telegrams became longer and more frequent as Backhouse announced coup after coup, and each text, having circulated in the Foreign Office, and gathered around it a cluster of sagacious comments, was converted into complacent intelligence for the War Office, the Army

Council and Lord Kitchener. These strategists in London were particularly delighted by a telegram which Jordan sent on 11 August, announcing a new triumph by the energetic agent in Peking.

On this day – the day after receiving the order to secure the arms from Hankow – Jordan reported that the Military Governor of Hupeh (the province in which Hankow lies) 'has made an arrangement here with Backhouse, with the *secret* connivance of the Chinese government, to dispose of such arms under control of himself and his friends in other provinces as are available for sale' – provided he was secured against demands for indemnity in the case of leakage. 'The execution of this arrangement', the Foreign Office was told, 'depends now only on the absence of German protest, which in turn depends on the degree of secrecy which can be maintained during the process of shipment and clearance from port.' Assuming that such secrecy could be maintained, the details had all been worked out. The material was to be moved by the Chinese themselves, but at British expense, to Hankow or Shanghai, whichever proved safer, and thence shipped to Hong Kong in a British bottom. To arrange such shipment, Backhouse himself would go to Hankow, and Barton – the only other man in the secret – would go to Shanghai. Payment was to be made in cash at the port of shipment. G.O.C. Hong Kong had been asked to have an officer ready to receive important orders. Thus everything had been prepared. But of course things could still go wrong in what was, in form, a purely private transaction between Backhouse and his Chinese contacts. Jordan asked that the War Office be warned that 'the success of this very delicate operation must depend on circumstances which are to a large extent beyond the control of either the Chinese government or myself.' It depended on Backhouse alone.

Meanwhile the indefatigable Backhouse was discovering more and more arms to add to his store. Would the War Office like 115 Skoda quick-firing field guns, of 1911, complete with carriages, ammunition waggons and limbers at £600 each? Or 100 Krupp field-guns, also of 1911, calibre 75mm., similarly complete at £950 per gun, with 25,000 rounds of ammunition at £8 a round? Or 100 Krupp machine-guns? This was in addition to

95,000 Mauser rifles of 1909–11 and 30,000 Mannlicher rifles of 1911, calibre 7mm., which had already been secured. . . . The War Office jumped at most of these offers and sent instructions to G.O.C. Hong Kong to be ready to inspect the arms on arrival. The whole consignment was now to be sent to Hong Kong: 'destination will be settled when it gets there safely'.

On 21 August Jordan, in Peking, was waiting impatiently for Backhouse to complete his elaborate negotiations, so that his Chinese friends could assemble at Hankow the complete tale of arms; whereupon the whole cargo would move at once down the Yang-tse Kiang to Shanghai, and thence along the coast of China southwards to Hong Kong. If all went well, it would reach Hong Kong on 15 September or soon afterwards. In London, the War Office also was impatient. The negotiations, it insisted, must not be prolonged: it was time for the action to begin. There was general relief when Jordan, on 27 August, was able to report that the negotiations were complete. All the material was now secured. On 8 September it would start to move majestically down the great river. Ostensibly, to preserve the appearance of a purely Chinese operation, it was bound for Canton, but in fact, of course, it would never arrive there: it would quietly slip aside into Hong Kong, where the British general was prepared to receive it. The whole journey would take ten days, so it now would arrive on 18 September.

A beautiful operation, perfectly arranged! No hitch was announced, the danger (it seemed) was past, and on 30 August the Foreign Office asked the Minister in Peking about the reckoning. What was the cost, and how was it to be paid? After making his calculations, Jordan replied that the total cost should not exceed one and three-quarter million pounds, but he suggested that a credit of two million pounds be placed at his disposal through the Hong Kong and Shanghai Bank. The manager of that bank in Peking had now been let into the secret, and Barton would be sent to Shanghai to explain it to the manager there. These arrangements were duly made, and Jordan was thus equipped to settle up once the arms arrived at Hong Kong.

Everything, as Backhouse insisted, depended on absolute secrecy. Unfortunately, at the last minute, secrecy was in serious jeopardy. On 11 September the British ambassador in Petrograd reported that the Russian government had asked him a curious question. Was it true, as the Russian minister in Peking had reported, that a large consignment of arms was being secretly bought in China by the British for delivery to Russia? This report caused a flutter of apprehension in the Foreign Office. There Alston set out the true position. 'Lord Kitchener', he minuted, 'has postponed the question of ultimate destination till he is quite sure that we have got possession on board a British steamer. His idea is that the rifles, etc., should go to Russia, but he does not want to raise false hopes.' It was just possible that they might suit Belgian or Serbian ammunition. 'We originally told the Chinese government that the ultimate purchaser would be Great Britain, but in the final contract' – that is, in the contract drawn up by Backhouse – 'no undertaking was required or given as to destination.' It was hoped that the material would be shipped at Shanghai about 20 September, 'but all now depends on the absence of German protest, which in turn depends on secrecy. . . .' On the basis of this minute, instructions were sent to the British ambassador in Petrograd. He was to tell the Russian government that 'negotiations have been conducted throughout by a private individual as a purely private transaction, and that their final execution depends entirely on the decree of secrecy' that could be maintained.

Four days later, on 15 September, it really seemed that at last the cargo must be on its way, and on that day the Minister wired to the G.O.C. Hong Kong telling him about the arrangements made and the part he was to play. Jordan apologised to the general for having kept him so long in the dark, but explained that the extreme delicacy of the operation imposed an altogether exceptional degree of secrecy. Next day, the Colonial Secretary, Mr Bonar Law, wired to the G.O.C. Hong Kong requesting him to give all possible help.

Another week passed: a week of anxious waiting. Then, on 22 September, Jordan was able to send welcome news to the Foreign Office. 'The Chinese officer in charge of the flotilla carrying material to Hong Kong', he wired, 'left Shanghai for Fu-chow last night at midnight. Ships are however moving south

separately to avoid attracting attention. They are to meet outside
Fu-chow and proceed together to Hong Kong, where they should
arrive at earliest on Saturday next. Above information is all
obtained by Backhouse from Chinese authorities who insist on
managing the whole business in their own way, and it is impossible to say whether it is accurate or not, as I have no means,
without attracting undesirable attention, of ascertaining movements of various ships carrying consignments. Barton was due to
arrive at Hong Kong last night.'

It was a tense period for Jordan. For over four months he had
been preparing for this operation, and now it was nearly complete. Within a few days the separate ships of the 'flotilla', loaded
with arms, would assemble at Fu-chow on the coast of Fukien.
Then there would only be the last lap to safety in Hong Kong.
But of course everything still depended on secrecy – secrecy and
the efficiency of Backhouse's organisation. For Jordan, far away
in Peking, had to rely entirely, now as always, on Backhouse. He
knew only what Backhouse told him. Ostensibly, the Legation
knew nothing about the affair, could not be seen, or even suspected, to be involved in it, could not mention it – except in
extremity – to the Chinese government, which also, officially,
knew nothing about it. Nor did other members of his own
Legation, except Barton; and Barton was now in Hong Kong.

Then, on 25 September, Backhouse announced a sudden hitch.
'Owing to strong protests from German and Austrian legations'
(so Jordan reported it to London), 'there is grave doubt whether
flotilla which has reached Fu-chow will be allowed to proceed
from there to Hong Kong.' The protest – according to Backhouse
– accused the Chinese government of selling arms to the Japanese
for eventual use by the Entente powers and Russia. 'Backhouse',
Jordan went on, 'is doing all in his power to persuade Chinese
authorities to order ships to proceed to Hong Kong without
delay, but they will do nothing without sanction of President
who is very nervous and agitated.'

Next day Jordan was able to report further. 'After great
hesitation', he wired, 'the authorities who are directing the
operation from here have, they state, telegraphed to the ships at
Fu-chow to proceed direct to Hong Kong, which they are ex-

pected to reach on Tuesday. As these orders are supposed to have
been given without the sanction of the President, and are accompanied by characteristic Chinese devices for getting over that
difficulty, there is still ample room for miscarriage. I have however warned them that any further delay will necessitate my
personal intervention with the President.' Jordan did not name
the 'authorities' who were directing the operation from Peking.
He was referring to Backhouse's Chinese friends with whom he,
as British minister, could have no direct dealings. Everything had
to go through Backhouse. To threaten a personal interview with
the President, cutting out both Backhouse and his Chinese
'authorities', was Jordan's last card. It might be effective if the
President was really being deceived. But it might be fatal, for it
would show that the British Legation, which had so carefully kept
out of the supposedly private transaction, was really interested
in it.

The Foreign Office, in its reply, did not refer to this last threat
but implicitly it urged Jordan to try all other means first. 'It is
of the utmost importance', he was told, 'that we should obtain
the arms. You need spare no expense to induce Chinese officials
or steamship captains to deliver them to Hongkong.' The Foreign
Office must have been relieved, next day, by Jordan's reassuring
message. It read, 'Telegram from Governor of Fukien to Chinese
authorities here, which has been communicated to B[ackhouse],
states that ships left Fukien Sunday night.' So all was well after
all. There was no need to cut out Backhouse, or appeal to the
President. The ships were on their way to Hong Kong.*

Now London and Peking could only wait for news of their
arrival. It did not come. After four anxious days a telegram was
sent to Jordan: 'Have you any further news? None has reached
us from Hong Kong.' Jordan's reply indicated that once again
there had been an inconvenient hitch. 'The Chinese explain the
delay in arrival of flotilla at Hong Kong', he wired, 'by statement
that the Canton governor, to whom the arms were ostensibly

---

* In the original telegram the initial 'B' has been extended by hand, by a Foreign
Office official in London, as 'B(arton)'. But this is clearly a mistake. Barton's name
is always spelled out in Jordan's telegrams; 'B' always means Backhouse. Barton
was anyway in Hong Kong.

consigned, and who is not a party to the transaction with us, sent a gunboat to meet the ships and convey them to Canton. Ships are now said to be outside Huichowon and have been ordered by Canton governor to proceed to Canton tomorrow morning. It is impossible to say whether above statements are true, but every effort is being made to induce Chinese authorities concerned to adhere to original plan.'

What news could have been more exasperating? After all those patient negotiations, all those tense moments and narrow squeaks, the long-awaited 'flotilla', laden with that indispensable cargo, had reached its destination only to sail past it into the wrong port! A feeling of helplessness overcame the experts of the Far Eastern Department: helplessness increased by their inability, with all their resources, to find Huichowon on the map.* Jordan's depressing telegram was passed round the office and picked up doleful comments. No doubt, observed one pundit, the Chinese plan was to throw on to the unsuspecting governor of Canton the blame for letting the ships find their way to Hong Kong, and the wily governor had outsmarted his enemies. However, perhaps the situation could still be saved: 'we must trust that the governor of Canton is open to "argument".' Yes, agreed the Under-Secretary of State, Sir Walter Langley: 'Sir John Jordan has full discretion as regards the argument which would appeal most strongly to the Canton Viceroy.'

Sir John Jordan did not try to bribe the governor of Canton to release the ships. He decided to play his last card. He announced that he would endeavour to see the President and would make 'a strong personal appeal to him'. Backhouse was at last to be cut out.

On the afternoon of 2 October, the interview took place. To Jordan's surprise, the President 'professed complete ignorance of the whole transaction, but said he would willingly assist us if I supplied the details to his Private Secretary; which I am now doing. The Chinese attitude throughout has been tantalising, but we should now be able to test the truth of the story given to Backhouse.' The President, Jordan noticed, was generally sympathetic to the Allied cause and willing to supply munitions; he

* I cannot find it either.

promised to grant special facilities for a large consignment which a British firm in Shanghai wished to send to Vladivostok for Russia; it was only this grandiose operation by Backhouse of which he disclaimed all knowledge.

The experts of the Foreign Office were highly indignant at the President's disclaimer. The Under-Secretary of State waxed facetious. The interview should have been dramatised, he minuted: the President solemnly pretending that he knew nothing about the operation only a week after he had received (as Backhouse had discovered) 'strong protests' about it from the German and Austrian ministers. . . . It was too ridiculous for words. The Under-Secretary had almost lost patience with these orientals.

Jordan did not lose patience. Four days later he called on the President's confidant, Liang Shih-i, 'the Machiavelli of China'. Liang, he reported, 'was fully aware of the transaction but had no information about the movements of ships. He thought the delay arose from the necessity of picking up different consignments on the way, but felt fairly sure that they would reach Hong Kong. He himself suggested that the ships should go to Canton and that the munitions should be conveyed thence to Hong Kong by rail'. 'Liang Shih-i's assurances', added Jordan, 'made me a little more hopeful of success.'

So long as there was any hope of success, the Foreign Office urged Jordan on. On 10 October Sir Edward Grey himself took a hand. He sent a private telegram to Jordan. 'It is more than ever urgent to get the Chinese rifles and machine-guns,' he told him. 'You should spare no expense that may secure this. If desirable, I would ask Japan to send a cruiser, which could wait for the ships outside territorial waters and escort them to Hong Kong, thus preventing them from being interfered with after they get outside territorial waters.'

On receipt of this urgent personal appeal from the Foreign Minister, Jordan resolved to get to the bottom of the matter and discover where in fact the obstacle lay. He obtained another interview with Liang Shih-i. Before calling on him, he drove to Backhouse's house in Shih-fuma Street. There he found Backhouse engaged in conversation with an American businessman. Jordan detached Backhouse and took him off in his own carriage for a confrontation with Liang Shih-i.

Once arrived at Liang's house, the Minister made Backhouse tell his whole story. Liang, as Jordan reported, was 'very sceptical'. He said that the amount of arms which Backhouse claimed to have collected was 'far beyond what China could spare' and that ships containing them could not possibly have moved without his knowledge. His earlier statements, which had given a gleam of hope to Jordan, had, he now said, been misunderstood: he was then referring to relatively small transactions – nothing on this huge scale. He assured Jordan that he was quite willing to supply Britain with a moderate quantity of rifles and send them by Chinese gunboat to Hong Kong, but that there could be no question of parting with machine-guns. All in all, 'he professed to think that Backhouse had been duped'. 'I shall continue to press the matter vigorously,' Jordan concluded his telegram, 'but have little hope of success.'

This telegram too caused a buzz among the minute-writing officials of the Foreign Office. Its content, they declared, was 'most disappointing and amazing'. Clearly the Chinese were trying to wriggle out of their promises. No doubt the explanation lay in high politics. There were those unfortunate leaks to the Russian Legation, those German and Austrian protests, the supposed involvement of Japan. And then there was 'the Monarchical Movement' – that is, the movement to make President Yüan Shih-k'ai Emperor of China, now gathering momentum. That movement was sponsored largely by the Chinese army; it might have to deal with opposition; if it came to a struggle, arms would be needed, and then it would look very bad if all the spare arms in China were found to have disappeared, having been corruptly turned into cash. . . . Altogether it was most annoying. Luckily the two million pounds credited to the Legation had not actually been paid out. But where were the elusive ships and arms now? Could nothing be saved from the wreck? Sir Edward Grey added a final memorandum in his own hand urging that Jordan should get whatever arms he could. 'Liang Shih-i can hardly refuse this after what he has said.'

On this basis a telegram was sent to Jordan. The Foreign Office, he was told, was most disappointed at the latest turn of events, but realised that the Minister had done all that was humanly possible. 'Could you tell me where the ships and rifles and guns are at present? Owing to urgent need of rifles, you should get all, or as many as possible, of the rifles sent at once to Hong Kong. Liang Shih-i can hardly refuse this after what he has said.'

Jordan's reply was defeatist. 'I know absolutely nothing about the whereabouts of the ships and rifles', he wired, 'and enquiries might do harm. Backhouse believes they are in Canton, while Liang Shih-i is convinced that not a ship has ever moved. There has evidently been a split between Liang and the party with which Backhouse was working, and the former has proved stronger.' Jordan added that he was now in close touch with Liang and 'now that I have the matter in my own hands' – i.e. now that Backhouse had been pushed aside and he was dealing direct with Liang – he felt fairly sure of obtaining a certain amount of arms. The Russian minister was also seeking arms through Liang, and Liang was willing to supply them, provided that the British would receive them in Hong Kong. Next day Liang promised, with the approval of the President, to deliver 20,000 rifles and an adequate supply of ammunition, and perhaps more later. 'We must be thankful for small mercies' was the comment of the Foreign Office.

The mercies in the end were very small. The 20,000 rifles did not materialise. As Jordan explained, 'arrangements made through Backhouse having completely collapsed, I have been working personally with Liang Shih-i, but business proceeds slowly owing to the difficulty of collection'. Besides, there was now a further complication. The affair of Chinese arms now really was entangled in high politics. Liang Shih-i had become the chief protagonist and organiser of the 'Monarchical Movement' and the British attitude towards that movement, which was one of hostility, 'will I fear put an end to the whole thing. The President and Liang will probably resent our intervention and withdraw their offers.' The Foreign Office minutes record gloom at this report. It was most unfortunate that the arms question should have to depend on our attitude to the monarchy, they lamented, 'but we are committed to the Japanese and must risk losing the arms'. For the Japanese government, whose support Yüan supposed that he had bought by huge concessions at his country's expense, were not in fact prepared to allow a revived military empire in China.

Jordan continued his efforts to buy arms in China. By now, everyone agreed, it was better to 'throw off the mask and deal openly'. The gains might be meagre, but at least there was some chance of something. So he waited patiently on Yüan Shih-k'ai and Liang Shih-i. The results were indeed meagre. Yüan and Liang were far more interested in their plans for a new imperial dynasty than in secretly trading arms to Europe; the shadow of the Backhouse affair lay across the whole business; and, as Jordan reported, 'I am obliged to take what I can get, and submit to interminable delays in getting it.' Early in 1916 a few rifles were scraped together and sent to Hong Kong. After that the issue died. The Ministry of Munitions was now working, and the British government found that there were better methods of arming its troops in Europe than by haggling with politicians in China.

Between the pressures of the European war, and the internal convulsions of the Chinese republic, there was little leisure for a post-mortem on the infelicitous Backhouse affair. The charitable view, which was adopted by Barton in Peking and by Alston in London, was either that the innocent Backhouse had been 'duped' by his unscrupulous Chinese collaborators, or that these collaborators had themselves been outmanoeuvred in political infighting by the machiavellian Liang Shih-i. These Chinese collaborators were never named in Jordan's communications, and it is clear that Jordan did not know – and for diplomatic reasons did not want to know – their identity. Only Backhouse knew who they were. To the Legation they were simply 'the authorities who are directing the operation from here', 'the authorities who insist on managing the whole business in their own way', 'the party with whom Backhouse was working'.

At first, Jordan also accepted this charitable view. He too presumed that the arms and the men of whom Backhouse spoke had a concrete existence; that the provincial governors had indeed given the undertakings which Backhouse ascribed to them; that the various consignments had indeed been loaded on to a 'flotilla' of real, material ships; and that these ships, having sailed secretly down the Yang-tse river to Shanghai, and then crept individually along the coast to Fu-chow had first been held up there by diplomatic protests, then released by the secret influence of Backhouse's friends, and finally, by the sudden intervention of the governor, whom Backhouse's friends had omitted to square, been diverted to Canton. Or, if he did not believe all this, at least he believed that Backhouse had been given, and had naïvely accepted, this elaborate story, the figment of his unscrupulous Chinese 'authorities'. If the story was not true, it was still 'the story given to Backhouse'.

But gradually, as he delved into the matter, Jordan found himself forced to a different conclusion: a conclusion that was both alarming and, to him, personally humiliating; for it implied that it was not Backhouse but he himself, who had been duped. For, after all who were these mysterious Chinese 'authorities' whom Backhouse had so regularly cited? What was the objective evidence for the story which, in successive telegrams, marked 'secret' and 'private', he had been sending, day after day, month after month, to the Foreign Office? The more he looked into the details of that story, the more difficulties he discovered in it. Whenever it touched real facts, it proved incompatible with them, and at no point could it be traced back to, or confirmed by, any identifiable source. So, ultimately, Jordan came to believe that the whole story, from beginning to end, was pure fiction – and, moreover, not merely a fiction told to Backhouse, but a private fantasy invented by him. The unnamed Chinese 'authorities', the provincial governors, the rifles and machine-guns so exactly described and dated, the flotilla of ships, and the whole dramatic history of their journey from Hankow to Canton, which had kept cypher clerks busy in Peking and London, caused legation officials to be sent to Shanghai and Hong Kong and commanding generals to be initiated into profound secrets; which had sent the British Minister Plenipotentiary to wait on the President of China, ruffled the diplomatic waters in Tokyo and Petrograd, fetched two million pounds from London to Peking, and nearly brought a Japanese battle-cruiser into the South China Sea; which had agitated pens in the Foreign Office and the War Office, exercised the Army Council and Lord Kitchener himself, drawn in the personal intervention of the Foreign Minister and the Colonial Secretary, been reported to the Cabinet, the Prime Minister and the King; all this, it now seemed, was an insubstantial pageant, the baseless fabric of a dream, now suddenly dissolved, leaving not a rack behind.

Such a conclusion must have been very mortifying to an experienced diplomatist, a man of sixty-three, who for the last forty years had served with distinction in the Far East, and who was now in his tenth year as head of the Legation in Peking. In the weeks immediately following the fiasco, it seems that Jordan was in a depressed state, and it was widely rumoured that he had resigned, or was resigning, from his post. This rumour was published in the Press and had to be denied in Parliament. A few months later, the Foreign Office decided to withdraw him from Peking for a year and to appoint Beilby Alston, the man who had handled the affair of Backhouse's 'arms and ammunition' in London, as counsellor and chargé d'affaires in his place. Once again it was presumed, and publicly stated, that Jordan was retiring, and the Foreign Office had to reassure the Chinese government: Jordan was merely taking a year's leave from his post in Peking, to which he would return. These widespread rumours cannot, of course, have been based directly on the affair of Backhouse's arms, which was a closely guarded secret; but they may well have arisen from Jordan's own depression of spirits after that affair. The Under-Secretary of State went out of his way to assure Jordan that the government wished him to stay in Peking as long as he could. In fact, he stayed in Peking till November 1916, when Alston arrived to replace him; then he left for nearly a year's leave. But he remained titular Minister Plenipotentiary, and in October 1917 would return to Peking to finish his active career there. We shall soon meet him again.

Backhouse too found it convenient to escape temporarily from Peking. On 6 November 1915 – the same day on which Jordan announced that he was now going to 'throw off the mask', dispense with secret agents, and deal openly with Yüan Shih-k'ai and Liang Shih-i – Backhouse informed the Legation that he proposed to leave for England, where he wished to inspect his recent gift to Oxford University and organise his work on a new Chinese dictionary. On arrival, as so often in times of crisis, he went to ground and declared himself very ill. This was the time when he wrote to Bland, whom he avoided seeing in London, those lamentable letters about his physical and financial sufferings: his bladder, his eyes, his poverty, the dreadful time with London doctors, the withering away of his investments, the prospect of a sightless and indigent old age. It was a sad decline after the elation of the summer months when he had been showering his munificence on Oxford University and commanding the attention of cabinet ministers, governors and generals, by secret operations in China.

However, let us not prematurely lament the blasted hopes of Backhouse. In his cyclical life, with its recurrent alternation of depression and euphoria, he would fall only to rise again; and already the springboard for his next adventure had been prepared. It had been prepared most recently on the evening of 11 October 1915.

To a superficial observer, it might seem that 11 October 1915, had been a black day for Backhouse. That was the day on which Sir John Jordan had called on him and taken him to be confronted by Liang Shih-i: a confrontation which had revealed that Backhouse's whole story was untrue, that, on the most favourable construction, he had been 'duped'. But in fact, for Backhouse, the episode could not have been more timely. That personal visit of His Majesty's Envoy Extraordinary and Plenipotentiary, who had carried him off to call on 'the Machiavelli of China', the closest adviser of the President of the republic, had been witnessed by Backhouse's companion of the moment, who was naturally impressed by such grand contacts. That casual companion was the American businessman, George Sylvester Hall, whom we have already met as the 'wrong-un', the 'partner' destined to cause such 'terrible trouble' to Mr James Cotton Minchin, the Backhouse family lawyer. Now it is time to introduce him fully into the story.

CHAPTER EIGHT

The Entrepreneur

GEORGE SYLVESTER HALL was an American businessman
employed by the American Bank Note Company of New York.
This company manufactured bank notes and transacted a large
business printing paper currency for foreign governments. Hall
worked in its Far Eastern Department, dealing with China and
Japan, and thus, in due course, he came into contact with
Backhouse.

They first met in September 1914, when both were travelling
to China on the same Pacific steamer. Hall was engaged on the
business of his company. Backhouse, we may remember, had just
resigned his chair at King's College, London, had declared himself a recluse, and was returning to China to rest his infirm and
almost sightless eyes. But on meeting Hall, Backhouse's eyes were
magically cured and his hermit instincts were suspended. He saw
a great opportunity, a social contact to be cherished. He therefore
introduced himself to Hall, explaining that he was an important
emissary of the British government, and was at this moment
carrying an autograph letter from King George V to President
Yüan Shih-k'ai. Hall already knew Backhouse by name, both on
account of his book on the Empress Dowager and on account
of the family bank, which was well known to his own bank note
company; and he afterwards travelled with him twice on the
steamer to and from America.

In conversations on these leisurely trans-Pacific journeys, and
in quiet social meetings in Peking, Backhouse impressed upon
Hall his own social grandeur and political influence. He made it
clear that he was a close friend of high Chinese officials, including
the President, Yüan Shih-k'ai. He indicated that he was not only

the agent of the important British shipbuilding company, John Brown, but also a trusted secret agent of the British government. Hall seems to have been a man of a singularly trusting nature; but if he had ever entertained any doubts, they were dissipated on 11 October 1915 when Hall, with his own eyes, saw the British Minister Plenipotentiary, the doyen and most respected member of the diplomatic corps in Peking, coming personally to call on Backhouse and taking him to visit the President's *éminence grise* and financial counsellor, Liang Shih-i. After this, Hall was satisfied that Backhouse was a man who counted. Therefore, when Backhouse suggested that, thanks to his grand contacts, he might be able to be of service to the Bank Note Company, Hall eagerly embraced the offer. With the agreement of his company, he enlisted him as a special agent to secure orders in China. He was to be paid two per cent commission on all orders obtained by him, together with his expenses.

The date of Backhouse's employment with the Bank Note Company is not clear, but it was probably after the impressive meeting of 11 October 1915: perhaps after Backhouse's return, early in 1916, from his visit to England. This was the time when Backhouse was uttering cries of economic anguish, which a new agency with a solid American firm might help to alleviate. The fiasco of the great arms deal was of course a closely guarded secret. The only man who knew about it in Peking, apart from Sir John Jordan, who had left, was Sidney Barton; and his interpretation was charitable. No visible shadow hung over Backhouse on that account. Moreover, political events in China were now moving fast, and the Bank Note Company had a particular interest in them.

The reason for the company's interest lay in its previous negotiations with the Chinese government. These negotiations, in which Backhouse does not seem to have been involved, had culminated in an order on 21 October 1915. This order was described as 'the hundred-million order', and was obviously of great value. Presumably it was for a hundred million Chinese bank notes. But it seems that this order was not specifically confirmed, and afterwards the changing political situation in China made it seem insecure. For we are now in the period of 'the

Monarchical Movement' and Yüan Shih-k'ai's attempt to make himself Emperor of China.

The monarchical movement did not in fact succeed. Yüan began with confidence. He took, like the old emperor, a new regnal title. The year 1916, instead of the fifth year of the Republic, was declared the first year of the Hung-hsien Emperor. Imperial ceremony was reintroduced; titles of nobility were distributed; and Yüan prepared to occupy the vacant Dragon throne. But foreign powers stood aloof from the new empire and, within China, all the republican parties united against it. The bourgeoisie of the south, always hostile to the imperialism of Peking, challenged the government, and Sun Yat-sen again became a power in the land. The Bank Note Company watched these developments with anxiety. If Yüan were overthrown, it was informed, 'the whole of the hundred-million order is useless and will have to be replaced'. Thus the pleasing vision of an unending snowfall of Chinese bank-notes had scarcely floated before the eyes of the businessmen in New York when it seemed about to dissolve again.

How fortunate that, by now, the company could rely on a real expert, with an intimate knowledge of Chinese politics, Chinese society, Chinese ways! Backhouse, at this time, was constantly offering his help. He was prepared to sell his house to the company for $30,000. He 'very kindly undertook' to intervene with the Chinese authorities and ask for the release of the company's chauffeur, who was in prison for knocking down a policeman. He assured the company that they would still get their money even if Yüan should go and a new government come in. 'I see Backhouse very regularly,' the company's agent in Peking reported in March 1916: he 'always seems to know what is going on earlier than anyone else.' Thanks to him, there were solid grounds for confidence, whatever should happen, for Backhouse did not only know Yüan himself, he was also on friendly terms with all those high Chinese politicians who were bound to constitute any successor government in Peking. He had long been a friend of the former Grand Secretary Hsü Shih-ch'ang, through whom he had formerly been able to assist Pauling & Co. and who had written such 'gracious' letters to him shortly before his (temporary) fall in 1910. Hsü was still a powerful figure in Peking, destined himself to be President of China. The Bank Note Company was also glad to know that 'Tuan Ch'i-jui, one of the men who is sure to be prominent in any reconstructed government, is Backhouse's closest friend'. Tuan was indeed a valuable friend to have. He had been Minister of War and acting Prime Minister under Yüan; he had the support of the generals; he could make or mar any government which might succeed the tottering Yüan.

For Yüan had indeed over-reached himself. The end came very quickly. On 6 June 1916, the ambitious President, deeply mortified by the failure of his schemes, suddenly died of nervous exhaustion. He was succeeded by the Vice-President, Li Yüan-hung, a man of no significance: he was, as the British Minister reported, 'all things to all men, and had no will or mind of his own'. Under him, Tuan Ch'i-jui once again became Prime Minister and Minister of War. Thus the Republic was saved and 'Backhouse's closest friend' became the indispensable strong man behind the new President's throne.

These appointments naturally pleased the Bank Note Company and made Backhouse more indispensable to it than ever. Hall, who had been in America, came out to Peking to discuss matters with him. Very soon after his arrival, he was able to tell the company that he was returning to New York 'on a special mission for the Chinese government'. Thanks to Backhouse, he had 'a guaranteed sizeable order': the company was to ·be the sole foreign printers of Chinese money for ten years, starting from 1 October 1916. But this coup, for some unstated reason, 'must be kept quite secret'. Backhouse had insisted on the greatest secrecy in all things.

At one point, Backhouse's insistence on secrecy was very inconvenient and seemed irrational. In order to clinch the new deal, it was necessary, in Hall's opinion, to secure the text of the previous 'hundred-million' contract made with Yüan Shih-k'ai's government, and he therefore cabled to New York asking for a photographic copy of it. This seemed natural enough; for how could a new contract be arranged with a new régime without full information about the old? But when Backhouse heard of this request, he expressed alarm, even indignation. He cabled direct to New York. It was absolutely essential, he said, that no reference be made to the previous contract. 'Above all', no copy of that contract, or of the documents relating to it, may be shown to anyone. In the present delicate state of Chinese politics, such an action, he said, would be fatal. It would blow Backhouse and prevent him from being of any further service to the company; it would destroy his good relations with the new Prime Minister; and it would destroy any hope of realising the new contract itself.

Hall hastened to reassure his principals in New York. He cabled to them that he would under no circumstances betray anyone. He authorised them to assure Backhouse that the copy of the contract 'absolutely will not be shown'. He only wanted it for his own guidance. But Backhouse was adamant. The old contract must be kept a dead secret. No documents may be shown to anyone. Everything must be left to his personal diplomacy. And that, too, must not be mentioned. If he were even named, in connexion with the October contract, he said, 'it would do him irreparable harm with his own government'. For of course Backhouse was not only the agent of John Brown and of the Bank Note Company, the confidant of Chinese Presidents and Prime Ministers, but also a secret agent of the British government.

Hall was very perplexed. He cabled to Backhouse (who was now in London) explaining that his reason for wanting a photograph of the previous contract and the Chinese characters in it was simply in order to have it confirmed by the new minister of finance, who was prepared to accept it as binding. The contract itself was no secret: people were talking about it; it had even been mentioned in the press; and the late President was said to have referred to it, although not to have approved of the large quantity of notes to which it committed him: he evidently thought a hundred million bank notes excessive. What then was the difficulty? Hall pushed aside Backhouse's arguments. 'Please telegraph me', he cabled to Backhouse, 'granting me permission to show the documents to the minister, that I may act as quickly as possible.'

Reading the agitated correspondence in the summer and autumn of 1916, we are left with the impression that Backhouse was

terrified lest the Chinese officials should deal directly with Hall or
any other agent of the company. Here, as in the great arms deal,
he wished himself to be the sole intermediary. Above all, he did
not wish the Chinese to see the contract of October 1915. He
did not even want that contract to be confirmed, for that, as he
said, would entail the payment of a commission to the original
signatory. He preferred that that contract be forgotten and
replaced by a new contract of which he would be the only
negotiator, and therefore, of course, the only person to be paid
commission. The company, naturally, did not care to whom it
paid commission so long as the contract was secured. To it, the
old contract was quite good enough, if only it could be confirmed;
and if it were confirmed, it would entitle its negotiators to a proper
reward: 'as to the matter of commission, that can be arranged
satisfactorily to all concerned.' Backhouse could only justify his
exclusive personal diplomacy if he could secure an even bigger
contract. He was playing for the highest stakes.

And he won. On his insistence, the old contract was forgotten.
Then, a few months later, he was able to report that he had
negotiated a new contract beside which the old hundred million
bank notes seemed mere chicken-feed. After arduous negotiations,
of which he gave detailed accounts, both orally and in writing,
including four personal interviews with the President of China
(which had cost him eighty dollars a time in gate-money), he had
prevailed. The Chinese government now undertook to purchase
from the Bank Note Company 650 million bank notes – fifty
million a year for thirteen years. Backhouse's chief agents in this
matter, he said, apart from the President and the Prime Minister,
were his old friend Hsü Shih-ch'ang and the ex-minister of finance
Chou Hsüeh-hsi.

Thus Backhouse had done it again. It was a repetition of his
technique in the great arms deal. Here, as there, it was the scale
of his operation which had constituted his triumph. Other
negotiators had been able to pick up small quantities of arms
here and there, but did such trifling gains justify the risk? Backhouse, operating in secret, by personal diplomacy, would produce
a flotilla of ships carrying mountains of arms gathered from remote
provinces, and the whole British war establishment, from the

Cabinet downwards, would commit itself to his dazzling schemes. So now, in this mere commercial transaction, the scale of his operations silenced criticism. The company would have been glad to save even part of the hundred-million order. They knew that the late President had thought it too large. But Backhouse insisted that, if all negotiations were left exclusively to him, he could do far, far better. And he had done so. The only difference between the two operations was in the internal disposition of the pieces. In the first, unnamed 'authorities' in China had been used to impress British cabinet ministers; in the second, named Chinese cabinet ministers had been used to impress anonymous businessmen in New York.

The news of this great scoop caused rejoicings in New York. Backhouse came to New York in person to report it, and was fêted by the directors of the company, and especially by the President, Mr W. L. Green. Hall himself received an increase of pay, and was made Vice-President of the Far Eastern Department of the company, merely for having discovered 'this treasure of an agent'. Hall then accompanied Backhouse back to Peking, where, on 7 December 1916, Backhouse triumphantly placed in his hands the contracts for the order. They were in Chinese, and were signed by the President of China, Li Yüan-hung, and the Prime Minister, Backhouse's 'closest friend', Tuan Ch'i-jui. Thereupon the delighted company laid in an ample stock of paper and had the plates designed by their staff. Backhouse received, 'in addition to unlimited praise', £5600 sterling as commission and various sums as expenses, including 320 dollars as a refund of the gate-money paid for interviews with the President.

So far, so good. The contract had been signed. But curiously, the order did not follow. Telegrams were sent, but nothing happened. The mails, it was explained, were uncertain in this time of world war: letters were being intercepted and opened by the Japanese. . . . Still, the failure of the Chinese government to follow up the contract with the essential order was very odd, and by March 1917 Vice-President Hall wrote to his agent in Peking declaring that Backhouse's failure to secure this order was 'a very grave and very serious matter'. Backhouse had been paid his commission in advance and had given an assurance that the text of the order would be handed over in exchange for it. That had not happened; and some explanation was needed.

As usual, Backhouse had his explanations. When pressed, he explained that he was having great difficulty in securing another interview with the Prime Minister. Finally, early in April, he reported that he had secured an interview, but it had not led to the desired result. In fact, the interview had been 'very stormy'. The Prime Minister had accused Backhouse of having stolen his 'remittance' – presumably the 'squeeze' which he had required the company to pay him in return for his co-operation – and had said that 'he would repudiate everything', including the contract, unless the 'remittance' were delivered to him. Backhouse implied that the British government had intercepted the remittance and had informed him, as its secret agent, that it would not return it unless China declared war on Germany, and 'even then, return appears doubtful'.

This remarkable story did not convince Hall's agent in Peking, who was now applying the pressure. He had had enough of 'Backhouse's repeated promises', and now he decided to act. 'If the matter be not settled satisfactorily in a few days', he cabled, 'I propose to arrange independently interview in order to ascertain what are real facts.' Inevitably, we are reminded of Jordan threatening to by-pass Backhouse and seek an interview with the President. Hall was reluctant to exasperate Backhouse by going behind his back, at least until Backhouse had been given a chance to explain himself. 'I think it best not to negotiate independently', he replied, 'until I have seen Backhouse.' Backhouse, with his family connexions, his grand Chinese contacts, his perfect knowledge of Eastern languages, and his powerful position as a secret agent of the British government, was still too important a person to slight on mere suspicion. Besides, Hall had other reasons for handling Backhouse gently: reasons of a more private nature, outside the affairs of the Bank Note Company.

For once he had become involved with Backhouse, Hall's appetite had been whetted, and he had entered into various private transactions with him. This was the 'partnership' mentioned by Minchin. For instance, Backhouse persuaded Hall to invest 15,000 Mexican dollars – the ordinary currency used in China – in a half-share with himself of a collection of Chinese 'curios' which he had been lucky enough to acquire. Hall was about to leave China at the time and acted, as he admitted, in too great haste. He trusted Backhouse's expert valuation of the curios, especially when Backhouse scrupulously reduced it by 2000 dollars in deference (as he said) to a second opinion given by the Dutch Director-General of the Metropolitan Museum in New York. Backhouse was adept at gaining credibility by such minute attention to detail, such pedantic and scrupulous self-correction.

Then there was the case of the old Empress Dowager's pearl jacket. This was a famous garment, the best-known item in her wardrobe, and it exercised a particular fascination on Backhouse, with his passion for jewellery. Backhouse approached Hall and informed him that he had an opportunity to purchase this valuable object, and he invited Hall to invest in a half-share of it. However, there were certain practical difficulties to be overcome before the Palace eunuchs would hand over the garment which (presumably) was not theirs to sell. In fact, Backhouse would have to make his way secretly into the Palace (which at that time was still occupied by the imperial family) and escape with his booty without alarming the Palace guard. This he proposed to do with the assistance, and in the company, of his 'secretary' – i.e. his boot-black factotum, Chang Ho-chai; but as the enterprise was risky, he intended to go armed. In other words, Backhouse, by his own account, intended to burgle the Palace in order to receive stolen goods.

Hall, by his own account, was ready to involve himself in the affair. He invested 50,000 Mexican dollars in the venture. He also lent Backhouse a revolver, which he had borrowed for the purpose, for self-defence in so perilous an undertaking. Then he sat back and awaited the return on his investment.

In due course Backhouse came to report the success of his burglary. According to his account, he had succeeded in penetrating the Palace, and although he had failed to secure the entire jacket, owing to an unseasonable panic among his Chinese accomplices, he had managed, with great difficulty and danger, which lost nothing in the telling, to cut 344 pearls from it. He had then made a dramatic escape, firing the revolver as he forced his way through the Palace guard. As evidence of his success,

Backhouse showed Hall one of the pearls, 'a drop-pearl of imperfect shape but beautiful lustre, which was valued by experts in America at 18,000 gold dollars'. He also returned the revolver with 'a cordial letter of thanks' to the original lender.

Lured by the bait of the single pearl, Hall waited to receive his share of the booty. He waited in China; he waited in America. But somehow it never came. He was fobbed off with a series of excuses, each more complicated and fantastic than the last. The pearls had been sent to London in the diplomatic bag with Backhouse's secret despatches to the Foreign Office. They had been valued at £600 apiece. They were insured for £100,000. They were in a London bank, in the joint names of Backhouse and Hall. There was competition to purchase them. Grander and grander names were dropped: ambassadors, maharajas, viceroys. . . . In the end, Hall could wait no longer: he was impatient of such excuses. So, with these melodious names ringing in his ears, but with empty hands, he retired to his home in Maine to reflect on this as on other strange Backhousian affairs.

By the autumn of 1917 the scales at last began to detach themselves from his eyes. In both his official and his private dealings, Backhouse, he now decided, was 'a crook'. Having reached this decision, he resolved on a personal confrontation. He would go forth and 'unmask the swindler'.

But where, in the autumn of 1917, was Backhouse to be found? The hermit of the Tartar city had suddenly become remarkably mobile. His plans, he had told Hall's agent in Peking, who was trying to pin him down, were 'very indefinite'. He was probably going to Japan . . . he would go to America as soon as business permitted. Then he announced that he would take a Dutch ship to Seattle. Altogether he was very elusive. But Hall was determined to intercept him. He demanded an interview. He proposed a meeting in Seattle. If Backhouse were delayed by his 'business', Hall would press on and meet him in Yokohama. Wherever he might be, Hall would discover him, and confront him.

Backhouse did not appear in Seattle; so Hall went on to Yokohama and waited to catch him there. Still Backhouse did not appear. Then Hall moved on to Peking. He arrived in mid-September, only to learn that Backhouse's plans had been changed again. While Hall was crossing the Pacific, Reuter had published the surprising report that Backhouse had been called to the Western Front as Director of Chinese Coolies. So Hall reached Peking just in time to learn that Backhouse, having received public congratulations on his patriotic response to the call, was about to set off for Europe via Canada. He would steam out of Tientsin on the *Empress of Asia* – the same ship on which Hall had just steamed in.

It seems, however, that Hall was in time for some conversation with Backhouse before he left; for on 23 September, Hall cabled laconically from Peking to New York that Japanese influence had caused the Chinese government to repudiate the contract, and that Backhouse had returned the commission advanced to him: 'will explain situation on arrival New York. I am to make new arrangement. . . .'

That indeed was Backhouse's latest explanation. Never at a loss for ingenious and detailed excuses, preserving his sang-froid and effrontery to the end, he announced, as he boarded the *Empress of Asia* that it was precisely because of this unexpected obstruction by Japan that he was leaving Peking so suddenly. On the way to his post on the Western Front, he would stop off in Japan in order to pay £100,000 to Baron Motono, the Japanese Foreign Minister, as a 'squeeze' to stay his objection to the purchase by China of seven battleships from John Brown & Co. He was doing this, he added, not only in order to secure the contract for John Brown but also to perform a service to his old friend Tuan Ch'i-jui and thereby persuade him to fulfil the bank-note contract after all. What was £100,000 compared with seven battleships and 650 million banknotes? Backhouse was now, at least by his own account, a wizard entrepreneur, conjuring with millions and managing the business of three continents.

Hall's first cable from Peking, with its factual assurance, suggests that Backhouse's explanation had convinced him. No doubt it had been both circumstantial and persuasive; his explanations always were. That silver tongue could charm away a mountain of concrete fact and give temporary credibility to the strangest fantasies. But later, when Backhouse had gone, and Hall in Peking began to piece together the evidence, this last magnificent fiction dissolved. It could not survive the first scrutiny to which it was subjected. On 3 October Hall cabled to New York, 'We have ended all relations with Mr Backhouse, who has been absolutely crooked. Deceived both Embassy and ourselves.'

He had indeed. In the first part of October 1917, Hall paid a series of visits in Peking which made the facts only too clear. The most shattering revelations followed his visit to the American Legation. There he produced the famous contract which had brought Backhouse such glory in New York. It was scrutinised by the Chinese Secretary, Dr Charles Tenney, a former missionary. Tenney looked at the signatures of the former President and the present Prime Minister and pronounced them perfect: he could not doubt that they were genuine. But afterwards he took steps to make sure. Together with the American Minister Dr Paul Reinsch, he took the document to the Prime Minister himself. In their presence, and that of his own private secretary, the Prime Minister examined it, and then, 'without hesitation pronounced his signature a forgery'. 'We also' (as Tenney afterwards wrote to Hall) 'asked the Premier if he knew or had ever met Mr Backhouse. He replied that he did not know him and had never met him.' So much for Backhouse's claim that Tuan was his 'closest friend'.

Next, Dr Tenney went to see Hsü Shih-ch'ang and asked him about his alleged interviews with Backhouse. Hsü's answer was categorical. 'He was not acquainted with the man', he said, 'and did not know who he was'; far less had he written him gracious letters proffering help and friendship, and met him in conspiratorial sessions over the past eight years.

Reeling from this discovery, Hall carried his story to the man who, if anyone, really knew Backhouse in Peking, the great Dr Morrison. When Morrison heard Hall's story, he must have smiled sardonically to himself at this implicit vindication of his unfavourable views on the authorship of the diary of Ching-shan. During the last five years, since he had become adviser to Yüan Shih-k'ai, and Backhouse had turned his interests to more exciting fields of activity than mere translation, there had been little contact between the two men and the few surviving letters between them refer only to their separation. Now, listening to Hall, Morrison decided to make a record of these interesting revelations. So he began the dossier which still survives among his papers. It is entitled 'Some Notes to Sir Edmund Backhouse, bart.', and is sub-headed, 'Edmund Backhouse the Sinologue and Author of the faked diary in Bland and Backhouse's book *China under the Empress Dowager*'. Thus defiantly Morrison reiterated his insistence that the famous document was a fake, and now accused Backhouse himself of faking it. We shall return to the diary. At present we are concerned with the occasion which produced the dossier.

Morrison's immediate reaction, on hearing Hall's story, was amazement that 'this shrewd businessman' could have been so completely taken in. But, asked Hall, would not anyone have been taken in? After all, Backhouse was the agent of John Brown, a very distinguished firm. He had shown Hall his contract with John Brown, and the British Naval Attaché at Peking, Commander Illtyd Hutton R.N., who happened to be travelling on the same boat with them, had confirmed that Backhouse had been introduced to him by the directors of John Brown as their agent in China. Hall's fellow-directors of the Bank Note Company did not blame him at all for his errors, for they themselves, particularly the President, had been equally deceived by this infinitely persuasive rogue. But of course everything was fraudulent. 'The contract itself is bogus', Morrison recorded, 'the signatures to it are forged.' Chang Ho-chai had himself confessed to Hall 'that Backhouse did not know any of the high officials with whom he was pretending he was in intimate intercourse'. The interviews with the President of China had never taken place: the 'gate-money' had been pocketed by Backhouse. That little detail riled Hall, in retrospect, more than any other: it made him mad to think of those refunds, eighty dollars a time, he told Morrison. As for Backhouse's private dealings with Hall, they were equally fraudulent. The curios were bogus – 'there is not a genuine piece in the collection'. The pearls did not exist, and the story of their acquisition was pure fantasy.

Morrison need not have blamed Hall for his gullibility. Too many others were gulled by Backhouse. Even the British Legation, in spite of the fiasco of the great arms deal, was a nest of gulls. This appeared when Hall went there to tell his dismal story to his old friend Commander Hutton, the naval attaché.

At this time there were two men at the British Legation who had been in the secret of the arms deal and involved daily in its details. They were Sidney Barton, who was still Chinese Secretary, and Beilby Alston, who had then been in charge of the case in the Foreign Office and was now chargé d'affaires in Peking in the continued absence of Sir John Jordan. Both Alston and Barton had evidently satisfied themselves that Backhouse, in that affair, had been an innocent dupe, a naïve scholar fooled by nefarious Chinese 'authorities', and Alston was himself a personal friend of Backhouse, involved with him in certain 'purely private transactions' – no doubt the acquisition of 'curios'. Morrison, who heard of these facts, and of rumours linking Backhouse with Alston, attempted to warn Alston; but Alston does not seem to have taken the matter seriously.

In his interview with Hutton, Hall recounted the whole tale of Backhouse's enormities. He told him about the contracts. He also confessed about the private partnership which had cost him, so far, 65,000 Mexican dollars. He added that, by now, he had 'a very large amount of evidence to prove that Mr Backhouse is a liar and a forger' and that he was 'collecting facts about sundry shady transactions in which Mr Backhouse was concerned several years back in America'; and he remarked that 'Dr Morrison also has a great deal of Mr Backhouse's past history at his fingers' ends'.

On hearing this alarming story, Hutton went off to see the acting counsellor at the Legation, Miles Lampson, afterwards well known in diplomacy as Lord Killearn. They discussed the matter together, and found it very embarrassing. The naval attaché was concerned in the interest of British shipping: he felt that he must warn the Admiralty and John Brown & Co. On the other hand, he had heard that Backhouse's contract with John Brown was now terminated; Backhouse had disappeared from China, apparently to take responsibility for Chinese coolies in France; and Hall's allegations, at present, were only hearsay. Besides there was the somewhat embarrassing fact about Backhouse's close association with Alston. In these circumstances, Lampson and Hutton decided not to report the matter to the chargé d'affaires.

The story, they thought, was on the face of it extremely unlikely to be true, and the less currency it obtained, the better. They hoped, as so many people so often hoped, that the problem of Backhouse, if only it were left alone, would go away. Unfortunately they were wrong. Backhousian problems never went away.

Moreover, precisely at this time, a formidable character appeared who was in no mood to leave the cosy gulls' nest undisturbed. Only a few days after Lampson and Hutton had agreed to bury the matter, Sir John Jordan returned to duty after a year's absence.* One of Jordan's early visitors was that other formidable character, his old friend – the man who had recommended him as minister – Dr Morrison; and Morrison, needless to say, told him all about the latest Backhouse affair. So Jordan, who had left Peking in the wake of one Backhouse scandal, found that he had returned only to be confronted by another. He was not pleased. He was even less pleased when he found that, although the matter had been reported to the Legation, his chargé d'affaires knew nothing about it. He insisted that it be cleared up. His object, as he minuted, 'was to warn the Foreign Office and forestall the issue of a commission to Backhouse in case there appeared to be reasonable grounds for crediting the charges'. In other words, Jordan intended to block Backhouse's commission as Director of Coolies.

The result was a flurry of minutes, memoranda, explanations, and a new dossier. Alston, who no doubt felt himself compromised, expressed great indignation against Hutton. Why had he not reported this 'important information' to the Head of Mission at once? Hutton explained himself; Lampson took the blame; and the storm subsided – but not before certain interesting details had emerged.

In the course of the recriminations, Lampson found himself answering the charge that he had suppressed a matter which was likely to compromise the Legation. In reply, he protested that he knew nothing about 'Backhouse's connexion with the Legation'. He knew that Backhouse was a personal friend of Alston, and

* Hall called on Hutton after Backhouse had disappeared, but while Alston was still chargé d'affaires – i.e. some time between 23 September and 6 October. Jordan resumed his duties on 6 October.

had some private dealings with him, but he was quite ignorant of any official relations. He knew also that Backhouse had left for France 'to take up a post in connexion with the censorship of Chinese coolies correspondence'. But the Legation had nothing to do with this appointment, 'which was offered to him direct by Colonel Fairfax, the officer commanding the coolie corps, in a letter dated from the War Office (Private) of February 2nd last. That letter is filed in our archives.' Therefore, said Lampson, he had no reason to suppose that the Legation was involved in, or could be damaged by, any private activities of Backhouse. What Lampson did not know was Backhouse's secret connexion with the Legation two years before – the great arms deal.

To Jordan, the memory of that episode was only too fresh. It was inseparable from the very name of Backhouse. When the internal enquiry was over, Jordan invited Hall to call on him and heard his story in full. Jordan consoled Hall by telling him that 'it would have been impossible for anyone to have suspected that man'. Clearly he was thinking of his own misguided confidence two years ago. How could he avoid thinking of it when Hall himself showed a disconcerting knowledge of it? For Hall, as Jordan afterwards reported to the Foreign Office, informed him that Backhouse had been 'employed by this Legation in connexion with attempted secret purchase of arms, and showed him some documents from us on the subject'. So Backhouse had not only cheated an American company and an American citizen: he had also, in the process, and for that purpose, broken the pledge of secrecy which he had given to his own government.

Having assembled all the evidence, Jordan reported to the Foreign Office. On 12 November 1917, he informed the Secretary of State that there was prima facie evidence that Backhouse was guilty of fraud against Hall and had betrayed the secrets of the Legation; and he therefore asked that no government appointment of any kind be given to him. Four months later, when the Foreign Office was seeking to locate Backhouse, who had disappeared, Jordan, thinking that it might be looking for its missing Director of Coolies, repeated his request. Backhouse, he wrote, was now in British Columbia, allegedly ill. It was said that, when fit to travel, he would return to China, to contest Hall's charges.

Even so, Jordan insisted, unless and until the charges were refuted, Backhouse was unfit for any commission.

Jordan's language was general: he did not refer specifically to
the post of Director of Coolies which Backhouse was allegedly on
his way to take up. Did he believe in that commission? Or did he
agree with Morrison that it was merely a ruse by Backhouse to
cover his flight from Peking? How genuine in fact was the
invitation? We cannot say. All we can say is that the appointment
seems, on the face of it, somewhat eccentric. The coolie corps was
raised in China in 1916 and the commissions in it were generally
recommended by the Legation, not initiated by the War Office. It
seems curious that Backhouse should have received a purely
private letter direct from the War Office, and that he should have
replied to it seven months later by a sudden public announcement.
Some may think it surprising that the correspondence of illiterate
Chinese coolies should need to be censored by a scholarly sinologist, or indeed at all. As for the letter from Colonel Fairfax, if
Backhouse could forge the signature of the President of China, he
could forge that of the commander of the coolie corps. In any case,
since Backhouse never arrived in Europe, the matter was not put
to the test.

Backhouse having disappeared, and his appointment in Europe
(if it was real) having been blocked, there remained the lawsuits.
The American Bank Note Company extricated itself without
difficulty. Thanks to Hall's prompt action, Backhouse had been
obliged to return the commission advanced to him – or at least, as
Hall told Morrison, £5000 out of the £5600. The company
thereupon washed its hands of him, preferring to regard him as
Hall's personal agent, not their own. That left Hall to pursue his
own case against Backhouse, and to utter, to all who would hear
them, his agonised expostulations. Backhouse, Hall concluded,
was a genius in his way, 'the most remarkable scoundrel ever
known in the Far East' – which was certainly saying a lot. He had
cheated everyone; so why should Hall have seen through him?
'I had no reason to suspect this man. He was the duly appointed
agent of John Brown, one of the largest firms of naval shipbuilders in the world. I personally saw his contract with them.
Their sub-agent in Shanghai came to Peking to see me.' But John

Brown too had been taken in. Hall had now heard that Backhouse had drawn 100,000 dollars 'before he bolted, on the strength of a forged contract for seven battleships'. Dollars or pounds – it does not much matter: no doubt this was the pretended 'squeeze' for Motono, the Japanese Foreign Minister.

It was some comfort to Hall to know that others besides himself had been cheated. At least he could say that he had been deceived in good company. All the same, the experience mortified him. He was particularly ashamed to recollect that he had himself been promoted to Vice-President, and his salary raised, solely on account of his achievement in recruiting Backhouse, who had now turned out to be such a scoundrel. In January 1918 he wrote to the company touching this sore point. 'You will remember', he wrote, 'that on my return to New York last year, on the strength of my securing these forged contracts, you made me a Vice-President. To save my face here in China, I would like to retain the title . . . but I would ask you to reduce my salary to the original amount I was receiving.' The company treated him with indulgence, but the affair clearly preyed on his mind. A fellow employee of the company who met him in Peking in April 1918 reported that he still seemed very depressed. 'I strongly urged him to get away for a rest as soon as he possibly can, for he surely is in a bad way. The Backhouse matter was a bad blow to him and is on his mind all the while – a veritable Banquo's ghost that will not down.'

It was particularly mortifying that Backhouse himself seemed beyond the reach of justice. At the British Legation, Hall was told that Backhouse 'had been at this game before, but it was hushed up, owing to the standing of his family.' Hall himself considered that it was not advisable to prosecute Backhouse for his frauds against the company 'on account of the high Chinese concerned'. The British Legation assured him that Backhouse would be arrested on arrival in England; but of course Backhouse was far too prudent to arrive in England: he went to ground in Vancouver Island. There he lay low, allegedly gravely ill, while Hall sued him in England, on his own private account, and the lawyers, in London, struggled to work out a settlement.

In the end they succeeded, and in the autumn of 1918 Backhouse, emerging from his seclusion in Victoria, British Columbia, re-crossed the Pacific and established himself in the Kyoto Hotel, Kyoto, Japan. There he was joined by Hall, and on 8 November 1918, the peace treaty was signed. By it, the partnership was formally dissolved. All the property of the partnership – that is, the 'curios' and the single pearl – were returned to Backhouse. The parties agreed to withdraw all allegations against each other, to bury the affair in total silence, to take no further action, and to live in outward amity thereafter. Backhouse also agreed to pay to Hall the sum of £10,650. 'His bill for legal expenses', as Morrison observed, 'must have been enormous.' A copy of the legal settlement was sent to the British Legation in Peking, and Sir John Jordan sent another copy, for information, to the Foreign Office in London.

In his covering letter, Jordan informed the Foreign Office – no doubt with considerable relief – that 'Backhouse is at present winding up his affairs here with a view to returning to England for good as soon as his health permits'. Which reminds us that this was the time when the election for the Oxford chair was impending. With him he was no doubt taking the 'curios' which he had been obliged to redeem at so high a cost. As itemised in the deed of settlement, they included two silk rugs, seven tap-estries, an embroidery, miscellaneous earthenware divinities, one pair of eggshell lanterns, various vases, 'one porcelain pagoda, date 1700, presented to the Dalai Lama by the Emperor', 'one pair bronzes (these are not genuine and were bought in error)', 'one roller painting of the Goddess of Mercy by Wu Tao Tzu 780', 'four scroll paintings', and 'one large pearl'.

Such, in brief, was the affair of Backhouse, George Hall and the American Bank Note Company. Bizarre though they seem, we have to admit that many of the details fit only too neatly into the pattern that we have already established. The letter from King George V which Backhouse was carrying to President Yüan Shih-k'ai reminds us of the letters from Lord Salisbury, Joseph Chamberlain and the Duke of Devonshire which he had brought with him to China twenty years ago. If the former deceived George Hall, the latter had deceived Sir Robert Hart. We can now feel sure that they too were imaginary, or, if they existed, forged. The interviews with Hsü Shih-ch'ang are familiar to us: now we know that they were as bogus when described to Lord ffrench, and paid for by Pauling's, as when described to Hall and paid for by the Bank Note Company. Morrison had been quite right when he told Bland, at Upper Helliford in August 1910, that Backhouse really had no friends or acquaintances among high Chinese officials. The bogus curios sold to Hall remind us of the bogus scrolls palmed off on the Bodleian. Now we realise why Mr Minchin sought from Madan a certificate that Backhouse was an expert in Chinese antiquities: it was in defence of the authenticity of those curios. In exactly the same way, Backhouse would protest that the eighteen scrolls were genuine, and that he could not be mistaken, being an acknowledged expert in such matters. The non-existent pearls are, by now, only too familiar. The story of the Empress Dowager's jacket is confirmed from other sources: it became well known in Peking that Backhouse had been involved in such an incident, which in the end had cost his family a pretty penny;* but of course, here too, it was said that his naïveté had been exploited by 'able and unscrupulous Chinese'. 'Ce génie de la Tour de Babel', writes M. Henri Vetch, who still believes in his innocence, 'était un naïf: il se laissait entrainer par des salopards dans des affaires véreuses.' This is precisely what Alston and Barton would say about the great arms deal. And now we can see why Sir John Findlay was so cautious in his correspondence with the Bodleian and was not on particularly good terms with his brother-in-law. The repercussions of the bank-note affair and Hall's lawsuit against Backhouse took place while Sir Jonathan Backhouse was in his last illness. No doubt Findlay had been involved in the settlement, for Backhouse's brothers were all serving in the armed forces at the time. Perhaps it was in settlement of those actions that Findlay, as Bishop Norris would state, had advanced '*a large sum of money*, not yet repaid', and in recollection of them that Findlay himself would declare that he too had learned, to his cost, not to trust his brother-in-law's alleged expertise in Chinese antiquities.

---

* It was known to Hoeppli, whose account, consistent with that of Hall, was presumably obtained from common knowledge in Peking in the 1930s. The mythical raid on the Palace had by that time become part of reality.

Moreover, another profane thought forces itself on our minds. What about those 'five very precious Chinese manuscripts' which were to be sold dirt cheap by Sotheby in the summer of 1920 and which were to be seen on application to Messrs Minchin & Garrett, Backhouse's lawyers? Were these perhaps some of the bogus 'curios' which had been palmed off on Hall and which he had now been obliged to buy back as part of the settlement? Possibly, possibly not; but at least the fact that they were in the hands of his lawyer indicates some comparable background.

The frauds which Backhouse was said to have perpetrated against the Bank Note Company and against Hall personally form only part, though the greater part, of the dossier drawn up by Morrison. On 28 September 1917, Hall told Morrison 'that he believed there was some crookedness' in connexion with the deeds of Backhouse's house in Peking. Backhouse had tried to sell the house to Hall, but Hall was suspicious and refused. The house in question was 19 Shih-fuma Street which Backhouse had occupied since 1912. All we know about its ownership is that by 1921, and perhaps earlier, the legal owner of the house was not Backhouse but Backhouse's servant Chang Ho-chai. Possibly, having found a gullible victim in Hall, Backhouse was trying to raise money by selling the house twice. Possibly Hall's suspicions were unjust and Backhouse, having failed with Hall, then sold the house to Chang. Not knowing the dates, we cannot decide the matter.

A little later, Commander Hutton told Morrison that Backhouse's 'swindle was even more complicated than I have indicated, involving large sums obtained for bogus furs'; and next year, while Backhouse was still at the Empress Hotel, Victoria, allegedly very ill, and the lawyers in London were desperately seeking to disentangle his affairs, still further malpractices were reported. One Moore Graham, Backhouse's new medical attendant, came to Peking on his behalf, presumably to protect his interests or to prepare for his return, and told Morrison that while staying in Victoria, Backhouse, undeterred by the failure of his Chinese enterprise, had entered into 'a wildcat scheme with Celsa, the Italian manager of the hotel, and was induced to part with $12,000 gold, a sum which he is now endeavouring to recover by law'. This at least was what Backhouse had told Graham. Knowing Backhouse, we may surmise that the $12,000 gold which he had given to Celsa, like the £100,000 'squeeze' which he was paying to the Foreign Minister of Japan, was notional and that only the attempt to recover it was real. No wonder Messrs Minchin & Garrett, in London, had their hands full, and Mr James Cotton Minchin was a worried man when he wrote to Bodley's Librarian for his help in his attempts to extricate his client from this imbroglio.

Somehow, in the end, he did. The cost to Backhouse's relations was heavy but at least the matter was buried, and in December 1918, as soon as the storm was over, Backhouse calmly returned to Peking and resumed his position as 'the well-known sinologue'. In 1919 he let it be known that he expected the chair of Chinese at Oxford and would be grievously pained if he should be passed over. He featured as an eminent scholar in *The New China Review*. The Curators of the Bodleian Library continued to trust and honour him until they too found themselves his victims in 1921. What is even more surprising is the comfortable oblivion which protected him in Peking. In the 1920s and 1930s few of those who are recorded as mentioning Backhouse seems to have had any idea of the elaborate frauds in which he had been involved. They would declare, even in the most confidential documents, that he was a scholar-recluse, eccentric indeed, but harmless, with no known vices. Only Weatherall would hint vaguely, in a private conversation in Oxford, that he was financially unreliable.

We may think this odd. Surely, we may say, the story of Backhouse's frauds must have been known in the Anglo-American colony in Peking and must have echoed round its convivial dinner-tables. No doubt it did, but very discreetly: for the cases being settled, and Backhouse being notoriously litigious, any public utterance would have been dangerous. Moreover, Backhouse benefited by an unpredictable accident. The man who built up the dossier which, even today, supplies the only authoritative contemporary account of his frauds, was Morrison. Morrison, as Bland had written, was 'amazingly indiscreet' and would no doubt have made capital out of these frauds which, if only by analogy, supported his claim that Backhouse had forged Ching-shan's diary. But here public affairs came to Backhouse's aid. In November 1918, before Backhouse had returned to China, the First World War came to an end. Before Morrison could complete his dossier, he was summoned to Europe to represent the interests of China at the Peace Conference. He was, by now, a sick man. He never returned to China. He died in London in 1920, aged fifty-eight, and the dossier which he had begun to compile remained incomplete among his private papers.

However, if Morrison disappeared from Peking, Jordan did not; and perhaps the last word should be given to that other strong man of the British colony. Like Morrison, Jordan had at first been persuaded by Backhouse's great gifts and had trusted him. Like Morrison, he had been disillusioned and now looked on Backhouse with an unclouded, critical eye. He recognised, as few others did, the sheer fantasy of his character. He also, it seems clear, deeply resented his own humiliation in 1915. How could he forget or forgive that absurd affair of the great arms deal, when His Majesty's Minister Plenipotentiary in Peking had been made so ridiculous, causing half the Cabinet Ministers of Britain, when the country was locked in the greatest war of all time, to dance to the empty tune of this absurd pied piper? For Jordan was convinced – and we may now believe that he was rightly convinced – that there never had been any 'Chinese authorities' behind Backhouse: Backhouse's wonderfully vivid imagination had created that whole elaborate charade.

That was hard enough. But there was also a further disagreeable consequence. For if Backhouse had invented the arms deal, it followed that he had also broken the secrecy imposed upon him: for how else could the Russian minister in Peking have reported to his government an operation of which there could be no objective evidence? This suspicion became a certainty when Jordan received Hall, and Hall told him about his relations with Backhouse: how Backhouse, to gain credit in Hall's eyes, had claimed to be, among other things, a trusted secret agent of the British government. We know, from Hall's own statements, both to his company and to Jordan, that Backhouse made this claim and supported it by showing Hall secret papers, which he had kept for the purpose, just as he supported his claim to represent John

Brown & Co. by exhibiting his contract with them. From the sequel, it seems clear that Jordan expressed his indignation to Hall, and that from Hall, or his lawyers, that indignation was conveyed to Backhouse when Backhouse surfaced after his long submersion in Canada and arrived in Japan to make the treaty of peace between them. At all events, it was from his hotel in Kyoto that Backhouse, on 29 October 1918, wrote a personal letter to the minister to exculpate himself from the charge of having disclosed to Hall 'my former connexion with the legation'.

This charge, he wrote, was quite untrue. 'I never gave to Mr Hall, nor to any other person, any such information, as I regarded the relation as entirely confidential and faithfully observed the understanding that it was not to be mentioned in any circumstances.' In order to explain away Hall's undoubted knowledge of these highly secret matters, Backhouse reminded the minister of that episode in October 1915 when Hall had been at Backhouse's house and 'Your Excellency called there in connexion with some negotiations which I had carried out at your request; and Mr Hall subsequently saw me drive away with Your Excellency.' Hall, if he were so minded, could have discovered that they had gone to visit Liang Shih-i, because Backhouse's carriage had orders to go and fetch him thence after their meeting. This, Backhouse now suggested, could have set Hall speculating. 'In any case, I never gave the slightest hint to Mr Hall that I was working for you, for the legation, or for Mr Barton, and I have kept the matter absolutely secret from first to last.'

On receiving this letter, Jordan passed it, for comment, to Barton; and Barton, who persisted in the belief, or the pretence, that Backhouse was the innocent victim of machiavellian Chinese plotters, sought to defend him. The existence of those secret papers was known, he said, to the Hong Kong and Shanghai Bank (which had handled the two-million-pound credit to pay for the operation) 'and also to certain Chinese, as well as to Backhouse'. Therefore, he implied, the leak need not be ascribed to Backhouse. Jordan was not impressed. He was sure, he wrote, that the bank 'did not betray our confidence' and he did not believe that any Chinese were in the secret: 'who were they, and how did they obtain the knowledge?' To Jordan, the unnamed

Chinese 'authorities' regularly cited by Backhouse, and still accepted by Barton, were mere phantoms, like every other element in Backhouse's story. 'I am convinced by my own experience of the whole case', he wrote, 'that the arms, ships, etc., never existed except in Backhouse's imagination.'

In a 'confidential note' which he attached to Backhouse's letter, and which was clearly intended for the record, Jordan stated why he could not accept Backhouse's 'ingenious explanation'. It was quite true, he admitted, that Hall had seen him in October 1915 'when I called upon Backhouse and took him to see Liang Shih-i'. But this was irrelevant, for Hall 'told me things which *must* have come from Mr Backhouse. He described the nature of the papers which we had given to Mr Backhouse in such circumstantial language as to convince me that he had either seen them or received very accurate information about their contents.' Then he added a note on the subject of the papers. 'As regards the transaction itself – the attempt to procure arms through Mr Backhouse for His Majesty's government – I was convinced long before I ever saw Mr Hall that Mr Backhouse's story was a myth from beginning to end. It cost me a summer's useless work, and HMG an equally useless expenditure of money in telegrams, etc.' A month later, Jordan's mind was still running on the same track. Sending to Barton a copy of Backhouse's deed of settlement with Hall, he remarked, 'it is preferable that I should make no comment on the transaction one way or the other. If I attempted to do so, it would lead me back to the arms business, which I have no wish to revive.'

That was in December 1918. At the same time Morrison, being about to leave Peking for good, made the last entry in his dossier of Backhouse's crimes. It reads, 'Commander Hutton tells me that there is an action pending by John Brown's against Backhouse for various frauds.' We therefore turn to Backhouse's major business activity in China, the agency for John Brown & Co.

This agency, which Backhouse had obtained in 1910, was central to his business activities in China thereafter. It was because he was known to be the agent of that great firm that the British Legation had regarded him as a suitable agent for the secret purchase of arms in China, and it was by the same reasoning that

Hall had accepted him as a reliable agent for the Bank Note Company. Unfortunately, it is not possible to document his activities in this capacity in the same detail, for the main archives of the company, are impenetrable. However, certain documents, including the company's minute-books, have survived; and from these, and from the records of the Foreign Office, it is possible to tell the story in outline, and with reasonable assurance of accuracy.

Backhouse's duties as agent were to persuade the Chinese government to order modern ships from John Brown & Co. We can see that, to the directors of the company, he must have seemed a useful agent. He came from a family well known in banking and business circles. His father was a director of Barclay's Bank. He was connected with the Fox family with their long-established shipping agency. He had already been employed by Pauling's railway construction firm and by Straight's syndicate of American bankers. He had a perfect knowledge of Chinese. He claimed personal acquaintance with influential Chinese politicians – Presidents, Prime Ministers, Grand Secretaries. And if there were any secret flaw in these credentials, it would not have appeared in correspondence or interview; for Backhouse, as everyone agreed, and as every event proved, was wonderfully plausible and never lacked convincing circumstantial evidence for his statements. To the shipbuilders of the Clyde, the sudden modernisation of China after 1900 must have offered huge opportunities. A vast and populous country was turning from junks and sampans to steamboats and ironclads. All that was needed was a solvent Chinese government and an effective agent in personal touch with it. The silver-tongued Backhouse could easily persuade these innocent industrialists that both conditions were fulfilled, and that he was their man.

Backhouse was engaged by the two associated firms of John Brown & Co. and Palmer & Co., in July 1910. It seems that his initial contract was for seven years, and he set out for China, in the autumn of that year, equipped with albums containing illustrations of ships suitable for sale to China and plans of battle-cruisers. Although well-informed persons, like Bland, were sceptical both of the Chinese government's capacity to buy and of Backhouse's capacity to sell, the company evidently entertained great hopes of his agency. In particular, they hoped that he would sell two cruisers of the 'Bristol' class. These hopes were encouraged by Backhouse, whose regular communications were discussed at Board meetings. In the spring of 1911, Lieutenant Edward Boyle, of the Royal Navy, was engaged by the company to be their agent in Japan, and for the next three years Backhouse and Boyle worked, or were said to be working, together. In January 1913 Boyle, after discussion with Backhouse, wrote to the company reporting that the Chinese government wished to buy eight 'Town class' battle-cruisers but that the Japanese government regarded such an investment as evidence of aggressive intent: therefore he proposed, as an alternative scheme, that John Brown & Co. should supply 'sea-going coast defence vessels' of 5000 to 6000 tons. A fleet of even eight such vessels, he wrote, could not be considered aggressive, and it would enable the Chinese government 'to gain "face" and show the flag in parts where there are large Chinese communities who seldom if ever see a Chinese man-of-war'. Backhouse must have been involved in this proposal: presumably it was he who reported the interest of the Chinese government in such an investment.

In January 1914 Boyle returned to England, but Backhouse, who remained in China, continued to discuss the sale of these coastal defence vessels, and in due course arrangements were made, or were thought to have been made, for the ships to be built in collaboration by John Brown & Co. and Palmer & Co. In August 1916 Brown and Palmer were discussing 'Backhouse and the Chinese business'. By this time, in spite of the fiasco of the great arms deal, of which his employers of course, knew no details, Backhouse seemed about to pull off a great commercial coup: a coup which, like so many Backhousian operations, grew larger and more impressive as it approached nearer to the moment of apparent realisation.

For in September 1916 Backhouse reported to his employers that he had been approached by certain Japanese firms 'with a view to their participation in the contract'. This was a welcome extension of business, but it also raised political issues, and Lord Aberconway, the chairman of the two companies, called at the Foreign Office to discuss the matter. He was received by Lord

Grey, the Foreign Minister, and Sir Walter Langley, the Under-Secretary of State. Lord Aberconway asked what would be the view of His Majesty's government on Japanese participation. He was told that 'since the Japanese were doubtless in a position to block the contract altogether, should they so desire, Messrs John Brown would clearly be wise to admit the participation of Japanese firms'. After discussion, it was agreed that Backhouse should continue his negotiations with the Chinese government, leaving the Japanese to make further proposals; and that if such Japanese proposals should be made, the company should accept Japanese participation in the contract. On this basis the company went ahead, and by the end of October the estimates and designs for six coastal-defence vessels of 10,400 tons for the Chinese navy were complete and the Japanese proposals for inclusion were expected. Thus by the end of 1916 it seemed that Backhouse had deserved well of his employers. He had arranged a substantial sale.

However, from now on, the phantom battleships began to slip away. In March 1917 the directors of John Brown & Co. noticed that they had had no word from Backhouse concerning his great Chinese contract. They evidently stirred up their agent, and a month later he cabled back to say that the contract had been signed. Then another three months passed – three months during which the affairs of China became more complicated as the impotent rule of President Li Yüan-hung crumbled and the Manchu Empire was briefly restored. In August, the directors again noticed the absence of any news concerning the contract, and again, presumably, they pressed Backhouse, just as the Bank Note Company was doing, for documentary confirmation. Finally, on 15 September 1917, Backhouse roused himself to reply. Through his friend Alston, the chargé d'affaires, he sent a private cable to John Brown & Co. It read: 'Detained hitherto. Leaving immediately, due London November. As my contract expired and no further business feasible pending peace, I assume you approve my taking post with Chinese labour in France to which I have been gazetted. Services at your disposal after war. Reporting fully on arrival. Telegraph nothing direct as delivery doubtful.'

With that last message to his company, Backhouse disappeared altogether from sight. George Hall was closing in, and it was time to go. As he left, he put out his story about the £100,000 bribe with which he was about to reconcile the Japanese Foreign Minister to his Chinese contract for John Brown, and Hall was informed that he had actually raised 100,000 dollars 'on the strength of a forged contract for seven battleships'. Neither the contract nor the battleships were ever heard of again – except perhaps in Backhouse's statement to Bodley's Librarian, four years later, that he was suing a shipbuilding firm for £30,000: presumably his commission on those ghostly battleships of 1917.

Such is the history of Backhouse's agency for John Brown as far as it is revealed by available evidence. The inference is obvious. The idea of the warships may have been reasonable when first advanced by Boyle but it became chimerical once it was taken over by Backhouse. The contract was presumably spurious: we cannot help noting that Backhouse announced it soon after returning from his triumphal reception in New York, when he had produced the forged contract with the Bank Note Company, and that he afterwards retreated and failed to produce the text just at the time when the Bank Note Company's contract was found to be a forgery. The chronological symmetry is remarkable and perhaps instructive. In any case the ships never materialised. The whole fantasy dissolved when Hall and the Bank Note Company closed in upon him and Backhouse judged it prudent, behind a patriotic smokescreen, to bolt from Peking and go to ground in Victoria, British Columbia. After that, the agency was over, and only the recriminations and lawsuits were left.

Of these recriminations, the files of the British Legation in Peking contain some tantalising hints. On 24 October 1918, the Foreign Office, prompted by John Brown & Co., cabled to the British minister in Peking about a sealed parcel of documents which Backhouse had apparently deposited in the Legation on the eve of his disappearance from Peking a year before. These documents, it was now said, were the property of John Brown & Co. The company had been seeking to trace both Backhouse and the documents for some time. Now that Backhouse had emerged from hiding, and the documents had been located, the Company had enlisted the help of the Foreign Office, and the minister was now instructed not to allow the said package to be opened except in the presence of the company's authorised representatives, or to be removed by anyone without their authority. If Backhouse should claim that the documents were his property, the minister was requested to hold them in the Legation until the title had been decided at law.

To this cable, Jordan replied that Backhouse had deposited the documents with a member of the Legation – presumably Alston or Barton – in a purely personal capacity, for safe-keeping during his absence, with certain instructions for disposal in the event of his death. Backhouse was now found to be alive in Japan and had 'declined absolutely to hand the papers over to John Brown & Co. pending settlement of questions at issue between them'. This being so, Jordan saw grave objections to the proposals of the Foreign Office. There was no reason to involve the Legation in a purely private controversy between Backhouse and his former employers; and he urged that the matter be left to the parties to settle between themselves. He had already allowed the legation to be involved with Backhouse once, and he had no wish to repeat that mistake. No doubt, by now, he was heartily sick of Backhouse and all his doings.

The Foreign Office accepted this argument and informed John Brown & Co. accordingly. However, the company was not prepared to give up. What was in the package, we do not know, but evidently the company regarded it as very important. Soon after making its formal application to the Foreign Office, and without waiting for a reply, the company followed it up with an informal approach. Miles Lampson in Peking received a personal letter from his friend and fellow Etonian, Stephen Gaselee: a classical scholar, bibliophile and Fellow of Magdalene College, Cambridge, temporarily employed in the Foreign Office and engaged in the dissemination of Allied war propaganda. Gaselee informed Lampson that one of his friends, a director of the associated firms of John Brown & Co. and Palmer & Co., had approached him with a specific request. These companies had for some time employed Sir Edmund Backhouse to work for them in China, but had parted company with him about August 1917. They had reason to think that, when this happened, Backhouse had left at the Legation a sealed packet containing documents, many of which were their property, with instructions that it was to be delivered only to himself or his agent. Could Lampson discover whether this was so, and, if so, arrange that the packet should only be opened in the presence of the Company's representative? His friend, Gaselee took care to add, was 'a good and generous supporter of our propaganda'.

The Minister having declared his objection, and the Foreign Office having endorsed it, Lampson prudently delayed his reply to this private approach. But John Brown & Co. did not accept defeat. A fortnight later Lord Aberconway decided to dispense with intermediaries and go to the top. He enlisted the support of the Foreign Minister, who thereupon re-opened the matter and sent a personal telegram to Jordan requesting him to hold the documents until the question of their proper disposal had been settled. Jordan, however, adopted delaying tactics. He did nothing. Then, on 5 December, Backhouse himself returned to China to resolve the deadlock. He went privately to his diplomatic friend and collected the packet. When Jordan finally yielded to the pressure of the Foreign Minister, he was informed that it was too late: the documents were out of reach. Jordan sent for Backhouse, and Backhouse stated that the papers were now in the hands of Mr J. G. C. Minchin, of Messrs Minchin & Garrett of Lincoln's Inn, who had instructions to arrange the terms on which the company might recover them. A letter from the company to Backhouse, sent through the Foreign Office for personal delivery in Peking, was similarly passed on to Mr Minchin.

Thus Backhouse's agency for John Brown, like his agency for the Bank Note Company, ended in the hands of the lawyers. What settlement, if any, was ultimately reached, we do not know: this time the terms were not reported to the Legation, which was glad to keep out of the affair. All that we know is that Backhouse claimed to be owed £30,000. Perhaps he was holding the documents as hostages for that sum. If so, he was disappointed. There is no record, in the available financial papers of the company, that Backhouse, after leaving its employment, received any payment from it.

So ended the story of Backhouse's career as an entrepreneur. It had been a glorious career – or rather a glorious pipe-dream –

while it lasted. Fleets of battleships, millions of bank-notes, arms for warring nations, imperial jewels, had been the substance of it. Cabinet ministers, industrial magnates, high financiers, envoys extraordinary of four nations had been involved. But now all was over. The dreadful Hall had been the catalyst who brought the whole speculative structure tumbling down. In future, ambassadors and businessmen would be more careful, and we shall hear no more of Backhouse as an entrepreneur. But the fantasy of selling imaginary battleships, first generated by the agency for John Brown & Co., did not so easily disappear. Long afterwards, in 1931, Backhouse would write to his brother, Admiral Sir Roger Backhouse, then Third Sea Lord, saying that he was acting on behalf of the Chinese government, and offering to buy any old British battleships. The letter, as always, was plausible and at first it was taken seriously; only afterwards was it found to be pure fantasy.

Apart from that last pale flicker, Backhouse's dream of wealth through commercial enterprise ceased with his final return to China in 1921. From now on, his speculations were confined to literature. From battleships and bank-notes we return to diaries, memoirs and *chroniques scandaleuses*.

CHAPTER NINE

The Diaries

WE have already seen that the core of *China under the Empress Dowager* (as also of *Annals and Memoirs of the Court of Peking*) consisted of the authentic Chinese documents which distinguished it from the numerous superficial biographies published at the time. These original documents were supplied by Backhouse, in his own translations; but Bland 'revised' those translations. That is, he went over them and sometimes modified the English style, 'without reference to the originals', most of which he had not seen, but without in any way altering the sense. There is no reason to suppose that he took any unreasonable liberties with the subject matter: he was solely concerned to present it in a simple and intelligible form. The most important single document was, of course, the diary of Ching-shan. It was this document which had attracted publishers and readers alike. But Ching-shan's diary, though by far the longest document, was only one among many. As Morrison had observed, 440 out of 500 pages had been supplied by Backhouse in the form of his translations.

We have also seen that, from the beginning, Morrison had challenged the authenticity of the diary of Ching-shan, roundly declaring it to be a fake. Such a challenge, from such a quarter, was, as Bland's publisher William Heinemann stated, very alarming: it could sink the credit of the book. Therefore Bland had pressed Morrison to prove or deny his allegations. Thus challenged, Morrison had denied them. But no sooner had he denied them, in writing, both to Bland and to Backhouse – somewhat disingenuously seeking to transfer his doubts to Bland – than he began to repeat them orally. It is clear that he regarded his own denial as a tactical necessity only. He believed, or at least was determined to have it believed, that the diary was a 'fake'. On what grounds he held this belief (assuming that he was personally convinced and not merely unscrupulous), we do not know; but since he did not know Chinese and had not seen the text, we have assumed, provisionally, either that he had circumstantial reasons for rejecting Backhouse's story of the discovery of the manuscript, or that he had been explicitly told of its fabrication by someone whom he was unwilling or unable to produce as a witness. As we do not know his authority we cannot judge its reliability.

Although Morrison was once again working closely with Backhouse in the period 1911–12, it does not seem that he ever challenged him directly on this delicate subject. Perhaps he thought it pointless to do so. If he was already certain in his own mind, why should he argue with someone who had an interest in maintaining an opposite position, and of whose services, at that time, he had need? There is indeed one letter from Backhouse to Morrison at the time of the publication of the book, in which Backhouse describes, briefly but circumstantially, his discovery of the diary; but Morrison, in answering this letter, did not take the matter up. It seems that his view was already fixed.

In the remaining ten years of his life, Morrison continued to maintain, in private, that Ching-shan's diary was forged, and this view, supported by his authority, was repeated by others. One of those who repeated it was Sir John Jordan. Jordan stoutly maintained that the diary existed only in English and 'emanated from the brain of one of the authors of *China under the Empress Dowager*'. Bland insisted that Jordan had never gone into the question: he simply took his opinion from Morrison. This was unfair: Jordan had a mind of his own; and we may recall (what Bland did not know) that after 1915 he knew something about Backhouse's powers of imagination. Morrison himself took care not to publish his opinion, for he knew that he could not sustain it in argument, and he had no desire to incur a second challenge. But his conviction never wavered. In 1918, when he had dropped Backhouse and was compiling the dossier of his frauds against Hall and the American Bank Note Company, Morrison saw no need for discretion: he then described Backhouse summarily as 'author of the faked diary' of Ching-shan.

Another man who took his views from Morrison was the Italian diplomatist Daniele Varè. Varè arrived in Peking in 1912 as secretary to the Italian Legation, and stayed there till 1920. In Peking, he soon became a close friend of Morrison. Nearly twenty years later, Varè wrote a popular biography of the Empress Dowager, in which he gave extensive extracts from Ching-shan's diary and noted, incidentally, that Morrison had believed it to be a forgery and had stated that Backhouse himself had forged it with the aid of his Manchu teacher. If it was really a forgery, wrote Varè, it was, even as such, a most valuable work of art: 'the point of view of the old China could not be better presented, or represented'. Since Morrison left Peking in 1918, and died two years later, it is clear that Varè heard this from Morrison between 1912 and 1918. Incidentally, in 1910, Heinemann had reported that if he remembered aright Morrison had been quoted as saying that the diary had been composed by Backhouse's 'boy': an idea which Backhouse had been able to ridicule. Probably he was even then referring to Backhouse's Manchu teacher.

We may even go a little further in speculation. In his letter to Morrison immediately after the publication of the book, Backhouse had made two interesting observations. First, after saying that he had found the diary in the house which he had occupied after the siege of the Legations, he added, 'you probably remember the insolence of the man En Ch'un, the son of old Ching-shan and his arrest and subsequent execution for patronising Boxers. It was he whose ears you boxed so violently.' This suggests that Morrison was present when Backhouse entered Ching-shan's house, or at least was closely involved with the occupation of it and the arrest of En Ch'un. Secondly, describing his custody of the diary, Backhouse told Morrison that 'your former landlord in the Imperial City, Mr Kung, who was at that time my writer' had copied out some parts of the diary for him, 'as at that time I had difficulty in reading the running hand'. Nearly three months later, Backhouse repeated this statement to Bland, adding that he still possessed parts of Kung's transcription. If Kung was both Backhouse's writer and Morrison's landlord, Morrison may well have had information from him, and this information may have been the basis of his allegations. That does not necessarily mean that the information was correct.

At all events, while Morrison kept to his view, Bland, relying on Backhouse's circumstantial assertions, kept to his. In his opinion – and it is an opinion regularly expressed by those who, to this day, have insisted on the authenticity of the diary – 'no one *could* fake it'. The manuscript was written in a very difficult 'grass-hand'. 'The man is not born who could fake a document like that,' wrote Bland, and he added that, anyway, the original manuscript was in the British Museum, where he himself had deposited it, available for the critics to see and expose if they could. In fact, nobody who had seen it, and was qualified to judge, had expressed any doubts about its authenticity. Backhouse himself took the matter in his stride, and soon after the publication of their first book he was discovering new diaries which he was offering to Bland, adding, rather wearily, 'No doubt the authenticity will be challenged, but I am getting used to that.' A week later he returned to the subject, adding 'I can get similar diaries if I remain in China, but it is thankless work if one is accused of fabricating them.' However, time and history, he felt, were on his side; Ching-shan's diary was accepted as genuine by the best judges: 'the diary is constantly quoted', he would write in 1915, 'in good Chinese papers by memoir-writers on the Manchus.'

So the matter remained for ten years after the publication of *China under the Empress Dowager*. Then, in 1920, after the death of Morrison, a serious attempt was made to settle the question. Encouraged by Lionel Giles, J. J. L. Duyvendak, a learned Dutch sinologue, undertook a scholarly examination of the manuscript now lying, in Giles's custody, in the British Museum. Duyvendak's intention was to publish the original Chinese text in the learned periodical *T'oung Pao*. In order to do this he needed the permission of Bland, as legal owner of the manuscript, and Bland, in correspondence with him, mentioned the doubts which had been cast on the authenticity of the document, but which he did not share. Others still entertained these doubts, and, because of them, the editors of *T'oung Pao* in the end declined to publish the disputed text. But Duyvendak finally published his own translation of the text, and his commentary on it, in another learned periodical, *Acta Orientalia*, in 1924.

In his commentary, Duyvendak made some criticisms of the

translation published by Bland and Backhouse. He observed that their version was very free and that some entries were even differently dated. He also noticed some rather surprising facts. For instance, in many respects Backhouse's text did not bear out his own description of the diary. Moreover, the speeches ascribed in the diary to the Empress Dowager were remarkably similar to the texts of imperial edicts. There were also some other curious features. However, he commented, none of these facts warranted distrust of the document itself. Duyvendak concluded that the diary was authentic; and he wrote to Bland that he hoped he had proved, 'to everyone's satisfaction, that Dr Morrison's statement was entirely baseless'. This was very gratifying to Backhouse and Bland.

Nor was this all. Duyvendak's decisive verdict was soon followed by spontaneous support from an equally disinterested source. This was Sir Reginald Johnston, the scholar-administrator whom we have already met as district officer of Weihaiwei. Since then, Johnston had been tutor to P'u-i, the last Emperor of China, and he was now Professor of Chinese Language and Literature in the University of London. In a learned review of Duyvendak's translation. Johnston endorsed Duyvendak's verdict of the authenticity of the diary. He had, he said, shown the fac-simile of part of the diary, which Backhouse and Bland had published, to two scholars, a Chinese and a Manchu, both familiar with the court of the Empress Dowager, and each had declared that he recognised the handwriting of Ching-shan. Duyvendak's authoritative work, Johnston now declared, proved that Ching-shan's diary, which 'constituted the most valuable and interesting chapter' in Bland and Backhouse's book, was unquestionably genuine, 'a document of high value' and a most important historical source. It established the true history of the attitude of the Chinese court towards the Boxer movement, and, in particular, of Jung-lu's strenuous efforts to protect the legations. Those who had questioned the authenticity of the document – and they included some, like Sir John Jordan, 'who should have known better' – were now finally refuted. Since Johnston (as we shall see) positively disliked Backhouse, his support in this matter was particularly valuable.

To complete the good work and enable the case to be declared closed, only one small task remained to be done. There still remained, in Backhouse's hands, those parts of the original diary which he had not translated and which, therefore, had not been deposited in the British Museum. In order to round off his work Duyvendak promised to translate and publish these parts also – of course with Sir Edmund's permission. Sir Edmund readily agreed to supply the manuscript. Later, when Duyvendak applied to see the manuscript, Sir Edmund put him off, saying that he had now decided to publish the document himself, with explanatory notes. The learned world could thus rest assured that it would soon see the remaining evidence.

Thus the question so maliciously raised by Morrison in 1910 seemed at last laid to rest, and Bland, whose credit was involved in it, was much relieved. Six years later, when Daniele Varè's Italian biography of the Empress Dowager was sent to him, for his opinion, by an English publisher, he could afford to take a high line. According to Bland, Varè had been taken in by Morrison; he had also made insufficient acknowledgments to Bland and Backhouse, whose work he had so extensively used; and he showed lamentable ignorance about the true history of Chingshan's diary. These comments were passed on to Varè, who, being no scholar and a practised diplomatist, knew when to surrender, and how to surrender gracefully. In the English edition of his book, when it appeared, he made proper acknowledgments; he flattered Bland personally and declared that his own work had been inspired by that of Bland and Backhouse; and although he still mentioned Morrison's doubts about the diary, he handled them more circumspectly. He referred to them only in a footnote and contrived to express them with diplomatic urbanity. If Morrison was right, he wrote, 'Sir Edmund Backhouse appears worthy to be classed with the famous translator of Ossian's poems'. In fact, if Morrison was right, Backhouse would have been in a higher class than Macpherson; for Macpherson, unlike him, never produced the original manuscript which he claimed to have translated.

That was in 1930–31. Next year, after many years of silence, Bland found himself in direct correspondence with Backhouse again. The question of Ching-shan's diary having been so happily settled, a new project had formed in that fertile mind.

The dialogue between the two old partners was reopened by Bland. He was now in his seventieth year, and he wished to make arrangements about copyright in their joint works in the event of his death. Backhouse roused himself from his hermit life to reply. He would gladly sell all his rights, he said, for ten pounds. Then, having regained contact with his old partner, he persisted in it. Three months later, in October 1932, he was writing to propose another joint venture. He announced that he had discovered a new diary, even more important, even more worthy of publication, than that of Ching-shan. In order to understand the significance of this new diary, and the part which it was to play in the repetitive Backhouse syndrome, we must go back to the last years of the Manchu dynasty, the years of the original collaboration of Backhouse and Bland.

We have seen that Backhouse, after the publication of *China under the Empress Dowager*, announced to Bland that he had discovered a new diary, and, indeed, was confident of discovering more, if he should stay in China; though he added rather wearily that it was thankless work if he were to be accused, as he probably would be, of fabricating them. He did not at that time specify the author of the diary which he had found, or might find, and the fragments which he sent to Bland in 1911 were described by him as unsuitable for use in *Annals and Memoirs of the Court of Peking*. However, on 17 January 1915, a year after that book had appeared, Backhouse, who was then in London, wrote to Bland a letter containing a cryptic sentence. Yüan Shih-k'ai, he said, would never forgive either of them for their book on the Empress Dowager, 'and I think, if we were Chinese, it would have been a case of "off with his head!" long ago. What he will say to the Eunuch's Memoirs when they appear, heaven only knows.' 'The Eunuch' can only mean the Grand Eunuch of the Empress Dowager, Li Lien-ying.

The Grand Eunuch, the head of the whole corps of eunuchs who administered the imperial household, was a figure of great importance at the court of the last Manchu Emperors, and Li Lien-ying, who held that post during almost the whole of the

Empress Dowager's long rule, acquired, in that period, immense and sinister power. We are told that he had originally been a cobbler in Peking; but one day he happened to witness the progress through the city of the Grand Eunuch An Tê-hai, with his numerous escort, saw the crowds driven from the great man's path, the pomp and arrogance of his manner and equipage, and, seeing all this, resolved himself to enter a profession which could bring such rewards. He therefore performed on himself the necessary operation and presented himself as a candidate for court service. In 1869 the Grand Eunuch An Tê-hai, on whom Tzŭ-hsi had become completely dependent, was summarily decapitated on the orders of her co-regent, and Li Lien-ying succeeded him. Throughout the next forty years he reigned over a huge and ever-growing corps of palace eunuchs, acquired by corruption, 'squeeze' and the sale of offices, a huge fortune, and was the political *éminence grise* of the Empress, dominating the politics of the Palace and always supporting the party of reaction; for the party of reform was committed to the abolition of the whole eunuch system by which he throve. One of the motive forces of the coup d'état of 1898 was Li Lien-ying's hatred and fear of the Kuang-hsü Emperor and of the 'Hundred Days' Reform' which so threatened his own privileges.

After that coup d'état, Li's power was greater than ever, and he is said to have boasted openly that he could make or mar any man and could defy the Emperor. In 1900 he threw his weight behind the pro-Boxer party at court; but, like his mistress, he contrived to disown it in defeat, and in the last years of the reign, when the obsolete monarchy was artificially preserved at the price of external concessions to the great powers, Li Lien-ying, with his domestic power and his corps of subordinate eunuchs, was preserved with it. In 1903 a Western visitor who was received in the Palace described him as 'a man of really exceptional ability', tall and thin, with 'a head like Savonarola', 'a Roman nose, a massive lean jaw, a protruding lip, and very shrewd eyes, full of intelligence, that shine out of sunken orbits. His face is much wrinkled and his skin like old parchment.' When the Kuang-hsü Emperor so dramatically and so narrowly predeceased the old Empress, it was naturally supposed that he had been murdered by the party of reaction, apprehensive of a return to the reforming policy of 1898, and Li Lien-ying was assumed to have organised his death. A year later, in November 1909, Li appeared at the Empress's ceremonial funeral, when her body was taken from its temporary resting-place in the Forbidden City to her specially prepared mausoleum in the Eastern Hills. Backhouse and Bland then described his appearance: 'smitten with age and sickness . . . scarcely able to totter the short distance which the cortège had to make on foot, he presented a pathetic and almost venerable spectacle, enough to make one forget for a moment the accumulated horrors of his seventy years of wickedness.'

Li Lien-ying might be a shadow of himself in 1909; but it was old age and the death of his patron, not any change of system, which had so reduced him. The eunuch system, which had so nearly been ended in 1898, had been saved by him, and it survived the death of Tzŭ-hsi and his own retirement. Under the nominal reign of the new infant Emperor, the new Empress Dowager faithfully continued the methods of the old. She modelled her rule, in every detail, on that of her aunt; and a new Grand Eunuch, Chang Yüan-fu, modelled himself no less faithfully on his predecessor, amassing for himself, by the same methods, immense power and wealth. However, the same methods could not be so successfully applied by different persons. The partnership of Tzŭ-hsi and Li Lien-ying had lasted nearly forty years; that of Lung-yu and Chang Yüan-fu lasted only three; and the eunuch system, which had led to the ruin of the last decadent Ming Emperors, and had been cut down by the Manchu conquerors, only to return and ruin their decadent successors, was finally swept away by the Republican reformers of 1912.

Li Lien-ying was still alive when Backhouse and Bland's book on the Empress Dowager was published. That book contained a whole chapter on 'Tzŭ-hsi and the Eunuchs', in which, of course, Li features at large, and the authors printed a facsimile letter of Li as evidence of his methods of extortion. In all his agitation about possible Chinese reactions to the book, Backhouse seems never to have worried about Li, who is so prominent in it and is represented throughout as the villain, though a fascinating and engaging villain, of the story. Presumably he considered that Li, old, ill and insulated from literature, would never know, or did not matter. Five months after the book was published, Backhouse wrote from Peking reporting Li's death. 'Poor old man,' he sighed, 'his last months were a time of cruel suffering.' 'I wonder that nobody wired the death of Li Lien-ying,' Bland replied. 'He was surely worth the honour of a *Times* obituary, if only as a picturesque figure in the human procession.' Bland sought to repair this omission by publishing an article on Li, presenting him as the central, and malevolent, influence at the court of the Empress. Backhouse (who had supplied the material for it) reported from Peking that Morrison declared Bland's article to be all wrong. Li, said Morrison, was 'a thoroughly good and honest man without any power, a sort of Chinese John Brown (of Balmoral) to Tzŭ-hsi. Hillier told him so. That settles it.'

Such was the man to whose 'memoirs' Backhouse enigmatically referred in 1915. This was the time when he was presenting documents to the Bodleian Library, applying for the Oxford chair, organising massive purchases of Chinese arms, crying poverty and declaring himself, in microscopic handwriting, too blind to read or write. At the same time Bland was contemplating a life of the Chinese statesman Li Hung-chang. Backhouse had warned him, in February 1913, that the memoirs of Li Hung-chang, which had just been published, authenticated by the former American Secretary of State, John W. Foster, were a fake, and Bland had been grateful for the warning, which proved that Backhouse was a skilful detector of forgeries. Bland's life of Li Hung-chang, on which Backhouse had offered to collaborate, was published in 1917.

After this brief and cryptic reference in 1915, we hear no more of the alleged diaries or memoirs of Li Lien-ying until 1923 when, as we have seen, M. E. Weatherall came to Oxford to check some of Backhouse's statements. Backhouse, according to Weatherall, claimed to have translated much or all of the diary of Li Lien-ying, and had stated in Peking that both the original diary and his own translation of it were among the documents which he had deposited in the Bodleian. Weatherall, however, sought for these documents in vain. He found no Chinese text and only two typed pages of alleged 'translation'. After that, silence falls for another nine years.

The silence was broken in October 1932 when Backhouse had resumed his long-interrupted correspondence with Bland. Backhouse then suddenly informed Bland that Li Lien-ying's great-nephew, also called Li, was about to publish the Grand Eunuch's memoirs, which, he said, were 'about as long as the Queen's journal' and 'very engrossing, although I have not read the whole in manuscript'. The memoirs contained reports of long conversations with foreign ministers, 'a meeting with Dr Morrison, whom he stigmatises as "a liar", a full narrative of the Boxers, the circumstances of the Old Buddha's death'. All this, of course, could be historically very important, and it was particularly useful to have Dr Morrison's veracity thus destroyed. No less useful was the confirmation which these memoirs brought to the judgment of Backhouse and Bland on the Empress Dowager. 'On the whole, you get the impression of a kind-hearted, playful, kittenish woman, amiable to a fault until she suspects you of tampering with her dignity, when she becomes simply *awful*. It amply confirms our view of her. . . . I have done a good deal of work, but fancy it is too long to publish or to find a market.' Then Backhouse went on to describe his way of life in Peking since he had ceased to travel to England. He had gone native and, 'by wearing Chinese dress (as is my habit now) I am able to go about with delightful freedom and in company with Chinese friends to pass as an *indigène*'.

Bland took up the offer at once. He was glad, he replied, to have 'your interesting account of your way of living, which seems the height of tranquil philosophy': Chinese-Manchu society was no doubt infinitely more interesting than that of the legations. He himself, at that time, was preoccupied with his battle against the dreadful Lionel Curtis and 'the Foreign Office School of Thought' which he regarded as 'one of the chief causes of the present rottenness of all things Chinese'; but he was attracted by the idea of another joint book, and he asked for more details about this new diary. Now that the critics of Ching-shan's diary had been so effectively repelled, and Duyvendak had given it his oracular confirmation, he could look back complacently on his previous experience of collaboration. Backhouse was now a respectable figure – in public at least. Bland knew all about his role as a benefactor of the Bodleian, but nothing about his later relations with that institution, or about his strange adventures as a secret or commercial agent. The record of these affairs was buried in the confidential files of the Foreign Office, of commercial companies and lawyers' offices, and in the private papers of Morrison, now safely dead. So Bland could take the new project seriously. He wrote off to his publisher telling him about Backhouse's new find. Backhouse, he said, 'is, as you know, a queer fellow', but the memoirs of 'that crafty ruffian' Li Lien-ying could not fail to be interesting, quite apart from the fact that they 'confirm at many points our story of the Empress Dowager'.

Thus encouraged, Backhouse wrote back. He offered to supply material from Li Lien-ying's memoirs for another historical book – provided, of course, that he could square the author's great-nephew. It would, he suggested, make exciting reading. 'There are some chapters in the Memoirs which suggest a page from Dumas and the doings of Catherine de Médicis. Poisons brought from Italy in the Ming dynasty which kill by the scent, or a glove steeped in a certain fluid which brings immediate death to the wearer; a horrid account of the Eastern Empress's murder; how Kuang-hsü died. And yet with all these atrocities you are left with the impression of a very lovable woman.' All this sounded very exciting, for although there were, inevitably, dark rumours of murder, the Eastern Empress was said to have died by suicide, and the Kuang-hsü Emperor was said to have died naturally. Then Backhouse added, '*your* memoirs should be interesting', and, more enigmatically, 'I have had an interesting life, although in a hidden way – behind the scenes, I mean.' What he meant by this Æsopian phrase, we shall soon see.

Two months later – on 3 March 1933 – Backhouse wrote to Bland reporting further progress. He had now seen Li Lien-ying's great-nephew, he said, and was able to describe the manuscript in detail. 'In all', he wrote, 'there are about one-and-a-half million characters and he is publishing the whole with a Chinese firm. I tell him it is too long, but he says, not from a Chinese point of view. However, that is his business. The question is, what to extract. I shall hope to send you a specimen shortly, so that you may judge.' It was gratifying, incidentally, that Li's account 'agrees entirely with us' on the Boxer Rising and the death of the

Pearl Concubine, and that 'Li says Morrison defrauded him, so he repaid him with false information'. That, of course, accounted perfectly for some of Morrison's deviations from the correct Backhousian version of events.

Bland again responded with interest and pressed for samples. He was sure such a book would go well. He was shortly going to lecture in America. Perhaps he could arrange for serialisation there. 'The revelations of the Chief Eunuch's diary' would surely attract the readers of that great continent.

Backhouse seemed reluctant to send samples, but he continued to feed Bland with tempting details culled from the memoirs and to describe new developments in the negotiations. These were not (he explained) entirely smooth. The Eunuch's great-nephew had published an extract from the memoirs in a Shanghai newspaper, and this extract contained adverse reflections on Sun Yat-sen, including the Empress Dowager's tart comments on him. Such irreverence towards its founding father had offended the Kuomintang government, which had forbidden the publication of the work in China. This was an inconvenient hitch, but it was not insuperable: the owner was now trying to have the original text published in Japan, and Backhouse had heard – though he could not yet confirm the report – that a German publisher was bidding for the German rights. He was himself trying to obtain the British and American rights and expected to succeed, though the English publisher John Lane had been in Peking and was interested. The owner, said Backhouse, wanted rather a large sum, $3000, but he had offered $2000, which he hoped would be accepted. Backhouse would then give Bland a half share gratis in return for his generosity in the old days, over *China under the Empress Dowager*.

The reference to John Lane the publisher, and his visit to Peking in 1932, might well have surprised Bland. John Lane, the founder of The Bodley Head publishing house, the publisher of the *Yellow Book*, the friend and patron of Aubrey Beardsley, Max Beerbohm, and all their circle, would indeed be the obvious publisher, in Backhouse's eyes, of a new work of chinoiserie. Unfortunately, he was in no position to bid for it. He had died in 1925.

The negotiations went on. The Chinese owner claimed that he had sold the German rights for $1500 and he offered the British and American rights for $3000 (an absurd price! said Bland). Gradually he came down to $2500: perhaps he would come down further. Then the Kuomintang government gave the last push which clinched the deal. The owner heard that the memoirs were about to be seized by the police; he appealed to Backhouse to receive and protect them; and 'they are now in my custody', 'packed in an enormous box'. Backhouse had undertaken (he said) to pay $2500 'for *all* rights', including the German.

Backhouse announced this last coup in October 1934. Curiously, the matter was then carried no further. The reason for this sudden silence is not apparent. Perhaps some of the correspondence is missing. However that may be, the memoirs of Li Lien-ying, having at last been physically secured by Backhouse, suddenly evaporate as mysteriously as they had arisen. I say 'mysteriously', because the attentive reader will not have failed to notice a strange inconsistency in Backhouse's story. These memoirs which, as Backhouse was now maintaining, had first been revealed to him in 1932, as an original untranslated manuscript held, for the last twenty-one years, by the Eunuch's great-nephew, had already, according to his own earlier story to Weatherall, been deposited by him, text and translation together, in the Bodleian Library before 1915. Nor would this be the last of their phantom appearances, or the last version of their history. Meanwhile, they receded into the shadows and were soon driven further back into them by the renewal of the great controversy over the manuscripts already supplied by Backhouse, and, in particular, by the most important of them, our old friend, the rival diary of Ching-shan.

CHAPTER TEN

The Controversy

EARLY in 1934, while Backhouse (according to his own account) was negotiating with Li Lien-ying's great-nephew, Bland found himself once again forced to fight a battle in defence of Backhouse's manuscripts and translations. This time the challenge came from an American scholar, Kenneth Scott Latourette, formerly a missionary in China, now Professor of Missions at the Divinity School at Yale University, and the author of the standard work on Christian Missions in China. In the bibliography of his new book on China, *The Chinese, their History and Culture*, published by The Macmillan Company of New York (then controlled by Macmillan & Co., London), Professor Latourette had cited both *China under the Empress Dowager* and *Annals and Memoirs of the Court of Peking*, but had seen fit to remark that the authors of these two works had taken 'melodramatic liberties' with 'improperly selected' Chinese texts. This wounding remark was duly drawn to the attention of Bland, already engaged in controversy with the supercilious grandees of Chatham House and somewhat impatient of the 'Westernised Chinese intellectuals' and their sanctimonious patrons in Britain and, especially, America.

Bland was very cross. Having seen the diary of Ching-shan finally (as it seemed) vindicated by Duyvendak, he now found these pestilential critics assailing, no doubt equally improperly, another part of his documentation. He therefore wrote direct to the American professor demanding an explanation. Latourette replied that he had accepted the criticism from 'the Chinese and foreign members, highly respected in scholarly circles, of the department of history in one of the better universities of China'. This vague and evasive reply incensed Bland still further, and he

wrote back to Latourette in strong terms. These loose and
defamatory criticisms, he wrote, were now admitted by their
author to rest not on any critical study of the documents but
merely on the irresponsible and undocumented opinion, or
prejudice, of unnamed persons in an unnamed Chinese university.
That would not do. Unless Latourette published a recantation,
he must expect a writ. Latourette stood his ground and replied,
giving specific instances. He cited several passages where material
had been selected for its 'romantic and startling qualities' and was
'too highly coloured'. Bland thereupon determined to deal with
this 'silly bloke' whose motive was only too clear: for obviously
he was seeking revenge for Bland's criticism of American mission
colleges in China. So he protested to his enemy's publishers. The
Macmillan Company replied that Professor Latourette was now
inaccessible: unfortunately he was preaching the Word in Mongolia; but Bland was not to be put off. He insisted on a withdrawal: if not from the author, then from the publishers. Backhouse, who was watching the battle from afar, congratulated him
on his dignified stand and offered to come from Peking to London
to bear witness in court. All the original manuscripts, he said,
were still available as evidence if necessary. In the end it was not
necessary to produce them. The publishers, without consulting
their author, inserted an apologetic erratum slip in his book.
Bland was satisfied with this victory. Macmillan's, he wrote to a
friend, had apologised for the Professor's silly remarks, though
he would not do so himself. Poor fellow, he saw everything
through Western missionary eyes: 'he should go a-fishing.'
Latourette's work was to prove a popular textbook and to be
frequently reprinted; but even after the deaths of Backhouse and
Bland, the criticism of their work was never reinstated in it.

The language used by Bland in these controversies, first with
Varè, then with Latourette, is the language of an angry man. Is it
also the language of a self-confident man? On the face of it,
Bland had grounds for self-confidence. He had, admittedly, taken
Backhouse's documents on trust. But all agreed that Backhouse
was a brilliant Chinese scholar, and even Morrison, while seeking
to undermine their joint work, had himself continued to rely on
his scholarship. In the case of Ching-shan's diary, Bland had seen

the text and was convinced that nobody could have forged it. Other good judges shared that conviction. Nobody except Morrison, and those who took their opinions from Morrison, had ventured to challenge its authenticity. Now Morrison had been routed by the internationally recognised expert Duyvendak, and Duyvendak's judgment had been confirmed by the impartial scholar Sir Reginald Johnston. In these circumstances, the borrowed phrases of a light-weight littérateur like Varè or the conventional wisdom of an American missionary like Latourette might well seem merely captious.

And yet, could Bland be quite sure? He had had his own experiences with Backhouse. He knew him to be 'a queer fish', 'erratic', 'weak', 'gelatinous'. Apart from Ching-shan's diary, he had never seen the Chinese originals of which Backhouse had provided the translations. He could guarantee nothing. Even if – thanks to Duyvendak – he could ward off these assaults, was it altogether prudent to commit himself to the authenticity of new Chinese memoirs authenticated only by Backhouse? There were so many bogus Chinese memoirs in circulation. There was the forged diary of Li Hung-chang. There were the memoirs of the bogus 'Princess' Der Ling, whose claims to have been a member of the Empress Dowager's court he was at this moment, in alliance with Sir Reginald Johnston, exposing. Perhaps the attack by Latourette, which so visibly exasperated him, made Bland doubt the wisdom of persevering with Backhouse's newly discovered 'memoirs' of Li Lien-ying. And then, before any samples of that work could arrive, the tide of confidence began to turn. In 1936, two years after forcing Latourette's publishers to eat humble pie on his behalf, and just after opening negotiations with an enterprising young French bookseller and publisher in Peking, Henri Vetch, for a new edition of *China under the Empress Dowager*, Bland had to face a new attack on Ching-shan's diary; and this time it could not be brushed aside.

This new attack was made by William Lewisohn, a British journalist who was then editing a local paper in Shanghai. Lewisohn was a good Chinese scholar and he also supported Bland's views on China as against those of Morrison and the 'Foreign Office School of Thought'. But he did not share Bland's confidence in Ching-shan's diary. In a letter to Bland he would afterwards explain how his doubts had been aroused. He had been writing an account of the siege of the legations, and he had found Ching-shan's diary both inaccurate and incredible. For instance, Ching-shan had quoted Jung-lu as saying, 'The attack on the Legations . . . is worse than an outrage, it is a stupidity.' Any literate European would recognise the well-known phrase of Talleyrand, and would have known 'that it was the last thing a Chinese would ever think of saying'.

Once aroused, Lewisohn made a close study of the document and then published his findings in the form of an article in the learned press. In this article he showed, by careful internal analysis, that the diary could not have been written as a diary, that it could not be the genuine work of one man, and that it could not have been written by Ching-shan. He showed that it was, to some extent, a pastiche, for it incorporated verbatim passages from the contemporary published account by the Grand Secretary Wang Wên-shao. Then, turning from analysis of the text to scrutiny of the circumstances in which it was said to have been discovered, Lewisohn asked some pertinent questions. In particular, how was it that Backhouse, who had so recently arrived in China, had been able at once to recognise the significance of a document written in a peculiarly difficult 'grass-hand' which even eminent sinologues could not read without help? And how was it that the diary, allegedly discovered in 1900, was never heard of by anyone until Backhouse produced it, and his translation of it, in 1910? When his article was complete, Lewisohn sent copies of it to both Backhouse and Bland.

When Bland read Lewisohn's article, he was deeply disturbed. Here at last was evidence, formidable evidence, which seemed to justify Morrison and his followers. In his anxiety he wrote at once to Backhouse. He reminded Backhouse that he himself had taken the diary on trust from him, having 'of course, no sufficient scholarship to be able to read that text or verify your translation'. Therefore it was for Backhouse to answer these formidable criticisms; and Bland pointed out that, unless they were answered, Latourette, whom he had so recently ground in the dust on Back-house's behalf, would be vindicated. Meanwhile Bland wrote to

Lewisohn and to Henri Vetch seeking to keep them at bay until Backhouse should answer. But his letters did not conceal his anxiety. Why, he asked, did not some Chinese scholar examine the disputed text? Why had Backhouse never fulfilled his promise to publish the untranslated portions of the text, with explanatory notes? And why had he never produced evidence – which in 1911 he had said that he could easily do – to prove that the writing was that of Ching-shan? 'I preserve an open mind', he wrote to Vetch; and he added, 'if the diary were proved to be a fake, it would rank as one of the most remarkable curiosities of literature, much more remarkable, as a feat of scholarship, than the bogus memoirs of Li Hung-chang'.

Everything thus depended on Backhouse. How would Backhouse answer the challenge: the most serious, the best-documented charge yet brought against his scholarship and his integrity as a scholar? Lewisohn in Peking and Bland in his retirement at Aldeburgh waited eagerly for his reaction.

To Lewisohn Backhouse replied with Olympian urbanity. He thanked him for the article, which, he said, 'will be a valuable addition to my library'. The content of the article he entirely ignored. To Bland he wrote at greater length, but again without facing the substance of the article. But with his letter he enclosed a long document, described as 'A Footnote to *China under the Empress Dowager*', in which he gave another account, fuller, more vivid, more detailed than ever, of the circumstances in which he had found the diary. This 'Footnote' – his last and completest word on the subject – was afterwards presented by Bland to the British Museum, where it remains, together with the diary itself, as the ultimate corroboration of its authenticity – or at least as clear evidence that Backhouse personally discovered it, in its finished form, in Ching-shan's own study, three days after the author's death. As such, it is a very persuasive document.

In his 'Footnote', Backhouse described in detail his visit to Ching-shan's house which, after the occupation of Peking by the Allies, had been allocated to him as his own residence. He named the British officers who had accompanied him and witnessed the events. He described the scene in Ching-shan's house and study: in the main room, Mme Ching-shan moaning and murmuring on the K'ang while her younger son and daughter-in-law tried to persuade her to take some gruel; the study littered with inextricably confused papers 'several inches deep': valuable books, some of them 'interesting Sung philosophical works', mixed with scattered manuscripts thrown about in the search for loot. He described his discovery of the diary, and his immediate recognition of its importance. He protested that, so far from keeping a mysterious silence on his find, he had reported it to several persons at the time: to Captain Rowlandson, of the Baluchistan Regiment, who was 'greatly interested', to General Barrow 'for whom I was acting as interpreter', and who was also 'much interested', and to several other named officers. Later, when Sir Ernest Satow had arrived in Peking as minister, Backhouse (he now said) had at once told him too of his discovery, and Satow had 'strongly advised publication, but recommended that it be deferred till after the Empress's death'. If those persons had not mentioned the fact at the time, or indeed at any time, that was too bad. He also described the various papers of which, in addition to the diary, he had taken possession: for Captain Rowlandson, he said, had told him that he could keep the whole lot.

Why then, it might be asked, did Backhouse not produce the untranslated parts of the diary to satisfy legitimate historical and bibliographical interest? Alas, he replied, that was now impossible. 'A higher and more immediate interest, viz., *Bread-and-Butter Interest* and *Res angusta domi*' had obliged him to sell them in 1932, 'to keep the wolf from my door'. Nor could he say where they now were, for 'my former comprador, Mr Chang Ho-chai, who effected the sales, was murdered in his home here before handing me a full list of the purchasers'. The sale, Backhouse would write in a later letter, had been very useful: it had provided him with a much-needed sum of $700. Of course he had never realised how inconvenient it would be. Poor Chang Ho-chai – 'I never foresaw his cruel murder . . . I suspect he handled some "squeeze" and didn't want me to know too much. But *de mortuis. . . .*' As for Lewisohn, Backhouse knew how to deal with him: he would issue a writ for libel. With these two answers Backhouse seemed to think that the questions raised by Lewisohn would go quietly away.

Alas, they would not go away, and soon Lewisohn was joined by a more formidable, because a more famous, ally. In Leiden University, Professor Duyvendak had long been kept waiting for Backhouse's promised edition of the missing portion of the diary. In 1934, to excuse his own silence, or to force Backhouse's hand, he had publicly referred to that promise, and in 1936 he had approached Backhouse, through Bland, offering to buy the manuscript – only to be told that the manuscript was no longer available: it had been sold, to unknown purchasers. At this Duyvendak's suspicions were aroused. Then, when Lewisohn's article was published, suspicion was joined in his mind by another emotion: professional pride or jealousy. It seems, from his subsequent behaviour, that Duyvendak was mortified by Lewisohn's article. His own last public statement on the subject had been his article of 1920 which had authoritatively endorsed the authenticity of the diary. Now, just as doubt was entering his mind and he was preparing to reconsider his view, he, the professional, had been forestalled and his published article had been publicly refuted by an amateur in the subject. It was very disagreeable. He therefore decided, for the sake of his own credit as well as of scholarly truth, to enter the fray and recapture the central position which Lewisohn had usurped; and he wrote to Bland advising him to suspend judgment, for the oracle was about to speak.

Bland was gravely troubled in mind. Naturally he wished to believe that the diary and the other documents which he had similarly taken on trust from Backhouse were genuine. He still believed that Backhouse could not have forged such a manuscript and would not have deceived him. But unless Backhouse would produce evidence, how could the critics be answered? And this storm was blowing up at a most inconvenient time, just when he was arranging with Henri Vetch to publish a new edition of the work. . . . He therefore wrote firmly to Backhouse, calling upon him to face the challenge. It was quite pointless to issue writs for libel, he said; what was needed was scholarly refutation: he must publish a frank, reasoned and convincing answer to Lewisohn. Bland assured Backhouse that he himself was convinced by Backhouse's circumstantial account of the discovery of the document, but his statement that he had sold the manuscript was most damaging: it would be 'seriously detrimental to your reputation if this were published' – especially after the promise made to Duyvendak. After giving such a promise, 'I should have thought that you would have preferred to sell your shirt rather than these papers. . . .'

Backhouse, in reply, tried his pathetic style. 'I suppose my quiet hidden life makes enemies,' he moaned. He had been 'in the greatest destitution' and had had to sell not only his manuscripts but also his wardrobe, his books, his family heirlooms. As a matter of fact, since Bland had referred to his shirt, he felt obliged to admit that he had sold his shirt too – a dozen new silk shirts, at knockdown prices. He had only sixty cents left in the bank. Bishop Norris had lent him small sums. 'I often wondered in the morning where my dinner was to come from and even contemplated begging in the public way. An old Manchu friend, of the Imperial Household, seeing I was in rags, sent me 100 dollars, a kindness that touched me deeply. . . .'

Bland, in his letter, had not mentioned – perhaps he had not noticed – a curious and unusual inconsistency in Backhouse's circumstantial narrative. The attentive reader will recall that three years ago, in 1934, when Bland was threatening legal action against Latourette, Backhouse had offered to come to London and give evidence, adding that the original manuscripts were all available. And yet now he was stating that he had been obliged to sell his manuscripts in 1932, two years before that date. But no doubt Backhouse, if pressed, would have found means to reconcile this apparent discrepancy.

There were other discrepancies too which Bland could not have noticed, for he had not seen all the evidence. In particular, he had not seen the letter which Backhouse had sent to Morrison in October 1910. In that letter Backhouse had admitted his nine years' silence about his discovery of the document and explained it by saying that he had never regarded the document as important 'until both ffrench and Bland strongly advised its publication'. Now he was saying that, from the start, he had been 'convinced of its interest', and 'so far from observing a mysterious silence about my find', had informed the authorities, both military and civil, including the new British minister Sir Ernest Satow. It is unfortunate that Backhouse had not mentioned this in 1910, when Satow was still alive, and could have confirmed the statement. By 1937 he was conveniently dead. In his despatches from Peking Satow had never showed any sign of having seen the document, whose importance, according to Backhouse's new version of the events, he had immediately recognised. In the same letter to Morrison, Backhouse had also admitted that he had had difficulty in reading the 'grass-hand' in which the diary was written, and had had it transcribed for him. Now he was declaring that, on arrival in China, he was perfectly competent to read grass-hand and did in fact read the whole diary by himself. These are very damaging discrepancies. They show that Backhouse gave, in 1910 and in 1937, two incompatible versions of his own action. Each version is detailed and circumstantial; and a critical reader will note that the details added in 1937 had only been introduced into the story when they could no longer be checked.

However, it was not such discrepancies of detail which disturbed Bland when he read Backhouse's lamentable letter. What shocked him was Backhouse's extraordinary admission that he had sold the manuscript beyond recall, and the extraordinary poverty which he gave as the reason for the sale. In his dismay, he wrote to Henri Vetch in Peking to ask in confidence about Backhouse's finances. Was he really destitute? Had he really been forced, by sheer poverty, to sell that essential document? At the same time he wrote to David Fraser, who had succeeded Morrison and himself as *Times* correspondent in Peking. 'What is the truth', he asked, 'about my friend Backhouse? Is he dotty? Some weeks ago he wrote me that his condition of destitution had reached a point where, having sold his clothes, even the shirts off his back, and all his manuscripts (including the unpublished fragments of the famous Ching-shan diary), he seriously contemplated begging his bread in the streets. . . . Is he really hard up, or is he merely following in his father's footsteps as a miser? I have written strongly advising him not to embark on litigation but to publish the story of the finding of the diary, and his work in connexion with it, in a dignified pamphlet. I preserve an open mind myself about the authenticity of the diary, but can't help thinking that Lewisohn has overshot his mark. After all, the worthy Duyvendak, a good scholar, pronounced it genuine.'

Alas, the worthy Duyvendak was not now so sure. Three weeks later, he wrote to Bland forewarning him of the judgment which he was about to deliver. The essential phrase in the letter was, 'I have been compelled to change my opinion'.

Bland still fought for time. He urged Duyvendak to give Backhouse a chance to explain himself. He wrote to Backhouse; he wrote to Vetch begging him to prod Backhouse into the correct action. Duyvendak replied that he would himself write to Backhouse, but would not wait indefinitely for a reply. 'In my opinion, I have mathematical proof. Were I a judge, I should not hesitate to hang anybody on this evidence.' Admittedly he could not discover Backhouse's motive for forgery: 'it is an insoluble riddle, and I can only explain it by ascribing it to a kind of morbid psychology, that delights in mystification. . . .' But the crime itself was certain, and the sentence must be executed. Poor Backhouse, he sighed, as he lovingly fingered his noose and checked that the trap-door of his gallows was working smoothly, he felt sorry for him. 'With all his great gifts, he must lead a miserable existence.'

A miserable existence? That was not what Henri Vetch discovered when, at Bland's request, he went and called on Backhouse to discuss the matter. Armed with Bland's letter, he arrived at the house in the Western City to which Backhouse had moved since the murder of Chang Ho-chai, and there was met, as he wrote to Bland, by 'a charming old gentleman full of life and reminiscences'. 'I believe', he added, 'Sir Edmund has been given a reputation for moroseness in Peking, which does not stand the test of a single moment. . . . He lives in a fairly spacious Chinese house and garden and appears comfortably off.' Backhouse had no difficulty in convincing Vetch that he was being maligned: 'Sir Edmund tells me,' Vetch reported, 'that Dr Morrison started the forgery tale.'

Today, nearly forty years later, M. Vetch still remembers vividly that visit to the professedly destitute hermit of Peking. 'Sir Edmund received me', he writes, 'in the garden house which he occupied in the Western City of Peking. He was a man of great charm, tall and spare, bearded like Tolstoy, whom, in his youth (as he told me) he had visited at Yasnaya Polyana.' We shall hear more about the visit to Tolstoy. 'In his hand', Vetch continues, 'he held a glass of whisky, which his doctor had prescribed, to raise his blood-pressure. . . .' Altogether, Vetch found Backhouse a genial and congenial old gentleman, enjoying a certain *douceur de vivre*, without any signs of 'destitution', *'res angusta domi'* or shortage of bread and butter.

If Vetch was delighted with Backhouse, Backhouse was no less delighted with Vetch. In his reply to Bland, he chatted happily about his visitor: 'a charming cosmopolitan I find him. It is pleasant to find a young man of such enthusiasm and civilisation. . . .' As to that boring old question of the diary, he had nothing to add to the narrative which he had already sent. 'I can only say, once for all – and if it were with my latest breath I could not say otherwise – "the facts are as I have stated. The document was found as I have written. The whole of my narrative is a cold hard statement of fact".'

Bland was not impressed by Backhouse's solemn asseverations of veracity. 'Confidentially', he wrote to Vetch, 'I may say that Backhouse is notoriously untruthful, and of late I have also thought that his mind must be a little deranged, for in one letter he will say that he is so destitute that he has to sell his warm clothes and is seriously thinking of begging his bread in the streets, and in the next he proposes to spend £500 in libel proceedings against Lewisohn. Let that pass.'

All attempts to gain time in which Backhouse might answer Duyvendak's article were doomed to failure, for Backhouse had no intention of answering it, before or after publication, any more than he intended to answer Lewisohn. Bland pressed him particularly on one of Lewisohn's points: 'I confess that I find it very difficult to imagine how a passage from Wang Wên-shao's diary can have got into that of Ching-shan, but the fact seems undeniable, and I await your explanation of the phenomenon with interest, not entirely free from anxiety.'

The phenomenon was not explained – at least not yet. Bland was frustrated by his inability to make any contact with his old collaborator, the sole possible defender of his own credit. One vital letter was returned by the Post Office, having been – not for the first time – 'refused by addressee' as under-stamped. Others were ignored. The personal emissary, Vetch, had been seduced. Duyvendak's own letter, like that of Lewisohn, was courteously acknowledged without any mention of its contents. If Backhouse did write to Bland, it was only to lament his poverty or his illness. He pretends not to receive letters, Bland wrote to Vetch, or to be ill, but 'the ailments are generally diplomatic and, as you say, he is an active and cheerful old gentleman in real life'.

In his next letter, Backhouse resumed the melancholy catalogue of his sufferings. He had been down with pneumonia for the last three and a half weeks, he wrote. 'If I recover, I shall occupy myself with the reply to Professor Duyvendak. My long privations and hardships over so many years have greatly affected a constitution which was never too robust.' A month later, he was still (he said) very ill: but for the care of Dr Aspland, the embassy doctor, 'I should, ere this, have been a denizen of the Yellow Springs'. However, he was well enough to issue writs. Lawyers had been instructed, counsel's opinion sought. He had had enough of this persecution, he declared. All his life he had been persecuted. It was true that, as a foolish youth, he had been rather extravagant – £5000 borrowed at sixty per cent interest from the Shylocks of London, a 'bogus racing debt' of £42,000. It was true that, at Oxford, he had had 'a prolonged mental breakdown'. But all other charges against him were pure calumny. He had even been slandered as '*homosexual*, the basest of untruths. . . . This since I knew Oscar Wilde in the days of his fame and admired his wit, knowing nothing of his perverted tastes. I knew him, Max Beerbohm, Aubrey Beardsley, H. Harland, Le Gallienne, Lionel Johnson, Edmund Gosse, Henry James, all at that time. But that did not make me one of their school of thought! I have no cause to fear exposure on *any* subject.' A little later he returned to the same topic. All this calumny, he declared, came from one source. 'I blame Morrison, that *improbus cinaedus* and *pathicus dévergondé* for most of these unspeakably false stories. I know what he was morally from certain things he said to me, things which I indignantly rejected, to say nothing about the stories of him at the race-course . . . and of his debauches *à l'instar de Tibère à Capri.* . . .' As for Wang Wên-shao's diary, that was unquestionably a fabrication based on the true diary of Ching-shan, 'as Wang himself told me he was publishing nothing and wanted Ching-shan's as a matter of interest to collate dates'. In other words, Wang borrowed Ching-shan's diary from Backhouse and then copied into his own the passages which Lewisohn had shown to be common to both.

Meanwhile Duyvendak had declined to wait longer and had published his article. Its form was strangely petulant. Duyvendak, it seemed, could not forgive Lewisohn, the amateur who had so impertinently forestalled him and made his own earlier article look foolish, before he had time to make his own dignified retreat. The Dutch pedant was prepared to correct himself, but not to be corrected. So he began by attacking Lewisohn's arguments, on the ground that they merely echoed his own and therefore could not lead to conclusions which he had not reached. Then, having pushed aside his impertinent competitor, he proceeded, by different arguments, to reach the same conclusion. Using refined philological reasoning, in which he had no fear of rivalry from an amateur like Lewisohn, he concluded that Ching-shan's diary, in its present form, 'cannot be authentic' but is a skilful literary fiction. Perhaps, he suggested, there did exist a real diary by Ching-shan, found by Backhouse in Ching-shan's study, and parts of this real diary were then incorporated into the present document: 'they have, however, been so elaborated that it has become practically impossible to extricate them from the additions.'

This attempt to argue that Backhouse found a genuine document and transformed it into a forgery does not seem to me very impressive. It seems to spring from a desire to reconcile the proven forgery of the document with Backhouse's circumstantial story of its discovery. Why anyone should entertain this desire is not clear. If Backhouse forged the document, or even transformed it into a forgery, he was perfectly capable of inventing its history. Indeed, if he forged it, he had to invent its history in order to account for his possession of it.

After the publication of Duyvendak's article, Backhouse bestirred himself. He decided to sue both Duyvendak and Lewisohn for libel. His lawyer in Tientsin, Percy Kent of the firm of Kent, Moundsey & Co., tried to enlist Bland as an ally. His client's good faith, he wrote, was unquestionable. No one who knew Sir Edmund, and had 'any real perception of mind', could possibly doubt his veracity. Sir Edmund himself might well go to London and bring the case to court there. Would Bland co-operate? Bland would not. This time he really had had enough of 'this gelatinous individual'.

Bland's last contacts with Backhouse were indirect, through Henri Vetch. Vetch's new edition of *China under the Empress Dowager* was now being printed, and all agreed that some reference must be made to the controversy, which had suddenly become so acute, about Ching-shan's diary. Vetch, who had been personally won over by Backhouse, sent William Sheldon Ridge, the editor of the *Peking Chronicle*, to see Backhouse, and Ridge, on the basis of Backhouse's story, as set out in his 'Footnote', wrote a 'note' on the subject for incorporation in the new edition. The note was seen and 'edited' by Bland, who otherwise declined to be involved. It is characterised by special pleading: that is, it is more concerned to advance hypotheses, how the diary *might* be genuine, than to face evidence, that it *is* forged. The new edition, incorporating this note, was published in Peking in 1939, and gave occasion to Lewisohn to publish a second article and to Backhouse to threaten him with a second libel action. Lewisohn's second article still further damaged the alleged diary by pointing out, in detail, the various sources from which it had been stitched together. Then the Second World War came to the Far East and the dispute over the authenticity of Ching-shan's diary was temporarily suspended.

The arguments of Lewisohn and Duyvendak convinced many scholars. Lionel Giles, of the British Museum, was convinced by them – he knew, of course, of the forged scrolls sent by Backhouse to the Bodleian, so he was open to conviction. Giles consoled Bland by telling him that the manuscript of the diary, which he had deposited in the Museum, was 'well worth preservation as the most masterly specimen of literary forgery in modern times'. Bland's own faith was shaken, but afterwards tentatively re-asserted itself: in his last year he would defend both the authenticity of Ching-shan's diary and the bona fides of his collaborator, whom he described as 'one of the greatest Oriental scholars'; but he hesitated to publish his defence.* Vetch believed that 'the controversy will always remain *sub judice*', and today he still asserts his belief that the diary is genuine.

Meanwhile Chinese scholars have joined in the debate. In general, they agree with Lewisohn and Duyvendak that the diary is a forgery. The Chinese scholar Chin-liang, the editor of the official history of the Ch'ing dynasty, had at first intended to include in that history a biography of Ching-shan, solely on account of the fame of his diary; but afterwards – in the 1920s – on looking more closely at the diary, he found so many 'errors and discrepancies' that he gave up his plan. The Chinese scholar Fang Chao-ying, writing evidently in 1938, pointed out that many of the speeches ascribed in the diary to Jung-lu are in fact taken from public memorials. Another Chinese scholar, Ch'êng Ming-chou, found reasons for suspecting that not only Ching-shan's diary but many other of Backhouse's documents were fabrications. However, in 1951, the Chinese collection of documents concerning the Boxer Rebellion, *I Ho T'uan Tzu Liao Ts'ung K'an*, quoted the diary as completely authentic.

In his book *The Boxer Uprising*, published in 1963, Victor Purcell devoted a special appendix to the controversy over Ching-shan's diary. After surveying the evidence, both Western and Chinese, he concluded that the document was a forgery, by persons unknown. Most scholars now regard it as forged; but the motive and circumstances of the forgery remain mysterious, and the controversy has never been declared closed. Perhaps, on the documentary evidence which has been used so far, it can never be closed.

I believe that it can be closed now, for we are now in a position to measure one factor which has hitherto been left unexamined:

* In November 1943 Bland was angered by the publication of Maurice Collis's play, *The Motherly and Auspicious*, which represented the Empress Dowager as 'a monster' and, in particular, by the author's claim to have superseded all earlier authorities and his dismissal of *China under the Empress Dowager* as 'interesting but valueless'. Bland wrote to Collis protesting that *China under the Empress Dowager* was the result of 'years of study on the spot, and based on authentic historical documents carefully translated by one of the greatest Oriental scholars'. Bland proposed to review Collis's play over his own name in order to force Collis to name his sources. In January 1944 he wrote a letter to the *Times Literary Supplement* on the subject. In the first draft of his letter, he cited Ching-shan's diary as a genuine source; but in the final form he prudently omitted all reference to it.

the character of Backhouse. Hitherto it has been assumed that any general conclusion about Ching-shan's diary has to respect the evidence of its history given by Backhouse. In other words, whether the document is genuine or forged, it is assumed that Backhouse discovered it, as he stated, in Ching-shan's house, on 18 August 1900, immediately after the Allied occupation of Peking. This fact was stated as a datum by Fang Chao-ying and was not disputed by Duyvendak or Lewisohn. They, of course, wrote when Backhouse was alive. But even Purcell, writing when Backhouse was safely dead and could no longer launch his writs, accepted his version. Indeed, in his appendix, having published, for the first time, Backhouse's 'Footnote' – his last and most circumstantial account of the discovery – Purcell explicitly stated that this document, though admittedly throwing no light on the authenticity of the diary, nevertheless 'makes Sir Edmund Backhouse's part in the episode perfectly clear and adds some valuable facts to our information'. I believe that it does no such thing – indeed, that it only increases the confusion. The beginning of wisdom, in this matter, is to recognise that it is at least possible that Backhouse's account of the discovery of the document, however circumstantial, contains no 'valuable facts' at all, but is a complete fabrication, a fantasy. Once we allow this possibility, the problem becomes soluble.

Both Fang Chao-ying and Purcell sought to reconcile the internal evidence of forgery and the circumstantial evidence of Backhouse by supposing that the forged document had been concocted with a political purpose and had then been skilfully placed in Ching-shan's house, 'where observant foreigners would find it'. But this is hardly possible. If the diary is a complete forgery, as they both believed, then Backhouse's story dissolves: for it is simply inconceivable that a forged diary of Ching-shan could be discovered in the real Ching-shan's study only three days after its last entry and his own death. Who could or would have fabricated so elaborate a literary artefact in those three days of convulsion, when the court was in flight and the city in turmoil, or placed the precious result of such scholarly fabrication where it might indeed be spotted and recognised by an accomplished English sinologue, but was far more likely to be destroyed 'by a party of Sikhs'? If the diary was really fabricated with a political purpose, there were better ways of ensuring that it reached Western hands, and was read by Western officials, than by putting it in a house that was about to be burned and hoping that a remarkable foreign scholar would come and rescue it, 'in the nick of time', from the flames.

Once we agree that the diary, as produced by Backhouse, is a forgery, we have no alternative but to regard his story of its discovery as fantasy; and if a man gives, and persists in, an entirely fictitious account of his acquisition of a forged document, there is no moral reason for supposing him incapable of forging it himself. Conversely, whoever forges a document must also provide it with a history which presupposes that it is genuine; and that history must of necessity be a forgery too.

There remains another possibility: the possibility of a partial forgery. It is conceivable, as Duyvendak seems to suggest, that Backhouse, in 1900, found a genuine document, in the circumstances which he described, and then transformed it into a forgery. But in that case, the transformation, as Duyvendak admitted, was total, and this unnecessary hypothesis does not in fact save Backhouse from any charge. The document which he produced in 1909 was still a forgery, and a forgery by him, and the story that he had found that particular document in Ching-shan's house in 1900 is still a fantasy, and a fantasy by him. Why then should we believe any part of his story? It is more rational to ignore his 'evidence' altogether and start our reasoning from a more solid base.

Assuming as certain that the document is a forgery, we naturally ask, who forged it, and for what purpose? It need not have been forged by Backhouse: it could have been supplied to him, already forged, at any time between August 1900 and April 1909, though not in the circumstances described by him. In that case, we must assume that it was forged in a particular interest, and we look at it to discover that interest. All who have studied it for this purpose agree that it could have been written to serve the political interest of Jung-lu. Jung-lu, according to Chinese officials who knew him, was an ambitious and selfish politician, talented indeed, but 'dangerous, treacherous and covetous'. He supported the attack on the foreigners, but afterwards tried to shift the responsibility

to others and pose as a man who had always supported the
Western powers and had vainly resisted the reactionary pro-
Boxer party at court. Although it is inconceivable that he would
or could have caused such a diary to be fabricated in time for
Backhouse to have discovered it in the circumstances described
by him, he might possibly have done so after the flight to Sian.
The Empress Dowager was then seeking to ingratiate herself with
the foreign powers by means of historical revision, and why not
the Grand Secretary too? The forged diary could then have been
conveyed to Backhouse in the hope that, through him, it would
be passed on to higher authorities. This could have happened in
1901 or soon afterwards. It would have been pointless after April
1903, when Jung-lu died. In that case we would have to assume
that Backhouse, having acquired the document, and defeated its
purpose by saying nothing whatever about it to anyone for several
years, then invented an elaborate story to authenticate it, and
inserted himself into that story.

However, such a theory, which does nothing to save Backhouse's credit (for it still leaves him guilty of forgery and fantasy
in supplying false credentials to a false document), is pure speculation, unsupported by evidence or probability. Once again, if
Jung-lu had wished to revise his own image in Western eyes,
there were simpler and more reliable methods of such revision.
The diary is too evidently the work of a scholar, not a propagandist.
It is a pastiche, artfully constructed out of a miscellany of Chinese
sources and European literary echoes, coloured with the faded
tints of contemporary European chinoiserie. Such a pastiche
argues a European, not a Chinese, hand, and every indication
points to Backhouse himself as the artist who created it.

Hitherto, scholars have sought explanations which leave
Backhouse himself innocent. They have argued – as Bland argued
– that it was impossible for any European to have executed so
masterly a forgery. They have asked what conceivable motive
could have impelled him to act as a retrospective propagandist for
Jung-lu. They have supposed that, here too, he must have been
the victim of 'able and unscrupulous Chinese'. They have been
unwilling to suppose that a distinguished English sinologue, a
cultivated baronet of known charm, could have been the author

of such a fraud. Besides, his account of his discovery of the document was so explicit, so coherent, so circumstantial, that it could not be ascribed to mere mistaken or confused recollections: it had to be either totally true or totally false, a record of 'valuable fact' or a cunning and unscrupulous tissue of lies. Neither those who knew him in his lifetime, nor those who read about him afterwards, were willing to see him as so heroic a liar. Scholars and administrators, journalists, publishers, lawyers, diplomatists, industrialists – all at first, and some to the last, were taken in by him. They agreed with Mr Kent of Tientsin, who found it inconceivable that any man of sense could doubt his complete veracity. We who have seen him palming off forged scrolls on libraries, forged contracts on manufacturers, forged 'curios' on individuals, forged letters of recommendation, forged reports of high-powered interviews, imaginary arms, imaginary battleships, imaginary libraries, imaginary pearls, all explained by elaborate, detailed, self-glorifying fantasies – flotillas of ships stealing down the Yang-tse river, carts laden with rare books creaking slowly through bandit-ridden provinces, nocturnal armed raids on the imperial palace, secret meetings with the great – may well feel differently. Certainly we need not boggle at a forged diary explained by a fanciful scenario in the desolate house of its alleged author.

Such a forgery may have demanded unique, even incredible, skill. But Backhouse evidently had that skill. It may presuppose unfathomable motives. We must seek to fathom those motives, or leave them unfathomed. Whatever they were, the truth can hardly be in doubt.

One man, and one man only, saw that truth from the start: Dr Morrison. It is clear that Morrison could not prove that Backhouse had forged the diary, but he knew it. How did he know it? We can only guess, but we can guess with some probability of accuracy. In the years 1900–1908 Morrison and Backhouse were on very close terms. Morrison was Backhouse's patron. He appears to have accompanied him to Ching-shan's house. Certainly he was involved in the arrest of Ching-shan's son. Morrison's landlord was Backhouse's 'writer'. Both Morrison and Backhouse were unmarried, and they must anyway have spent much time together. By 1910 Morrison had taken the measure of Backhouse. He had discovered something about his past. He had discovered that he did not really know any of the important persons with whom he claimed to be familiar. It is reasonable to suppose that he had discovered other things too: that from straws of evidence, from things seen but not mentioned, from casual gossip and questions, conversation with servants, etc., he knew what Backhouse had been doing, knew that he had not found a diary at Ching-shan's house, knew that he was cooking up a Chinese diary, guessed that it was being ascribed to Ching-shan. He could not prove it and therefore was not prepared to argue the matter; but he knew.

CHAPTER ELEVEN

The Recluse

IN January 1933, when he was seeking to interest his old collaborator in the newly discovered memoirs of the Grand Eunuch,
Backhouse had casually remarked, '*your* memoirs would be
interesting'. Bland was at that time seventy years old; and at some
time in the next decade he began, in 'septuagenarian detachment',
to write his memoirs. Unfortunately they were never finished: the
manuscript covers his years in China, but stops short of his
collaboration with Backhouse. Indeed, the name of Backhouse
does not occur in them. Perhaps he stopped there because he found
that subject too difficult. He could write objectively about Morrison, that 'erratic genius' from whose company, as a colleague,
he was glad to have been set free. In retrospect, the character of
Morrison had set in a clear and definite mould. But how could the
gelatinous Backhouse ever be fixed in a firm, coherent shape?
Even in his old age, he was as slippery as ever. The uncertainty
surrounding Ching-shan's diary made it impossible to write
confidently about their collaboration, or indeed about anything
else in which he had been involved. It looks as if Bland despaired
when he came to that collaboration, and laid down his pen.

However, there is one passage in Bland's memoirs which he
clearly wrote with Backhouse in mind. Describing his own study
of the Chinese language, he remarks that by a year's concen-
trated work, he acquired fluency in the spoken language and
familiarity with enough written characters for everyday purposes.
After this, he continued his studies in the intervals of an active life,
but soon concluded 'that there was nothing in Chinese literature,
ancient or modern, likely to compensate any normal individual' –
perhaps we should italicise the word 'normal' – 'for the vast

amount of labour involved in studying it'. He reached this conclusion, he says, partly as the result of the acute mental indigestion produced by painfully ploughing through two classics of Chinese fiction, 'and partly because I observed that the mentality of Europeans who become absorbed in the intensive study of Chinese gradually assumes an oriental complexion and, in the end, becomes estranged from the European outlook on life, habits of thought and standards of conduct'. This passage needs no commentary. It is Bland's real reply to Backhouse's statement that he had now gone native, that he regularly wore Chinese dress, and that thereby he enjoyed a 'delightful freedom', being able 'to pass as an *indigène*'.

It was evidently in 1921 that Backhouse radically changed his outward way of life. That was his climacteric year. Till then, he had travelled widely, making regular, almost annual visits to England. In that year came the visit to the Findlays, when he arrived in London in Chinese dress and suddenly disappeared from Edinburgh in distressing circumstances. After 1921 he lived continuously in China: indeed, according to Weatherall, that was a condition of his allowance. He was now merely an *émigré*, for it was inconceivable, after the affairs of the Bank Note Company and John Brown & Co., that any business organisation would make use of his undoubted talents; and, being an *émigré*, cut off from his own country, he allowed himself to be assimilated into Chinese society. He had very few English friends. Two successive Anglican bishops, Dr Scott and then Dr Norris, kept an eye on him and administered his allowance for him. He also, being something of a *malade imaginaire*, had much to do with doctors. At first, we are told, he liked to retain special private doctors, in personal attendance. However, there were hazards in this profession, as one of them discovered. This was Dr Kirkby Gomes, a half-caste doctor whom Backhouse brought to court in May 1917, accusing him of breach of contract for having failed to look after his health adequately. The case was heard by Sir Havilland de Sausmarez, the Judge of the British Supreme Court for China, in Tientsin. Backhouse lost it. He also relied on legation doctors, of whom the first was Percival Yetts and the last Dr Aspland. There was also his personal friend, Mrs Danby. Except for Bland, with whom he corresponded on such practical or controversial matters as their two books and the two diaries, his contact with England was slight. 'He had little respect for his family in England', writes M. Vetch, 'and they, on their side, regarded him as a black sheep, the scapegoat of the Backhouses, packed off to China, a remittance-man.'

He also became even more of a recluse. He had always been a recluse, to some extent. He had shown symptoms of withdrawal from reality at Oxford. He had been described as a recluse when he first came to China. In the first period of their collaboration, Bland had respected his 'hermit instincts'. But in those earlier years retreat alternated with society. Bland's diary, in 1909–10, recounts numerous social meetings and meals with Backhouse, often in the company of ffrench, and there were those regular visits to England, Scotland and America. However, with time, the hermit tendency increased. Sir Alwyne Ogden, arriving in Peking as a student-interpreter in 1913, found him well known as a complete hermit. But when necessity or opportunity had drawn him into society, he had always been sociable enough and could delight his companions by his urbanity and charm. These characteristics remained constant in his character; but in China, after 1921, his seclusion became more absolute, at least as far as Europeans were concerned. He maintained – as he wrote to Bland, as he informed Mrs Danby – that he still enjoyed the society of the old Manchu nobility and the members of the imperial family; but we cannot be sure of this. His social commerce with Manchu grandees may well have been as mythical as his previous interviews with President Yüan Shih-k'ai and Grand Secretary Hsü Shih-ch'ang.

One man who might have shed light on this matter, and whose view of Backhouse would be particularly interesting, was Sir Reginald Johnston, who has already appeared in this narrative as a supporter of the authenticity of Ching-shan's diary. Johnston had come out to China in 1898, the same year as Backhouse. He was an administrator who acquired an intimate knowledge of China, its language, its history, its philosophy. On the face of it, he would appear a natural ally of Backhouse: for he was a scholar, a Confucian, and a hater of missionaries. He also had close contacts with the imperial family and the Manchu aristocracy. In 1918, he was appointed European tutor to the last Ch'ing Emperor, P'u-i, known as the Hsüan-t'ung Emperor, and lived for six years in the Forbidden City; for the abdicated imperial family continued to live in their palace, and enjoy their titles, privileges and ceremonies, until the coup d'état which evicted and dispossessed them in 1924. Through his imperial friends, as well as through his own experience, Johnston must have known a great deal of previous court history. What, we may ask, did he make of Backhouse, an exact contemporary, a fellow-sinologist and, like him, a historian of the Manchu court? If Backhouse really maintained close contact with the imperial family and the Manchu nobility, he must have been familiar also with Johnston.

Unfortunately, there seems to have been no contact at all between these two distinguished scholars. Their relations were described by Johnston in a letter to Bland in 1934. Johnston had then just published his book, *Twilight in the Forbidden City*, and he told Bland that he was quite sure that Backhouse would have nothing good to say of it 'for personal reasons'. He added, 'I had my reasons for disliking the man and did not go near him all the time I was employed in the Palace. I met him twice *before* that time and dined with him once. But I did not wish to renew my slight acquaintance with him, and didn't do so. I have been told that he resented it.'* What lay behind this antipathy we do not know. The tone of Johnston's letters at the time of the meetings and the dinner, which were in the spring of 1914, already express mutual aloofness. Beyond that we can say nothing. The discreet Scotchman saw to it that, on his death in 1938, all his personal papers were destroyed.

If Johnston, who lived among the Manchu nobility, did not see Backhouse, other Westerners, who lived in the legation area, were even less likely to do so. He lived apart from them, in the Tartar City, on the far side of the Forbidden City, first, since 1912, in No. 19 Shih-Fuma Street, the house which he shared with Chang Ho-chai, then, from April 1937, after Chang's murder, in the Western City, at 28 Yangjou Hutung, the spacious garden-house

---

* He did indeed: Backhouse's memoirs contain some savage remarks about Johnston.

in which Vetch would find him so comfortably lodged. There he kept to himself, avoiding the society of his compatriots. It is said that, when he went out, he would send his Chinese boy ahead of him to warn him if any Western foreigner were in sight. If he met a Westerner on his occasional walks on the old city wall, he would turn on his heel. If he passed them in his rickshaw, he would cover his face with a handkerchief. He particularly avoided Western officials. He affected to despise the diplomatic corps and regularly declined its ritual invitations. However, if Westerners had occasion to penetrate his house, they invariably found him friendly and ceremoniously polite. We have seen Weatherall, who had criticised him so strongly in England, seduced again by his personality in Peking. We have seen Soothill, who visited him in 1926, won over to him. We have seen Henri Vetch enchanted by him in 1937. The same effect was felt by other visitors whom, for good reasons, he occasionally admitted to his house.

One of these was Sir Humphrey Prideaux-Brune who, in the 1920s, was a member of the Chinese Secretariat. This was a department of the Legation which supervised the Chinese studies of new recruits to the Chinese consular service. On one occasion, the department decided to compile a new Chinese reader for students of literary Chinese, and, having chosen the texts, thought of commissioning Backhouse to help with translations and explanatory notes. Backhouse, of course, was glad of such small commissions, which added to his tenuous allowance and ministered to his self-importance, and he welcomed the visitor with old-world civility. 'He lived as a hermit', Sir Humphrey writes, 'in a large mansion belonging to a Chinese friend' – that is, in his own former house, now controlled by Chang Ho-chai. 'My wife and I used to visit him there and he was always courteous and friendly with us, and I enjoyed the visits as a complete change from official life.' Sir Humphrey admired him particularly as the co-author of *China under the Empress Dowager*, 'a really splendid work. . . . This book and Pierre Loti's *Derniers Jours de Pékin*', he writes, 'are the two books which give a real impression of the atmosphere of Peking in the imperial time.'

Some years later, in the mid-1930s, one of Prideaux-Brune's successors in the Chinese Secretariat similarly called, with a colleague, on Backhouse to commission translations from him. They found him in his home, 'which was in the untidy and rather sordid state traditionally expected of recluse scholarly eccentrics. However he received us with unexpected cordiality and took on several odd jobs effectively.' In the course of several such visits Backhouse once or twice revealed 'his sudden fear of his Chinese major-domo who had been with him many years' – that is, once again, Chang Ho-chai – and also, later, a conviction that he was being pursued by the secret agents of certain powers, in particular of China, Japan and Russia. This, he said, was because of work which he had done for other countries; and he hinted that he had supplied translations of secret documents to the Bulgarian government, 'which struck us as odd and improbable at the time'. Altogether he exhibited a well-developed persecution-complex, 'which, added to an already existing Walter Mitty idea of being an important link in a secret service chain, convinced us that he was "bonkers" but not a dangerous nut'.

Another visitor who met Backhouse in the mid-1930s was Sir James Marjoribanks, a young diplomatist who was sent out to China in 1934. Sir James's father was a first cousin of Sir John Findlay, and when the Findlays learned that he was going to Peking, they asked him to do what he could to 'find Edmund' who had disappeared so dramatically from their house thirteen years ago. Sir James soon discovered that the way to Backhouse lay through Dr Aspland. From Dr Aspland he learned that Backhouse lived in somewhat squalid conditions, under the tyranny of his Chinese servant. 'However,' he now writes,

when I called on him at his house in the Tartar City, I found a small but neat and tidy establishment adjoining the house of the Mayor of Peking, who was at that time notorious as the Japanese puppet-administrator. A moon door in the wall gave access to the mayor's house. I found Edmund sitting in the courtyard in a long Chinese gown and with a mandarin hat on his head. He greeted me very warmly, although he was obviously very nervous and unused to accidental visitors. His conversation was lively and scholarly: Chinese and Latin expressions kept popping up. He was a quite delightful interlocutor, full of fun and enthusiasm. I wish I had kept a record of our conversation. I remember discovering that the Mayor had been responsible for getting him this house as he found it handy to have Edmund on tap to translate documents, Edmund being adept in both Russian and Japanese as well as Chinese. As a result of this conversation, it was arranged for texts of some of the documents he translated to be passed to the Embassy for information. One, I remember, was in Russian, in red ink and with a signature which looked like a large *S*. The explanation of the Mayor receiving such correspondence was that, besides posing as the Japanese puppet, he was at the same time a leading official of the Chinese communist party and received instructions straight from Moscow. . . .

So at least Backhouse told Marjoribanks; but we must remember the Walter Mitty aspect of his character, and his ability as a forger, unsuspected at that time. His self-importance is illustrated by his contemporary entries in *Who's Who*. Here he solemnly recorded each of his 'penny-a-line translations', and sometimes inflated them into formal appointments: honorary translator to the British embassy, honorary adviser on this and that. He did not fail to record that he was a Fellow of the Royal Geographical Society – that is, one of 6,000 subscribers to its Journal – a member of the Standing Council of the Baronetage (a very shadowy member of a very shadowy body), and a Member of the no less shadowy 'Académie Diplomatique Internationale in Paris'. As only states, not persons, can be members of this last body, the record (solemnly repeated by Mrs Danby in *The Dictionary of National Biography*) must have been somewhat confused. He would simplify it, in his later years, by describing himself, more briefly, as a 'Member of the Academy, Paris'.

Backhouse's close association with the Japanese puppet-mayor need not cause any surprise. He sympathised with the Japanese conquerors, although he might be afraid of their soldiery, and did not like to see them too close at hand. In March 1933 he expressed delight at the Japanese victories in Manchuria. After all, the Japanese had restored the Manchu dynasty with which Backhouse now romantically identified himself. They had set up, as 'emperor' of their new puppet state of Manchukuo, the last of the Ch'ing emperors of China, the helpless human cypher P'u-i, whom, as an infant, the formidable old Empress Dowager had appointed to succeed her doomed victim, the Kuang-hsü Emperor, and who would end his days as a brain-washed exhibit to advertise the communist China of Mao Tse-tung.

Later in the 1930s, the British diplomatic corps came to know Backhouse better. On 7 July 1937, occurred 'the Lukouch'iao incident', when Japanese forces, allegedly engaged in permitted exercises, demanded admittance to the city of Wanp'inghsien near Lukouch'iao (or Marco Polo Bridge) and, on being refused, fired on the Chinese garrison, killing or wounding 200 of them. This incident was correctly seen at the time as the beginning of a new Japanese aggression in North China: indeed, it is now recognised as the beginning, in the Far East, of the Second World War. The foreign embassies in Peking immediately took precautions and invited all their nationals to move into the legation area, as they had done during the Boxer rebellion. In the British embassy there was some speculation how Backhouse would receive such an invitation. Would he, as in 1900, seek safety in the Legation, or would he prefer his self-imposed isolation in the Tartar City?

To their surprise, he accepted it with alacrity. When the refugees arrived at the Legation, two young British diplomatists were waiting to receive them, sitting at two tables underneath the great *ting'rh* at the front of the Residence. One of them has described the scene. 'About half-way through, a dear old boy with a white beard came up and in the gentlest voice announced himself as Sir Edmund Backhouse. We nearly fell over backwards, and duly allocated him to Dr Aspland. I can recall no significant conversation – all I do remember vividly was that he had the most beautiful hands I have ever seen: white, with long tapering fingers – I can still see them.'

Once in the Legation, Backhouse still further surprised the diplomatists by quickly settling down 'and becoming a jovial occupant and a social member of the evacuees' mess'. He showed great courtesy, especially to the women of the party: indeed, he seemed to delight in feminine company. The diplomatists who only knew him by repute, were astonished to discover the human side of his character, his ready response to friendly overtures, and they listened with delight to his vivid reminiscences of the days of the Empire. He appeared to them a wide-ranging scholar whose conversation would have graced the panelled rooms of a senior common room at an ancient university – which indeed had been his ambition when he had dreamed of the chair of Chinese at Oxford. Then, as order returned to Peking, he disappeared again, back to his hermit life in the Tartar City.

Next year, a fleeting glimpse of Backhouse was caught by Sir Harold Acton, who was then living in Peking as Lecturer in English at Peking University. Sir Harold found him very frail – 'he seemed a nervous wreck' – but a nimbus of fame surrounded him. 'He was reputed to know a dozen oriental languages, even Mongolian and Sanskrit. He lived in Peking as a complete recluse, in Chinese garb, looked after by a trusty Chinese factotum, who even drew his income from the British embassy, since Backhouse suffered from agoraphobia and never left his house. . . .' 'I heard', Sir Harold goes on, 'that his English relations tried to induce him to return, but he broke down at the railway station and refused to leave.' This story, which shows a certain change of heart among his relations, is confirmed by them. Hitherto they had paid him to stay in China: now, with the Japanese occupation of Peking, they were prepared to reclaim him. To ensure his return, they sent him a ticket back from China to England. Backhouse did in fact get as far as Tientsin. But then he had second thoughts. He sold the ticket and spent the proceeds on continued life in Japanese-occupied Peking.

At this time Backhouse was sixty-five years old. He was living in his new house in the Western City, with the new factotum mentioned by Sir Harold Acton, who had presumably replaced the murdered Chang Ho-chai, and he was apparently still busy with those two great works of scholarship of which Mrs Danby tells us: his Chinese-English dictionary and the lives of the Ch'ing Emperors. The former of these two works is already familiar to us, as a long-standing but 'visionary' project of which, after more than ten years, only a few unintelligible notes had come into existence. Of the latter we know nothing, nothing at all. Perhaps it was no less visionary than the dictionary. But all questions on this subject are now academic, for in August 1939 all Backhouse's papers in China, together with his library and other possessions, were destroyed.

The history of this episode, which has been briefly mentioned by Mrs Danby in *The Dictionary of National Biography* is obscure. It seems that, at this time, being the eve of the Second World War, the Japanese authorities in China showed their solidarity with their German allies by opening a propaganda campaign against both Britain and America. This campaign created more noise than damage, and nowhere, as far as is known, led to violence or looting. But Backhouse was suddenly seized by such fear that he abandoned his house and, carrying with him only a few personal belongings, took refuge within the embassy compound, in 'the ex-Austrian legation'. This was the old legation of the Austro-Hungarian Empire, which had been incorporated into the diplomatic quarter after the Boxer Rising and, until 1918, had enjoyed extra-territorial rights. After 1918 these rights were forfeited and the building ceased to be an official diplomatic residence. It became a convenient hostel for miscellaneous fugitives; for it was still within collective diplomatic jurisdiction. The Chinese had no authority there and even the Japanese occupying authorities did not interfere with it until the outbreak of the Pacific War. Consequently, as a former diplomatist in China has it, 'it was a likely funk-hole for anyone in Backhouse's situation'.

In this new home, Backhouse was visited, early in October, by his faithful publisher, Henri Vetch. Vetch reported to Bland on the visit: 'Backhouse I saw the other day, in the compound of the ex-Austrian legation, where he has moved to, fleeing from his house in the West City, as his servants turned anti-British, so he says. He seems to be in very good health, rather sad at the passing of his brother, the Admiral' – that is, of Sir Roger Backhouse, who had died in July. 'I shall be calling on him again in a few days', Vetch went on, 'to hand him three presentation copies of *China under the Empress Dowager*' – the new Peking edition, elegantly published, with Sheldon Ridge's note demonstrating, to those whom it could persuade, the authenticity of the diary of Ching-shan.

To the Europeans who knew of it, this second flight of Backhouse, which was in response to no invitation and occasioned by no real danger, seemed 'somewhat strange'. We may make allowances for an elderly man, frail, solitary, and subject to paranoid fears. But what seemed inexplicable was his complete abandonment of his possessions, which he made no attempt to recover. Afterwards he would repeatedly lament the loss of jewels, manuscripts, heirlooms, souvenirs and, above all, his library. Whether his manuscripts were really burnt by the suspicious Japanese, as Mrs Danby states (perhaps on his authority), or were rifled, as Backhouse would afterwards maintain, by 'unfaithful servants and treacherous friends', is not clear. All we know is that he abandoned them to their fate and they disappeared. On one occasion he would admit that the loss had been caused 'largely through my own fault'.

Two points may however be made about this strange episode. First, if it is put in the context of Backhouse's whole career, it becomes less strange. Backhouse was always liable to sudden changes of mind, sudden disappearances, sudden evasions. As Bland had written, 'I rely not on his going or staying.' At Oxford, he had disappeared suddenly from his own dinner-parties. After Oxford, he had disappeared from the record. He had disappeared suddenly from London in 1912, from Edinburgh in 1921. He was continually disappearing from Peking. Each disappearance was an escape from something: from some commitment, some problem, the burden of possessions or obligations. He had escaped from his Oxford debts. His generosity to the Bodleian was, in one sense, an escape from the books and manuscripts which he had collected. He had extracted himself, in turn, from every human association which, from protective, had become oppressive. Now he was escaping from his books and manuscripts again. In 1912, when he gave his collection to Oxford, including all his material for the history of the Chinese revolution, he had intended (he said) to work on it himself; but in fact he never went near it again: he simply dumped it in the Bodleian and was free. In 1939 his escape from the accumulated books and papers of the next twenty-seven years was a similar emancipation. The pressure which forced him to it was psychological: there is no need to rationalise it by calling in objective dangers, anti-British servants, or the Japanese.

Secondly, the critical reader may observe that, if we believe Backhouse's own earlier statements, he had, by now, no jewels, manuscripts, heirlooms, etc., etc., to lose, for had he not sold them all, in 1932, to relieve his destitution and save him from begging his bread in the public way? Either the earlier or the later statement must be untrue. But, as Bland would say, 'let that pass'.

Backhouse remained in the ex-Austrian legation for two years, a hermit still, though in a new hermitage. Then, in December 1941, with the outbreak of war with Japan, his position became more difficult. The British missions in Japanese-occupied China were now closed and his remittances consequently ceased. As an enemy alien, he was liable to be interned. However, because of his age, he was excused the rigours of internment. Nor did he wish to be repatriated. At his own request, he was allowed to live on in Peking, in a single room in a house in the British Legation compound, with a single Chinese servant. The servant, we are told, was treated by him with great consideration, but 'in return often played the rôle of the master'. It seems like a repetition of the role of Chang Ho-chai: one of the many recurring syndromes in Backhouse's repetitious life.

One of the last British subjects to see him was his old friend Mrs Danby. She was one of those awaiting repatriation, and her last days in Peking were spent in his company. He told her that, if he should survive the war, he would then retire to spend the remainder of his days in a temple in the Western Hills. 'It is a favourite spot of mine', he said, 'and the abbot is an old friend. He has often invited me to take up my abode with him.' Perhaps he was referring to the Buddhist temple of Pi Mo Yen, to which a Manchu general, a cousin of the Ch'ien-lung Emperor, had retired to write a book, *Footsteps in the Snow of a Solitary Goose*, in the eighteenth century, and in which Daniele Varè would afterwards begin the life of the Empress Dowager to which he had been inspired by the work of Backhouse and Bland. So Mrs Danby pleased herself with an imaginary picture of 'the Professor's' last days: days of renunciation and contemplation in monastic peace, philosophic conversation with the old abbot, and veneration by the young monks, who would look upon him as a great scholar. It did not occur to her that the old rogue had one last game to play. But how could she foretell that, even at this late hour, he would find a new friend, the protector, physician and chronicler of his last two years, the midwife of his last and most extraordinary birth? This new friend, the last successor to Morrison, Bland, Jordan, Barton, Hall, Chang Ho-chai, the Anglican bishops and the embassy doctors, was Professor Reinhard Hoeppli.

CHAPTER TWELVE

Dr Hoeppli

PROFESSOR REINHARD HOEPPLI was the new Swiss representative in Peking. He was not a career diplomatist. By profession he
was a physician, specialising in parasitology. A bachelor, free to
move and fond of travel, he had roved over the world, and since
1930 had served on the staff of the Peking Union Medical College,
an American foundation. By now he had travelled widely in China
and knew it well. In January 1942, when the Swiss government
took over the protection of American, Dutch and British interests
in Japanese-occupied territories, it needed a reliable man with
local knowledge to assume these large responsibilities, and since
Dr Hoeppli was available on the spot, and had such long experience of China, it appointed him as its honorary consul-
general. Hoeppli carried out the duties of this post throughout
the years of war, and won golden opinions for his work. One of
the many who were indebted to him was Backhouse, whom he
helped in a double capacity, both as consul and as doctor. For
Backhouse had by now quarrelled with Dr Aspland, the Legation
doctor, and they had parted 'by mutual consent'.

It is clear that Hoeppli took great trouble for Backhouse. It is
also clear that he was fascinated by him: by his personality, by his
genuine charm, and by his remarkable conversation. To the Swiss
doctor, *bon bourgeois* and perhaps somewhat naïve, this destitute
English baronet, with his graceful features, his exquisite manners
of a *grand seigneur*, and his strange, hermit instincts, was a figure
from another world. And what an extraordinary world too! It
was quite different from anything hitherto experienced by the
good doctor – 'a stiff, tight-lipped, old-maidish person, with an
ambiguous expression and a secretive manner', as he has been
described to me. For of course, Dr Hoeppli did not know

Backhouse's true history. He did not know that, just like himself, Backhouse came from good Protestant bourgeois stock. He knew nothing of the Quaker bank, the youthful extravagances, the agency for railway contractors, shipbuilders, bank-note printers, the forgeries, the frauds, the fantasies. He only knew what Backhouse told him; and Backhouse – as must now be only too clear – was a most persuasive talker. In Hoeppli, he now discovered the perfect listener, and Hoeppli, fascinated by his character and his company, encouraged him to talk. So Backhouse talked and, talking, carried his enchanted listener up to dizzy social heights, back to forgotten eras of literature and politics, and into dark, forbidden recesses.

Dr Hoeppli has himself described his first encounter with the bewitching English baronet whose personality was to haunt him for the rest of his life.

The impression I got when meeting Sir Edmund first, was that of a distinguished-looking old scholarly gentleman dressed in a shabby, black, somewhat formal, suit who had a definite charm and spoke and behaved with exquisite, slightly old-style politeness. His long white beard gave him a venerable aspect, his walking was slow and somewhat unsteady, so that one feared he might fall down. His hands were well-shaped and white, slightly feminine; they moved nervously and often showed tremor. His eyes were remarkable for the very different expressions they were able to show in rapid succession, as I could observe in the course of many visits. They might at one moment have the quiet look of an old scholar, quite in line with beard, dress and refined politeness; suddenly they became the eyes of a monk in religious ecstasy, to change again into the eyes of an old salacious profligate with a very clever cunning look which gave the face a certain resemblance to that of Aretino in Titian's painting in the Pitti Palace in Florence. It was his eyes which betrayed the fact that the first and dominant impression of an old scholar represented only a part of his personality. Gradually, after somewhat closer contact, one obtained an entirely different impression, that of a person who, notwithstanding age and ailments, still harboured a strong sexuality and who, after some external inhibitions had been overcome, revealed with lascivious pleasure the erotic part of his personality. In such moments, he presented occasionally the very picture of an old satyr enjoying happy memories.

By preference he used to wear a long Chinese gown of dark colour which made him timeless in the sense that he might have looked in place in a Roman house at the time of the late emperors, in a Renaissance setting, and in the study-room of one of the Jesuit fathers at the time of K'ang-hsi. When sitting on the verandah of his residence in the British Embassy Compound, he used to wear a black Chinese cap with a large piece of rose-quartz fastened to its front part in the old Chinese fashion. During the hot summer months, he would wear a light yellow Chinese gown of grass-cloth.

He was a gourmet, and occasionally indulged in small luxuries such as strawberries and asparagus out of season, which he could hardly afford in view of his very limited funds. He was also fond of good wine, especially Bordeaux and Burgundy. As far as I could ascertain, he had never indulged in opium-smoking but took daily much caffein in crystals and during the last year of his life sleeping-powders and pills in large quantities.

His conversation was always interesting, dealing as a rule with a great variety of topics, but giving preference to historic matters, literature and erotic subjects. He was a bibliophile who had given (as he told me) a very large collection of Chinese and Manchu books and manuscripts to the Bodleian Library in Oxford. . . .

In this account, one detail at least is totally new. 'An old salacious profligate', 'strong sexuality', 'lascivious pleasure', 'an old satyr', 'erotic subjects' – in his previous history we have seen no trace of this. It is true, he had selected some passages about eunuchs and concubines – harmless in our eyes – for translation in the *Annals and Memoirs of the Court of Peking*. But even before they were published, he had panicked at the thought of them and protested that they were indecent, that they made the book itself disreputable: a view dismissed with contempt by the robust sense of Bland. In the 1920s those who knew him best in China – Weatherall, Bishop Norris – were quite positive that he had 'no vices'. Later, indeed only three years before, he had indignantly repelled the slander that he was homosexual and had expressed his revulsion from such 'perverted tastes' – which, however, he had been quick to ascribe to others. But perhaps, hitherto, he had had no friendly psychotherapist like the good Hoeppli, to help him to 'overcome some external inhibitions'. At all events, those inhibitions were now overcome and the old satyr, emancipated at last, would sing his paean of triumph over them to some tune.

Another inhibition which Backhouse shed in his last years was his British patriotism. This, perhaps, had never been strong. He had always seen himself as a cosmopolitan, an aesthete. He had never liked British policy in China. He had always supported Japan. But now he became positively violent in his hatred of his own country. Even Dr Hoeppli, who would take almost anything from Backhouse, was shaken by the violence of his expressions. Never, during the Pacific war, he says, had he heard, 'from any Englishman, especially one of high education and good social standing, such unkind remarks on Great Britain, the British government, and the British character in general, as were made by Sir Edmund. On the other hand there was nobody in the Peking British community who spoke so highly of Germany and Japan. . . . He seemed to enjoy Japanese victories just as if he were Japanese, and recorded with sadistic pleasure the various defeats of the Allies, especially of the British, during the first period of the War.' On this subject, Hoeppli felt obliged occasionally to remonstrate with him: he was, after all, the official representative of British interests in the Far East.

For two years Hoeppli ministered regularly to the real or imaginary physical needs of Backhouse, and listened with increasing fascination to the stories which he elicited. During many months he visited him daily. He found the experience unforgettable. Long afterwards he would thank the good fortune which had brought him 'into contact with Sir Edmund, who, having moved for many years in a vanished world, brilliant in art and literature, and at an extraordinary oriental court, could in his conversation bring all back so colourful and vivid that the historical persons whom he had once met seemed alive and spoke through him'. But why, Hoeppli asked himself, should he alone enjoy this rich, if vicarious, experience, these remarkable and authentic stories? Backhouse was old and poor; and yet he had these priceless memories to impart. Surely an arrangement could be made. . . . 'Whatever the historic value of these stories may be', wrote Hoeppli, 'it seemed regrettable that they should be lost, and in order to preserve them, and to have at the same time a good pretext to provide him with additional funds from my private means', he persuaded Backhouse to write down his experiences 'and to sell the manuscripts to me, as would a professional writer.'

Backhouse was delighted by the proposal. It is clear that, for some years, he had been thinking over his own past. Had he not seen and savoured the memoirs of Li Lien-ying which, by his own account, had surfaced in 1932 (if not before), only to dive out of sight again in 1934? Had he not suggested to Bland that 'your memoirs should be interesting'? And had he not, at the same time, darkly hinted that he too had had an interesting life 'in a hidden way, behind the scenes'? But always Backhouse needed a collaborator, an 'editor', who would drive and organise his own work. In the past, Bland had supplied that function. Now Bland had been replaced by Hoeppli as Morrison had once been replaced by Bland. So once again Backhouse would supply the authentic documents of the past to an 'editor' who would present them to the public. Only this time it would not be translations that he would supply: it would be the direct recollection of his own experience. He would not now be controlled, however loosely, by pre-existent texts. Nor would he be conditioned by any previous knowledge on the part of his editor. For what did Hoeppli know about the early life of Backhouse? Nothing but what Backhouse had told him in those fascinating monologues: monologues which Backhouse, with his quick, vivid, circumstantial and marvellously coherent imagination, was now deliciously free to expand and elaborate, in any direction.

So Backhouse set to work. The reconstruction of his past life revived his spirits. The removal of those 'external inhibitions' liberated his pen. Writing itself proved a form of therapy. His physical health improved visibly as he wrote. His spiritual health had already been improved by his reception into the Roman Church. This had taken place in the summer of 1942.* He now took himself seriously as a Catholic and signed himself, for preference, Paul Backhouse, after a more famous convert.

Hoeppli was somewhat perplexed by Backhouse's conversion. He could not detect in it any spiritual content. He concluded that it had other causes: that it was motivated partly indeed by love of

---

* Mrs Danby says 1941; but Hoeppli's memory for dates seems to me more reliable.

'beautiful ceremonies', but largely by material need. Alone and somewhat lost in enemy-occupied Peking, the old man (Hoeppli thought) 'hoped that by accepting the Catholic faith he would be provided by the Church not only with money, which he always needed, but eventually also with some peaceful abode, secluded and sheltered, such as a monastery with an old garden where he could sit and contemplate, removed from the world and safe'. It was a well-worn theme: we may recall that, a few months before, he had told Mrs Danby that, after the war, he would retire to a Chinese temple, under the protection of a benevolent abbot, for similar contemplation, no doubt on the same unedifying topics. However, if this was his hope, it was to be deceived. In spite of lamentable pleas to the Roman Catholic bishop of Peking, to whom he now turned, as he had previously turned to the Anglican bishops Scott and Norris, Backhouse obtained no material relief from his new church. As Hoeppli says, the Roman Catholic hierarchy was far too prudent to risk its position in Japanese-occupied China by giving special treatment to an enemy alien, who anyway was perhaps no great catch. All the comfort that Backhouse received from his conversion was in the visits of an un-educated Irish confessor, soundly anti-British indeed, but otherwise, as his penitent complained, 'better suited to convert coolies than people like myself'. This uncongenial evangelist would arrive in Backhouse's room with a supply of religious pictures mass-produced for plebeian devotees. Sir Edmund, says Hoeppli, kept them on his table for months and contemplated them devoutly while writing some of the most scabrous chapters of his memoirs.

Thus doubly regenerated, in body and soul, Backhouse wrote quickly, and with *élan*. From the end of that year, Hoeppli received 'in regular succession, sheets covered with the thin, highly nervous products of his penmanship, rather difficult to read'. By May 1943 the first volume had been completed. It was a work of nearly 150,000 words, which Backhouse entitled 'Décadence Mandchoue', and it described, in vivid, personal detail, his own secret history, and his hitherto undivulged relations with the Manchu court, from his arrival in Peking in 1898 until the death of the Empress Dowager ten years later. Then he began a new volume. With quickening pace, he delved still deeper into his remarkable memory, and by the end of June he had written another 70,000 words, forming a second work. This second work, which he entitled 'The Dead Past', was a series of essays concerning his own early life, friendships and travels before coming to the East.

Hoeppli intended to publish Backhouse's two volumes of memoirs, when the time should be ripe. He was proud of his own modest role as Backhouse's 'editor'. He realised, truly enough, that he, and he alone, was responsible for the existence of the Memoirs. As M. Henri Vetch has remarked, Backhouse was not 'un génie créateur': without the driving co-operation of Bland, we should not have had 'those two marvellous books *China under the Empress Dowager* and *Annals and Memoirs of the Court of Peking*', and without Hillier and Barton we would not have had the revised Anglo-Chinese dictionary. When Backhouse worked alone, his work came to nothing. He needed an external force to shape his work; and the force which shaped his last two volumes was Hoeppli.

By the time when he finished 'Décadence Mandchoue' Backhouse had moved to a new address in Peking. In April 1943, on account of high blood-pressure, dizziness, and prostatic and urinary troubles, he could no longer stay in his German boarding-house, and Hoeppli arranged that he should be moved to St Michael's Hospital, a French Catholic hospital in the legation quarter, run by nuns. There he was given a private room, which was to be his home for the rest of his life.

The French hospital was under the control of the French embassy and it happened that one of the French diplomatists then in China was no stranger either to Peking or to the name of Backhouse. He was M. Roland de Margerie, whose father, Pierre de Margerie, had been French minister to the court of Peking from 1909 to 1911. M. de Margerie has told me how, as a boy of twelve, he had returned with his parents from Peking to Paris, and had there discovered, and read and re-read with fascination, the newly published French translation of *China under the Empress Dowager*. Now, thirty years later, he had returned to China as French consul-general in Shanghai, and finding, on a visit to

Peking, that the aged author of that great work was in hospital there, he welcomed the opportunity to visit him.

'I found him', M. de Margerie goes on, 'very frail, but well cared for. He greeted me very warmly, on account of my own early days in Peking, and also – but less warmly! – because I had known his brothers, the distinguished admirals, in England. He was an impressive figure, with a long white beard, very much the man of letters, and he showed real pleasure as he told me about his literary friendships, when young in Paris, with Wilde, Verlaine and Mallarmé. Need I tell you that I was fascinated, especially when, by questioning him, I obtained a promise of further instalments? He then told me that he had even known Rimbaud at the time of his liaison with Verlaine, and gave me details on that subject. Unpublished eye-witness testimony on Rimbaud and Verlaine, found in Peking! That was something to turn the head of any lover of poetry. . . .' So de Margerie questioned this precious source, which he had discovered in the nick of time, and compiled 'a whole dossier of notes, based on my conversations with Backhouse, which now lies somewhere at the bottom of a trunk'. . . .

For later, on reading Backhouse's memoirs, lent to him by the enthusiastic Dr Hoeppli, M. de Margerie began to entertain some doubts. There were certain chronological difficulties which the Swiss doctor had not noticed, but which were exposed by the 'very rich French libraries in Peking'.

Backhouse's conversations with de Margerie were not only on a high literary level. Like Hoeppli, de Margerie found that his new friend was, in conversation at least, 'an old salacious profligate'. In particular, he was 'obsessed with homosexuality' and recounted his own experiences with relish. 'The assurance with which he spoke,' writes de Margerie, 'and the extreme dignity of his appearance, were in perfect contrast with his known morals, of which he boasted freely. I revisited him several times; but he became visibly weaker.' He died on 8 January 1944. He was buried in the Catholic cemetery of Chala, outside P'ing Tze Men, near the burial-place of the Jesuit fathers who had been active in China in the reign of the K'ang-hsi Emperor.

A few hours after Backhouse's death (Hoeppli tells us), a young Chinese called at the Swiss consulate-general and inquired whether the contents of his will were known. In particular, he asked whether Backhouse had left him, as he had promised, a large and beautiful diamond. There was no such provision in the will, and no such diamond among Backhouse's possessions: evidently it was another of those imaginary jewels which he periodically tried to turn into real assets. By his will, dated 11 February 1943, he left small legacies in money to Chinese servants and the residue to his relations in England, whom he asked to provide 'for the recital of a mass for the repose of my soul on the anniversary of my death'. It is unlikely that there was much residue. His personal property, at his death, consisted only of worn clothes, an old Victorian travelling-clock, and a few books, almost all cheap editions and practically worthless. 'He had hardly any linen, no watch, no cuff-links, and, apart from the piece of rose-quartz fastened on his Chinese cap, no jewellery of any kind.' But he had kept, in a red leather case, the document recording his succession to the family baronetcy. At the end of his will, Backhouse expressed 'to Dr Reinhard Hoeppli, Consul of Switzerland, my deepest gratitude for the unfailing kindness, patronage, goodwill, which he has so freely accorded and which is beyond my power adequately to acknowledge'.

Backhouse's legacy to Hoeppli consisted in fact of the two volumes of his memoirs. For the rest of his life, Hoeppli preserved this precious deposit, waiting for the time when they could be given to the world; for Backhouse had made it quite clear that he wished them to be published, and Hoeppli was anyway convinced that they were an important contribution to literature and history. Unfortunately, he had to admit, they were unpublishable – at least at present. They were grossly, obsessively obscene. But who could tell? Times might change: the climate of opinion might become more tolerant, more permissive; the unpublishable might become publishable. So he had them prepared for publication. He had that illegible handwriting transcribed and typed, those numerous ideograms – for Backhouse could not resist the temptation to quote, and to exhibit his calligraphy – exactly and elegantly copied. He had several copies made, and neatly boxed in Chinese covers. He supplied the necessary annotation. He had photographs taken of the author, both alive and dead, to serve as frontispieces to the two volumes. He himself, as editor, wrote a 'postscript' about Backhouse, his own relations with him, and the genesis of the two works. It is from this postscript that I have derived most of my information about Hoeppli's part in the story. Then he waited. Meanwhile he told his friends that he possessed this great literary treasure, and that he would ensure its preservation: for although he admitted that it was scandalous, he had no doubt of its truth.

Indeed, why should he doubt? He had known Backhouse personally, even intimately, for two years. He had never seen any sign of abnormality in him. Backhouse appeared to him 'shrewd', intellectually alert, of strong and exact memory, and patently honest. What motive had he to deceive his benefactor? As his previous 'editor', Bland, had once written, after knowing Backhouse, and knowing him well, for thirty years, 'he would not have sold a fake to me'. And then, his story, however surprising it might seem if baldly paraphrased or summarised, was in itself so coherent, so detailed, so circumstantial. It argued direct experience.

It also had the emphatic authentication of the author. To each of the two volumes Backhouse prefixed a distinct and solemn protestation of absolute veracity, in the form of a deposition on oath. He admits that after so many years, 'the *exact* time' of any episode 'may occasionally have escaped my recollection', but apart from such occasional and trivial lapses, he asserts his bona fides, 'solemnly and seriously, *urbi et orbi* without the shadow of a shade of reservation. As Shylock says, would I lay perjury on my soul? No, not for Venice!' If, at any point, his memory has failed, or even if he is in doubt, he has scrupulously left a blank; for he has a nice sense of honour and would be ashamed to allow even a word of fiction in his factual memoirs in which 'no romance nor embroidery finds a place'. In the body of the work, too, he occasionally reminds his reader, and himself, of his conscientious adherence to the truth. His work, he insists, owes 'nothing to art'; it is a meticulous record of 'things actually seen and heard at first hand'; it is 'veracious from alpha to omega'; 'every syllable is under oath'; '*la devise* of J. J. Rousseau, *vitam impendere vero* is ever my motto also'. Such solemn, not to say portentous asseverations, by a man who had recently 'turned to religion' and expected shortly to meet his Maker, can hardly be ignored, and Dr Hoeppli took them seriously. He 'saw no reason to doubt' that Backhouse's memoirs, even if the detail was occasionally coloured by a particularly vivid imagination, were 'fundamentally based on facts', and that any deviation from strict truth was in matters of detail only, and quite unconscious: 'Sir Edmund, in writing "The Dead Past" and "Décadence Mandchoue", firmly believed that he was stating the truth.'

Besides, the story told in such exact and persuasive detail by Backhouse was not without external corroboration. Before ever reading the lurid revelations of 'Décadence Mandchoue', Hoeppli had received a surprising piece of information from an aged rickshaw-man who, being himself a Manchu, might have some reason to know what he said. After seeing Backhouse pass, this old man told Hoeppli that that venerable Englishman was said to have been, in the distant past, the lover of the Empress Dowager, Tzŭ-hsi.

CHAPTER THIRTEEN

The Memoirs – One

THIRTY years after they were written, Hoeppli still possessed the precious documents which he had hoped to edit for publication. He was now an old man and wished to ensure their future safety. The climate of opinion had not changed – at least not that far. What should he do? Looking again at that scabrous document, he found that there was one chapter which was not obscene and which might well be of historical importance. This was the chapter of 'Décadence Mandchoue' which gave the 'true' history of the dramatic imperial deaths of 1908 – the death of the Kuang-hsü Emperor on 14 November, and the death of the old Empress Dowager next day.

In this chapter, Backhouse had given a completely different version from any that had previously been published – completely different, far more detailed, and extremely readable. It was also far more authoritative; for he had had it, he explained, at first hand, from the chief actors in the drama: from Li Lien-ying, the Grand Eunuch, who had been the organiser, and another eunuch, Ts'ui Tê-lung, one of the perpetrators, of the murder of the Emperor. For by now Backhouse no longer maintained, as he had written in 1910, that either the Emperor's or the Empress's death had been natural. He now stated, categorically and circumstantially, that both had been violent: that the Emperor had been murdered on the orders of the Empress (which indeed has always been believed by many) and that the Empress herself had been murdered by none other than the grand traitor, the maker and unmaker of Emperors, who would seek to found a new dynasty, Yüan Shih-k'ai. All previous accounts, said Backhouse, including his own, had been based either on hearsay or on official propaganda.

They were therefore of no value. He himself had always known the truth but in 1910 he had not dared to publish it. He wished to stay in Peking and therefore had no alternative but to repeat the official version; and the pressure of the Chinese government was reinforced by the explicit orders of the British government, determined not to jeopardise its relations with Yüan Shih-k'ai. Why he had to wait quite so long in order to reveal the truth is not made clear. However, it is enough for us to observe that Backhouse, like the Byzantine historian Procopius, had a public version for the contemporary record and, for posterity, another, a secret history.

Persuaded of the historical importance of this one publishable chapter in Backhouse's memoirs and completely satisfied by his explanation of the different account which he had published in 1910 (and republished in 1939), Hoeppli extracted it and prepared it for separate publication. To it he appended his own 'postscript' on the author which presented him as a reliable authority and gave, in decent language, some account of his interesting life as revealed in the still unpublishable memoirs. By this time the view of Backhouse as a devoted and entirely reputable scholar had been confirmed by the publication of Mrs Danby's article in *The Dictionary of National Biography*. The document, thus edited and supplemented, was duly submitted to a learned Swiss orientalist journal, whose editor, being convinced of its value, accepted it for publication.

The rest of the memoirs Hoeppli did not attempt to publish. But he took steps to ensure their preservation. In January 1973, a month before his own death, he passed both the original manuscript and the annotated typed copies of it which he had prepared for publication to the director of the Swiss medical institute of which he was a member, with the request that they be conveyed, after his death, to public libraries for safe keeping. He particularly mentioned the Bodleian Library, which had already benefited by Backhouse's generosity. The director, seeing the nature of the works and being, no doubt, somewhat embarrassed by them, decided to seek the advice of competent Swiss colleagues before sending them abroad. Those whom he consulted were two distinguished scholars: one a professor of history, the other a professor of English literature. Both expressed lyrical admiration for the work, and neither questioned its basic truth. Apart from Backhouse's solemn protestations, the narrative itself, they said, was its own guarantee: it was so circumstantial, so immediate, so alive, that its truth simply could not be questioned. They also declared that Backhouse was 'a great writer', whose 'literary gifts and incomparable narrative power appear on every page', and they endorsed Hoeppli's wish that 'this precious legacy' be published. It could not be published in Switzerland, of course: that, they admitted, 'would be quite impossible'; but might it not be accepted by a learned press in England? A university press, they suggested, would have a double advantage: it might be prepared to meet the cost of printing all those Chinese ideograms which Sir Edmund had so liberally sprinkled through his work, and it would not fear the imputation of pornography.

The two professors may, of course, have been helped towards their conclusion by Hoeppli's 'postscript' which had been sent to them together with Backhouse's text; but however that may be, they clearly endorsed Hoeppli's view, and the director of the institute, now fortified by three concurrent opinions, offered the document to me. All three sponsors of the work – Hoeppli and the two Swiss professors – had proposed that I should be the final arbiter, partly because it was thought that I had spent some time in the British Secret Service of which Backhouse, in his memoirs, claimed to have been a trusted agent. Had he not been sent, by Lord Curzon, on delicate missions to Mongolia, and had he not reported from Peking, in secret, to correct the inexpert views of official British diplomatists, directly to 'my chief at home' Sir Edward Grey?

I mention these grave judgments by the Swiss professors, not to claim any superiority over them – for at first I too was disposed to take the documents seriously – but simply to show Backhouse's extraordinary plausibility. To anyone who has read his personal history, as I have now reconstructed it, it must be obvious that the old fraud was at his tricks again. But in 1973 that biography had not been established. The only biography available was the article by Mrs Danby in *The Dictionary of National Biography*. The few persons whom I could discover who had known Backhouse in his now distant and anyway secluded days had no inkling of his real character. And although it was known, to Hoeppli as to others, that there were doubts about the diary of Ching-shan, nobody had yet publicly suggested that Backhouse himself had deliberately forged it. Henri Vetch, who had discussed it with Backhouse, still insisted that it was genuine. Victor Purcell, writing twenty years after Backhouse's death, though convinced that the diary was a forgery, had nevertheless treated Backhouse's account of his 'discovery' of it with respect, as a necessary piece of evidence in the case. But indeed, Backhouse's whole career, as now reconstructed, is evidence of his remarkable gift of plausibility. Not only by loose, general speeches, but by precise and detailed written documents, throughout his life he imposed his fantasies and forgeries on otherwise critical men. Hoeppli himself was an experienced medical man, familiar with psychological problems, and he had been chosen by his government for a practical task of great responsibility which he discharged with universal commendation. He cannot have been a fool. If he too was taken in, he could say, with the American businessman George Hall, that, faced with Backhouse, anyone would have been taken in.

Therefore, when I first read these extraordinary memoirs, without any biographical context into which to fit them, and against which to check them, or any apparent means of constructing such a context, there was no alternative but to test them internally, by their content. At first this was very difficult. Backhouse's statements about persons, in so far as they were neutral and factual and did not involve himself, turned out to be remarkably accurate; and the accuracy and detail of his memory, after so long a time, could not but inspire a certain confidence. Where he involved himself with famous persons, there was no means of disproof. I merely noted that none of these famous persons – Lord Rosebery, Paul Verlaine, Oscar Wilde, Walter Pater, Aubrey Beardsley, Sir Edward Grey, Lord Curzon, and a dozen others – had left, as far as I could discover, any record of having known Backhouse even by name. As for the Empress Dowager and her courtiers, with whom Backhouse had claimed personal familiarity – and he had claimed it long before he wrote his memoirs: at least as early as 1921 – that was an area which I could not penetrate. I could only note that the few writers who had claimed knowledge of her court evidently did not associate him either with her or with it. The central events in the memoirs, both before and after Backhouse's arrival in China in 1898, were by their nature unverifiable; and it was impossible to test them against the known movements of Backhouse, because his movements, from the time when he left Oxford to the time when he first became known in China, were and still are buried in obscurity. Even now, apart from a few casual references, the only source for the whole period from 1895 to 1908, if source it can be called, is his memoirs, which I was seeking to test.

However, little by little, as I pressed the evidence, the inevitable discrepancies began to appear and I was able to satisfy myself that the memoirs were not merely erroneous here and there, not merely coloured by imagination in detail, but pure fantasy throughout – and yet fantasy which was spun with extraordinary ingenuity around and between true facts accurately remembered or cunningly bent to sustain it. It seemed as if Backhouse had devised his fantasies with infinite care and skill not only in order to avoid ruinous collision with objective evidence, but also so that, however improbable in themselves, they would appear to be positively supported by such evidence. They were not random hallucinations, the wandering visions of a weakened mind: shot through though they were by grotesque sexual obsessions, they were highly rational constructions, artfully designed not only to be coherent in themselves, indestructible by obvious fact, but also to corroborate other, earlier, now threatened figments of the same mind.

Since establishing, to my own satisfaction, the true character of Backhouse's memoirs, I pursued such evidence as I could find about his life and reconstructed it, as objectively as I could, without (naturally) making any use of the memoirs. I could not exclude the possibility that those memoirs might occasionally deviate into veracity about their author, but they could never be trusted. Now that his true biography has been set out, I do not believe that it is necessary for me to expound or examine the memoirs in any detail, or narrate the process by which I was convinced that, even when most circumstantial, and least verifiable, they were totally imaginary. The reader will already be predisposed, by Backhouse's previous history, to dismiss in advance his unedifying revelations, and to wonder how anyone can ever have taken them seriously. It is therefore enough to summarise them very briefly, not for their own sake, but for the light which they shed on two problems: first, on the psychology of their author, and secondly, on the still unresolved question of the purpose and method of his literary forgeries.

Outwardly, the two volumes of Backhouse's memoirs relate his personal experiences, first in Europe, until 1898, then, from 1898 to 1908, in China. In Europe, he appears as a man of letters, an aesthete, an intimate personal friend of all the best known poets and writers of the 1880s and 1890s in both England and France, and a man of the world who moves in the *beau monde* and is admitted to the company of royalty. In China he is a privileged observer who, thanks to his linguistic gifts and sympathetic manners, is adopted into the imperial court. But these scenes of literary, social and courtly life provide only the colouring of the story: its internal unity, its only organising principle, is not social or literary but sexual. Both volumes are grossly, grotesquely, obsessively obscene. Backhouse presents himself as a compulsive pathic homosexual who found in China opportunities for indulgence which, in England, owing to repressive laws and Victorian hypocrisy, could be only dangerously and furtively enjoyed; and in his old age, once the benevolent Hoeppli had removed 'certain external inhibitions', he clearly derived an exquisite lubricious pleasure from minutely and unctuously describing every detail of such perversions. Whatever their claims as literature or history, the two volumes can in fact be best entitled 'The imaginary sexual life of E. T. Backhouse, 1. in the literary and political world of the 1890s, 2. in the court of Tzǔ-hsi'.

Like many men whose life excites conventional disapproval, Backhouse ascribed his eccentricity to a misunderstood childhood. His early years, he wrote, had been 'ideally unhappy'. He detested both his mother and his father, and uses the most violent language about both of them. Indeed, he twice describes the scene of his mother's funeral, in October 1902, when (he tells us) he stood at the graveside and, much to the surprise of his widowed father, cursed her 'detestable memory' in 'ten different tongues'. He was then thirty years old and, according to his own account, had not seen his mother for eight years; but time and absence had not abated his detestation, his need to avenge the sufferings of the past. Nor was he any happier at school than at home; for St George's, Ascot, the school to which he had been sent at the age of nine, was, he tells us, merely another scene of torture. It was 'a nursery of stereotyped intellects', and the boys which it turned out were 'prigs and snobs': only the companionship of Winston Churchill, Maurice Baring and some others made life bearable. The headmaster, Herbert Sneyd-Kynnersley, was 'a sadistic tyrant of colossal self-adulation, who loved to flog his pupils' and who, he suggests, had homosexual relations with some of them. However, after four years, the horrors of school life at Ascot were suddenly compensated, says Backhouse, by the arrival of a new teacher to whom he became devoted and who was to be the greatest influence in his life, redeeming it from insularity and philistinism. This new master, who arrived in February 1886 and stayed till July of the same year, teaching French, was none other than the poet Paul Verlaine.

Verlaine, according to Backhouse, stayed at St George's, Ascot, for six months teaching French. His departure was precipitated by an untoward event. On 16 July 1886, *albo lapillo notanda dies*, the headmaster died suddenly of a heart-attack while ferociously flogging a boy, who is scrupulously named as Dermot Howard Blundell, and the school broke up for a premature vacation. Verlaine disappeared, and Backhouse and his fellow-pupils took an exquisite revenge on their sadistic tyrant: 'we boys were so thrilled by the tidiness of his fatal syncope that, with the friendly co-operation of a kindly house-maid who laid him out in his coffin, we managed to have the broken rod inserted in his shroud, like the Egyptians who buried familiar objects with their dead; so birch and crucifix (for he was an extremely high English church-man) found place together in his dishonourable grave.'

On Verlaine's arrival at St George's, Backhouse (he tells us) at once became his favoured friend and protégé. With the consent of his parents (which seems surprising), he accompanied Verlaine to Paris in the Easter holidays, and thus found his way, at an early age, into French literary circles. Through Verlaine, then or on later visits, he became familiar with most of the French writers of the time, and the Ganymede of some of them. He mentions Mallarmé, Barrès, Villiers de l'Isle Adam, Pierre Loti, Pierre Louys, J. K. Huysmans. In the first draft of 'The Dead Past' he also mentioned Rimbaud, but when Hoeppli pointed out an insuperable chronological difficulty, he deftly changed the poet into a cobbler called Rimbot whose name had occasioned a temporary and pardonable confusion. Meanwhile, at Winchester, Backhouse was discovering the tastes which (he says) he was afterwards to indulge so freely. His six years there (he tells us) were 'a carnival of unbridled lust': he was 'the desired of many' and enjoyed 'carnal intimacy with at least thirty (perhaps more) boys, ascendant and descendant' – including, inevitably, 'Bosie', Lord Alfred Douglas. But he admits that he derived some subsidiary pleasure from the classics, of which he still imperfectly remembered the more indecent passages; and so, with his flair for languages, he obtained his Oxford award.

At Oxford (if he can be believed) Backhouse at once became friendly, not to say intimate, with all bearers of famous names. Walter Pater was 'my outside college tutor' and 'I fell completely under his spell'. He was soon having luncheon with Pater, discussing 'Greek love' with him, and whether Michelangelo was passive as well as active in that respect; but he resisted the surprising propositions of his tutor, finding his equipment under-size. Within a few days of his first arrival, he was invited to meet the Prime Minister, Mr Gladstone, who had come to deliver the Romanes lecture, on 'Medieval Universities'. Backhouse, he tells us, had an interesting conversation with the great man, who was pleased to meet a relation of the whig hero Charles James Fox. Backhouse also entertained Verlaine, and provided him with facilities for casual enjoyment with a good-looking and compliant undergraduate whom he had spotted at mass in the Catholic church. He was entertained by Haverfield, taught by Jowett. He was also taken up by Charles Gore, the first Principal of Pusey House, and took to ritualism, both in its Tractarian form at Oxford and in its Roman form at the Jesuit church in Farm

Street, London. Among undergraduate friends, he only mentions Max Beerbohm and a few peers. He was often in London, where he enjoyed regular dinners *à quatre* with Max, Oscar Wilde and Alfred Douglas, and in Paris, where he enjoyed a different kind of intimacy with Wilde, Douglas and the actor Harry Stanford. He was also a close friend of Aubrey Beardsley and his circle – indeed, at the age of twenty-one, he helped Beardsley to edit *The Yellow Book*, and himself wrote an essay for it arising out of his experiences in Greece. However, he withdrew it before publication to avoid offending his host, Frank Noel. Meanwhile he enjoyed 'an association . . . which was by no means platonic' with Beardsley's friend and patron André Raffalovich, who, we are told, 'has spoken of it' in his memoirs.*

Backhouse's memories of Oxford, apart from relations with Pater and Max Beerbohm, meetings with Gladstone and visits by Verlaine, seem very thin. Most of his activity, in those years, was extra-curricular. At one time he 'started a career as a prodigal plunger of the turf' and had a narrow escape from the sharpers. At another, we find him at the tables at Monte Carlo. In London, he sits at the feet of Henry James, Edmund Gosse, George Moore, Joseph Conrad; he visits the homosexual *hammam* in Jermyn Street, where he meets all his old friends, including Henry James as a neutral voyeur 'who held nothing human alien from his theory of life' – as well as similar institutions in Paris. He is even to be found at the feet of Herbert Spencer in the Athenæum; and in the intervals of such company, he is eating dinners at the Inner Temple and taking 'a high degree in law'.

But above all, in those undergraduate years, he travelled. His travels are indeed extraordinary. In his first long vacation he is in Greece. There we find him staying in Euboea with that hospitable English landlord, Frank Noel, who, he tells us, was still under a cloud on account of his supposed involvement in the sensational

* André Raffalovich was the son of a rich Jew from Odessa (Backhouse, who did not like Jews, calls him Croatian). In Oscar Wilde's phrase, he attempted to set up a salon in London and ended by setting up an eating-house. In 1895, after the trial of Oscar Wilde, he published in France a treatise on homosexuality. He also wrote poems and novels. I cannot discover any memoirs by him, or any reference to Backhouse in those of his writings which I have seen. His personal papers, including Beardsley's letters to him, are now in the University of Texas.

Dilessi murders of 1870, when a party of innocent tourists, mostly English, had been captured by bandits on the battlefield of Marathon and four of them held to ransom and killed.* Then we hear him discussing the same delicate but ancient subject with the King and Queen of the Hellenes at a royal garden party at Tatoi. If we object that, by 1893, that famous episode had been forgotten in Greece, we should consider that it was remembered in north Yorkshire, the home of one of the victims, Frederick Vyner; and Backhouse had something of a fixation on the Vyner family. Next long vacation he is on the way to Canada, exciting the jealousy of Henry Irving by his evident attraction to Ellen Terry: we may recall that he had a similar fixation on Ellen Terry.

By September he is back at home, staying with Lord Rosebery at Dalmeny and enjoying with him 'a slow and protracted copulation which gave equal pleasure to both parties'. These delightful experiences, interlaced and heightened by port and elevated political conversation, took place in a 'detached and solitary house' called Barnbougle, and the pace was made by the great man: for, as Backhouse puts it, 'my readers will agree that when a young man is privileged to have sexual intercourse with a Prime Minister, any proposal regarding the *modus operandi* must emanate from the latter'. By this time Backhouse is describing himself as unofficial private secretary to the Prime Minister, translating documents for him.† But he has time also to set up in Paris with an actress, 'la belle Otéro', much to the chagrin of Sarah Bernhardt. . . . Meanwhile he has, at some unspecified time (as he would explain to the Empress Eugénie) 'beaucoup voyagé en Espagne', and he has been learning some of the forty-eight languages which he could afterwards claim to know, including Japanese. Finally, in 1895 'after completing my Oxford course' (in fact he never completed it), 'I went to Japan'.

In January 1896 he was back in England, in time to intervene with Lord Curzon to save the life of Dr Sun Yat-sen, who, as is well known, had, at that time, been lured into the Chinese

* The accusation that Frank Noel was involved in the murders was a Greek libel. See Romilly Jenkins, *The Dilessi Murders* (1961).

† Backhouse always refers to Rosebery as Prime Minister, though he did not become so till March 1894. In September 1893 he was Foreign Secretary in Gladstone's government.

Legation in London and imprisoned there: for by this time he was unofficial private secretary to Curzon too. Then, almost at once, he set off, via Paris, to Russia. Two years before, he tells us, he had written to Tolstoy inviting him to contribute to *The Yellow Book* (an enjoyable thought). Tolstoy had declined but had invited the unknown young Englishman to Yasnaya Polyana. Now was the time to cash that blank cheque. Backhouse spent, as he tells us, all that summer in Russia, including a month at Yasnaya Polyana enjoying the stimulating conversation of the great man, who also gave him – what is rather surprising, since Tolstoy was then in deep disfavour, hated at court, disowned by society, and excommunicated by the church – a letter of introduction to the Tsar. In Moscow he was 'a privileged guest' at the coronation of Nicholas II at the Uspenski Sobor and enjoyed familiar conversation with the Empress and the Empress Mother. He also (according to his later statements) was made a Russian baron, and became 'intimate, too intimate' with Alyosha, nephew of Prince Lobanoff, who introduced him to new homosexual refinements. On his return – if his dates are correct – he appears in England, visiting Swinburne at The Pines. Next spring he is in Paris, studying the theatre under M. Got of the Comédie Française and appearing on the stage with Sarah Bernhardt, who gives him his introduction to the Empress Eugénie. He enjoys an agreeable conversation with the Empress – his third Empress in a year. Then he is off via Constantinople (where he discovers the pleasure of copulation with eunuchs, afterwards to be refined in China) to Cairo, where the pleasure derived from an amorous night with an easily identifiable Ottoman princess is increased by the contrast which she draws between his prowess and the frigidity of Lord Kitchener. Later, Backhouse would be able to chaff Lord Kitchener (whom he would oblige by purchasing Chinese porcelain for his collection) on this unflattering comparison. The great man, we are told, was not at all put out, but candidly admitted his different proclivities. 'Where there's no will, my boy,' he said knowingly, 'there's no way.'

Meanwhile, at an uncertain date but probably in 1894, when he last saw his hated mother, Backhouse has contrived to be in Yorkshire long enough to become engaged to a suitable *partie*, 'Doris V.', a relation of the Marquis of Ripon. It is easy to supply the surname: once again we note the Vyner fixation. Who knows, Backhouse rhetorically asks, what would have happened had that marriage come off? Perhaps he would have become respectable and settled down as a Yorkshire squire. . . . Perhaps; but it was not to be. At the last minute, a few days before the wedding, when the copious gifts were already displayed, the prudent lady changed her mind, married a less eccentric neighbour, and then, returning from her honeymoon, broke her neck in the hunting-field. That was one way to dispose of a purely imaginary person. After that, Backhouse had no further thoughts of matrimony.

It was in the autumn of 1897 that Backhouse was complimented by the Ottoman princess on being 'un bimétalliste des plus séduisants'. In November he was back in England in time to see the dying Aubrey Beardsley. Next spring he was arriving, from Tokyo, in Shanghai. The *Wanderjahre* were over. From now on, Backhouse is a Chinese figure, or legend. 'The Dead Past' is dead; and we move on to the even more extraordinary adventures of 'Décadence Mandchoue'.

'Décadence Mandchoue' opens, appropriately, in a high-class homosexual brothel, the Shu Ch'un T'ang, or Hall of Chaste Joys. This establishment, Backhouse tells us, was patronised by the Manchu aristocracy, and he had been introduced to it, in April of 1899, by Prince Ch'ing, an imperial clansman and President of the Tsungli Yamen or Foreign Office. The Prince was one of its regular customers, being 'himself homosexual in the "forme active et passive" of the word.' Once introduced, there is no delay. We are initiated, in great detail, into every practice, every refinement, of the institution. It is a subject of which the reader will have more than enough long before the end of the book. But with the next chapter we are relieved to find ourselves back in the open air. This is the essential chapter which sets the stage for the whole drama. It shows how Backhouse first came to the notice of the Empress Dowager.

We are now in 1902, but in order to understand the course of events we must look back two years, to the summer of 1900, the period of the Boxer Rising. In the course of that rising, the foreign legations in Peking had been besieged. They had been relieved, in the end, by an Allied army, and the imperial court had fled to Sian. For a time, the deserted Summer Palace had been occupied by Russian troops; then the Russian government, as a conciliatory gesture, had withdrawn its forces and British and Italian troops took over. At once, says Backhouse, looting began, and he decided, on his own initiative, to rescue the imperial treasures from the vandalism of our 'counterfeit Caucasian civilisation'. So, with the aid of a party of 'trusty Manchus', he caused the removal of 'bronzes, jades, porcelain, ivories, paintings, calligraphy, cloisonné, lacquer, tapestries, carpets (some 600 pieces in all)', and about 25,000 volumes – for Backhouse is always exact and circumstantial in such matters – 'to a place of safety, not my own house, as I did not wish my name to appear, knowing as I do the inveterate calumnious suspicions of my unctuous hypocritical compatriots'. Sixteen months later, in January 1902, when the court returned to Peking, Backhouse (he tells us) got in touch with the all-powerful Chief Eunuch 'with the object of returning personally Her Majesty's property intact'. The Chief Eunuch was, of course, our old friend Li Lien-ying.

The Eunuch, says Backhouse, was gratified by this unusual honesty of a Foreign Devil. He reported that the Empress Dowager would receive Backhouse personally, on delivery of the treasure at the entrance to the Palace in the Forbidden City. Accordingly, in May 1902, 'the long, long procession of porters and bearers wound its serpentine trail into the Eastern gate of the Forbidden City'. There it was met by Li Lien-ying himself, who ticked off each package against the previously submitted inventory, and then engaged the author in desultory but intimate conversation. They discussed the Boxer Rising, secrets of state, Ching-shan; and Li asked particularly, in the name of the Empress, whether John Brown the ghillie had been 'cut off from the family' – i.e. made a eunuch – like himself, and if not, why not? Surely, in such a case, it was the duty of Parliament to intervene, to protect the Blood Royal. Meanwhile the Empress was counting her restored treasures, rejoicing particularly in the recovery of her favourite piece, 'an enormous block of jade, most beautifully carved and dating from 1420', and preparing to receive and thank their restorer.

If this remarkable scene, the restitution, by a single just man, of the imperial treasures of China, somehow – like so many other episodes in Backhouse's life – escaped the notice of contemporaries, that (says Backhouse) is easily explained. Her Majesty had providentially chosen for the occasion the day of the Peking spring races, when all Europeans were out of the city and 'not even the inquisitious and perfidious correspondent of the London *Times* had wind of the matter, nor associated me, whom he regarded as his enemy, with part or lot in the transaction'. Only the Japanese-owned newspaper *Shun T'ien Shih Pao*, we are told, mentioned the episode, and that somewhat inaccurately; but in any case an oriental paper would not have been intelligible by *The Times* correspondent; for that inquisitious and perfidious creature was of course, Dr Morrison. In his memoirs, Backhouse would never mention without expressions of detestation the man who first doubted the authenticity of the diary of Ching-shan.

Having thus unexpectedly recovered the treasures of her Empire, the Empress graciously received her benefactor, and Backhouse, who now found himself in the presence of his fourth Empress, was thanked and rewarded. He was given 'the brevet of a Board President, or Shang Shu, the First Button of official rank (jewelled, not coralled), a hereditary II class nobility, the coveted twin-eyed peacock's feather, a set of court spring and autumn robes decidedly on the small side for my inches, and a sable robe with yellow riding jacket, the coveted privilege (of which I never availed myself) of riding on horseback across the Forbidden City, a special gold tablet, 3 inches by 2, with the ideographs Huang T'ai Hou T'ê ("by H.M. the Empress Dowager's special favour") which would gain my admittance at any hour at the gate of all the palaces when Her Majesty might happen to be in residence, besides a gold *ju-i* weighing 28 oz. and a fine collection of books now in a European library, a painting by Her Majesty's own hand' – the painting, presumably, which is reproduced in *China under the Empress Dowager* – 'and a manuscript history of the Yehonala clan' – the Manchu clan to which she belonged. These rewards were to be increased later, for further services of a different kind. The hereditary nobility conferred upon Backhouse made him a marquis in the Manchu peerage, and the same title was also granted retrospectively to his ancestors for three generations, thus compensating Sir Jonathan for his failure to attain an English peerage.

In the course of his interview, Backhouse, he tells us, enjoyed some interesting private conversation with the grateful and bountiful Empress, whose personality he set out almost in the terms ascribed by him, in his letter to Bland, to the memoirs of Li Lien-ying, adding that she reminded him, particularly, of that famous Victorian *grande dame* and Lady Bountiful, the Baroness Burdett-Coutts. She too dwelt on the recent Boxer troubles and rattled away indiscreetly about the actions of her ministers at that time. She also volunteered the true story of the fate of the Chen Fei, or Pearl Concubine, the Kuang-hsü Emperor's favourite consort who had angered the Empress by trying to keep the Emperor in Peking when the court was preparing to flee, and had addressed the Empress in injurious terms. This was the last of many provocations. The Empress gave the impertinent girl short shrift: she had her thrown down a well and then ordered the distraught Emperor to mount the peasant cart which would take him to Sian.

So at least Ching-shan had recorded in his diary, as quoted by Backhouse and Bland, although others had given a less dramatic version of the episode. Now, as Backhouse recalled, the Empress herself had endorsed the version of Ching-shan in even more dramatic terms. She described the insolence of the concubine. 'I heard her to the end', she said, 'and bade Li and another eunuch take her up and throw her into the well, as a warning to monster-hearted birds which peck out their parents' eyes. I waited to leave in the carts until her shrieks had ceased and the servants had placed a great slab over the well.' Then, after a pause, the Empress turned to Backhouse. 'You are a foreigner', she said: 'tell me, was I right or wrong? Dynastic house law decrees death for any concubine who insults the imperial ancestors'. 'She brought her fate upon herself', said I. 'Your Majesty could no other'. . . . 'The attendant eunuchs looked greatly relieved at my reply: Li Lien-ying told me later that he had half feared some remonstrance on my part, which, as he said, would have been bad for me and worse for him'.

This interview, says Backhouse, marked the beginning of his close relations with the Empress Dowager. Soon afterwards, he tells us, he was summoned for a no less interesting interview with the most powerful politician at her court, the man who, in political matters, ruled both the Empress and the Empire: the Viceroy and Grand Secretary Jung-lu, 'the father-in-law of the future Regent and grandfather of the present emperor of Manchukuo'. Already, he tells us, his admiration for Jung-lu knew no bounds: 'I had already idealised him, partly from Ching-shan's diary and partly knowing that, but for him, every alien in North China would have been massacred'. This was indeed the thesis which Jung-lu's propagandists would soon be putting out and which would be so conveniently documented in Ching-shan's diary.

It was also documented by Jung-lu himself in conversation with Backhouse. Indeed, it seems that Jung-lu had summoned Backhouse expressly for the purpose of giving him the correct version of events at court during the Boxer crisis. After discreetly discovering the correct amount of 'gate-money' to be paid to the attendants (we recall, inevitably, the 80 dollars charged to Hall for the imaginary visits to the President), Backhouse duly set out. He found that he had to wait, for Jung-lu – most opportunely, as it turned out – was giving audience to the Grand Secretary Wang Wên-shao, the author of the rival diary whose entries had become so mysteriously intertwined with that of Ching-shan; and Wang was staying to luncheon. So Backhouse was served a delicious refection in his host's 'inner study' and there was able to imagine the past history and admire the present furniture of this secret power-house of the Empire. Was it not from this room that the all-powerful catamite of the T'ien-ch'i Emperor ruled the Empire for six years, inducing his infatuated master to erect shrines in his honour as a divine sage? Jung-lu had only recently acquired this imperial residence, but its furniture already reflected his aesthetic and intellectual tastes. Among the books, mainly historical, was 'a fine Ming edition of the Tso Chuan annotated by Jung-lu. I did not think then', says Backhouse, 'that this work would pass to me by purchase after Jung-lu's death, and it is now in the Bodleian'.

After luncheon, Backhouse was summoned, and the conversation began. Jung-lu answered all questions freely and provided Backhouse with ample evidence of his own sound views and meritorious actions in the days of crisis. He spoke freely about the less sound views of the other politicians and courtiers. He also spoke of Ching-shan and confirmed the authenticity and veracity of his diary about which he had just heard from Wang Wên-shao. Wang, who had asked to be remembered to his friend Backhouse, had told Jung-lu how Backhouse had found the diary and how he himself had read it. That explained much. At the end of the interview, Jung-lu presented to Backhouse an interesting bibliographical rarity: a poem by the Ch'ien-lung Emperor copied by Grand Secretary Liu Lun and bound in jade, which, says Backhouse, 'is now in a European library' – as indeed it is, for it is one of the books presented by him to the Bodleian. In this respect at least it is more real than the annotated Ming edition of the Tso Chuan, which cannot be traced.

If only Jung-lu had lived! sighs Backhouse. He would have prevented the dismissal of Yüan Shih-k'ai in 1909, and perhaps there would have been no revolution in 1911. . . . But alas, by 1904 he was dead, and by his death he left a void in the Empress's heart. No doubt this explains, in part, the next striking episode in Backhouse's life. For in August of that year Backhouse (he tells us) received a message from the eunuch Li Lien-ying commanding him to come to the Summer Palace. He was to leave his chair at a discreet distance and arrive at the palace in a closed palanquin 'so as to attract less attention'. He had no doubts what this meant. As the palanquin was carried 'along the water-logged country by-paths, some eight or nine miles distance, to the Wan Shou Temple's imperial road', where two eunuchs met him to escort him on foot for the rest of the journey, he felt himself a second Königsmarck or Potemkin. His doubts were solely about his performance. 'Was I sexually adequate for Her Majesty's over-flowing carnality?' Might he be so unfortunate as to 'present to the Old Buddha a *telum imbelle sine ictu*, a tool unwarlike and devoid of thrust, like the faltering sword of Priam, slain by Pyrrhus at the fall of Troy?'

He need not have worried. Although Her Majesty's demands, in her seventieth year, were both exacting in number and unusual in form, delicious refreshments, sophisticated devices, well-tempered aphrodisiacs, supplied any defect of strength in her partner; and in the intervals of action he was able to enjoy intimate conversation about Queen Victoria and John Brown (a subject to which the Empress continually returned), the Jewish origin of the Prince Consort ('a court secret of which my family have sure and certain cognizance'), the unfortunate circumstances of the death of the French President Félix Faure, the English laws against homosexual practices, and Backhouse's intimacy with the Queen's lifelong friend, Sir John Clark, baronet, of Tillypronie (near Balmoral).

Ex uno disce omnes, as Backhouse is fond of quoting, though he does not often follow his own precept. The rest of the book consists largely of an alternation of two themes, tediously and minutely reiterated: homosexual relations with eunuchs, professional catamites and Manchu *jeunesse dorée*, and command performances for the Empress Dowager. At one point the two threads are intertwined. In conversation with Backhouse, the Empress expressed an interest in a fashionable homosexual *hammam*, and turning to the eunuch Li Lien-ying said, 'after our return to town, you must arrange for me to go there in disguise: it would amuse me to see all you dissolute young men diverting yourselves'. As she ordered, so it was done. The young men were indeed diverting themselves, when 'a peremptory voice shouted from the foot of the short flight of stairs, "Kuei Hsia, kneel down",' ...' and who should enter the room but Her Majesty, 'who had disguised herself with a Feng Ling or windproof cape round her head and was wearing a yellow riding jacket and masculine trousers and wadded shoes'. Her Majesty ordered the diversion to continue while she engaged in light badinage with those not immediately occupied. Backhouse, as always, described the diversion in revolting detail, but the badinage reads well. When the Empress had gone, 'Prince Kung asked me if my queen would have come out incognito on such a visit. I replied that customs differ and that such spectacles, though existing in London and Paris, were concealed from publicity by the cloak of hypocrisy, though equally libidinous'.

In counting up his experiences, Backhouse concluded that he

had in Peking 'many hundred (perhaps a thousand) love affairs'
with his own sex and 150 to 200 with the Empress Dowager.
We need not seek exactitude in such matters, nor follow Backhouse in his indefatigable reiteration. We read on, and, with some
relief, find ourselves in the cleaner air of mere conspiracy and
murder: the last chapter of 'Décadence Mandchoue' is the chapter
on the death of the Emperor and the Empress, which Hoeppli had
sought to publish. I have already mentioned this chapter and its
conclusions. Here I shall add a little illustrative detail; for the
story shows Backhouse's style of *histoire romancée*, reminiscent of
the popular writers of his time, Stanley Weyman and Anthony
Hope.

According to Backhouse the events of 1908 were a crisis
comparable with the crisis of 1898–1901. Now, as then, factions
at court competed to control puppet emperors, and this time the
struggle was intensified by the failing health of the Empress and
the prospect of a vacuum at the centre of real power. This time,
also, there was a new character in the dramatis personae: for
Backhouse inserts himself into the story as the Empress's faithful
confidant.

The story begins when the confidant receives an urgent summons from the Grand Eunuch. Backhouse, ignoring the agitated
pleas of his ten servants, who apprehend disaster, boldly sets off
wearing his twin-eyed peacock-feather, his yellow riding-jacket,
and the rest of his court robes, and carrying the golden tablet
which admits him to the Forbidden City. There he is received by
the Empress, 'resplendent in jewels and wearing the famous pearl
jacket'. The Empress describes the intrigue against her; how the
dominant faction among the councillors, taking advantage of her
recent illness, is scheming to end her regency and restore the
Kuang-hsü Emperor to power. She herself is to be assassinated or
banished to Jehol. But she protests that she is not defeated yet.
Soothsayers have prophesied that she has still several years to live,
and she has plans to thwart the threatened coup d'état: 'I am not
one to let the grass grow under my feet, and I mean to anticipate
these traitors. Consequently (and Li Lien-ying is cognisant of the
plan) I feel it my bounden necessity to dispose of the Emperor,
because in so doing I shall deprive these treason-workers of their

puppet figurehead. I shall deal with each of them later', she added grimly. But of course, the Emperor's death was to seem natural; and this is where Backhouse comes in: 'What I want is that, if you hear of the Emperor's sudden passing, dragon-borne, to Heaven, you will be at pains to let your government know that it was a natural death'. Once the Emperor had been disposed of, she proposed to put aside the infant P'u-i, whom she had herself designated as the next emperor, and replace him by P'u-lun, the more legitimate heir, who had been passed over in 1875. . . . Backhouse obediently agreed to misinform Sir Edward Grey, with whom, he said, he had direct connexion. The Empress then provided him with a cover-story for his summons to the Palace. If anyone should ask the reason for his visit to the Palace at such a time, he was to say that it was in order to convey an autograph birthday greeting from the Empress to Queen Alexandra 'which I wish you to send direct and not through the Foreign Office'; as indeed, we are told, he then did, sending the letter via Siberia; and it duly reached the Queen 'on 2nd December, the day of her nativity'. Backhouse was, by now, according to his own account, a practised bearer of royal messages. After these arrangements had been made, the tension was relaxed in an affable conversation on more agreeable topics, and in particular, the liaison between Edward VII and Mrs Keppel.

A few days later, the Empress's plan was carried out. Two eunuchs waited on the Emperor, followed by a servant carrying stuffed cushions and a silken cord. They found him reclining on the k'ang 'reading the novel *Chin P'ing Mei* (not one of the most reputable Chinese novels)', and after some preliminary civilities, informed him that the Empress had made new arrangements for the succession, put the noose round his neck, and suffocated him slowly with the pillows.

When the news was brought to the Empress she was much relieved. 'Thank God, I feel a new life within my veins,' she said: 'it's the most blessed of all events'; and she summoned the Grand Council in order to proceed to the next stage of her plan: the proclamation of a new emperor. The infant P'u-i, so recently adopted as heir-apparent, was to be set aside and the mature P'u-lun was to reign under the title of the Heng-ch'ing Emperor.

All seemed to go smoothly, as planned, There were no objections. But afterwards Yüan Shih-k'ai and the Minister of War, T'ieh-liang, demanded a private audience, to submit their humble views on a matter of state:

Yüan kotowed thrice and T'ieh followed his example. 'Your Majesty is full of years, riches and honours. You should pass your remaining years in the profound seclusion of Yi Ho Yüan and not be troubled by multitudinous state affairs. . . . I ask Your Majesty, and T'ieh-liang (who nodded assent) joins me in the prayer, to issue one more decree announcing your irrevocable abdication and appointing us as Grand Imperial Preceptors, T'ai Shih, who will advise the new emperor on all governmental business as Joint Regents.

The Old Buddha's wrath kindled even as thunder. She shouted in her rage and fury, 'You traitor, nay you two traitors. After all I have done for you, is this the way you repay my benevolence? I dismiss you both from your offices and shall order that you be handed for trial to the Minister of Justice. Though you die a thousand deaths, your retribution will be too light. The cup of your treason and iniquity is full to the brim. Leave the presence and await my orders.'

At this, Yüan drew out a six-chambered revolver and fired three shots, at point blank range, into the Empress's belly. The court apothecaries, the women of the bed-chamber, the eunuchs, hearing the shots, rushed in; but it was too late. After a few dramatic last words, the Empress, in a pool of blood, 'expired amidst the wailing of the eunuchs and of the household, who called upon her spirit not to leave the tenement of her body'. Once she was dead, the Council met, reversed the Empress's last decrees, and re-instated the infant prince, P'u-i, on the throne left vacant by the death of the Kuang-hsü Emperor. After their successful counter-coup, the councillors declared that both deaths were natural; their statement was endorsed, out of loyalty to the Empress in one instance, out of self-interest in the other, by Backhouse; and the European legations being 'as usual, in blissful ignorance' of real events, never discovered the truth.

Such is the authentic story of the two imperial deaths of November 1908 as recounted by Backhouse from first-hand evidence: the death of the Emperor from the eunuchs who carried it out; that of the Empress from those who witnessed it. The only

objection to this dramatic and circumstantial story is that – *pace*
Dr Hoeppli, and apart from the fact that it defies both evidence
and probability* – there is not the slightest reason for believing
a word of it.

After describing this tragic dénouement, which ended his
personal history as a privileged guest in the imperial court,
Backhouse's memoirs end with general reflexions, including an
epilogue on the desecration, twenty years later, of the imperial
tombs. For in 1928 thieves broke into the mausolea of the Manchu
dynasty in the Eastern Hills, and the bodies of three of its
Emperors – the Kang-hsi, Hsien-fêng and T'ung-chih emperors –
and of Tzŭ-hsi herself, stripped of their funeral ornaments, were
thrown to the scavenging dogs. Backhouse, as he tells us, went
out, soon afterwards, to see the melancholy scene, and was able to
strike his most sentimental note, recording this last indignity to
his revered mistress. It was a subject on which he had dilated
before, at Mrs Danby's dinner-table. The new revelations of old
intimacy now gave the story an added but, alas, spurious pathos.

* It defies probability because the Empress had an obvious interest in the succession of the infant P'u-i whose power must have been exercised by a regency
controlled either by herself or, after her death, by her niece Lung-yu. She had no
such interest in the succession of P'u-lun, a grown man independent of her clan.

CHAPTER FOURTEEN

The Memoirs – Two

In thus brusquely summarising the two volumes of Backhouse's memoirs I have, I fear, done them an injustice. Stripped of their supporting circumstantiality, of the verve and vigour of the writing, and of the entertaining conversation pieces which give the appearance of authentic experience, the accumulated improbabilities are too many, the cascade of dropped crowns and coronets is too absurd. So let us forget that such things were ever believed, even by him (if he did believe them), and examine the memoirs not censoriously, as if judging their veracity or their morality, but in a clinical, friendly spirit, looking not for truth or falsehood but for a psychological pattern which may help to explain them, and to answer further questions.

The dominant pattern is clear enough. Backhouse has a series of social or sexual relations – preferably both – with a series of persons distinguished by social grandeur or literary fame. All these relationships are almost certainly imaginary, but all are deliberately constructed within a historical framework which has been carefully studied, and they are illustrated by an elaborate and historically plausible apparatus of circumstantial detail. Finally, in every case Backhouse identifies himself with, and substitutes himself for a distinct person. This can be shown if we take a few particular instances. In chronological order they are Verlaine, Lord Rosebery, the Empress Dowager.

Backhouse's pretended relations with Verlaine are central to his whole romance about his own early life and literary friendships, and he took great trouble to ensure that his account of them was irrefutable by the factual knowledge available at the time. Unfortunately, in this case his ingenuity was in vain. Later research has filled the gaps in our knowledge of Verlaine's life, and consequently Backhouse's story dissolves, dragging down with it the whole elaborate edifice of the literary part of the memoirs and, by a logical consequence, everything else too. This is bad luck. No such positive frontal disproof can be opposed to his fantasies about Lord Rosebery and the Empress, but they crumble in the general ruin precipitated by the case of Verlaine.

When Backhouse wrote about his relations with Verlaine, he had beside him – it is clear because he quotes page-references – the biography of Verlaine by his friend Edmond Lepelletier. Now Lepelletier leaves a blank in Verlaine's life between 10 February 1886, when he wrote from Paris after the death of his mother, and July 1886 when he entered the Tenon hospital in Paris. Backhouse knew that Verlaine had, on several earlier occasions, taught French briefly at English private schools, and he knew that, on one of these occasions, he had been accompanied by his young protégé Lucien Létinois. What Backhouse has done is to fill in this convenient blank period, bringing Verlaine to another English school – his own – between those two dates, and substituting himself for Létinois. The operation has been artfully carried out, known dates are respected, contemporary events worked in, predictable inconsistencies avoided. His story would be technically irrefutable if that blank period had not since been filled in from authentic sources which show that Verlaine was in Paris during the whole time.

Exactly the same process can be observed in the case of Lord Rosebery. Here the external circumstances are clear enough, and Backhouse was remarkably well informed about them. The 1890s were a decade in which homosexuality was fashionable in certain aesthetic circles and allegations of homosexuality were no less fashionable among their critics. The trial of Oscar Wilde in 1895 brought these tensions to a head. One of those about whom such allegations were made, or insinuated, was Lord Rosebery, who was anyway disliked by the respectable late Victorian bourgeoisie for his olympian magnificence, his esoteric, epicurean tastes and his love of the race-course. Dark suspicions were whispered about his private life, and seemed to be confirmed by his secretive protection of it.* His proclivities were said to be more openly

* George Murray, who had been Gladstone's secretary, and who became

indulged in his villa in Naples, which was anyway somewhat too near to Capri for conventional tastes.* One of the great sniffers of homosexuality in those days was 'the mad marquis' of Queensberry, whose younger son, Lord Alfred Douglas, seemed to him far too close to Oscar Wilde. Queensberry's eldest son, Lord Drumlanrig, was private secretary to Rosebery, and for him Rosebery secured a peerage of the United Kingdom, as Lord Kelhead. This was represented as a measure of political convenience, so that Drumlanrig could be with his Minister in the House of Lords. Queensberry was consulted before the peerage was conferred, and at first consented to it; but afterwards it riled him to think that his son sat in the House of Lords, where he, as a mere Scottish peer, had no right to sit. He thereupon began a vendetta against Rosebery, writing offensive letters to him, and about him to the Queen and Gladstone. These letters were ignored. Then, in October 1894, Drumlanrig was killed by his own gun while crossing a stile out shooting in Somerset. The circumstances were suspicious, and it was said that Drumlanrig had committed suicide to prevent a scandalous exposure. The scandal was then extended to embrace Rosebery. It was suggested that Queensberry's indignation with Rosebery was not merely on account of the peerage but because Rosebery was 'a bad influence' on his son.

Whether there was any truth in this can hardly be discovered. It may well be that Drumlanrig's death was not accidental. The eleventh marquis, Drumlanrig's nephew, certainly believed – presumably on the authority of his father – that his uncle had committed suicide to prevent the revelation of a scandal, and there are other hints which support the suggestion.† But this, even if true, does not necessarily involve Rosebery. Rosebery himself treated Queensberry's letters as a joke, and his own

Rosebery's secretary when Rosebery succeeded Gladstone as Prime Minister, was diverted, but not pleased, by the change in his office. He told Lewis Harcourt that Rosebery insisted on opening all his own letters – which, Harcourt recorded in his diary, was not surprising 'considering some of the things which, to my knowledge, some of them must contain'.

* Norman Douglas, and others who lived at Posillipo, used to relate circumstantial stories of Rosebery's activities there.

† In his manuscript diary, Lewis Harcourt recorded, on 1 October 1894, 'Drumlanrig is going to marry General Ellis's daughter. It makes the institution of marriage ridiculous.' Less than three weeks later, Drumlanrig shot himself.

reaction to Queensberry's behaviour suggests that he did not fear the worst that the mad marquis could do. Rosebery's latest biographer, Mr Robert Rhodes James, having seen all the material, and concluded that there was no evidence to justify any suspicion, said nothing about it.

These then are the twigs: twigs of gossip rather than fact; and on them Backhouse spun his web. He invented details about Drumlanrig, transferred other details from the Wilde case, threw in names of places and persons, made the story exact and coherent, every strand neatly placed and artistically tied, involved himself with Drumlanrig, and then, substituting himself for Drumlanrig, both as secretary and as alleged ganymede, displayed himself proudly in the centre, describing, in slow motion, his *nuits d'amour* with the Prime Minister in September 1893, at Barnbougle in the grounds of Dalmeny House. . . . To the reader who is unprotected by knowledge of Backhouse's character, the story, like so many of his stories, seems too circumstantial to be false. All that detail, so solemnly stated, so scrupulously documented, that apparently exact knowledge of Rosebery's houses, his library, his political associates, his interests, his character, his insomnia, his private tastes, seems its own warrant. It is a repetition, *mutatis mutandis*, of the case of Verlaine.

Finally Tzŭ-hsi. Although the Empress Dowager is said to have shown great interest in, and admiration for, Queen Victoria, the moral views of these two long-lived empresses were very different. Backhouse undoubtedly knew a great deal about the court of Tzŭ-hsi and he knew, of course, what was said about that court by its Chinese critics, who were vocal and uninhibited. A letter from Bland to W. T. Stead, in 1910, just after the publication of *China under the Empress Dowager*, summarises their public voice. 'The Cantonese and other critics of her morals', wrote Bland, 'assert that she used to introduce students and other young men into the Palace, with the help of the eunuchs (this was done during the first Regency); but the charge cannot be proved'. The Empress's first Regency was from 1861 to 1873; but if it had happened then, when she was young, why should it not happen again in her third Regency, though she was old? Like Verlaine's school-teaching in England, or Rosebery's alleged romance with

Drumlanrig, the scenario could be repeated with a new actor; and the new actor, of course, here as there, would be the same.

However, to Backhouse, with his love of high rank, it was not enough to deputise for a nameless Chinese student. He must find a particular individual with whom he can identify himself and thereby a particular satisfaction. In the case of Verlaine, it had been 'that sweet youth' Lucien Létinois about whom he can only have read. In the case of Rosebery, it was Drumlanrig with whom he felt, he says (for he pretends to have known him in the drawing-rooms of the great), 'an immediate sympathy'. And so, in the case of Tzŭ-hsi, he evidently identifies himself with Jung-lu, the Empress's great minister and – he believes – lifelong lover. When he arrived for his first performance for the Empress Dowager, he felt, he says, 'very self-conscious, as if I were the cynosure of every eye. Of course the eunuchs and palace-women guessed the purpose of my evening visit: in fact, I heard one Manchu girl of great beauty say, "There goes the foreign Jung-lu" '. Backhouse tells us in his memoirs that he idealised Jung-lu; and he had already made him the hero of *China under the Empress Dowager* on the strength of that authoritative document to which he always appeals for evidence, the diary of Ching-shan.

This then is the pattern, which is regularly repeated. Once we recognise the method, we easily see its recurrence. Nor does Backhouse identify himself only with persons whom he pretended to know, and could have known. He identifies himself with characters from past history. The boundaries of time and space are dissolved, and a fabulous autobiography is constructed out of the Memoirs of Saint-Simon, the impostures of Cagliostro, the *chroniques scandaleuses* of all ages and all places. In this imaginary autobiography, though so carefully constructed, Backhouse himself may well have come to believe. Believing it, he could recount it with conviction and plausibility, and could persuade Hoeppli that, in his conversation, he was bringing back to life the historical persons 'whom he had known'. To Hoeppli this distinguished-looking old man, with the delicate feminine hands and seductive voice and gross imaginings, was an 'English noble-man' who 'had known personally Verlaine, Mallarmé, Beardsley, Pater and Wilde, not to speak of Tzŭ-hsi and her court'.

In this dream-world of Backhouse's autobiography, two re-current features deserve attention. One is the uncertainty of the boundary between fact and fiction. The iridescent centre of the web is too obviously a work of art, deliberately spun. But where exactly does the web of fantasy meet the solid thorns of fact? Through the mysterious Backhousian twilight it is difficult to distinguish the gossamer from the twig. Sometimes a shaft of external light enables us to do so at one particular point; but without such external aid we can never be sure. We know that fiction, at some point, is joined to reality; but the point of contact escapes the naked eye.

Thus Backhouse's account of his school at Ascot is often accurate. His description of the headmaster and his tastes – or some of them – is borne out by other memoirs. His account of the long natural history expeditions, the precocious electric lighting, the rigid toryism, the severe discipline, are all borne out by reliable witnesses. But what of the headmaster's death? That he died suddenly of a heart attack during term is indeed true; but the rest – the story of the birch-rod inserted into the coffin – is fiction. We can prove it to be fiction, because he died, not on 16 July 1886, the date so engraven in Backhouse's memory, but four months later, on 1 November; he died not at Ascot, while beating Master Blundell, but at Moor Green, Birmingham; and Backhouse, by then, was no longer at Ascot: he had left the school and was already at Winchester. At this point we can separate fact from fantasy because the facts are publicly recorded. In Back-house's private life we have no such external checks and so, while we can never believe anything on his authority, we can never be sure that some even of his improbabilities may not be true. His motto – since he was so ready to drop into foreign languages – could be that of Hesiod:

ἴδμεν ψεύδεα πολλὰ λέγειν ἐτύμοισιν ὁμοῖα,
ἴδμεν δ᾽ εὖτε θέλωμεν ἀληθέα γηρύσασθαι*

The second recurrent feature which is of some interest is his conversion, to his own use, of historical or literary episodes or phrases. This is a regular mannerism. The court of Catherine de

* We know how to tell many lies, which seem true; and we know, when we want, how to tell the truth.

Médicis and Henri III of France, or the intrigues of the dying Roman republic, supply the phrases, or the gestures, of the Manchu dynasty; and the Empress Dowager herself dies uttering the last words of Catherine of Aragon. This mannerism is worth noting, in the memoirs, because the same mannerism had been noted by Lewisohn in the diary of Ching-shan, where Jung-lu echoed, during the Boxer Rising, the phrase used by Talleyrand of the murder of the Duc d'Enghien.

But all these tricks of detail, significant though they may be, are subordinated, throughout both volumes of the memoirs, to one central, unifying theme: Backhouse's sexual obsession. This obsession, we have observed, is relatively new. As far as we can see, it entered into Backhouse's fantasies in their last stage; or at least, in his earlier years, it had been repressed. The process of its emergence is illustrated, in part, by his correspondence with Bland, in the 1930s, on the diaries of Li Lien-ying and Ching-shan.

In January 1933 Backhouse had remarked to Bland, while on the subject of memoirs, that he too had had 'an interesting life, though in a hidden way, behind the scenes'; and this enigmatical remark suggests that already, at that time, he was fabricating or imagining a romantic autobiography, an expression of those old 'Walter Mitty' fantasies which had deceived his business partners as far back as 1909. No doubt it consisted of imaginary adventures in the literary world, in high life, and in the Forbidden City. After all, he had always pretended to know the great, from the time when he invented, or forged, the grand letters of recommendation which impressed Sir Robert Hart in 1899. A few years later, in August 1937, when Vetch first called on him, he produced a detail from these new recollections, remembering how he had once visited Tolstoy in Yasnaya Polyana. In October of the same year he was telling Bland about his friendship with Oscar Wilde and his circle. But even then he disclaimed any knowledge of their 'perverted tastes' and rejected, as 'the basest of untruths', any suggestion that he shared them. Thus it is clear that the elements of the imaginary memoirs were already forming in his mind, although the co-ordinating sexual fantasy had not yet taken over these disconnected fragments and given them their lurid, obsessive form.

No doubt, *in pectore* at least, Backhouse did share those tastes. His detailed knowledge of the fashionable and literary homosexual world of the 1890s, even if purely platonic, is at least evidence of his interests. But no one accused him of a scandalous life. Morrison, it is true, declared that he had been involved in the Oscar Wilde scandal, but Morrison's information was at third hand* and the only evidence that we have is Max Beerbohm's contemporary statement that Backhouse was collecting money for Wilde's defence. From what we know of Backhouse's financial activities, we may suspect that the money – like that collected for his dictionary – may not have been applied to that purpose. Later, in Peking, his life was declared by all to be blameless. It probably was blameless. The very crudity, the grotesque exhibitionism, of the memoirs would seem to indicate not an exaggeration of real indulgence but a release from long repression, the desert mirage of a starving man. Such fantasies no doubt flourish and expand in the social vacuity of a hermit life. Since reading the memoirs of Sir Edmund Backhouse, I feel that I understand better the lurid visions of the desert fathers, the luxuriant but imaginary temptations of St Antony in the wilderness.† It was only in his last years, when the old inhibitions had weakened, when the British colony in China, with its conventions and conformities, had disappeared, and when Dr Hoeppli (who was credited with similar tastes) had applied his solvent psychotherapy, that these repressed fantasies were released to inform and inflame the old, and equally unreal, fantasies of exalted and esoteric social and literary life.

However, even the most irresponsible fantasies have their inner rationality, and it is interesting to turn from the overt obscenity of Backhouse's memoirs to the ingenuity of purpose which is concealed within them. We may pass over the absurd story by which Backhouse pretends to have acquired his famous collection

* According to Backhouse, Morrison learned about his early life from Valentine Chirol, who had heard it from 'my old friend Sir Hugh Bell'. Bell was a Yorkshire industrialist and landowner, Lord Lieutenant of the North Riding of Yorkshire.
† The same exaggeration can be seen in the work which, though far less outrageous than Backhouse's memoirs, seems to me most comparable with them: the 'Black Diaries' of Sir Roger Casement – much of which seems also to have been pure fantasy. See Jeffrey Meyers 'To die for Ireland: the Character and Career of Sir Roger Casement' in the *London Magazine*, April–May 1973.

of books and manuscripts and thus excuses himself from the charge of having participated in the general loot of Peking. We do not know exactly how he acquired these treasures – whether by plunder during the Boxer Rising, when we know that he was arrested for looting, and when he himself claims to have looted Ching-shan's diary and many other valuable books and papers, or by purchase afterwards, from the easy trade in rifled treasures which accompanied the revolution of 1911. The question is of no great importance. More interesting are the cunning devices whereby Backhouse, in his memoirs, seeks to reinforce the pretended authenticity of his most successful forgery, the diary of Ching-shan, and to undermine the specific criticisms which had been made of it. Here we see no random fantasies generated by subconscious pressures, but the workings of an acute critical intellect, conscious of its aim, deliberate in its choice of means.

Thus, in his memoirs, Backhouse describes his own pretended conversations, in 1902, with both Jung-lu and Li Lien-ying. In both cases, he tells us, conversation fell upon Ching-shan, whose diary he had allegedly possessed for two years, although he would unaccountably fail to mention it to anyone else for another seven. To both Jung-lu and Li Lien-ying, Backhouse – as he tells us – casually put the same question: how deaf was Ching-shan? Could he really hear and understand a conversation? Both, we are told, gave the same reply: Ching-shan was only slightly deaf, 'his deafness was largely put on' for political reasons, to avoid having to commit himself: 'he feigned deafness when asked embarrassing questions'. The casual reader of the memoirs might wonder why the subject of Ching-shan's deafness should loom so large in these alleged conversations. The answer is simple. Lewisohn, in his critique of Ching-shan's diary, had found it odd that Ching-shan, being evidently stone-deaf, had recorded in his diary such detailed conversations. Backhouse, in 1943, was calling up the ghosts of Jung-lu and Li Lien-ying so that they might appear to forestall, in 1902, the objections made by Lewisohn in 1937.

While on the same topic, Jung-lu, according to Backhouse, paid a passing tribute to the reliability of Ching-shan's information. 'He was an inveterate gossip', he explained, 'and liked to be in the know. Old Wang Wên-shao supplied him with much news and in fact lent him his own journal to copy more than once'. How beautifully that last observation disposes of Lewisohn's most damaging discovery – the discovery which so shook Bland – that Ching-shan's diary had been constructed out of other documents, and in particular, out of the published journal of Wang Wên-shao! Thus fantasy supports fantasy, forgery forgery, so that the whole baseless edifice seems, until touched, self-supporting, rational and coherent. This final version presumably superseded the previous version which Backhouse had given privately to Bland in December 1937, viz.: that it was Wang Wên-shao who had borrowed Ching-shan's diary 'as a matter of interest, to collate dates'.

But Backhouse, in his last memoirs, would not stop at mere conversations: he would fabricate whole archives in support of his present and previous forgeries. To corroborate his story of his own life in China, and his personal familiarity with the court of the Empress Dowager, he appeals to two particular sources. The first is his own records. He assures us that he 'kept an unusually close record of my secret association with the Empress and with others, possessing notes and manuscripts written to me by Her Majesty'. How unfortunate that all his personal effects were destroyed by his own 'unfaithful servants', in 1939, 'so that my large collection of books and manuscripts was lost *in toto*'! Thus, for their contents, we only have his word, which, by now, we may have begun to distrust. Fortunately, the second corroborative source, according to Backhouse, is still extant. It is also more objective. For it is, once again, an independent Chinese diary: the diary (need it be said?) of our old friend, the Grand Eunuch, Li Lien-ying.

How constantly Backhouse's mind returns to Li Lien-ying! The Grand Eunuch dominates *China under the Empress Dowager*. His work, variously described as diary or memoirs, emerges from the haze at regular intervals, like some fabulous sea-monster which is sighted every nine years or so, and then disappears again. It first swims into Backhouse's correspondence in 1912–15, a looming, indistinct bulk, unexplained and undescribed. It breaks the surface a second time in 1923. By this time it has been captured by Back-house and is imprisoned, together with his translation, in the

Bodleian Library. But when Weatherall goes there to inspect it, it has escaped again, back to Chinese waters. In 1932 it appears again, as if hitherto unknown, in the possession of the author's great-nephew, – who, we are told, has had it all the time, direct from his great-uncle – only to sink for the third time, when the attack on Backhouse's documents was resumed in earnest, in 1934. But even then it did not drown. It bobs up again in 1943, in Backhouse's own memoirs, and we are then told that it has been in his possession since 1911. . . . The new version would no doubt have surprised Bland, who had been prepared to join Backhouse in buying the Eunuch's memoirs from his great-nephew in 1934; but readers of Backhouse's memoirs would not be expected to pay attention to Bland. Backhouse had already warned them against that unworthy collaborator with whom his own genius had once been so unequally yoked. Bland, whose generosity, skill, constant support and 'exquisite style' had once been so praised, had now become 'a detestable personality, *la lie du peuple*', 'my enemy, J. O. P. Bland'.

But we return to the diary of Li Lien-ying. As so often, Backhouse is lucid and precise in describing his acquisition of this precious document – as lucid and precise as he had been when he described his discovery of Ching-shan's diary. The story begins in 1902, when he first (he says) met the Grand Eunuch on his famous visit to the Forbidden City to restore to the Empress the imperial treasures which he had been protecting in her absence. On that occasion, he tells us, Li Lien-ying confided in him 'that he had kept a journal ever since he entered the Palace, which he would gladly lend to me, in which he recorded every event in the Old Buddha's life of which he had cognizance'. He does not seem to have lent the document at that time, and indeed it would have been very odd if he had done so, when his old mistress was alive and Backhouse a new, untried acquaintance. His predecessor An Tê-hai had been decapitated for less. But six years later, when Backhouse and Li had become (according to Backhouse) familiar friends, and when the Old Buddha had but recently died – or rather, as Backhouse now says, been assassinated – Li (says Backhouse)

came to my house, looking twenty years older, with eyes marred by the mists of pain, and we both shed burning tears together as we spoke of our bereavement. He had brought with him a case containing his journals from the year V of Kuang Hsü (1879), when he first entered the palace, meticulously written right up to Tz'ŭ-hsi's death, when, like the Blessed Sage, he *Chüen Pi* 'laid down his pen.' He asked me to take charge of the diary which consisted of thirty to thirty-five ordinary large account books as used by tradesmen in China, *Chang Pen*, on coarse paper. 'My position is very uncertain since the Old Ancestress became a guest of Heaven', said he, 'and the New Regent has no love towards me. I hope he will have the traitor Yüan Shih-k'ai decapitated, for my own life will be in danger while he lives: only I and Ts'ui Tsung Kuan know for certain that he killed the Old Buddha. Please oblige me in preserving the papers, but do not read them for (say) ten years after my death, because I have written frankly my own thoughts and there might be passages you would find fault with. Believe me, I have been your loyal friend ever since I met you in the 28th year, 1902! After my death, you may consider the papers your property; for my heirs these journals will be of little meaning, *Tui Niu T'an Ch'in*, like playing a fiddle to a cow, as they know nothing of all that I have seen.'

So much for the great-nephew, who, according to Version Three, still possessed the original documents in 1932. But I return to Version Four and continue the account from Backhouse's memoirs.

'Naturally', says Backhouse, 'I could not refuse so earnest a request', and so (he tells us) he accepted the diaries. It was with more difficulty that he complied with the other request and restrained himself from looking into those tempting volumes during the long closed season. Since Li died in 1911, this lasted till 1921 – which conveniently explains why we find no reference to this primary source in Backhouse's publications of those years. But as soon as the ten years were up, he tells us, he opened the precious package and 'inspected' it. He cannot have inspected it very thoroughly, for it is, he says, of enormous length: with $1\frac{1}{2}$ million ideographs it would, in a European language, fill fifteen volumes; and in the same year in which he was first authorised to open it, he brought it with him on his last visit to England and deposited it in Lloyds Bank, 16 St James's Street, Piccadilly – where, he tells us in 1943, it still is, among 'masses' of other papers, similarly deposited by him and available to confirm his story, 'if not bombed by the eagles of mighty *Grossdeutschland*'.

However, in spite of the brevity of his study of the document, Backhouse was evidently able to take the measure of its style and contents, which he remembered with remarkable accuracy after more than twenty years. He speaks of its engaging naïvety, its occasional faults of style and scholarship, its 'convincing ring of truth'. It is, he says, 'a human document of extraordinary interest', comparable with the *Journaux-Memoires* of Pierre de l'Estoile in sixteenth-century Paris or the diary of Samuel Pepys in seventeenth-century London. Of course it could never be published *in extenso*: quite apart from its length, 'much of it is unprintable'. There is 'an infinity of veiled allusion to the Old Buddha's erotic adventures'. Besides, much of the detail has lost interest now that 'the Manchu dynasty is one with Nineveh and Tyre'. However, perhaps Backhouse would one day publish 'a careful selection', 'some salient extracts' . . . although no doubt there would be people like 'that arch-liar Dr G. E. Morrison (now howling in the deathless flames of Hell)' who would suggest that he had forged the document, as he had suggested of Ching-shan's diary – which, incidentally, this new diary of Li Lien-ying completely confirms, with even greater authority: for it is 'more revealing' than Chingshan's diary, being based not on hearsay but on direct personal experience. It also confirms 'all the events that I have tried to describe, albeit in less detail and without the pathetic aspect, which did not appeal to his matter-of-fact disposition'. And Backhouse quotes, with complacency, the Eunuch's references to his own 'wit and charm', his 'colossal orgasm', so pleasing to the Old Buddha, his amorous eccentricity ('ten males could not satisfy his lusts'), and his 'plethoric carnality, which is even as the sea which can never be filled up'.

When I read about this important document, which so conveniently confirmed all the stories of 'Décadence Mandchoue', my first thought was to seek it out. And not only it, for there were all those other 'masses of papers' which, having been deposited in the same bank, had escaped the alleged Japanese holocaust of 1939. Among them, I noted, was the entire correspondence between Backhouse and Verlaine, 'which still survives, as far as I know, in a London bank's custody'. There was also a drawing by Verlaine of Backhouse and another boy at St George's, Ascot.

That too, according to Backhouse, would be found in the vaults of 16 St James's, Piccadilly – with the usual proviso, 'unless incendiary bombs have paid to my bank a visit'. Sometimes it seems as if Backhouse almost hoped that the bank had been bombed. How convenient for his fictions if it had been! How convenient, incidentally, was the holocaust of 1939, which now begins to wear a somewhat different aspect. Was it too a device to create, retrospectively, a lost archive which would have supported other forgeries? Certainly Backhouse made good use of that lost archive. In it, he tells us, were not only his contemporary notes on his relations with the Empress Dowager, and his correspondence with her, but also his secret political correspondence with 'my chief at home', the Foreign Minister, Sir Edward Grey, from which, however, he recalls, almost verbatim, one highly flattering letter dated – as near as he can remember (for, as usual, he is precise even in his uncertainties) – 15 June 1907. . . .

However, although the Peking archive had so conveniently perished, Lloyds Bank, Piccadilly, somehow escaped the German bombers. Therefore the mass of papers deposited there in 1921 should still, in 1973, be easily traced. I took the necessary steps to trace them. The answer did not take long to come. Neither the bank nor Backhouse's heirs knew anything about any such deposit. The only document held by the bank from Sir Edmund was a power of attorney, which lapsed at his death. Li Lien-ying's massive diary sank again out of sight, this time for good. This, by now, will not surprise anyone.

When a man, to prove the authenticity of a disputed document, fabricates imaginary corroboration, we can take it, first, that the disputed document is a forgery, and secondly, that he knows it to be a forgery: in effect, that he forged it. The imaginary conversations with Jung-lu, the imaginary diaries of Li Lien-ying, are circumstantial but sufficient proof not only that the diary of Ching-shan is a forgery but also that Backhouse himself forged it. In Victor Purcell's phrase, but in a somewhat different sense, the part played by Sir Edmund Backhouse is now quite clear.

CHAPTER FIFTEEN

The Portrait

ALAS, it must be admitted, Backhouse's 'memoirs' are not an edifying work. They are a pornographic novelette. No verve in the writing can redeem their pathological obscenity. But let us be charitable. Let us treat this whole phenomenon as a morbid eruption of senility, always remembering the psychological pressure of a hermit life on an anyway abnormal personality. Then we can happily forget the novel sexual fantasies which, in his last years, under the benign encouragement of the good Dr Hoeppli, suddenly broke out from their ancient, repressive prison to dominate and reorganise all other fantasies, and we can consider the memoirs only in so far as they illuminate Backhouse's whole life. For in their general character, they do not interrupt, rather, they illuminate the personality which we have come to know.

For in spite of this last explosion of repressed and distorted sexuality, Backhouse's career is all of a piece. His peculiar tendencies may have grown upon him, but they were always there. The final discharge of his fantasies may have been morbid, but they themselves were not. They were inseparable from his personality; and that personality, in itself, was complete, coherent and sane.

Yes, sane. For to live in a world of make-believe does not necessarily indicate an unsound mind. Many men have been liable to self-glorifying (or self-damaging) fantasies without prejudice to their sanity. They have been promoted to responsible office, trusted in business. They have become oracles of the media, heads of university colleges – and why not professors of Chinese? Part of T. E. Lawrence's spectacular career, it now seems, was pure fantasy. The late Harold Laski, who once laid down the laws of

The Portrait

politics to his mute, spell-bound followers, lived in a mental world
of fantasy, assuring those who could not check his statements that
he was the confidant and adviser of prime ministers and kings.*
Perhaps the phenomenon is more common than historians, in our
rational age, are pre-disposed to allow. Who knows what apparently factual evidence has been accepted from sources no less
plausible, and yet no more accurate, than the letters of Laski or
the memoirs of Backhouse? As far as I can discover, no contemporary judged Backhouse to be more than mildly eccentric.
All would have agreed with Bishop Norris who, having known
him for thirty years, pronounced him odd indeed, but fundamentally 'sane'.

If Backhouse was abnormal, it was in the exceptional vividness
of his imagination and the exceptional weakness of the restraints
upon it. He lived in a world of imagination. That world, created
by romantic vanity, suspended between distant points of truth,
and yet internally coherent and rational, was more real to him
than the objective, external world, with which, somehow, it
seldom collided. When the two did collide, it was the external
world which was made to yield. It yielded intellectually, in the
victory of fantasy over fact. It yielded physically in the actual
forgery of such documents as might be necessary to sustain the
illusion. So complete was the victory of imagination over reality
in Backhouse's mind that we cannot assume that he was even
aware of the conflict. His instant rationalising capacity took care
of every objection, spinning ever new figments to resolve inconsistencies in the old. Even when he was physically forging
documents, he may have been unconscious of the fraud involved.
He may have supposed that he was merely supplying the accidental
defects of a total picture already known to be true, like a classical
scholar supplying the missing letters of a text whose general
meaning is already clear. For reason does not always create
certainty: sometimes it conforms with it.

By the force of his own conviction, Backhouse easily convinced

* Laski's habitual mendacity was familiar to those who knew him, but could
deceive at a distance. His letters to Oliver Wendell Holmes, a tissue of self-glorifying
fantasies, were solemnly published, in two volumes, as a contribution to English
political history, by a Harvard professor. See *Holmes-Laski Letters, The Correspondence
of Mr Justice Holmes and H. J. Laski*, ed. M. de W. Howe (Cambridge, Mass. 1953).

others. His success in this was amazing. However extravagant his fancies, everyone, at first, was persuaded by him, and those who were persuaded included highly intelligent, practical men of the world: Sir Robert Hart, Dr Morrison, Sir John Jordan. After ten years of intimate personal contact with Backhouse, and reliance upon him, Morrison saw through him; but Bland, a man of great intelligence and understanding, who collaborated no less closely with him, could never bring himself to suspect him of forgery. In 1915, when Jordan accepted him as the sole manager of a vast and costly secret enterprise, Backhouse had been known to the British Legation in Peking for seventeen years. Jordan himself had been head of that legation for nine years. And yet no one saw reason to distrust him. After the grotesque failure of that operation, Jordan himself realised the truth; but the two diplomatists who had personally handled the affair – Barton in Peking and Alston in London – persevered in their illusions. Always it was said that there were 'able and unscrupulous Chinese' who were manipulating the innocent Englishman: Chinese forgers who had palmed off on him the diary of Ching-shan, the bogus 'curios', the forged scrolls; Chinese palace officials who had lured him into the affair of the Empress Dowager's pearl jacket; mysterious 'Chinese authorities' who had 'duped' him over the arms and munitions. These nameless Chinese manipulators who were regularly invoked by rational men to explain away successive deceptions were in fact just as unreal as any of the rationalising fantasies of Backhouse himself.

Part of Backhouse's extraordinary plausibility evidently lay in his great personal charm and appearance of transparent honesty. But part of it came from his apparent realism. For this spinner of absurd fantasies did not appear fantastic. Outwardly, there was nothing of the dreamer about him. He could impress his victims as a tough-minded, acute, practical negotiator, in command of all the details of any business and fully equipped to cope with all difficulties. His American victim George Hall was deeply impressed by Backhouse's legal astuteness, his precise legal language, his anticipation of legal problems. The document which so impressed him survives. It would impress anyone if seen in isolation from the rest of the story. Backhouse's last victim, Dr

Hoeppli, was similarly impressed by his practical 'shrewdness'. Backhouse's seclusion no doubt helped him in this. The general context of his life being invisible, each episode was seen in isolation. It is only now, when that context has been reconstructed, that the pattern appears and we wonder that anyone could have been deceived by him.

Backhouse's practical toughness, his cunning and sang-froid, even when he was most extravagant, is evident from his behaviour in 1917–18. How calmly, how skilfully, he then handled the crisis caused by the sudden collapse of his visionary empire of banknotes and battleships! In the autumn of 1917, the Bank Note Company and George Hall were closing in on him from one side. John Brown & Co. were pressing from the other. The legations were being mobilised against him. Sir John Jordan, who knew all about the great arms affair, was returning to Peking. Dr Morrison, who knew about the forgery of Ching-shan's diary, was already there. But did Backhouse panic? Not at all. As in 1915, after the collapse of the great arms fantasy, he moved quietly out of the way till the storm should have blown over. He conceded nothing. He exposed himself to no danger. He retired to the safety of British Columbia and protected himself by a smoke-screen of grave illness. But before disappearing, he took specific and practical precautions. He was in possession of certain vital documents. He deposited them in safe hands. John Brown & Co. were determined to recover those documents, and used every means to do so. The chairman of the company demanded them. The Under-Secretary of State, and then the Foreign Minister, intervened. But all intervention proved vain. In his own time, Backhouse would emerge from his Canadian retreat, re-cross the Pacific, and, having bought off his assailants at others' expense, recover the documents for future self-protection and resume his career as a respected scholar in Peking, the candidate for a professorial chair in Oxford University.

Another element in the plausibility of Backhouse's fantasies was their extraordinary circumstantiality, their minute and scrupulous detail. Backhouse's language was never loose or vague. He impressed everyone by his remarkable 'memory', which in turn seemed a guarantee of truth. He would supply the names and regiments of the British officers whom he had accompanied to Ching-shan's house. He would describe the scene at the house: the Sikh soldiers hunting for loot, the litter of papers, Madame Ching-shan moaning on the k'ang, her family vainly tempting her with gruel. He would state the number, the make, the year, the calibre, of the rifles and machine-guns which he was collecting from the provinces of China, recount, in lively detail, their adventurous journey down the Yang-tse river, the hazardous passage of the flotilla which was carrying them along the China coast to Fu-chow and Canton. He would specify the number of boxes in which the great Palace Library was being conveyed from bandit-ridden Kansu, emphasise the political disorder of the province, the state of the roads, the creaking carts which were slowly bringing their costly burden to Peking. He knew the exact number of pearls taken from the Empress's jacket, could calculate and adjust their value with scrupulous honesty, explain the causes of their unfortunate devaluation. He would describe the paper on which Li Lien-ying's memoirs were written, state the number of ideograms in them, comment on their style and tone, criticise their grammatical idiosyncrasies. He would recall the circumstances in which the manuscript had been delivered to him, name the bank in which he had deposited it, identify the other documents deposited with them. He would remember the books and furniture in Lord Rosebery's houses; the places and dates and attendant circumstances of his meetings with Verlaine; the furniture, the menus, the guests, the subjects of conversation at his visits to the Empress Dowager.

All these things we now know to be fantasy; but can we penetrate behind those fantasies and discover the real personality of this ingenious literary forger? Even fantasies reveal something of the person who devises them, and although we know so little about Backhouse's early years (those years so fully and fancifully depicted in the memoirs), we can perhaps, even out of those memoirs, deduce something of the forces which made him what he was.

Consider the time and the social context in which he grew up. The eldest son of a rich and successful family, he was the first member of that family to be born outside the cohesive Quaker fold and the shadow of the provincial family bank. Against this inheritance he clearly rebelled. From the middle-class traditions of his family he fled to an imaginary aristocratic world; the long Quaker inheritance was cast away; and from the materialism of late Victorian England, he took refuge in the fashionable nonconformity of his time and class: the 'æstheticism', the febrile eroticism, the aggressive, insolent deviation of the 1890s.

In other words, Backhouse was, both socially and intellectually, a snob. His social *snobisme* exudes from his memoirs. There he is always ready, while repudiating his immediate parents, to exalt their lineage. His family, according to his own account, was friendly with royalty, had access to court secrets, was related to two Prime Ministers, had received personal favours from the Tsar Alexander I, etc., etc. He hints at a dormant peerage which he could claim and ascribes to himself a titular Russian barony and a Chinese marquisate (which would have become a dukedom had the Empress lived longer). He claims descent from Charles James Fox. He was indeed descended from Charles Fox; but his ancestor of that name was not the statesman: he was a Quaker merchant of Falmouth. Backhouse is careful never to mention his family's Quaker background, the provincial shipping agency in Falmouth or the provincial bank in Darlington. Those would not, in his eyes, have been proper subjects to mention in the salons, or the beds, of Empresses and Prime Ministers.

His intellectual *snobisme* was equally unjustified. He was indeed a marvellous linguist and even those who disliked him in China admitted that he was a first-class sinologue and scholar of Japanese. He was tolerably well read in the conventional classics. But his writings show no power of thought, no familiarity with philosophy, with science, with other than anecdotal history, other than fashionable current literature. He would quote the later poems of Tennyson, the slip-slop of Tom Moore, the mindless melody of Swinburne, but there is no depth in him, even of literary sensibility, and the conversations which he invented between himself and distinguished writers are pitifully thin. His intellectual *snobisme* was in fact a kind of supercilious élitism which rested, solely and sufficiently, on hatred of the *profanum vulgus*, in literature as in society: for as he despised his own middle class socially, so he despised them in literature too, and would write with contempt of 'the unimaginative English of the middle class'. It was this double élitism which drew him – in desire, if not in reality – into the aesthetic world of the 1890s, the esoteric, not to say etiolated world of private culture, of art for art's sake, pleasure for pleasure's sake, of Wilde and Beardsley and their hangers-on, of whom he may, or may not, have been one.

This essentially empty élitism, this complacency in adhering to a côterie which, by mere moral nonconformity with the 'philistinism' around it, held itself to be intellectually and socially superior, pervades Backhouse's writing. He expresses his hatred of 'the sordid Philistinism of the Victorian era and the drab self-satisfaction of the British middle-classes, scarce other than children playing at the edge of the abyss, into which', he adds with relish, in 1943, 'they have now fallen'. The disasters of the Far Eastern War were to him the nemesis of the 1890s, the aesthete's revenge on the once confident bourgeoisie which had persecuted his tribe.

To Backhouse all English society, in the 1890s, was vulgar, bourgeois, materialist, and the duty of an aesthete, a superior spirit, was to set itself free from that society, and to signalise its freedom by outraging its conventions and denouncing its whole life and being. From this artificial height, first in the real or imaginary circles of Wilde and Beardsley, then in the uninhibited seclusion of Manchu China, he would express his hatred of England and all things English, including its 'dynasty of Saxe-Coburg' and, in particular, the monarch who, to him, typified its complacency, the friend of plutocrats and Jews, King Edward VII. Rejecting England and English history, he found his heroes in the strong men of the Continent: in Napoleon and, second only to him, Bismarck. Among English statesmen, his only hero was his supposed kinsman Charles James Fox; but that was not on account of any love of 'liberty': it was because Fox would not have resisted Napoleon. In his own time, he reserved his admiration for despotic states which kept the bourgeoisie in order: for Tsarist Russia and feudal Japan.

Admittedly, these views, as known to us, were expressed in later life, but there is no reason to suppose that they were a late development. The flower grows naturally from the seed, and the seed was planted in the days of his youth, in the warm spring of aestheticism, in the early 1890s. But then came the sudden frost which nipped those early flowers. In 1894–5 both he and the world with which he identified himself ran into trouble. For himself, it was the nervous breakdown, the inglorious end of his Oxford career, the bankruptcy and breach with his parents. Looking around him, he saw the trial and ruin of Oscar Wilde, the prosecution and disintegration of that aesthetic, narcissistic, homosexual côterie to which in desire, if not in fact, he belonged. From the débâcle of his ideal world in England, after what intermediate experiences in those years 1895–8 we do not know, he escaped to China and a new phase of his life began.

In saying this, we have slid over the problem of the missing years, those years from 1895 to 1898 which are so imaginatively documented in his memoirs: the years of travel, in Greece, in Spain, in Egypt, in the Turkish Empire, in Russia, in America, the encounters with kings and queens, emperors and empresses, poets, actresses and philosophers: Swinburne, Sarah Bernhardt, Tolstoy – all those adventures which dazzled and convinced the good Hoeppli. None of these encounters can be believed, and therefore we are left totally without guidance: there is not a single stone of firm evidence upon which we can stand in the swirling stream of fantasy. We can only speculate, guiding our tentative speculations by the general pattern of his mind.

Perhaps Backhouse did spend those years in travel. He evidently knew modern Greek and Russian when he arrived in China; which suggests that he knew both countries. The mere fact that Backhouse said something does not necessarily make it untrue. Indeed, his fantasies are always interwoven with truth, which is what makes them so tantalising: the difficulty is to trace the dividing frontier between truth and fiction. Sayce, who knew him before 1912, remembered him as a traveller and sightseer, and we have seen him regularly moving between Britain and China, Japan and America. I have observed that the circumstances of his bankruptcy suggest that he had gone abroad, soon after leaving Oxford, in order to evade his creditors, and it may well be that he stayed abroad while the lawyers worked out a settlement – just as he would do afterwards, in 1917–18. There is also the visit to

America, which his sister remembered, and ascribed to that period, and the early frauds in America which Hall claimed to have discovered, but did not date or specify. But if Backhouse did spend those years in travel, we can be sure that it was not in such elevated social circumstances as he would afterwards pretend. Those pretences were part of his mental furniture, which he carried around with him, to illuminate and quicken his prosaic, solitary life. He was an inner hermit even on his outwardly sociable journeys, living mentally in one world while moving physically in another. We have seen him on a Pacific liner, imagining himself the trusted emissary of royalty, or sailing from Tientsin to Yokohama and pretending that he was carrying a magnificent bribe to the imperial ministers of Japan.

When he arrived in China, we are at last on firmer ground. In what precise circumstances, and for what precise purpose Backhouse went to China, we cannot say. Perhaps he just drifted thither. Perhaps, like other social casualties of his time and class, he was sent away to redeem himself, if he could, on the far side of the globe. In either case, his flair for languages and his particular knowledge of Chinese and Japanese, would have drawn him to the Far East.

He evidently had some other qualifications too. It is clear that, at some time, he had picked up considerable legal knowledge, which would serve him well in some of his scrapes. In 1901 he could be made a professor of literature and law in Peking. How, we may ask, had he acquired this knowledge? He himself spoke of his legal studies in London, his membership of the Inner Temple, the 'high degree in law' which he had taken after leaving Oxford. All this is fantasy. However he had acquired his knowledge, it was not thus. But the knowledge itself was real enough and argues some experience.

There is also evidence of experience in the world of commerce, and particularly of shipping. In one of the few passages of his memoirs which have a certain plausibility, because in it he drops no grand names and claims no sexual adventures, and actually admits that he envisaged involvement in the otherwise unmentioned world of trade, Backhouse remarks that, in April 1898, he arrived in China bearing not only the inevitable letter from the

Prime Minister to the Envoy Extraordinary but also 'private recommendations to several heads of firms in Shanghai', including one from Sir Thomas Sutherland, the chairman of the P. & O. shipping company. Afterwards, his father, as we know, arranged his employment as a responsible agent of the shipbuilding company of John Brown & Co. From these hints and facts we may infer that Backhouse had some experience in the world of shipping, and it may well be that he had been placed, for some time, in a shipping office. When we remember that his Fox cousins ran a shipping agency in Falmouth, and that one of them, Charles Masson Fox, was Russian consul in that town, we may even conjecture that Backhouse may have acquired his knowledge of Russian in places less brilliant or romantic than Yasnaya Polyana or the imperial palace of St Petersburg. However, all this is pure speculation: all that we can say with confidence is that, having somehow acquired some legal and business knowledge, he arrived in Peking, already practised in the arts of plausible fabrication. At first, exploiting those arts, he sought a place in the famous 'kindergarten' of Sir Robert Hart. Then, having failed in that attempt, he was swept into the wake of that other dominant personality, Dr Morrison.

From that moment, his course was set. Under Morrison's patronage, as Morrison's client, or ghost or slave, he was able to indulge his genuine love of scholarship. With his miraculous linguistic flair and his taste for solitude, he mastered one language after another, and soon became indispensable to Morrison, supplying that powerful patron with the one essential gift which he lacked. Always in need of such patronage, always ready to be dominated, he quickly succumbed to Morrison's forceful personality. There was a honeymoon period, a period of protected security, in which his scholarship easily expanded into fantasy: into delusions of grandeur which fed his own vanity and compensated him for his obscure and subject state.

One of Backhouse's functions was to discover, for Morrison, the secrets of Chinese politics. He was Morrison's contact man, who picked up the gossip, and translated the documents, of the impenetrable, monoglot Chinese world. Here he was free, within the limits of plausibility, to exercise his fancy: to embroider, to imagine, even to forge. The temptation was irresistible. Ultimately, Morrison would see through Backhouse's tricks, but he continued to call on his undoubted talents. Ultimately, Backhouse would resent Morrison's patronage, but he could not escape from it. He continued to serve his patron's need and his own vanity. Meanwhile, he sighed for delivery from a domination which his pliant and submissive character both needed and resented.

The opportunity came in November 1908, when a series of dramatic public events, coinciding with the absence of Morrison from Peking, threw Backhouse into the arms of Bland and Bland's friends, ffrench and Straight. To these new patrons Backhouse lightly transferred his services and his affections. There was a new honeymoon, new opportunities, new fantasies. For Bland he produced translations of literary and historical documents. No doubt they were largely genuine translations. For ffrench and Straight he produced political reports. No doubt some of them too were genuine. At first these new patrons were delighted with his services. They spoke, as Morrison had done, of Backhouse's 'genius'. Bland welcomed his documents for their book. ffrench marvelled at the acumen of his political reports. But how could the leopard change his spots? Backhouse habitually exploited his patrons, and these patrons lent themselves to exploitation. Bland took all the documents on trust. ffrench, like Morrison, knew no Chinese. So the indispensable slave enjoyed the delicious sensation of mastery as he fed, to one of them, a bogus diary, bogus state papers, to the other, bogus reports of bogus interviews.

With ffrench and Straight, Backhouse soon overplayed his hand. Between inexperience and *folie de grandeur*, he moved too fast. He sought to supplant ffrench as direct agent of Pauling & Co. in Peking. He overvalued his services to Straight. But these failures did not check the commercial ambition which had been aroused in him: they merely made him more cautious in pursuing it. Soon he would establish himself as sole agent of John Brown in China, and the agency for John Brown would lead to the splendid contract for the Bank Note Company, the stupendous fantasy of the great arms deal.

With Bland, Backhouse's success was far more lasting. Here he was less ambitious, and he was on his home ground, playing a game which suited both his own genius and the taste of the time. For if *China under the Empress Dowager* was a 'masterpiece', it was a masterpiece of timing. Decadent Manchu China appealed naturally to the intellectual decadence of the European *fin de siècle*, which had its own preconceptions of the Far East: it was, after all, the time of *The Mikado* and *Madam Butterfly* and the rage for Japanese colour-prints. Backhouse easily infused the chinoiserie which he knew into the China which he had discovered. Hence those 'melodramatic liberties' with arbitrarily 'selected texts' of which Latourette would afterwards complain. Hence also that masterpiece of the forger's art, the diary of Ching-shan.

It has been suggested by some – it was put out as a hypothesis by Duyvendak – that the diary of Ching-shan, as supplied by Backhouse to Bland, was the transformation, by Backhouse, of an original diary which was either authentic, and had been found by Backhouse more or less as he had stated, or a Chinese forgery, manufactured for propagandist purposes. But as Backhouse always maintained that he had translated the diary 'exactly as I had discovered it, without the addition of a syllable of extraneous matter', his veracity is anyway past salvation, and since Duyvendak had to admit that the transformation, if it had occurred, was so complete that no trace of the original could be discerned, there is no need of such a hypothesis. If Backhouse discovered anything in Ching-shan's house, it was not the diary, or anything resembling it, but the idea.

The diary, as Backhouse presented it to the world, does indeed contain a thesis, and that thesis has been cited as evidence of an independent origin. The thesis is that of the pro-Western Jung-lu. According to Ching-shan, the Grand Secretary Jung-lu had not really supported the Boxers, or the reactionary party at court, but had been opposed to both: he had tried to prevent the court from yielding to the Boxers, tried to prevent the attack on the legations, but had been overborne. This was indeed a thesis which was put about in the period immediately after the defeat of the Boxers, in Jung-lu's interest: like the Empress Dowager herself, he found it prudent to disown, even falsify, his past in order to secure his future. But in order to disseminate such a story, Jung-lu did not need an elaborate literary artefact. Discreet hints by obedient officials were sufficient – and more likely to be heard. Thanks to such hints, many Westerners accepted this view of Jung-lu, as Bland's correspondence shows; and clearly Backhouse chose to accept it too. He made it the thesis not only of Ching-shan's diary, but of the other diaries that he pretended to have discovered, and of the conversations which he retrospectively invented* Sometimes he ascribed his idealisation of Jung-lu to the evidence of Ching-shan's diary. In fact, he constructed Ching-shan's diary around his idealisation of Jung-lu.

Why did Backhouse idealise Jung-lu? We do not know. Perhaps he just chose to do so, as he chose also to idealise the Empress Dowager. If so it was a purely literary idealisation, after they were both dead. It would become a fixation, a formalised cult, growing in intensity as the persons cultivated receded into historical time.

We may add that although, by that time, Backhouse could not serve the political interest of Jung-lu, his retrospective historical vindication was very effective. 'I was very pleased to read your rehabilitation of Jung-lu', an old friend from the Chinese Customs wrote to Bland after the publication of their book; and Daniele Varè, in the 1930s, while allowing that Ching-shan's diary might be a forgery, would nevertheless uncritically accept its picture of Jung-lu, whom he would praise for his 'courageous defence of the foreigners' and his constant opposition to the Boxers.

From a view of his whole life, we can infer something of Backhouse's literary methods. In China, he collected a mass of material – contemporary documents, historical evidence, gazettes, ephemera. He would have liked to construct them into some great literary work. But he lacked the architectonic gift, and in the end would use his documents only to create another document like them: a pastiche, a tour de force. By 1909 he had constructed Ching-shan's diary. Then he met Bland. Under Bland's formative pressure, Backhouse's material suddenly took shape. His diary of Ching-shan became the nucleus of a real book. His historical collections crystallised into another book. Afterwards, Backhouse

---

* 'Reading these extracts' – i.e. of the new diaries which he pretended to have found – 'I take it Jung-lu never meant the guns to be fired at the Legations' (Backhouse to Bland, 20 January, 1912).

went on collecting: he collected historical material and material for the contemporary revolution in China. But this time the formative pressure never came. The material accumulated till it became oppressive. It never yielded another book, or even another diary of Ching-shan.

As a forgery, Ching-shan's diary was Backhouse's masterpiece. It deceived the experts for a generation at least. If Morrison, from the start, saw through it, that was not because he could detect the forgery in a document which he could not read and had not seen. It was simply because he knew the facts, although he could never prove them. He also knew his Backhouse. To his death he would confidently assert that Backhouse had forged the diary. But he asserted in vain when learned Orientalists, like Duyvendak and Johnston, authoritatively pronounced the work to be genuine.

A scholar who has once attempted forgery, and apparently succeeded, can rarely be prevented from trying it again. There is a subtle temptation which leads a man on, from mere disinterested craftsmanship, through a positive delight in his own virtuosity, to the exquisite private satisfaction of deceiving the elect. Many of the great forgers – François Lenormant, T. J. Wise, Henricus van Meegeren* – have been scholars tempted by the prospect of a double, if private triumph: the vindication of their own skill and the discredit of the established experts. So, as soon as he had seen his diary acclaimed as genuine, and important, Backhouse was eager to try his hand again. He began, cautiously and tentatively to devise new diaries, and float them before the collaborator whom he had so successfully deceived. There is a pleasant irony in this little episode; for even while he was seeking to tempt Bland with these new diaries of his own imagination, he was using his genuine critical scholarship on other forgeries and warning Bland against the forged memoirs of Li Hung-chang which had been accepted as genuine in America. Later, in the memoirs, he would indulge a similar irony, citing instances of persons who had apparently believed convenient fantasies about their own lives, as George IV convinced himself that he had commanded a brigade at Waterloo, and the Empress Dowager believed that, in

* See page 301.

the year of the Boxers, she had saved the lives of many mission-aries. It is little episodes like this which oblige us sometimes to wonder whether Backhouse really deceived himself and was not, all the time, enjoying an exquisite game.

Having come so far, we find ourselves faced by another question. If Backhouse himself forged Ching-shan's diary, did he also forge the eighteen manuscripts and scrolls which he palmed off on the Bodleian Library? Unquestionably he had the will to forge, and we cannot believe a word of his explanations. On the other hand the amateur nature of one forgery contrasts strongly with the professional skill of the other. The same expert who had described Ching-shan's diary as 'the most masterly specimen of forgery in modern times' would dismiss the scrolls as gross and palpable forgeries which could not deceive any educated Chinese. However, we need not take this difference too seriously. It is one thing to forge a contemporary document, in which only the handwriting and the content must be made plausible, and another to manufacture an ancient document, avoiding the perils of anachronism not only in writing and in content but also in paper and ink. And of course we do not know what assistance Back-house may have had on those two separate occasions. On the whole, we must suspect that, though the forgery was different, the forger was the same.

However that may be, the successful forger soon becomes the prisoner of his forgery. Once the experts begin to suspect him, he loses the initiative. Then

> The same arts that gain
> A power must it maintain,

and new forgeries must be brought in to maintain the old. Circum-stances must be invented to counter circumstances discovered. New documents must be forged, or imagined, and back-dated, in order to refute, or forestall, new documents revealed. So Ching-shan's diary, which at first rested comfortably on its own claims, had to be supported, twenty-seven years later, by a new account of its discovery; a second diary would be devised to sustain it; that second diary must also be provided with a circumstantial pedigree;

and newly fabricated conversations, back-dated forty years, would be called in to authenticate both the original forgery and its later authentication.

Meanwhile, Backhouse was engaged on a new operation. In the opportunities provided by the looting of Peking in 1900 and the revolution of 1911, he had begun his great collection of books and manuscripts, and in 1912 he conceived the idea of depositing them in the Bodleian Library. Having deposited them, he proposed to come himself and catalogue them; and ideally he would do so with the authority of a Professor of Chinese. In 1913 he secured a chair of Chinese, in London; but what he really coveted was the chair at Oxford, his own university, whose vacancy could not long be delayed. That chair was, in fact, almost promised to him. He only had to sit still and enjoy his present fame, and all his ambitions, it seemed, would be fulfilled.

1910 to 1923 – those, for Backhouse, were the years of outward triumph and respectability. His forgery had deceived the elect. Morrison's smear-campaign had been silenced. Every year improved his public image. He was established intellectually, as a scholar and author, in 1910; academically, as a munificent benefactor, in 1913; socially, as a baronet, in 1918. With Couling's blessing in 1919, and Morrison's death in 1920, and Duyvendak's endorsement from 1920, it seemed that he could not go wrong. He had missed the Oxford chair, indeed, but that was a mere private failure, soon to be redeemed by public honour. The name which had floated on the uncertain breath of an electoral board would be inscribed permanently on the marble record of the university.

Such was the public appearance. The reality, as we now know, was very different. All through those years of apparent triumph, Backhouse was continuing his career of forgery and fantasy. Unknown to the public, or to the world of scholarship, he was concocting new documents, perpetrating new frauds on British and American companies, leading the cabinet ministers and war leaders of his country in a grotesque, irrelevant dance. Behind the scenes, lawyers were seeking desperately to extricate him from a series of extraordinary scrapes, over which his family were able, for a surprisingly long time, to draw a costly veil.

How are we to explain the contrasts of those years: the spectacular munificence of an apparently indigent scholar who, at the
same time, was seeking to raise large sums by elaborate frauds?
Was Backhouse really, as he maintained in 1915, penniless? How
then could he afford such generosity? But if he was not poor,
what was the real motive of those frauds, which, in the end,
brought him nothing? For although two million pounds were
transferred from England to China to pay for his imaginary cargo
of arms, not a penny in fact reached his pocket; although he
claimed £30,000 as commission on his imaginary battleships,
nothing was ever paid on that account; and although he received
£5600 as commission on his forged contract for bank-notes, most
of it was soon recovered. The only real transactions of those
years were the costs of his frauds, which fell on his family and the
Foreign Office, and his gifts to Oxford, which, whatever their
origin, were acts of real generosity by him.

When we put these various transactions together, it seems clear
that Backhouse's frauds were not inspired by need or greed.
Money entered into his fantasies, but not into his calculations. In
times of euphoria, he would squander real or imaginary sums; in
times of depression he would cry abject poverty. His early Oxford
extravagance, which led to bankruptcy, his later Oxford benefactions, which led to fame, were one part of the manic-depressive
syndrome; his lamentations of penury, the rags worn to impress
Soothill, the threat of mendicancy in the streets of Peking, were
another. Both were part of his dream-world: a world of high life,
secret power, lavish gestures, compensated, on the return to
reality, and through reality, by an equally illusory world of
solitude, penury and gloom. But Backhouse's real world was
quite different. He was not really poor, at least until his last years.
He had a salary from the university of Peking and an allowance
from home. He had money from Pauling's – they offered him £720
a year in 1909 when they were paying ffrench himself £1000 –
and occasional payments from Straight; and from 1910 to 1917
he had the contract with John Brown, which even he admitted
was liberal. His treasures probably cost him very little: if they
were loot, they may have cost him nothing. Even in the 1930s,
when his cries of economic anguish were so piercing, Vetch found

him living in elegant comfort, sipping whisky in his spacious garden-house.

Thus he could afford his generosity. But what were its motives? Perhaps it was mere love of fame, a desire to find an identity of his own. Throughout the years of their collaboration Bland had urged him to stand on his own feet, to claim his just credit as a scholar, to publish in his own name, not to be a mere anonymous ghost-writer working for the greater glory of Morrison. And Morrison, most unjustly, turned the tables on Bland, encouraging Backhouse to believe that Bland was stealing his credit. Both his patrons, in fact, agreed that Backhouse was being overshadowed by other men: that he was an unfairly exploited genius who should step forward and claim his due recognition. It would be understandable if Backhouse, who secretly resented his dependence, and was so easily turned by one against the other, had ended by seeking to establish himself independently of both by discovering a new area of fame. He wanted his 'measure of notoriety'. A munificent gesture was one way to personal fame. Brilliant forgeries would be another. There is a pleasant unconscious irony in Backhouse's choice of that word 'notoriety'; and a pleasanter still in Bland's dry rejoinder, '. . . "a measure of notoriety" (is that the word you meant?)'.

Love of fame, even notoriety . . . a desire to smooth his way into a coveted chair . . . a compulsive extravagance. . . . Perhaps all these were merged together. But perhaps also there were other ingredients in that lavish gesture. Conceivably Backhouse's gift to Oxford, his offer to catalogue the gift, and the pursuit of the chair, are parts of the same process. The events which followed, in 1921, would show that Backhouse was quite capable of presenting forged documents to the Bodleian. One of the best protections of a forger is to be accepted as the authenticator of his own forgeries. Thus T. J. Wise, having printed forged editions of nineteenth-century English poets, authenticated them by including them in his own authoritative bibliographies. If Backhouse had been elected Professor of Chinese at Oxford and had, in that capacity, compiled the official catalogue of the Chinese books and manuscripts presented by him, we can be sure that he would not have exposed the 'impudent forgeries' which he presented in

1921; and if there were other, less impudent, forgeries among those which he had presented in 1913, we can be equally sure that they too would have been authenticated. This may seem too suspicious an interpretation of motive, but it cannot be entirely excluded. The man who could invent the diary of Li Lien-ying to authenticate his own fabulous memoirs was not incapable of compiling a catalogue to authenticate the forgeries in his own collection.

However, there are other syndromes in Backhouse's life, which perhaps we should remember in explanation of his generous gesture. Lavish expenditure had characterised his life at Oxford. Sudden withdrawal, impulsive, unexplained escape from inconvenient commitments, was a recurrent expedient in his career. Perhaps he just unloaded his possessions, which had become oppressive to him, involving him in projects which, without a Bland or a Hoeppli to give him force and direction, he would never bring to completion: the history of the Chinese revolution, the lives of the Ch'ing Emperors, the Chinese dictionary. Perhaps the suggestion that he would come, later, to work on his books and manuscripts, to list and catalogue them, was a mere pretext, a convenient rationalisation. Certainly he would never make the slightest attempt to do so. The disposal of his collected treasures, with the work which they implied, in 1913, may be psychologically comparable with his even more impulsive escape from his accumulated books and manuscripts in 1939.

Backhouse's motives are one problem; his immunity is another. All his life he seems to have been almost magically protected from the effects of his own actions. This was partly because his own actions were so skilfully concealed, and mere rumour could not compete with his extraordinary plausibility. In all the documents that I have read, I have only found one reference to his early bankruptcy. It is the letter of the Oxford jeweller, Mr Payne. But for that single chance allusion I would never have discovered the fact. The great arms deal was buried in total silence and even disbelief. The one man who realised what had happened, Sir John Jordan, never wished to be reminded of it, and therefore never spoke of it. Had he not made one reluctant reference to it in a confidential note, I would never have known about it, or been moved to seek out the documents which, once examined, would reveal the whole incredible story. The affair of the Bank Note Company was similarly buried, and silence legally enjoined on the parties. But for Morrison's note of his conversations with Hall, I would have known nothing of it, nor pursued the evidence into the records of the astonished company.

Thanks to such concealment, such plausibility, and occasional good fortune, Backhouse sailed calmly through the stormiest seas. While his successive victims sank spluttering in his wake, he sat, benign and complacent, in the prow of his charmed vessel, like some heaven-protected sage in a Chinese tale; for was he not Sir Edmund Backhouse, baronet, 'the well-known sinologist', unmistakably 'a scholar and a gentleman', unconcerned with the noisy vulgar world of politics and trade? So complete was his self-assurance that, in the 1930s, he could re-emerge with a projected new diary. His lawyer in Tientsin could write to Bland that no one 'of any real perception of mind' who knew Backhouse could conceivably doubt his complete veracity. Henri Vetch, in Peking, would be similarly convinced by him. Of all the British diplomatists or other residents in Peking at that time who have recorded their impressions of him, not one has admitted to any knowledge of his frauds and forgeries. Bland, who survived him, died unconvinced of the charges against him in respect of Ching-shan's diary and unaware of his other exploits. Hoeppli, after ten years in Peking, did not suspect his good faith, and retained his innocence till his own death thirty years later. Mrs Danby, to the very end, admired his learning and judgment. Victor Purcell, in 1963, could not bring himself to doubt the truth of his circumstantial 'Postscript'. To all these, it was inconceivable that Backhouse was a forger: they saw him simply as a somewhat eccentric hermit scholar, 'a studious sinologue', as Sir Harold Acton has described him, 'living as far as possible from the beau monde'.

Today that spell is broken. Whatever plausible explanation might be offered of any one episode, seen in isolation, dissolves when all are added together, and the last evidence – the imaginary memoirs of Li Lien-ying and the grotesque 'memoirs' of Backhouse himself – are conclusive. After reading his solemnly alleged fantasies about his life with Verlaine and his amours with the Empress Dowager, we can no longer doubt. Those successive forgeries, so skilfully constructed to sustain each other, only serve, in the end, to pull each other down.

But we must return to Backhouse as a social phenomenon. For he was not only a forger: he was also a social type. However eccentric in certain directions, he belongs to a certain category and a certain date. I have described him as an aesthete who repudiated the materialism, the philistinism, of Victorian England, and took refuge, mentally at least, in the spiritually and intellectually empty élitism, the social and sexual non-conformity, of the 1890s. This trivial aestheticism, this sense of superiority, this hatred of Western materialism, continued to be the central thread of his life in Peking. As the outer world became more and more distasteful to him, he retreated ever further into personal seclusion, an inner citadel.

He also took refuge in history: European history, Chinese history. He had 'more intimate knowledge of Chinese history', writes Mrs Danby, 'than anyone I had ever known'. But Backhouse's knowledge of history, like everything else about him, was peculiar. History to him was not a discipline, a means of understanding the world, but a compensation, a means of escape from it. These characteristics are already visible in the *Annals and Memoirs of the Court of Peking*, of which he claimed, truly enough, to be the main author: for not only do we know that he provided the raw material: its dislike of the West, its emphasis on eunuchs and concubines, so deplored by English reviewers, also denote his hand. The same characteristics would no doubt have been clearer in the biographies of the Ch'ing Emperors which he was said to be writing afterwards and which are said to have been destroyed in 1939. And they are apparent in his memoirs: in his historical allusions, his choice of historical periods. His favourite periods of history are periods of 'decadence': periods in which a residual political authoritarianism, however weak, irresponsibly maintains a functionless elegance, a corrupt *douceur de vivre*. His mind rested most happily in the last years of Valois France, under Henri III and his *mignons*; in the last heedless years of the Bourbon ancien régime, under Louis XV and his mistresses; in the last years of the

Manchu dynasty in Peking, under the Empress Dowager, with her eunuchs and her intrigues, her outdated courtly etiquette, her amateur theatricals at the Summer Palace, her amorous picnics on the lake.

History might be a compensation; politics were a fact. In his later years, even Backhouse could not escape the impact of politics in China. The sympathies which he then expressed, though they surprised some observers, seem to me entirely consistent with his own history, his own social type. The old aesthete who had once admired authoritarian, Bismarckian Germany and Meiji Japan, now transferred his admiration to authoritarian Nazi Germany and 'fascist' Japan. Both, after all, were making war on 'pluto-democracy', the last phase of Victorian bourgeois liberalism. After December 1941, when Britain was apparently in extremis under the victorious attacks of Germany and Japan, Backhouse did not conceal his vindictive glee. The sight of 'the collapse, unwept and unsung, and the practical obliteration from the map, of a once great power' was nothing to him, he said, compared with the pathetic death, thirty-five years ago, at the age of seventy-four, of the Empress Dowager, whom in fact he had never known.

So, as Hoeppli records, he positively revelled in the defeat of his own country. In his memoirs he shows himself, again and again, its open enemy. No Englishman is there mentioned but with resentment. The English proconsuls in China in his early days – Sir Robert Hart, Sir Claude Macdonald, Sir John Jordan, Sir Reginald Johnston – are all now denigrated and slandered; the English journalists, Morrison, Bland, and 'the Semitic correspondent of Reuters' – that is, his reviewer Leveson – receive only hatred and contempt; and of Sir Winston Churchill he is pleased to remember, or invent, only a discreditable story from their common childhood at St George's School, Ascot. Backhouse's vindictiveness against his own country, in its hour of apparent defeat, is obvious in his memoirs; but Hoeppli tells us that the original manuscripts 'contained even more virulent observations' which, at his request, 'were omitted or changed when the manuscripts were typed'. On the other hand he is still, he says, 'an admirer of German *Grossmut*'. As a final repudiation of his country, Backhouse even claimed for himself German ancestry and was pleased when imagined foreign royalty used 'the original German form of my name'.

Thus the empty aesthetic élitism of the late nineteenth century was converted gradually into the brutal, hollow, glittering, sadistic élitism which was one of the constituent elements of fascism. The phenonemon is familiar in France in the development of *Action Française*. It can be seen in Germany, in the Wagner circle. It is less obvious in England, where the aestheticism of the 1890s petered out and fascism was never to acquire a native base. Only in the purulent atmosphere of the decaying Manchu court could a pale reflection of English decadence linger on until it could be ravished and possessed by the brutal, but still perverted masculinity of fascist *Führerprinzip*.

It is against this background, I suspect, that Backhouse's ultimate conversion to Catholicism must be seen. Dr Hoeppli was somewhat perplexed by this conversion, and could ascribe it only to the hope – a barren hope – of material comfort. But is it not, after all, of a piece with Backhouse's adopted loyalty? He saw himself as one of the aesthetes of the 1890s – one who, by the accident of his linguistic genius, had transplanted himself from 'la décadence anglaise' to 'la décadence mandchoue'. And had not his fellow aesthetes all, or almost all, ended thus? Long ago, Catholicism had been the last refuge of the atomised aestheticism of the 1890s. Verlaine and Huysmans, Wilde and Beardsley, André Raffalovich and his friend John Gray,* and several other hangers-on of the movement, ended, individually, as converts or *dévots* of Holy Church; and was it not reasonable for the last and outermost, and therefore the most clinging, of all the hangers-on to follow, in the end, their example?

Backhouse, of course, maintained that he had always had a leaning towards Rome. In his memoirs he sees his conversion foreshadowed from his childhood. Had he not managed, at the

---

* The love affair, and conversion, of Raffalovich and his fellow-poet John Gray is well known. The unregenerate couple set out together on a Mediterranean cruise in Raffalovich's yacht, which was painted black and called 'Iniquity'. They returned pious Catholics. Gray afterwards went as a Catholic priest to Edinburgh. Raffalovich followed him and set up, in that less sophisticated city, the salon which he had failed to establish in London. It was the newly converted Raffalovich who, in 1896, persuaded Aubrey Beardsley to become a Roman Catholic.

early age of five, to have an audience with Pio Nono, then in his last year? Had not the aged Pope addressed him, 'Caro fanciullo, sia ricevuto nella fede'? Had he not at the age of seventeen, received a similar appeal from Cardinal Newman, also in his last year (trust Backhouse always to scrape in, just in time, at the very top)? Had he not, as a child, been impressed by Titian's portrait of St Ignatius Loyola, 'of which my family possessed the original' – a curious heirloom to be transmitted in a Quaker family – 'there being a copy at Windsor Castle'? But these early incentives are no doubt as mythical as the Titian, which is unknown to art-historians. No less mythical, I am sure, is the letter from Aubrey Beardsley, also on his last legs in Menton, begging 'dearest Trelawny' to see the light and follow him on the only way to salvation. But at least, I suspect, it was rather the real example of Beardsley than the alleged injunctions of Pio Nono and Newman which caused Sir Edmund Backhouse, forty-five years later, to creep, on his last legs, without conviction or repentance, into that capacious bosom.

At the end of his memoirs, Backhouse attempted to draw a portrait of himself. As usual, it was a mixture of truth and fantasy, intelligently perceived truth and wild fantasy; and the frontier between the two, as usual, is hard to draw. As usual, there is self-dramatisation and self-pity. His sexual excesses, he says, over which he has hitherto drawn a conventional veil, but which now, yielding to his natural 'candour and simplicity', he has revealed, have not affected his brain – that brain which an Edinburgh alienist had once described to him as 'purely mimetic, without creative power', – but they have occasioned 'a lesion to my will, which is weak, and my judgment, which is hesitant and nebulous'. 'I have ever been veracious, kind-hearted, true to myself. My *fatale dono* is a woeful indecision, a halting between two opinions, a feebleness under pressure, even from my own domestics, whose truculence bullies and distresses me.' He has been much misused by ungrateful men who have exploited his labour: by 'pressmen' (Morrison and Bland), by 'sharpers' (those rapacious creditors, 'the Shylocks of London'), by '*chevaliers d'industrie*' (Pauling & Co., Straight, the Bank Note Company, John Brown & Co.). As for his hidden life, there are some who have ascribed it to pride or

guilt, a desire to conceal the fraudulency of his claims to scholarship. But this is a monstrous slander. 'In truth, none was ever
more socially disposed (if time permitted) than I, none ever
worked harder or more patiently.' Even his sexual adventures
were but 'parerga' to his life of study. It was to gratify his passion
for work that he had become a hermit. He was 'a most laborious
worker', as industrious as the ant, and 'merits comparison with
the chiefest and most painstaking of my contemporaries'. Has he
not translated documents from Chinese, Japanese, Manchu,
Mongol, Tibetan and Russian? Has he not written 'innumerable
papers and articles on divers subjects, political, literary, philosophical, historical and social', for several periodicals? Was he not
'principal author' of *China under the Empress Dowager*, which so
many good judges had praised as a masterpiece? 'Be that my
epitaph,' even though, in that book, 'the story was left half-told',
for it contained little about the intimate life of the Empress,
'which I have left to the present study to portray'. All in all,
Backhouse concludes, he is not dissatisfied with his achievement.
'Were I to live again, I would lead the same life, except that I
regret having so long postponed my Holy Baptism.'

There we may leave Sir Edmund Backhouse: the spendthrift
aesthete of the 1890s who became the sinologue and recluse of the
next century, the spiritual fascist of the Second World War; the
brilliant linguist who used his gifts to diddle successive patrons;
the enchanter whose spells softened the hard heads of businessmen and diplomats; the collector whose generosity enriched his
old university and who inexplicably abandoned his own papers to
meaningless destruction; the secret war-time agent who led his
own government on a ludicrous wild-goose chase; the scholar
who created a 'masterpiece' of historical writing and produced a
masterpiece of forgery; the ghost-writer who created a whole
world of ghosts; the mystery man, the calligrapher, the porno-
grapher. However he may be judged, he was, in his self-expression,
an original. But we are all creatures of our time, and behind his
specific and perhaps pathological originality, he belongs recog-
nisably to his own age: an age which produced not only the most
ingenious of learned forgers, T. J. Wise, and the most aggressive
of sexual pretenders, Frank Harris, but also another deviant

character who, in his brittle aestheticism, his social snobbery, his personal plausibility, his persecution-complex, his paranoid ingratitude, his delusions of grandeur, his bogus titles of nobility, his refuge in Catholicism, his literary fantasies and last pornographic effusions, is, of all men, most comparable with him: Frederick Rolfe, self-styled 'Baron Corvo'.

Baron Corvo – how he haunts these pages! Always, as I have explored the strange career of Sir Edmund Backhouse, self-styled 'marquis Pa k'o-ssu' in the Manchu peerage, I have been reminded of that contemporary poseur. It was the outrageous last letters from Venice, casually purchased from a homosexual bookseller in London, which prompted A. J. A. Symons to undertake his 'quest for Corvo', and it was the outrageous last memoirs from Peking, so gingerly placed in my hands at Basel airport, which prompted me to embark on a similar quest for Backhouse. Only when I thought that I had completed this book did I discover the curious coincidence that Corvo's Venice letters had been addressed to Backhouse's first cousin, the Cornish Quaker, Charles Masson Fox. Whether this is more than a coincidence – whether Backhouse had been initiated by his cousin, or had seen Corvo's letters, and been inspired by their explicit suggestions, which sometimes seem to point directly to Backhouse's memoirs* – we cannot say. Backhouse must have known his cousin, and perhaps knew him well during his early years in Cornwall, but how could he refer to him, or identify his Fox relations, in his memoirs, when he had already pre-empted their name, and detached it from their identity, in order to claim descent from ͺa more famous homonym, Charles James Fox?

However that may be, we may still end on that note. As a

---

* In his letters to C. M. Fox, Corvo offered to write for him, against payment, 'two books which would have a rattling good story in them, told artistically, with a vividness and plain-spokenness hitherto unheard of', and presented as 'my personal experiences'. As a tempting sample, he offered an account of a homosexual brothel with all its refinements. Backhouse's two books of memoirs written against payment for Hoeppli, and beginning with that scene in the 'Hall of Chaste Joys', seem the fulfilment of Corvo's offer. That Backhouse had seen Corvo's letters is not impossible. Fox evidently circulated them to like-minded friends, for they found their way on to the market in his lifetime. But there is no evidence, and no necessary connexion between the two documents.

scholar, a man of letters, Backhouse is a very minor figure. But he may still claim a little niche in the temple of literary history, or at least literary fashion. We need not lament the loss of 'the priceless records and labour of half a century' which are said to have perished in the alleged 'holocaust' of 1939. But by his eccentric generosity he deserves his commemorative inscription in the Bodleian Library, and by his still more eccentric career of fantasy and fabrication he deserves his notice – though now, I venture to believe, a revised notice – in *The Dictionary of National Biography*. He may yet be remembered not, as hitherto, as the grave scholar and historian who declined 'distinguished posts in Europe' in order to pursue his researches in China, nor, as he himself wished, as the lover of the Empress Dowager, but as the unsuspected original of *Our Man in Havana*, the T. J. Wise of Chinese manuscripts, the Baron Corvo of Peking.

Appendices and Source Notes

Appendix One

Three learned forgers (see p. 287)

François Lenormant (1837–1883), classical and oriental archaeologist, philologist and traveller, was the author of numerous important works of scholarship (in particular *La Monnaie dans l'Antiquité*, 1878–9, and *La Grande Grèce*, 1881), and also of numerous elaborate forgeries – Greek, Latin and Oriental manuscripts, funeral inscriptions, sherds – which occupied his leisure for twenty years, and were accepted as genuine by a succession of grave scholars. He was finally exposed by German scholars: see the articles by J. H. Mordtmann, Theodor Mommsen, A. Kirchhoff, and especially the two heavy-handed articles by H. Rohl 'in Franciscum Lenormant Inscriptionum Falsarium', in *Hermes* XVII (1882) and XVIII (1883). Soon after his exposure, Lenormant died, aged 46. The standard works of reference, in their notices of Lenormant, make no reference to his forgeries, although Larousse, *Grand Dictionnaire Universel du 19e siècle*, admits that Lenormant's scholarly work was impaired by some 'very grave errors' ('les plus lourdes bévues').

Thomas J. Wise (1859–1937) was an authority on Victorian literature. Until 1934 he enjoyed an unchallenged reputation as 'England's foremost book-collector and supreme bibliographical pontiff'. But in that year his reputation was shattered by the classic work of J. Carter and G. Pollard, *An Enquiry into the Nature of Certain 19th century Pamphlets*. By unanswerable arguments, Carter and Pollard showed that Wise was a forger, a vandal and a thief. Throughout his long life, he had skilfully manufactured, authoritatively authenticated, and profitably sold not merely individual bogus copies but more than fifty whole bogus 'first editions' of English poets. He too died almost immediately after being exposed.

So did the third of my three great impostors, Henricus van Meegeren (1889–1947). Van Meegeren's paintings, fraudulently ascribed to Vermeer and de Hooch, had deceived the elect for many years, and had been purchased at high prices by international museums, when an accident forced him to confess, and afterwards to prove to an incredulous court, that they were all his own work. He was exposed because one of his 'Vermeers' had been acquired, during the Second World War, by Hermann Goering. Allied authorities, seeking to discover the legitimate owner, could not trace the supposed seventeenth-century masterpiece beyond van Meegeren, who had in fact originated it. He was sentenced to a year's imprisonment but died before serving it.

All these learned forgers were exposed during their lives and died in, perhaps of, discredit. Backhouse did better. He died questioned indeed, but not convicted, and serene in his defiance.

Appendix Two

A ghost Backhouse collection

The many mysteries generated by and around Backhouse are increased by the appearance of a 'ghost' Backhouse collection in the British Museum. This was first mentioned, as far as I know, by Arundell Esdaile in his work *The British Museum Library* (1946) pp. 318–19. According to Esdaile, the collection was acquired in 1908 and is 'distinguished by a number of fine Ming editions, a large thesaurus entitled *Yu Hai* or *The Sea of Jade*, and a complete set of the 24 dynastic histories, among many rare and valuable books'; and he refers to the '*Catalogue of the Backhouse Chinese Library* by Lionel Giles, 1908 (unofficial)'. This 'important Backhouse collection of rare Chinese books' catalogued by Giles is cited, from Esdaile, in Edward Miller, *That Noble Cabinet, A History of the British Museum* (1973) p. 341. Since Esdaile was Secretary of the Museum 1926–40 and Lionel Giles spent forty years in it, ending as Keeper of Oriental Books and Manuscripts, this would seem authoritative. However, no such collection, and no such catalogue, can now be identified, and the Museum records show that the two Chinese works specified, which do exist in the Museum and were acquired in 1908–9, were bought from the oriental booksellers Luzac & Co. without any reference to the name of Backhouse. These may have been sold, through Luzac, by Backhouse, who informed the Bodleian, in 1912, that he had already sold some items to the British Museum; but if so, the fact is unrecorded in the Museum. I can only conclude that Esdaile's statement rests on a misunderstanding by him of information supplied by his colleague Giles. In any case, I am assured that there is no 'Backhouse collection' in the British Museum.

Source Notes

Where the source of a statement is clear from the text I have avoided the unnecessary pedantry of references to individual documents. The main MSS sources are: 1. *London, Public Record Office:* Foreign Office papers: FO 228/3434, 'Affairs of Sir Edmund Backhouse' (Peking file on Hall's charges and some later matters); FO 228/191-2, 160, 167, official London–Peking correspondence 1915-17; FO 371/2327, telegrams, minutes and other documents on search for Chinese arms and ammunition 1915; 2. *Oxford, Bodleian Library:* Library Records: LR 551/56-7, correspondence on Backhouse's gifts; LR 551/60-1, internal correspondence on cataloguing Chinese collections; 3. *Edinburgh, National Library of Scotland:* Correspondence of Sir J. H. S. Lockhart; 4. *Glasgow, University Library:* Records of John Brown Shipbuilding & Engineering Co.; 5. *New York:* Archives of American Bank Note Company; 6. *Toronto, Thomas Fisher Rare Book Library:* Papers of J. O. P. Bland; 7. *Sydney, Mitchell Library:* Papers of G. E. Morrison.

page

3 *early Manchu court.* Hope Danby, *My Boy Chang* (1955) p. 107.

5 *at Casanova's dictation'.* A. J. A. Symons, *The Quest for Corvo* (1935).

9 *publisher's hands.* The Correspondence of G. E. Morrison, ed. Lo Hui-min, vol. 1 (Cambridge, 1976).

14 *a Quaker missionary.* For the Backhouse family in its Quaker days, see the *List of the Backhouse Papers* compiled by Miss M. S. McCollum and published by the University of Durham, Department of Palaeography and Diplomatic, January 1973; *The Descendants of John Backhouse of Yealand Redman, yeoman, d. 1690* (1894); James Backhouse, *Select Family Memoirs* (York 1831); *Extracts from the Letters and Journals of Hannah Chapman Backhouse* (privately printed 1858); Sarah Backhouse, *Memoir of James Backhouse* (1870); Edward Backhouse, *Early Church History* (1880).

16 *orientalist Charles Fox.* For Caroline Fox and Charles Fox the orientalist, see *D.N.B.*

16 *I have referred.* For details of Charles Masson Fox, see Donald Weeks, *Corvo* (1971); Timothy D'Arch Smith, *Love in Earnest* (1970).

17 *absolute truthfulness.* Harry Graf Kessler, *Gesichter und Zeiten. Erinnerungen* (Berlin, 1935) pp. 127-60.

Source Notes

18 *conveniently be exploited.* Max Beerbohm, *Letters to Reggie Turner*, ed. Rupert Hart-Davis (1964) p. 117.

18 *a book on the Empress Dowager'.* W. Rothenstein, *Men and Memories* (1931) vol. I, p. 147.

18 *famous prosecution.* Beerbohm, *Letters to Reggie Turner*, p. 103.

19 *declared to be satisfied.* The details of Backhouse's bankruptcy are in the records of the High Court (no. 1424 of 1895).

21 *I can't afford it'. The I.G. in Peking. Letters of Robert Hart, Chinese Maritime Customs 1868–1907*, ed. John K. Fairbank, Katherine F. Bruner, Elizabeth M. Matheson (Harvard, 1976) no. 1132.

34 *besieged in the Legations.* Lancelot Giles, 'Diary of the Boxer Riots', in *The Siege of the Peking Legations*, ed. L. R. Marchant (Nedlands, University of Western Australia, 1970) p. 131.

34 *sergeant-major'.* Letter from Sir Charles Marjoribanks to the author.

34 *looting and robbery'.* Mitchell Library (Morrison MSS.) ML 312/31.

35 *Empress Dowager's bedroom.* The detail about Morrison comes from Bland's memoirs. For a general account of the plundering see 'B. L. Putnam Weale' [i.e., Bertram Lenox Simpson] *Indiscreet Letters from Peking* (1922).

38 *guidance of him.* Morrison MSS., Mitchell Library MSS. 312/121 9 Nov. 1905, 25 Feb. 1906.

38 *in our story.* For this episode, see *Correspondence of G. E. Morrison*, vol. I p. 354.

39 *what I feel'.* Morrison MSS., ML 312/121, 31 Mar. 1906, 11 Mar. 1907, 13 Apr. 1908.

43 *coming generation'.* Wu Lien-teh, *Plague-fighter: the Autobiography of a Modern Chinese Physician* (1959) p. 304.

51 *no finality in it'.* Arthur H. Smith, *China in Convulsion* (1901) p. 596. Duyvendak, in a letter to Bland of 10 Aug. 1937, suggested that this letter might have inspired the forgery of Ching-shan's diary.

63 *competent to judge'. Annals and Memoirs of the Court of Peking*, p. 466. *Efficiency and Social Progress.* The editor was Chalmers Roberts.

63 *rehabilitation of Jung-lu.'* Alfred E. Hippisley to Bland, 8 Aug. 1911. Bland MSS.

71 *by resignation. History of The Times* (1947) p. 740.

72 *World's Work. The World's Work, an Illustrated Magazine of National Efficiency and Social Progress.* The editor was Chalmers Roberts.

82 *a horrible document.* It is printed in *Correspondence of G. E. Morrison*, vol. I pp. 610–11.

92 *work of great rarity.* This is the *Yung-lo Ta-tien*, the 12,000-volume encyclopaedia compiled on the orders of Ch'eng Tsu, the third Ming emperor, whose regnal name was Yung-lo. The original, and one sixteenth-century copy, were destroyed by fire in the eighteenth century. The residue of the last surviving copy was burnt in the Han Lin Academy during the Boxer Rising; but the

greater part of it had already escaped into private hands. The largest single portion of it is in the Library of Congress in Washington. The largest portion in Europe is in the Bodleian (nineteen volumes, eleven of which came from Backhouse). See H. A. Giles, 'A Note on the *Yung-lo Ta-tien*', in *New China Review*, vol. II (1920) p. 1143; A. F. L. Beeston 'Seven New Volumes of the *Yung-lo Ta-tien*', *Bodleian Library Record*, vol. III (1951) p. 198.

93 *known about it in time*. Reginald Johnston to Sir James Lockhart, 22 Apr. 1913 (National Library of Scotland, Lockhart MSS.).

97 *in his place*. Johnston to Lockhart, 25 Dec. 1913 (Lockhart MSS.).

98 *for the Oxford chair.* Parker to Lockhart, 21 Apr. 1914 (Lockhart MSS.).

101 *to rest his eyes*. MSS. of the Minutes of the Delegacy of King's College, London.

102 *decide to revive it*. Johnston to Lockhart, 31 Aug. 1916 (Lockhart MSS.).

113 *curios and jewellery*. Letter to author from Mr William Lewisohn, 22 Sept. 1973.

124 *dubious authenticity*. Hsiang Ta's report, translated by Hughes, is among the archives of the Bodleian. The descriptive part of it was published by Hughes, under the title 'The Bodleian Chinese Collection', in *Bodleian Quarterly Record*, vol. VIII (1936) pp. 227ff.

124 *further purchases*. *Oxford Magazine*, 1938.

146 *denied in Parliament*. Hansard, 16 Dec. 1915.

146 *he would return*. Langley to Jordan, 19 Mar. 1916 (FO 228/1960).

159 *the past eight years*. Copies of two letters from Tenney to Hall describing these interviews were supplied to the British Legation and are now included with Jordan's despatch of 12 Nov. 1917 (PRO. FO 228/1967).

162 *and a new dossier*. FO 228/3134. Dossier 1451, 'Affairs of Sir Edmund Backhouse'.

175 *a substantial sale*. The discussions with the Foreign Office, reported baldly in the Company's minute-books (28 Sept. 1916), are given in more detail in a despatch from the Foreign Office to Peking on 4 Oct. 1916 (FO 228/1960).

175 *delivery doubtful*. Alston to Foreign Office. FO 228/1967, item 427A; cf. Company minute-books, 28 Sept. 1917.

182 *or represented*. Daniele Varè, *Yehonala* (Florence, 1933) pp. 177–94.

184 *authenticity of the diary. Chinese Social and Political Science Review*, Oct. 1926. The review is signed 'Reginald Irving' (Irving was Johnston's mother's name).

187 *like old parchment*. Katherine A. Carl, *With the Empress Dowager of China* (1906) p. 125.

189 *court of the Empress*. The article, entitled 'The Late Eunuch', was printed in *The Times*, 11 Apr. 1911.

Source Notes

189 *detector of forgeries.* The *Memoirs of Li Hung-chang*, with an introduction by John W. Foster (1913). Foster was a lawyer-politician who had represented the Chinese Government in the peace negotiations with Japan in 1895 and at the second Hague conference in 1907. He had been American Secretary of State 1892–3. The 'memoirs' were a forgery by W. F. Mannix.

197 *learned press.* W. Lewisohn, 'Some Critical Notes on the So-called Diary of His Excellency Ching-shan', *Monumenta Serica* (1936).

198 *he entirely ignored.* Backhouse's original letter was kindly given to me by Mr Lewisohn.

198 *author's death.* The document is published in V. Purcell, *The Boxer Uprising* (1963).

206 *published his article.* See J. J. L. Duyvendak, 'Ching-shan's Diary: a Mystification', *Toung Pao*, vol. XXXIII (1937).

207 *stitched together.* Lewisohn's second article is in *Monumenta Serica* (1940).

208 *public memorials.* Arthur W. Hummel, *Eminent Chinese of the Ch'ing Period (1644–1912)* (Washington, 1943–4) p. 409. I deduce from his citations, which include works published in 1937 but omit relevant works published thereafter, that Fang's article was written in 1938.

208 *were fabrications.* Ch'eng Ming-chou's arguments were published in the *Yenching Journal of Chinese Studies*, no. 27, June 1940, and are recapitulated by Duyvendak in his article 'Once More: the So-called Diary of Ching-shan', *Toung Pao* vol. XXXVI (1942) pp. 85–6.

211 *pro-Boxer party at court.* See Hummel, *Eminent Chinese*, p. 409; also, for further evidence of Jung-lu's propaganda, Purcell, *Boxer Uprising*, p. 284, and *Correspondence of G. E. Morrison*, vol. I, pp. 173–4.

215 *the last Dr Aspland.* Information from W. Lewisohn.

221 *see them'.* Letter of Sir Colin Crowe to the author, 24 Nov. 1973.

222 *into existence.* I am informed by the Clarendon Press that all the correspondence concerning Backhouse's proposed Chinese dictionary was destroyed in 1946.

225 *the work of Backhouse and Bland.* Daniele Varè, *Yehonala* (English translation) dedication.

225 *as a great scholar.* Danby, *My Boy Chang*, p. 218.

239 *for publication.* The Swiss journal was *Asiatisches Seminar*. The article was never published. It was withdrawn in Nov. 1973, after I had pointed out the true character of Backhouse's memoirs.

254 *to the Bodleian.* It is Bodleian Library, MS. Backhouse 11.

262 *revelation of a scandal.* H. Montgomery Hyde, *The Other Love* (1970) p. 147.

286 *publication of their book.* A. E. Hippisley to Bland, 8 Aug. 1911.

286 *opposition to the Boxers.* Varè, *Yehonala*, pp. 171, 180.

Index

Index

(In this index 'B.' stands for Sir Edmund Backhouse, for whom there is no distinct entry.)

Index

Battleship syndrome, B.'s, 60, 78, 88, 95, 100, 115, 174–5

Beardsley, Aubrey; a friend of B? 192, 205, 241, 246, 249, 264, 280; edits *Yellow Book*, 246; leads B. to Rome?, 296–7

Beerbohm, Max, 70, 192; a college friend of B., 18, 205, 246; finds him pluckable, 18; cited, 18, 267

Bell, Sir Hugh, Yorkshire magnate, 267 n

Bell, Moberly, managing director of *The Times*, 26, 67

Bernhardt, Sarah, 247–8, 286

Bland, John Otway Percy: his papers, 9–10; his character, 30–3; association with B., 39–45; his 'exquisite style', 43, 46; proposed collaboration, 46; its character, 180; buys out B.'s interest in book, 54; but continues to pay him, 63; problems of collaboration, 51–7; success of work, 60–5; tries to divert B. from commerce to scholarship, 60; sceptical about sale of battleships to China, 60; and about B.'s reports of Chinese reactions to book, 64; and about Chinese Revolution, 87–88; contest with Morrison over B., 66–90; Morrison seeks to ruin him, 67–8, 71; succeeds, 82–4; Bland passes heat on to B., 81–5; collaborates with B. on new book, 77–8, 81; its publication, 89–90; decides to end relations with B. (1914), 100; renews them (1932), 190–193; convinced of genuineness of diary of Ching-shan, 182–5, 194–6; shaken by Lewisohn's attack, 196–7; and by B.'s reaction, 200–6; declines to give evidence for B., 207; but remains a believer – up to a point, 208; writes his memoirs, 214–15; B.'s revenge on him:

'a detestable personality', 270

Blomfield, Sir Reginald, architect, 114

Bodleian Library, Oxford: B.'s real benefactions to, and correspondence with, 1–2, 6, 8–9, 91–125, 254, 289; his bogus curios palmed off on, 108–10, 118–21, 124, 167, 169, 288, 291; his mythical deposits in, 116–117, 193, 269–70; and gifts to, 253–4; commemorative inscription in, 1, 114, 300

Boxer Rising (1900), 3–4, 23–4; surprises Morrison, 29, 41; B.'s contribution to defence of legations, 34; Chinese court and, 50, 62, 184; B.'s historical revision of, 187, 191–2, 250, 252–3

Boyle, Lieutenant Edward, R.N., agent of John Brown & Co. in Japan, 174, 176

Braham, Dudley, acting foreign editor of *The Times*, 82–4

British Museum: B. to have job in? 60; buys K'ang-hsi Encyclopaedia, 93; Ching-shan's diary deposited in, 3, 51, 73, 183, 185; ghost Backhouse collection in, 302

Brown, Sir John & Co. (and Palmer & Co.): do not co-operate with historians, 10; early history of, 57–8; employ B. as agent, 58; rosy prospects, 58–60; lend B. to H.M. Government for secret work, 131–4; a good name to drop, 152, 160, 164; B. raises money from, 165; B.'s achievement as agent, 172–176; last recriminations, 176–8; B. claims £30,000 from, 114–15

Buckle, G. E., editor of *The Times*, 71, 83

Bullock, T. L., Professor of Chinese at Oxford, 95; B. wants to succeed him, 95, 97–8, 101–2

Index

Burdett-Coutts, Angela, Baroness: English version of Empress Dowager? 252

Casement, Sir Roger: compared with B., 267
Celsa, Italian manager of Empress Hotel, Victoria, B.C., 168–9
Chang Ho-chai, B.'s bootblack, secretary, comprador, etc.: takes over B.'s house, 113, 168, 218; and his money, 117, 120; and B. himself, 123, 219; to assist B. in burgling Palace, 156; makes a damaging confession, 160; murdered, 199, 203, 217
Chang Yüan-fu, Grand Eunuch 1908–12, 188
Chatham House (alias 'Foreign Office School of Thought'): its invertebrate liberals, 32; and supercilious grandees, 194
Chavannes, Édouard, sinologist, 106
Ch'eng Ming-chou, Chinese scholar, 208
Chiang Kai-shek, 32
Ch'ien-lung Emperor (1735–96), 254
Chin-liang, Chinese scholar, 208
Ch'ing, 2nd Prince (I-k'uang), President of Tsungli Yamen (Board of Foreign Affairs), 249
Ching-hsin, President of Hu Pu (Board of Revenue) 1895–1900, 69
Ching-shan, Chinese courtier, 49, 182; B. occupies his house, 34; finds his diary, 46, 48–51; manuscript lodged in British Museum, 51, 54; reaction to its publication, 62–3; Morrison doubts authenticity, 69, 72; but withdraws charge, 73; and then renews it, 160, 180–3; authenticity defended by Duyvendak (1920), 183–4; and by Reginald Johnston, 184; B. to publish

untranslated parts, 185; authenticity now admitted, 195–6; attack reopened by Lewisohn (1936), 196; B.'s last stand, 198–205; summary of evidence, 207–13; vindicated by B.'s memoirs, 252–4, 268–9; and vindicates memoirs, 264; B.'s masterpiece of forgery, 285–8
Chirol, Sir Valentine, foreign editor of The Times: employs Morrison, 67–8, 70–1, 82–3; knows too much about B., 267 n
Chou Hsüeh-hsi, Chinese Minister of Finance, 153
Ch'un, 2nd Prince (Tsai-feng), brother of Küang-hsu Emperor and Regent of China 1908–1912, 40, 45, 87
Churchill, Sir Winston, 128, 244
Cochrane, Dr, attends B. from Peking to London, 38
Collis, Maurice: produces new image of Empress Dowager, 208
Corvo, Frederick Rolfe, 'Baron', 5, 16, 299–300
Couling, Samuel, 106, 289
Cowley, Sir Arthur, Bodley's Librarian 1919–31, 7, 10, 104, 107–10, 113, 119, 121–3
Craster, Sir Edmund, Keeper of Western MSS., Bodleian Library, 116–17
Crowe, Sir Colin, 221
Curtis, Lionel: represents 'Foreign Office School of Thought', 190; a bête noire of Bland, 32
Curzon, George Nathaniel, Marquis, Foreign Secretary: his view of Morrison, 28; alleged relations with B., 240–1, 247–8; to buy B.'s precious manuscripts for Bodleian? 109

Danby, Mrs Hope, 2–4, 6–7, 36, 215–16, 220, 222–3, 225, 231–2, 239–40, 259, 293

309

Duyvendak, 200; returns to the attack, 207–8; B. calls up ghosts to refute him, 268

Li Ching-fang, Chinese minister in London, 63

Li Hung-chang, Chinese statesman, 96, 189; his bogus memoirs, 189, 198, 287

Li Lien-ying, Grand Eunuch of the Empress Dowager, 186–9; B.'s article on him, 189; B.'s fixation on him, 269; his alleged diaries or memoirs, 186; deposited by B. in Bodleian?, 116–17, 189; re-emerge in Peking, 190–3, 214, 231; B.'s alleged source for important historical revision, 238; new story of acquisition of his memoirs, 269–73, 278, 292–3; deposited in a London bank, 271; Li in B.'s memoirs, 250–1, 254–6; B. in Li's memoirs, 272

Li Po, Chinese poet, 38

Li Yüan-hung, President of China, 151, 153–4, 159–60, 175

Liang Shih-i, Chinese politician: close friend of B. in 1909, 44; the *éminence grise* of Yüan Shih-k'ai, 130; 'Machiavelli of China', 131; involved in the great arms deal, 130–1; and in monarchical movement, 143–4; confronted with B., 141–2; B. turns confrontation to his advantage, 149, 171–2

Liu Lun, Grand Secretary, 254

Lo Hui-min, Dr, 8

Lockhart, Sir James, 97

Loti, Pierre, 245

Lukouch'iao (Marco Polo Bridge) incident, 221

Lung-yü, Empress Dowager 1908–12, 40, 56, 63, 86, 188

Macdonald, Sir Claude, British Minister to Peking 1896–1900, 23–4, 36

Macmillan, Messrs, publishers, 195

Macpherson, James ('Ossian'), 185

Madan, Falconer, Bodley's Librarian 1912–19, 7, 10, 91, 98, 99, 101, 104–5, 107, 167

Mallarmé, Stéphane, 234, 245, 264

Mannix, W. F., author of forged memoirs of Li Hung-chang, 189 n

Mao Tse-tung, 33, 221

Margerie, Roland de, 6, 233–4

Marjoribanks, Sir James, 219–20

Meegeren, Henricus van, artistic forger, 287, 302

Minchin, James Cotton, Backhouse family lawyer, 104, 109, 147, 155, 167–9, 178

Morrison, George Ernest, *Times* correspondent in Peking: early life, 26–7; character, 27–9; first patron of B. in China, 33–9; visits B.'s family, 37–8; misses a scoop through love of wildfowling, 41; loses B. too, 45; bent on revenge, 64–5; exploits revolution in *The Times*, 66–8, 70–1; out to ruin Bland, 67–8, 71; his manœuvres in England, 69–74; returns to China, 75–6; woos B. away from Bland, 76–81; his triumph, 84; adviser to Yüan Shih-k'ai, 88; declares Chingshan's diary a forgery, 69, 72–5, 180–3; consulted by Hall on B., 159; mounts general attack on B., 160–2; leaves China and dies, 169–70; B.'s posthumous revenge, 190, 192, 205, 251; 'now howling in the deathless flames of Hell', 272

Motono, Baron, Japanese Foreign Minister, 158, 165, 169

Müller, Friedrich Max, Professor of Comparative Philology, Oxford, 107

Index

Tolstoy, Count Leo, 203–4, 248, 266, 281

Tuan Ch'i-jui, Prime Minister of China, B.'s 'closest friend', 151–2, 154–5, 158; their 'very stormy interview', 155; an unfortunate showdown, 159

Tsai-i (Prince Tuan), 24

T'ung-chih Emperor (1862–74), 22, 46, 259

Turner, Reggie, 18

Tzŭ-hsi, the Empress Dowager of China 1861–1908: her reign to 1900, 21–5; last years and death, 39–40; her death is B.'s opportunity, 41–3; proposed book on her reign, 45–7; scandalous tales of her life, 61; B. and Bland give standard account, 62–5; B. gives her autograph to Bodleian, 96; claims familiarity with her, 112; offers to steal her pearl jacket, 156, 167, 276, 278; a rival biography of her, 182, 225; a new source: the Grand Eunuch's memoirs, 190–2; B.'s new claim, 237; his new version of her death, 238; and of her private life, 249–59; origin of the new version, 263–264; documentary evidence – of a kind, 269

Vanishing Trick, B.'s, 18, 95, 103, 112, 147, 175, 224

Varè, Daniele, Italian diplomat and writer, 182, 185, 195, 225, 286

Verlaine, Paul, 234, 241, 244–6, 260–4, 272, 278, 296

Vetch, Henri, bookseller and publisher, Peking, 6, 167, 198, 200, 202–5, 208, 216, 218, 223, 241, 266, 290–1, 293

Victoria, Queen, 255, 262–3

Vyner family: B.'s fixation on, 247–9

Waley, Arthur, 13 n

Wang Hsi-chih, breathtaking Chinese calligrapher, 101

Wang Wên-shao, Grand Councillor 1898–1901: part of his diary incorporated in diary of Chingshan, 197; a grave problem, 204; easily, but variously, explained away by B., 205–6, 253–4, 268–9

Waugh, Evelyn, 128

Weatherall, M. E., a disturbing visitor to Oxford, 116–18; sends disturbing letter from Peking, 120–1; protests by B., 122; mentioned, 124, 169, 189, 183, 215, 218, 229, 270

Weitzen, Edward H., 11

Wilde, Oscar: his trial, 261–2, 281; B. collects money for his defence, 18; association with, reported to Morrison, 70, 267 n; claimed by B., 205; improved, 264, 266–7; his influence on B., 280–1, 296

Wise, T. J., learned forger, 287, 291, 298, 300–1

Wylie, Alexander, missionary and sinologist, 124

Yehonala, Manchu clan, 40, 56, 251

Yetts, Percival, physician and sinologist, 13 n, 93, 102

Yüan Shih-k'ai, Chinese general: his treachery (1898), 23, 29 n; later career, 87–8; said to be annoyed by *China under the Empress Dowager*, 186; President of China (1912–16), 88, 95, 126; Morrison becomes his adviser, 88, 159; involved in great arms deal, 129–31, 138–41, 143–6; tries to make himself emperor, 142–4, 150–1; B.'s alleged mission to, 148, 166; involved in Bank Note affair, 149–50, 152; death, 151; biography revised in detail by B., 238–9, 258–9; mentioned, 216, 254, 271

A NOTE ABOUT THE AUTHOR

Hugh Trevor-Roper was born in 1914. Educated at Charter-house School and Oxford University, he served in the British Army (Intelligence) from 1939 to 1945. Returning to Oxford after the war, he was a student and tutor at Christ Church, becoming Regius Professor of Modern History in 1957. Among his many books are *The Last Days of Hitler* and *The Rise of Christian Europe*. Professor Trevor-Roper is a frequent contributor of reviews and essays to *The New York Review of Books*, *The New York Times*, *Horizon*, and a number of British periodicals.

A NOTE ON THE TYPE

This book was set on the Monotype in a type face called
Garamond. Jean Jannon has been identified as designer for
this face, which is based on Garamond's original models but
is much lighter and more open than Garamond's original
form. The italic is taken from a fount of Granjon, which
appeared in the repertory of the Imprimerie Royale and was
probably cut in the middle of the sixteenth century.

Printed and bound by The Haddon Craftsmen, Inc.,
Scranton, Pennsylvania